# The PC Upgrader's Manual

## How to Build and Extend Your System

Revised Edition

**Gilbert Held**

John Wiley & Sons, Inc.
New York • Chichester • Brisbane • Toronto • Singapore

386/PC, Above Board, Inboard, and Intel are trademarks of Intel Corporation.
Bridge-File is a trademark of Sysgen Corporation.
CuRAM 32 and CuRAM Module-SP are trademarks of Cumulus Corporation.
FileSafe is a copyright and Mountain is a registered trademark of Mountain Computer, Inc.
HBASIC and Hercules Graphics Card Plus are trademarks of Hercules Computer Technology.
IBM and PS/2 are registered trademarks of IBM Corporation.
MicroRAM 386 is a trademark of Tecmar, Inc.
Quadboard and QuadEMS+ are trademarks and Quadum and Silver Quadboard are registered trademarks of Quadram Corporation.
Rodime R-Card 35 is a trademark of Rodime Inc.
SixPak Plus is a trademark of AST Research, Inc.

In recognition of the importance of preserving what has been written, it is a policy of John Wiley & Sons, Inc., to have books of enduring value published in the United States printed on acid-free paper, and we exert our best efforts to that end.

This publication is designed to provide accurate and authoritative information in regard to the subject matter covered. It is sold with the understanding that the publisher is not engaged in rendering legal, accounting, or other professional service. If legal advice or other expert assistance is required, the services of a competent professional person should be sought. FROM A DECLARATION OF PRINCIPLES JOINTLY ADOPTED BY A COMMITTEE OF THE AMERICAN BAR ASSOCIATION AND A COMMITTEE OF PUBLISHERS.

Copyright © 1988, 1991 by John Wiley & Sons, Inc.

All rights reserved. Published simultaneously in Canada.

Reproduction or translation of any part of this work beyond that permitted by section 107 or 108 of the 1976 United States Copyright Act without the permission of the copyright owner is unlawful. Requests for permission or further information should be addressed to the Permission Department, John Wiley & Sons, Inc.

**Library of Congress Cataloging-in-Publication Data**
Held, Gilbert, 1943–
   The PC upgrader's manual : how to build and extend your system / Gilbert Held. — Rev. ed.
      p.    cm.
   Includes bibliographical references.
   ISBN 0-471-52452-2
   1. IBM Personal computer.  2. Microcomputers—Upgrading.  3. IBM-compatible computers—Upgrading. I. Title.
TK7887.5.H45   1990                                                               90-12585
621.39'16—dc20                                                                   CIP

Printed in the United States of America

91 92 10 9 8 7 6 5 4 3 2 1

# Contents

**Chapter 1**  **PC Series Hardware Overview**  1
System Components  2
The PC and PC XT  4
Keyboards  4
System Unit  8
Diskette Drives and Media  13
RAM  15
ROM  17
Configuration Switches  17
Bus  21
Adapter Cards  21
Parallel Versus Serial Ports  23
System Unit Rear  28
PC XT System Unit  29
The PC AT  36
Keyboard  37
System Unit  37
Device Housing Area  37
Diskette Drives  48
The PC XT Model 286  49
Monitors and Display Adapters  52

Monochrome Display and Adapter 53
Color Displays and Adapters 55

**Chapter 2**    **PS/2 Hardware Overview**    **61**
Major PS/2 Components 62
Keyboard 62
System Unit 63
Disks and Storage Media 72
Video Display Support 75
Monitors 76
Model 25 79
Model 30 80
Features 81
Limitations 82
Model 30 286 83
Features 83
Model 50 83
Features 84
Limitations 84
Model 50Z 85
Model 55 SX 85
Model 60 86
Model 70 86
Model P70 386 88
Model 80 89
Comparison to PC Series 89

**Chapter 3**    **PC Series Third Party Hardware Overview**    **93**
I/O Address Space 94
Port Categories and Addresses 95
Addressing Conflicts 95
Representative Hardware 97
AC Power Protector 98
Keyboards 99
Multifunction Boards 104
Memory Cards 113
Accelerator Cards 118
Fixed Disks 123
Fixed Disk Card 133
Tape Backup Units 137

|  |  |  |
|---|---|---|
| | Mouse 145 | |
| | Display Adapters 148 | |
| | Monitors 159 | |
| **Chapter 4** | **PC Hardware Upgrade Strategies** | **163** |
| | Performance Constraints 164 | |
| | RAM 164 | |
| | Processor Performance 167 | |
| | On-Line Storage 168 | |
| | Removable Mass Storage 175 | |
| | Expansion Slot Availability 178 | |
| | Upgrade Strategies 182 | |
| | IBM PC Upgrade 182 | |
| | PC to PC XT 185 | |
| | PC or PC XT to PC AT 189 | |
| **Chapter 5** | **PS/2 Hardware Enhancements** | **193** |
| | On-Line Storage Devices 193 | |
| | 5¼-inch Diskette Drive 194 | |
| | Tape Backup Unit 198 | |
| | Other Internal Enhancement Products 199 | |
| | Model 25/30 Hardware Options 200 | |
| | Micro Channel Hardware Options 204 | |
| | PS/2 Upgrading 211 | |
| **Chapter 6** | **Printers** | **213** |
| | Types of Interface 214 | |
| | Printer Type Formation 214 | |
| | Impact Printers 214 | |
| | Dot Matrix Printers 215 | |
| | Laser Printers 222 | |
| | Printer Control Codes 224 | |
| | Escape Sequences 226 | |
| | HP Printer Command Language 228 | |
| | Control via BASIC 228 | |
| | Expanded Printer Control 231 | |
| **Chapter 7** | **Modem Installation, Operation, and Selection Considerations** | **233** |
| | PC Series System Unit 234 | |
| | Obtaining a Serial Port 238 | |

PS/2 System Unit   246
Modem Modulation Methods and Operational
Classification   249
Nonstandard Modems   275
Asymmetrical Modems   278
Intelligent Modems   279
Modem Selection Considerations   288

**Chapter 8**  **Clone Construction**   **299**
Individual Components   300
System Board   300
Power Supply   304
Cabinets   304
Clone Tailoring   305
Keyboard   306
Bundled Software   306
Bundled Hardware   307
Warranty   308
Purchasing Sources   308
Assembly Techniques to Consider   310
Clone System Board   311
System Construction   312
The Assembly Process   314
Clone Operation   319

**Chapter 9**  **Problem Resolution**   **323**
POST   323
Parity Check Errors   325
Keyboard Malfunctions   328
The Diagnostic Disk   330
Troubleshooting Tips   331
Internal Failures   332
Summary   334

**Appendix A**  **PC Components to Consider**   **335**

**Appendix B**  **Vendors to Consider**   **345**

**Index**   **351**

# Preface

Although it may not be obvious, personal computers, like automobiles, can provide you with long and useful service. For the same reasons most of us would not buy a new car every time there is a model change, most of us will not purchase a new computer each time a new advance in microprocessor technology occurs. In recognition of this, this book focuses on how to prolong the useful life of the original IBM PC series and compatible computers, techniques to improve performance of members of the IBM PC series, and upgrades to the more recently introduced family of IBM PS/2 computers. Thus, whether you were the original purchaser of a PC, PS/2, or compatible computer, or you acquired one of these computers at a later date, this book will assist you in maximizing its potential.

The basis for writing this book was a series of personal computer seminars I conducted in the United States and Europe over the last few years. Although these seminars covered hardware, software, and communications, common concerns of the delegates included the differences among members of the IBM PC and PS/2 series, techniques to upgrade the performance and capabilities of different members of the IBM PC and PS/2 series, and information about the use of IBM compatible personal computers. In writing this book I have attempted to answer these questions and more. Because the utility of a personal computer is based to a great degree on techniques used to maximize its performance, I have also added information to assist you in isolating and resolving problems should they occur. In revising this book I would be remiss if I did not significantly expand coverage of the second series of personal computers IBM introduced in April 1987: the PS/2 family.

Members of the PS/2 family differ from the original PC series in several areas, including the type of data storage media used, types and number of expansion slots contained in each computer's system unit, and video display capability. Although these differences are not trivial, it is important to recognize the fact that both generations of personal computers support DOS. Due to this, over 99 percent of the software developed for use on the IBM PC series will operate on PS/2 computers. Similarly, with the correct hardware most members of the IBM PC series can execute software written for the PS/2 family of personal computers.

Although the PS/2's use of $3\frac{1}{2}$-inch diskettes with rigid outer cases significantly reduces the potential for corrupting data during normal handling in comparison to the use of $5\frac{1}{4}$-inch floppy diskettes used on the original PC series, for a few hundred dollars you can upgrade your older computer to support this technology. Whereas the new video standards incorporated into PS/2 computers provide enhanced clarity in displaying data, with an appropriate hardware upgrade you can also obtain a PS/2 video display capability in your PC series computer. Only in the area of desktop footprint and the Micro Channel capability do PS/2 computers offer features not obtainable with the use of a PC series computer. Concerning capabilities, the Micro Channel design permits adapter boards containing independent microprocessors to operate in conjunction with the microprocessor on the system board of a PS/2. This design permits up to 15 additional processors to be supported by a Micro Channel-based PS/2, providing a significant expansion capability that may enable its design to support new technological developments into the next century.

In addition to expanded coverage of IBM's PS/2 family this revised edition of the *PC Upgrader's Manual* includes three additional chapters. One chapter examines PS/2 hardware upgrades; the other two chapters cover two of the most common peripheral devices that can be used with both PC and PS/2 computers—modems and printers.

I sincerely welcome readers' comments; they assist me in tailoring future editions to the requirements of the public. Therefore, please feel free to write me if you have any suggestions or comments concerning information which should be incorporated into future editions of this book.

Gilbert Held<br>
Macon, GA

# *Acknowledgments*

The preparation of a book is a comprehensive task that requires the cooperation and assistance of many individuals and organizations. I would like to take the opportunity first to thank my family for their patience and understanding for those countless hours I had parts of computers disassembled all over our house as I took apart and reassembled different systems to ensure the accuracy of vendor claims. To AST Research, Cumulus Corporation, Genoa Systems, Hercules Computer Technology, Intel, Keytronics, Logitech, Mountain Computer, Quadram, STB, Seagate, Tecmar, Toshiba, and IBM I would like to extend my thanks for their cooperation and assistance. To Mrs. Carol Ferrell, who has diligently prepared this book and others for me, taking my notes and converting them into a manuscript suitable for publication, a special thanks is extended. To Teri Zak, who sponsored this project, I am once again indebted for her backing.

CHAPTER 1

# PC Series Hardware Overview

One of the major reasons for the market success of members of the IBM PC series is the open architecture policy followed by IBM in the design of personal computers. Publishing the technical specifications for each computer, including the interface structure that third party vendors could design their products to work with, resulted in hundreds of manufacturers developing products that can be used with one or more members of the IBM PC series. The variety of products enables you to configure your system to satisfy just about any requirement imaginable. Unfortunately, the differences among members of the IBM PC series impose some constraints on how you tailor your hardware to meet your needs. To understand the nature of these constraints, as well as the options available for customizing a system to obtain different degrees of functionality, you must first obtain a firm understanding of the hardware.

This chapter describes the major components of an IBM Personal Computer system. The description will form a foundation for a later, more detailed, exploration of both the similarities and the differences among the various members of the IBM Personal Computer series, as well as provide a means to compare and contrast IBM PC hardware and functionality with the more recent IBM PS/2 family of personal computers. In addition, the information you gain will help you to understand the constraints and limitations (covered in later chapters) that are associated with upgrading the functionality of your IBM or compatible personal computer.

This book uses the term *PC* when the hardware or function under discussion is common to all or most members of the IBM PC series. When referring to hardware or functions specific to certain individual members of the series, the text identifies each member by its appropriate name, such as the IBM PC, PC XT, XT 286, or PC AT. Similarly, when referring to members of the PS/2 family, this book uses the term *PS/2* when the hardware or functions under discussion are common to all or most members of the PS/2 family. When referring to specific members of that family, we will identify each member by its model number, such as the PS/2 Model 30 or PS/2 Model 50.

# System Components

Figure 1.1 illustrates a "typical" IBM PC system, which consists of four major components—keyboard, monitor, system unit, and printer. This is a typical system because you can connect a variety of keyboards, monitors, and printers to the personal computer's system unit, and you can install different types of storage devices such as diskette drives, fixed disks, and tape backup units inside or outside the system unit. In addition, a variety of adapter cards, ranging in scope from memory expansion boards to modems, can be installed in slots formally known as *system expansion slots*, inside the system unit. All of these devices modify the operating characteristics or increase the functionality of your PC.

The keyboard illustrated in Figure 1.1 is the original 83-key device that was introduced with the IBM PC in mid-1981. In examining individual members of the IBM PC series in detail later in this chapter, we will note the existence of the IBM Enhanced keyboard and discuss its similarities to and differences from the original IBM PC keyboard. We'll also discuss the compatibility of various keyboards with different members of the IBM PC series.

The system unit illustrated in Figure 1.1 contains two full height 5¼-inch diskette drives, one of the more popular storage configurations used with some members of the IBM PC series. The locations where the diskette drives are installed are known as the *device housing areas* and can accommodate a variety of storage devices to include both 5¼- and 3½-inch diskette drives, fixed disks, and tape backup units.

Some of the constraints governing specific types of devices that can be installed in the system unit's device housing area include the power consumption of the devices to be installed, the types of adapter boards used to control storage devices, and the availability of free expansion slots for the installation of adapter boards. Each of these constraints will either be discussed in detail later in this chapter or will be covered in later chapters when hardware upgrade strategies are discussed.

Although Figure 1.1 shows an IBM monitor and printer, in actuality a large number of PCs are equipped with third party monitors and printers. When the original IBM PC was introduced, IBM did not market a color monitor, nor did the company offer a letter-quality printer for use with that computer. This omission created a void that was rapidly filled by a large number of hardware vendors who captured a major portion of the market for these two components, in spite of IBM's later introduction of color monitors and letter-quality printers to fill these product voids.

**Figure 1.1.** "Typical" IBM PC system consisting of four major components—keyboard, monitor, system unit, and printer. *Photograph courtesy of IBM Corporation.*

# The PC and PC XT

Because the IBM PC and PC XT personal computers have numerous features in common and both use the Intel 8088 microprocessor for their computational capability, this section examines both computers. This will help you to understand the hardware similarities and differences between the two computers, how you can upgrade a PC to a PC XT, and how you can add functionality to each computer by installation of various adapter cards into its system unit.

## Keyboards

### Original (83-Key) Keyboard

The original keyboard sold for use with PCs and PC XTs manufactured prior to mid-1986 is illustrated in Figure 1.2. This 83-key keyboard is attached via a 6-foot coiled cable to the rear of the system unit of a PC or PC XT. The keyboard contains all of the keys found on a conventional typewriter as well as special keys shaded in gray. These shaded keys help users perform such tasks as programming, editing, updating, and executing programs.

At the left side of the keyboard are 10 keys, labeled F1 through F10, arranged in a matrix 5 keys high by 2 wide. These keys are called *function keys*, because they can initiate special functions, such as bringing a menu or help information to the screen. Because each function key emits a unique (but nonprintable) code when you press it, an application program can assign special meanings to these keys, such as commands to load a data file, or to terminate the program and return to the DOS command level. With the help of special utility programs, you can assign your own definitions to these keys; for example, you could make a single keystroke initiate some complex command sequence that you use often.

IBM assigned predefined functions to the function keys for editing Disk Operation System (DOS) command line entries and for generating BASIC language commands. For DOS command line editing, only the first 6 function keys have a predefined meaning. In BASIC, all 10 keys are initially assigned meanings in the form of BASIC commands that are

**Figure 1.2** Original PC and PC XT 83 Key Keyboard—The original keyboard used with the IBM PC PC XT personal computers contained 10 function keys and lacked visual indicators to denote the status of the Caps Lock, Num Lock, and Scroll Lock Keys. *Photograph courtesy of IBM Corporation.*

generated when each key is pressed. You can change the meaning of one or more function keys in BASIC to correspond to a function or sequence of operations you more commonly perform; hence, the use of these keys can be viewed as a labor saving device because they reduce a sequence of keystrokes to a single keystroke. Table 1.1 lists the BASIC commands initially assigned to each function key.

Most application programs—such as word processors, spreadsheets, and database managers—take advantage of the function keys by assigning a program function or operation to each key. As an example, pressing F2 when you are using a word processing program might invoke a spelling checker, and F5 could center the data on the line where the cursor currently resides.

At the right-hand side of the keyboard is the numeric keypad, which

**Table 1.1** Initial Function Key Assignment in BASIC

| KEY | COMMAND | KEY | COMMAND |
|-----|---------|-----|---------|
| F1  | LIST    | F6  | LPT1:   |
| F2  | RUN     | F7  | TRON    |
| F3  | LOAD    | F8  | TROF    |
| F4  | SAVE    | F9  | KEY     |
| F5  | CONT    | F10 | SCREEN  |

is useful for the rapid entry of numeric data. Because most keys in this area have dual meanings, you must enable their numeric usage by pressing the Num Lock key, which is above the 7/Home key. Note that there is no indicator on the keyboard to denote whether the numeric function is enabled or disabled. Similarly, the Caps Lock and Scroll Lock keys lack indicators to inform you of the current state of these keys. However, some programs show the current state in a portion of a status line on the screen. The status line is the 25th line in the display and is normally used by application programs to display special instructions and/or error messages. One example of its use is to display the abbreviations NUM and CAPS when the Num Lock and Caps Lock keys are set.

In the upper left portion of the typewriter area on the keyboard, to the right of the F2 key, is the Esc or escape key. As its name implies, this key is typically used by application programs as a request to escape from a current activity. However, because it's so close to F2, you can easily press Esc when you mean to press F2, with possible disastrous results to your work.

Although the keyboard may not appear from outside to be a sophisticated device, it in fact contains an Intel 8048 microcontroller that provides a significant degree of intelligence. The microcontroller supervises all keystrokes, generates a unique code for each key, and transmits these codes to the microprocessor located inside the system unit to which the keyboard is cabled. Other tasks performed by the 8048 include a diagnostic test of the keyboard when power is applied to the system unit; preventing one keystroke from being interpreted as two, which is more formally known as *debouncing*; and checking the keyboard for stuck keys.

When you press a key, it generates an identifying number known as its *scan code*. For the keys on the keyboard illustrated in Figure 1.2, the scan codes are numbered 1 through 83 to correspond to the number of keys on the keyboard. When you press a key, the 8048 transmits the scan code of the key to the system unit. Similarly, when you release the key, the 8048 transmits the key release code to the system unit; the release code is the regular scan code of the key plus 128.

When a key is pressed, released, or repeated by holding it down, its action is recorded into a 20-character buffer inside the keyboard. The keyboard generates an interrupt to the system unit, in effect requesting the servicing of the key action. In response to the interrupt, part of the operating system code, known as the *Basic Input Output Service (BIOS)*—which is contained on a read only memory (ROM) chip in the system unit—reads the scan code from the keyboard and sends instructions back to the keyboard. These instructions tell the 8048 microprocessor in the keyboard to remove the key action from the keyboard's buffer.

The ROM BIOS routines in the system unit are responsible for monitoring all keyboard activity. That is, they keep track of the scan codes and release codes to determine whether you pressed a sequence of alphanumeric keys; held down one key to make it repeat the character; or held down the Alt, or Ctrl, or Shift key while you pressed other key(s) in order to initiate some special function. The routines also keep track of the current status of the toggle keys (Caps Lock, Num Lock, and Scroll Lock). In the light of all this information, the BIOS routines are able to translate your keystrokes into the appropriate ASCII codes for processing purposes.

## Enhanced PC Keyboard

In 1986, IBM introduced the Enhanced PC Keyboard, containing 101 keys, which is illustrated in Figure 1.3. Unfortunately, this keyboard is not compatible with the original IBM PC and can be used only with new versions of the PC XT, XT 286, and the PC AT. The addition of a few keys results in a new set of scan codes that can be correctly interpreted only by new versions of BIOS in those computers.

In comparing the keyboards illustrated in Figures 1.2 and 1.3 you'll notice several major and minor differences. Three major differences between the keyboards are the number of function keys, their locations, and the inclusion of visual indicators to denote the status of the Caps Lock, Num Lock, and Scroll Lock keys.

**Figure 1.3** The IBM Enhanced PC Keyboard contains 12 function keys that were relocated to a row across the top of the keyboard. *Photograph courtesy of IBM Corporation.*

The enhanced keyboard contains 12 function keys, which were relocated to a row across the top of the keyboard. Another major difference between keyboards is the inclusion of two Ctrl and Alt keys opposite sides of the space bar on the Enhanced PC keyboard. Other changes on the IBM Enhanced PC keyboard include the relocation of the Esc key to the upper left corner of the keyboard to reduce its inadvertent usage; the enlargement of the Tab, Caps Lock, Backspace, and Shift keys; the provision of separate screen control and cursor keys in a four-key keypad between the typewriter and numeric keypad areas on the keyboard; the inclusion of an Enter key on the numeric keypad; and the addition of three dedicated function control keys to the left of the three visual indicators. These dedicated keys reduce the number of keystrokes needed to initiate certain functions. For example, on the original keyboard you would have to hold down the Shift key and press the Prt Sc key in order to print the contents of the screen; on the enhanced keyboard you merely press the Prt Sc key, by itself.

## System Unit

Figure 1.4 illustrates the exterior of the system unit of the IBM PC from an angle that shows the position of the power switch on the right side of the unit.

**Figure 1.4** The system unit exteriors of the PC and PC XT duplicate one another, the label above the ventilation grill and, upon occasion, the devices installed in the device housing areas. *Photograph courtesy of IBM Corporation.*

## System Unit Exterior

The PC and PC XT system units are very similar in external appearance, the only differences being the look of the emblem label on the upper left front of the unit over the ventilation grill, and the devices installed in the device housing areas.

Two full-height 5¼-inch diskette drives are installed in the system unit illustrated in Figure 1.4. The original IBM PC introduced in 1981 was equipped with a single 5¼-inch disk drive installed in the left device housing area; a black faceplate covered the empty right device housing area. You could order that system with two drives, in which case the computer store would install the second diskette drive, or you could purchase a one-drive system and add another drive yourself. You could do the installation quite easily by unfastening several screws at the rear of the system unit, sliding the cover of the unit forward, and lifting it at a 15-degree angle to remove the cover. Then, removing the black faceplate permitted you to install and connect a second drive.

The original IBM PC XT's system unit contained a 5¼-inch disk drive in the left device housing area and a 10M-byte, full-height fixed disk in the right device housing area. Later versions of the PC XT were sold with one and two 5¼-inch diskette drives as well as one 5¼-inch diskette drive and one 20M-byte fixed disk. In fact, during periods of high sales activity, many computer stores were known to have sold PC XTs with no storage devices installed in the device housing areas, permitting users to tailor the computer to their specific storage requirements. In such cases the prevalent question "What do you call a PC with no storage devices?" was answered by the retort "A bargain."

## System Unit Interior

Figure 1.5 illustrates the interior of the system unit of an IBM PC after removal of its expansion slot covers and all cards previously installed in

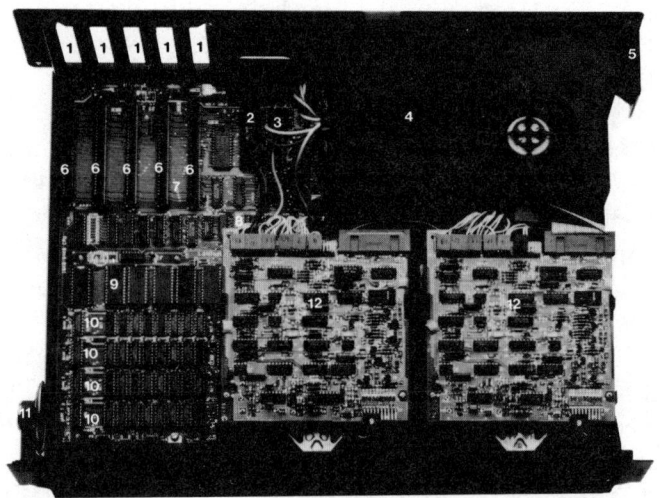

1. Expansion slot covers removed
2. Intel 8088 microprocessor
3. 8087 coprocessor socket
4. Power supply
5. Power switch
6. 5 expansion slots
7. Input/output bus
8. Dip switch
9. ROM BIOS and cassette BASIC
10. RAM memory banks
11. Speaker
12. 5¼-inch diskette drive installed in device housing areas

**Figure 1.5** IBM PC System Unit Interior—Two versions of the IBM PC were manufactured. Early versions of the PC used 16K RAM chips and could have a total of 64K of memory on the motherboard. A later version of the PC was designed to use 64K RAM chips and could have a total of 256K of memory installed on the motherboard. *Photograph courtesy of IBM Corporation.*

its expansion slots. To obtain an appreciation of the key components of the system unit and their functionality, take a tour of the interior in a clockwise direction, starting in the upper right corner.

The power supply converts alternating current (AC) into the direct current (DC) required to operate the solid state electronics installed in the system unit. The PC's power supply wattage is 63.5, with a maximum of 7.0 amps. This was sufficient for powering all options that could be installed in the system unit in 1981, when the original PC was introduced. Today, its wattage is usually insufficient to operate an internal high-speed modem, as well as a full complement of adapter cards and a fixed disk. Thus, you may have to replace your original power supply with a higher-wattage device if you want to upgrade your computer with hardware add-in devices. Chapter 3 contains additional information concerning the PC's power supply.

The power cables protruding from the center of the left side of the power supply terminate in two connectors. These connectors plug into the underside of the diskette drives and can also be used to power other devices installed in the device housing areas.

Two full-height 5¼-inch floppy disk drives are shown installed in the two device housing areas. When the original PC was introduced only full-height storage devices were available. Later, when half-height storage units were introduced, it became possible to install as many as four devices. Figure 1.6 illustrates five popular device housing area configurations. Note that IBM did not market half-height or full-height fixed disks or a half-height tape backup unit for use with the PC. However, all of these devices are now readily obtainable from numerous third party vendors and will be discussed when upgrade and performance strategies are covered in later chapters in this book.

The configuration shown at the top of Figure 1.6 represents the storage devices available for inclusion in the system unit of an IBM PC when that computer was introduced in 1981. Two diskette drives did not provide a significant amount of data storage capability, so one of the earliest third party products for the PC was a full-height fixed disk. This resulted in a device housing area configuration illustrated by the second drawing in Figure 1.6. Later, IBM "sanctioned" this configuration with the introduction of the PC XT, whose device housing area configuration is the same as that illustrated for the modified PC.

The manufacture of half-height storage devices considerably expanded the number of device housing area configurations PC users could consider. The lower portion of Figure 1.6 illustrates three configuration options that use half-height storage devices. The third configuration from

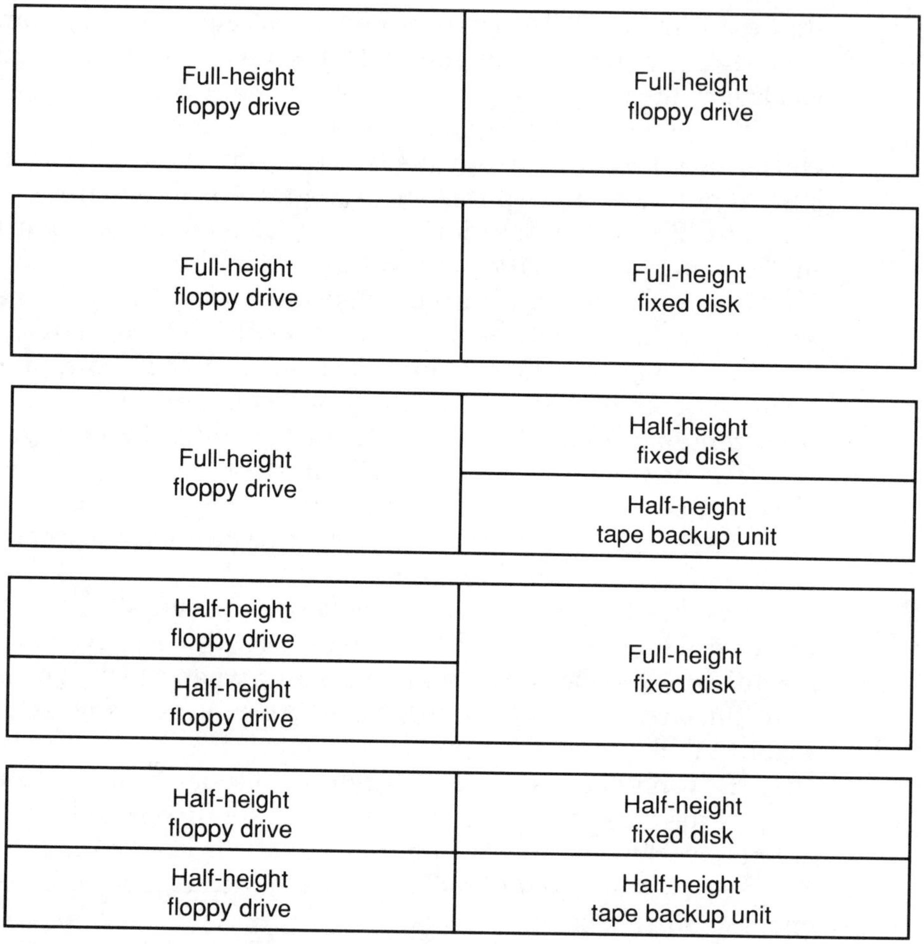

**12** The PC Upgrader's Manual

| Full-height floppy drive | Full-height floppy drive |

| Full-height floppy drive | Full-height fixed disk |

| Full-height floppy drive | Half-height fixed disk / Half-height tape backup unit |

| Half-height floppy drive / Half-height floppy drive | Full-height fixed disk |

| Half-height floppy drive / Half-height floppy drive | Half-height fixed disk / Half-height tape backup unit |

**Figure 1.6** Device Housing Area Configuration Options—By using a mixture of full- and/or half-height devices, a variety of storage configurations can be considered to satisfy your requirements.

the top of Figure 1.6 uses a half-height fixed disk and half-height tape backup unit mounted in one full-height device housing area. This configuration provides the storage capacity of a fixed disk as well as the speed associated with backing up data onto tape rather than diskettes.

The fourth and fifth configurations both use two half-height diskette drives mounted in one device housing area, providing the ability to easily copy the contents of diskettes. Although DOS can copy the content of one diskette to another using a single diskette drive, if more than a few files are to be transferred the procedure can be very time consuming. This is because DOS prompts you to insert and remove diskettes as it copies data to your computer's memory from one diskette and then writes the data onto a second diskette you "swap out" in the drive. Thus, the two configurations shown at the bottom in the figure are more popular when the use of a fixed disk is required.

## Diskette Drives and Media

When the IBM PC was introduced in 1981, the operating system known as DOS 1.0 supported only single-sided floppy disk drives. Within a few months, however, IBM revised the operating system to version 1.1, which added support for double-sided diskette drives.

Figure 1.7 illustrates the cross section of the 5¼-inch diskette used with IBM PCs and compatible computers. The diskette is a circular sheet of Mylar plastic, coated with ferric oxide, enclosed in a square protective jacket. The disk rotates clockwise in its jacket.

Before you can use a blank diskette, you must *format* it; that is, you must command the computer to write dummy data to all tracks in such a way that it can later identify precisely which part of the disk is currently

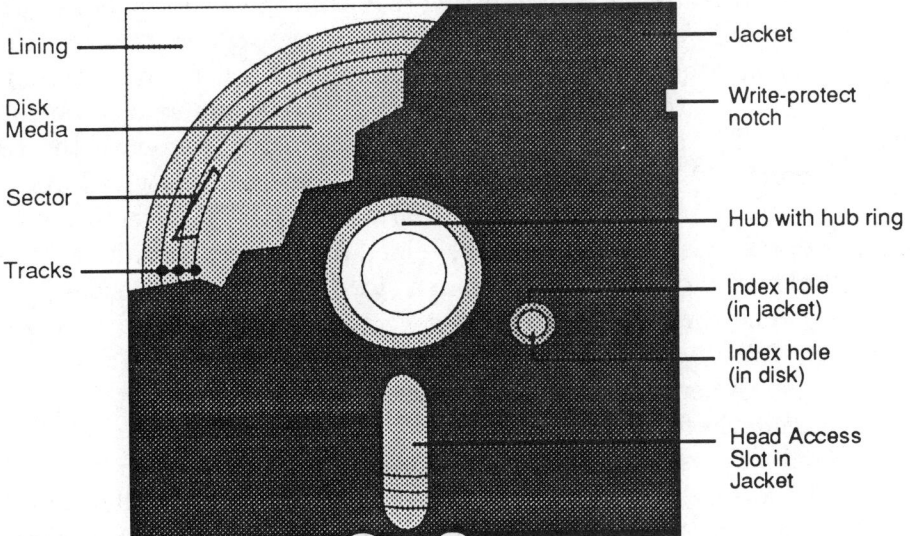

**Figure 1.7**   Cross Section of a 5¼-inch Diskette.

under the read/write heads. During this formatting process, the computer divides the recording space into *tracks*, which are concentric circles numbered from 0 at the outer edge to 39 at the inner edge for a total of 40 tracks. If the diskette is double-sided, there are two such sets of tracks, one on each side of the diskette surface. These upper and lower tracks are numbered identically but are differentiated by the number of the head that reads or writes them (0 for the upper, 1 for the lower head).

The computer identifies the start of each track as the point at which the index hole in the diskette becomes aligned with the index hole in the jacket and allows a beam of light to pass through both holes. A photocell detects the light beam and generates an index signal. At this time, the computer writes a special pattern called the index mark onto the diskette.

The computer then divides each track into storage allocation units called sectors by writing a synchronization pattern consisting of the track number, head number, and sector number, followed by the appropriate number of bytes of a special character (usually E5 hex) that denotes an empty data area. After the last data byte, the computer writes two check bytes that will allow the detection of reading errors. The computer repeats this sequence of sector ID, data bytes, and check bytes as many times as there will be sectors on the track.

Note that the maximum number of bytes per track is determined partly by the diskette rotation speed and partly by the encoding method employed by the disk controller. Within these limits, however, the number of bytes per sector and the number of sectors per track can vary according to the requirements of the operating system. For this reason, disks that are formatted by the process just described are said to be soft-sectored.

The original single-sided diskette drive used with the IBM PC supported 40 tracks with 8 sectors per track. This resulted in a total storage capacity of 40 tracks * 8 sectors/track * 512 bytes/sector, or 163,840 bytes of information. When double-sided drives were introduced, the use of double-sided diskettes resulted in a storage capacity of 2 sides * 40 tracks/side * 8 sectors/track * 512 bytes/sector, which doubled storage capacity to 327,680 bytes of information.

When the IBM PC XT was introduced, version 2.0 of DOS became available for use on both the PC and PC XT. Under DOS 2.0 and other minor versions of that operating system, such as DOS 2.1, a diskette could be formatted with 9 sectors per track. Doing so resulted in a double-sided diskette obtaining a storage capacity of 2 sides * 40 tracks/side * 9 sectors/track * 512 bytes/sector or 368,640 bytes of information. Table 1.2

**Table 1.2** Diskette Support and Capacity

|  | OPERATING SYSTEM | | |
| --- | --- | --- | --- |
|  | DOS 1.0 | DOS 1.1 | DOS 2.X |
| Diskette Support | | | |
|   Sectors/Track | 8 | 8 | 8 or 9 |
|   Single sided | yes | yes | yes |
|   Double sided | no | yes | yes |
| Diskette Capacity (bytes) | | | |
| Single Sided | 163,840 | 163,840 | 163,840 or 184,320 |
| Double Sided | N/A | 327,680 | 327,680 or 368,640 |

compares the diskette support and storage capacity based upon the three commonly used versions of DOS used with IBM PCs and PC XTs.

# RAM

Random access memory (RAM) is the working memory of your computer. This is because programs must be loaded into RAM from diskette or fixed disk storage prior to being executed.

The four random access memory (RAM) banks on the system board are numbered 0 at the top to 3 at the bottom. Approximately the first 300,000 PCs were manufactured using 16K-byte (*where K is 1024*) memory chips. Only the top bank, bank 0, was populated at the factory, resulting in 16K of installed system board memory. Customers could either have the dealer install additional memory or they could do so themselves. If the three lower banks of memory were populated, a total of 64K RAM was obtained.

If you look closely at the memory bank, you'll see that there are 9 chips in each row. Eight of these hold a byte of data; the ninth is a parity bit that provides a means of error detection. When the computer stores a byte into memory, it counts the number of bits that are set to 1, and then sets the parity bit so that the total number of 1s is even (for even parity) or odd (for odd parity). For example, a capital A, whose ASCII code is decimal 65, would have bit positions 0 and 6 set to one. This is an even number, so for an odd-parity scheme, the computer would also set the parity bit, as follows:

| Bit position: | P | 7 | 6 | 5 | 4 | 3 | 2 | 1 | 0 | |
|---|---|---|---|---|---|---|---|---|---|---|
| Weight: | 256 | 128 | 64 | 32 | 16 | 8 | 4 | 2 | 1 | |
| Contents: | 1 | 0 | 1 | 0 | 0 | 0 | 0 | 0 | 1 | (64 + 1 = 65) |

When the computer next reads that location, it checks the parity bit, finds a 1, and therefore expects to find an even number of 1s in positions 0 through 7. If the computer in fact finds an odd number of 1s, it knows that an error has occurred in reading or writing the data and executes an error-handling routine, which is part of the operating system to determine what action to take.

When power is applied to the PC, a BIOS routine initiates what is known as a power-on self test (POST). During POST, the PC writes data into each memory location, computing the proper parity-bit state, and checks the parity bit to determine whether a parity error occurred. If so, a memory chip is considered to be defective, and the PC displays a code in the upper left corner of the monitor to denote that a parity error occurred. The code defines the bank and chip in the bank that caused the error. This information can then be used to replace the failed chip. Detailed information concerning the power-on self test and potential error codes is given later in this book.

In 1982, IBM changed the system board of the PC to support the use of 64K-bit memory chips. Again, the top memory bank was populated at the factory, whereas the remaining three rows were populated either by the computer dealer or by the purchaser. Through the use of 64K-bit memory chips, a total of 256K bytes of RAM could be installed on the PC's system board.

When you purchase memory chips, you usually have a choice of several different speeds. The speed of a chip refers to the maximum time the chip needs in order to respond to a request to store data. Memory chips must be at least as fast as the computer system; otherwise, they cannot respond fast enough to storage requests, and the data stored in the chips could be inaccurate. Both the PC and PC XT require RAM chips with speeds of 250 nanoseconds (ns) or faster. Faster chips, with access times of 150 ns or less, are more expensive and do not increase the speed of the system, because that is determined by the 8088 microprocessor and the system clock-pulse generator.

Although faster chips can be used in a PC or PC XT, they should not be mixed with slower chips in the same bank. That is, all chips in a given bank should have the same speed. Fortunately, most chip manufacturers use a numeric code with a suffix that indicates the speed of the chip. As an example, a chip with the suffix −20 would indicate a 200-ns chip.

Another important consideration in purchasing memory chips is to ensure that the chip contains the correct amount of memory. Most memory chips are labeled 41XX or 41XXX; the 41 numbers indicate that the chip is a memory chip, and the suffix XX or XXX indicates the amount of memory on the chip. For example, a 4116 chip holds 16K bits of memory, while chips labeled 4164 and 41256 hold 64K and 256K bits of memory, respectively.

## ROM

Directly above RAM bank 0 is a row of read only memory (ROM) chips that contain instructions or program statements that can only be read and are nonalterable—hence the name ROM. The five ROM chips illustrated in Figure 1.5 contain approximately 40 kilobytes of code divided into BIOS (Basic Input/Output System), Cassette BASIC, and POST routines.

The purpose of the BIOS is to present a common interface to programs by isolating hardware usage to a set of predefined routines; such routines include displaying information on a monitor or writing data onto a file. Programmers can invoke BIOS routines by using a set of interrupts that are routed to various BIOS entry points. This usually simplifies the programming effort because, as an example, a programmer can simply load data into a register and invoke an appropriate interrupt to display information on the monitor. Without the BIOS the programmer would have to know the address of the monitor port as well as how to control it.

Programmers are encouraged to use standard BIOS calls in writing programs. Although writing directly to the hardware is faster than calling a BIOS routine, it can result in problems if a new version of the operating system uses an area in memory that a programmer previously used in developing a "custom" routine.

## Configuration Switches

Directly above the top left corner of the left diskette drive (Figure 1.5), labeled with the number 8, you can see a portion of one of the two configuration DIP (dual-inline package) switches. The second switch is to the right of the switch labeled in the photograph but is hidden from view by the cables at the rear of the diskette drive. Each DIP switch contains eight individual switch elements whose settings define the display adapter to be used when the PC is powered on, the amount of memory installed, the number of diskette drives installed, and other equipment information. The top portion of Figure 1.8 indicates the DIP switch settings for different hardware options. Note that there are some slight differences in the meanings of DIP switch settings, depending on the manufacturing date of the PC they are using. PCs manufactured prior to August 16, 1982, used a BIOS chip that supported a maximum of 576K bytes of RAM, whereas later versions of the PC support a maximum of 640K of RAM. The lower portion of Figure 1.8 indicates the DIP switch settings required to define the total amount of memory installed in an IBM PC, including the system board and memory adapter cards in which the computer contains ROM BIOS chips manufactured on or after August 16, 1982.

To determine the date of the BIOS chip installed in any member of the IBM PC series, you can use the following four-line BASIC program, which was executed on an IBM PC AT whose ROM BIOS is dated 01/10/84. The BASIC program listed here can also be executed on IBM PS/2 computers to determine their ROM BIOS date.

```
Ok
LIST
100 DEF SEG = &HF000
110 FOR I = &HFFF5 TO &HFFFD
120 PRINT CHR$(Peek(I));
130 NEXT I
Ok
01/10/84
Ok
```

As explained later in this chapter in a review of the addressing characteristics of the Intel 8088 microprocessor, IBM PCs use a segmented addressing technique to address memory. In segmented addressing two 16-bit numbers are used to reference memory locations, where the first number is known as the segment address and the second is referred to as the *offset* or relative portion of the address. To obtain the actual memory location, the first number (segment address) is multiplied by 16, which is equivalent to adding four binary zeros to it, making the segment address 20 bits long. The second 16-bit number is used as is, providing a relative address to the

PC Series Hardware Overview   19

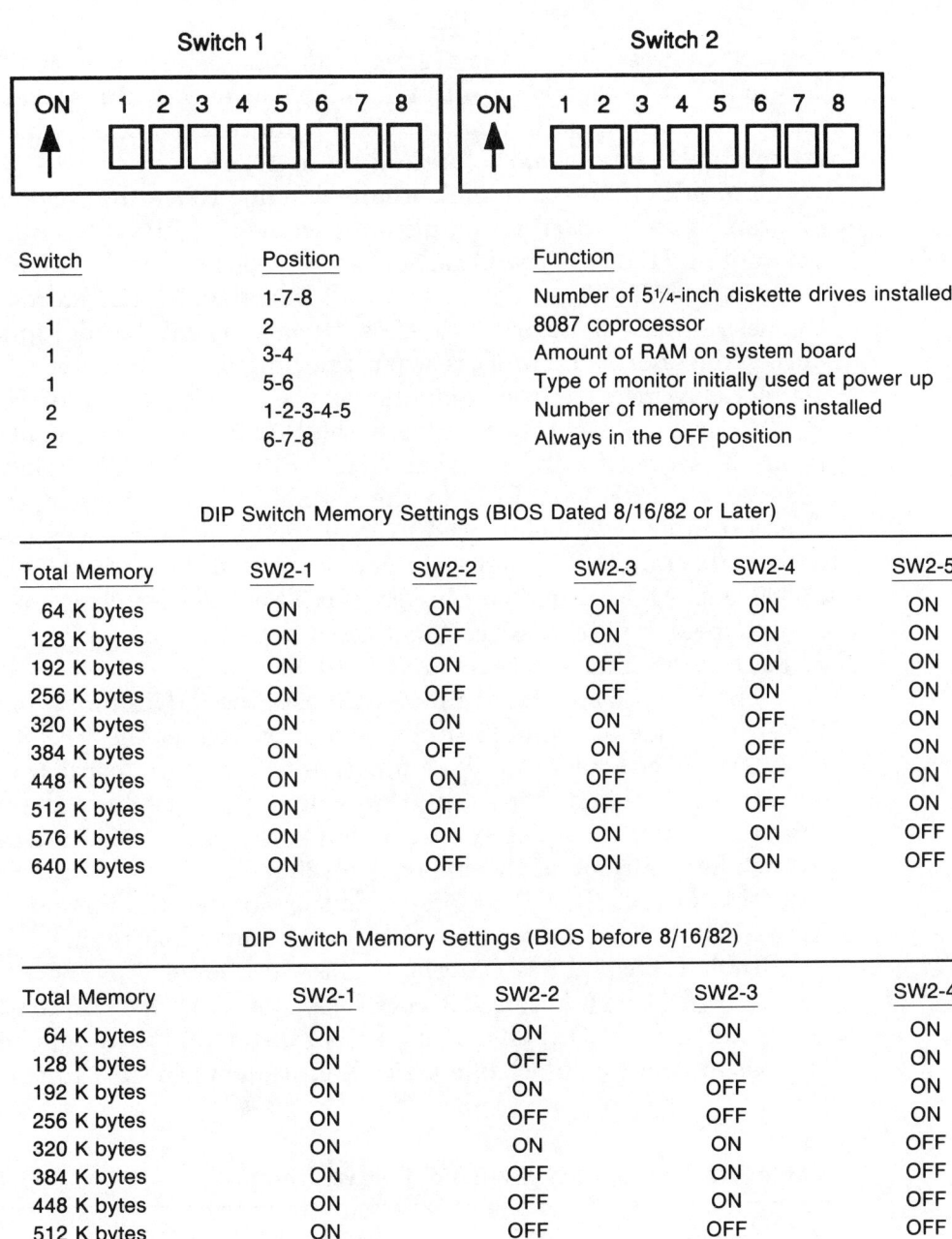

| Switch | Position | Function |
|---|---|---|
| 1 | 1-7-8 | Number of 5¼-inch diskette drives installed |
| 1 | 2 | 8087 coprocessor |
| 1 | 3-4 | Amount of RAM on system board |
| 1 | 5-6 | Type of monitor initially used at power up |
| 2 | 1-2-3-4-5 | Number of memory options installed |
| 2 | 6-7-8 | Always in the OFF position |

DIP Switch Memory Settings (BIOS Dated 8/16/82 or Later)

| Total Memory | SW2-1 | SW2-2 | SW2-3 | SW2-4 | SW2-5 |
|---|---|---|---|---|---|
| 64 K bytes | ON | ON | ON | ON | ON |
| 128 K bytes | ON | OFF | ON | ON | ON |
| 192 K bytes | ON | ON | OFF | ON | ON |
| 256 K bytes | ON | OFF | OFF | ON | ON |
| 320 K bytes | ON | ON | ON | OFF | ON |
| 384 K bytes | ON | OFF | ON | OFF | ON |
| 448 K bytes | ON | ON | OFF | OFF | ON |
| 512 K bytes | ON | OFF | OFF | OFF | ON |
| 576 K bytes | ON | ON | ON | ON | OFF |
| 640 K bytes | ON | OFF | ON | ON | OFF |

DIP Switch Memory Settings (BIOS before 8/16/82)

| Total Memory | SW2-1 | SW2-2 | SW2-3 | SW2-4 |
|---|---|---|---|---|
| 64 K bytes | ON | ON | ON | ON |
| 128 K bytes | ON | OFF | ON | ON |
| 192 K bytes | ON | ON | OFF | ON |
| 256 K bytes | ON | OFF | OFF | ON |
| 320 K bytes | ON | ON | ON | OFF |
| 384 K bytes | ON | OFF | ON | OFF |
| 448 K bytes | ON | OFF | ON | OFF |
| 512 K bytes | ON | OFF | OFF | OFF |
| 544 K bytes | OFF | OFF | OFF | OFF |

**Figure 1.8**  DIP Switch Settings.

segment address. Thus, the segment address can be considered to be a base address to which an offset is added to obtain the actual memory address. By adding both numbers a 20-bit address is formed, which enables a reference to any memory location up to 1024K.

The DEF SEG statement contained in line 100 in the previously listed program is used to define the memory segment address. In this example, the address HF000 is the hexadecimal (H) address F000, which is binary 1111 0000 0000 0000 or decimal 61,440. In actuality, this address is $1/16$ of the desired base or segment address, because it will be multiplied by 16 during the addressing process when the program is executed. Thus, line 100 actually instructs the computer to use a base address of HF0000 or 983,040 decimal. Next, line 110 uses the BASIC FOR statement to increment the value of I from hexadecimal FFF5 to FFFD, in effect, adding hexadecimal FFF5 to FFFD to the segment. This results in the PEEK function in line 120 being used to read the value of memory assigned to the variable I. In this example, the actual values of I vary from hexadecimal F0000 plus FFF5 to F0000 plus FFFD. Thus, the resulting memory addresses read by the PEEK function are hexadecimal FFFF5 through FFFFD, or decimal 1048565 through 1048572.

The PRINT statement in line 120 uses the CHR$ function to covert the ASCII code of the data in memory retrieved by the PEEK function to its character equivalent. This function is necessary, because all data is stored in ASCII code representation where numerics have the values 48 through 57, uppercase letters are assigned the values 65 through 90, and so on. The semicolon at the end of line 120 results in the output from each execution of the PRINT statement as the variable I is incremented by 1 in the FOR-NEXT loop continuing on the same display line.

Table 1.3 lists the BIOS release dates and some differences that exist among them. If you have a BIOS release date of 4/24/81 or 10/19/81 you can obtain a new ROM chip that you can install on the system board that will permit the PC to act like a PC XT; it allows the PC to boot from a

**Table 1.3** PC and PC XT BIOS Release Dates

| RELEASE DATE | PC/FUNCTION |
|---|---|
| 04/24/81 | IBM PC (recognizes 576K bytes of RAM) |
| 10/19/81 | IBM PC (fixed some bugs in original BIOS) |
| 08/16/82 | IBM PC XT |
| 10/27/82 | IBM PC (recognizes fixed disk and 640K bytes of RAM) |

fixed disk and recognize 640 K bytes of RAM. This chip has a release date of 10/27/82, and is more formally known as the IBM PC BIOS Upgrade Kit. Although this kit is no longer sold by IBM, it is still available for purchase from many computer stores.

It is a good idea to check the date of the ROM BIOS installed in your system, especially if you purchased your PC from another person or you're unsure of its date of manufacture. This release date checking is important if you plan to install an Enhanced Graphics Adapter or a local area network adapter, or if you wish to boot your system from a fixed disk. A release date prior to 10/27/82 precludes using the previously mentioned hardware or booting the system from a fixed disk.

## Bus

The bus illustrated in Figure 1.5 is the path along which data moves from the Intel 8088 microprocessor to each of the system expansion slots into which various types of adapter cards can be inserted. The lines that are visible between system expansion slots are known as *trace lines* and are part of the bus. These lines contain three types of data paths or circuits—addressing, control, and data. The control circuits direct the flow of information to and from the expansion slots, whereas the addressing circuits enable data to reach its appropriate destination or to be read from a specific destination. The data circuits carry a byte of information to or from the CPU.

## Adapter Cards

Table 1.4 lists adapter cards that IBM offered for sale for use with the IBM PC and briefly describes the function each card performs. Although IBM no longer manufactures either the first six adapter cards listed in Table 1.4 or the expansion unit, many third party vendors produce compatible products. In addition, hundreds of computer resellers actively market both new and used PC series components and provide a viable source for personal computer parts that can be used to extend the functionality of the PC, PC XT, and PC AT computers.

Figure 1.9 shows eight of the more popular IBM adapter cards originally marketed for use in the PC and PC XT. Note the extension of the Color/Graphics board to the rear of the edge connector, which is inserted

**Table 1.4** IBM PC Adapter Cards

| ADAPTER CARD | FUNCTION |
|---|---|
| Monochrome Display and Parallel Printer | Drives the monochrome display and provides a parallel printer interface |
| Parallel Printer | Provides the parallel printer interface necessary to operate a printer |
| Color/Graphics Monitor | Permits the attachment of an RGB monitor or TV frequency monitors or sets; also contains a light pen interface |
| 5¼″ Diskette Drive Controller | Permits the attachment of up to two internal and two external 5¼-inch diskette drives |
| 64/256K Memory | Increases memory by 64K or 256K above the maximum on-board memory |
| Enhanced Graphics Adapter | Permits the attachment of several different types of monitors to include the monochrome display or a color display to the PC |
| Asynchronous Communications | Converts parallel data into a serial format for communications or to drive a serial printer |
| Bisynchronous Communications | Converts data into a bisynchronous protocol format for communications with another similarly operating device |
| SDLC Communications | Converts data into a synchronous bit oriented protocol format for communications with similarly operating devices |
| Expansion Unit | Permits the PC to be connected to an expansion unit that then adds 7 additional expansion slots that can be used for other adapters |
| IBM PC Network | Permits the PC to be connected to the IBM PC Local Area Network |
| IBM Token Ring | Permits the PC to be connected to the IBM Token Ring local area network |

into a system expansion slot. The extension is known as a "skirt" and restricts the insertion of boards with this physical structure to a subset of the system expansion slots built into the PC AT and XT 286. These machines have only five system expansion slots, so there is a limit to the degree of functionality you can obtain through the addition of adapter cards. Recognizing this limitation, a large number of third party vendors have incorporated two or more functions onto one card. These multifunction cards are discussed in Chapters 3 and 4.

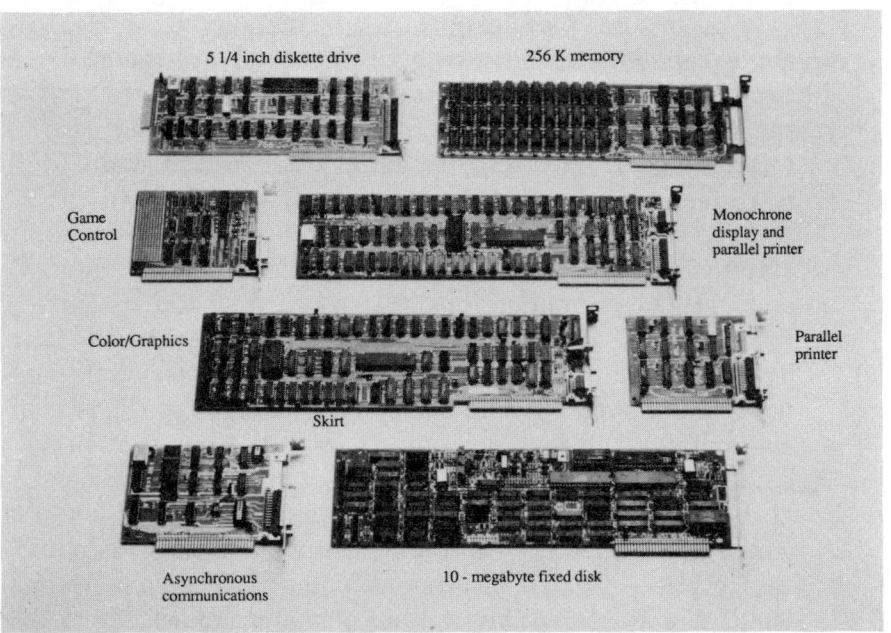

**Figure 1.9** Popular IBM Adapter Cards—The bottom edge of the color/graphics card extends down further than any other adapter. This extension restricts the insertion of boards with skirts into some expansion slots in the PC AT and XT 286. *Photograph courtesy of IBM Corporation.*

## Parallel Versus Serial Ports

The parallel printer and communications cards listed in Table 1.4 provide two of the more popular methods by which IBM PCs can communicate with devices cabled to their system unit. The parallel printer card and the parallel printer interface on the Monochrome Display and Parallel Printer card transmit data from your computer in parallel, 8 bits at a time. Each parallel port can be identified by a 25-pin female (socket) connector at the rear of the card, which, when the card is installed in the computer's system unit, is located at the rear of the unit. The 25-pin connector includes 8 data lines, as well as control lines, and the connector is formally referred to as a DB-25S connector by cabling companies, where the $S$ stands for socket. On the IBM Monochrome Display and Parallel Printer card illustrated in Figure 1.9, the parallel printer port is located directly below a smaller 9-pin video output port used to connect the adapter card to a monochrome display.

Up to three parallel ports can be installed in an IBM PC. These ports are designated LPT1 through LPT3, which are their DOS addresses. Due to the high data transfer rate at which data is sent over the parallel port, the width of the data bits is very narrow, making them susceptible to interference. Because of this, parallel cables are usually limited to a length of 15 feet or less.

The second popular method by which IBM PCs communicate with external devices is through serial ports. The asynchronous, bisynchronous, and SDLC communications adapter cards listed in Table 1.4 all contain serial ports. Each of these cards includes electronics that convert 8-bit bytes that your computer operates on into a serial stream of 8 bits that flows over a single wire in the serial connector at the rear of the card. You can install up to four serial ports in your computer. Serial ports are designated COM1 through COM4, which are their DOS device names. These ports are also referred to as EIA RS-232 ports, which is the method by which the Electronics Industries Association (EIA) denoted a standard for this interface. In this instance, RS stands for *recommended standard* and 232 is the identification number of the standard.

Serial ports can be identified by a 25-pin male (plug) connector, formally referred to as a DP-25P, which is the reverse of the connector on a parallel port. This should normally prevent you from plugging a serial cable into a parallel interface or a parallel cable into a serial interface. A second type of serial port uses a 9-pin connector. This type of serial port is used with IBM PC AT computers and is discussed later in this chapter and in Chapter 7.

Common data rates supported by serial communications range from 110 to 19,200 bits per second. In addition to supporting data transmission via a modem, serial ports can be used to operate serial interface printers, plotters, and scanners, as well as some mice. With a serial interface, a cabling distance of up to 50 feet can be used to connect the serial port to a serial device.

## Cabling

The key to successfully cabling a port on an adapter card to an external device is obtaining the appropriate cable with the correct connectors. Because there are few things more frustrating than purchasing hardware with an improper cable and then being unable to use the system until the mistake is rectified, I examine here some steps you can take to ensure that you obtain a cable that is compatible with your hardware.

The first step to consider before you order a cable is the type of cable required—parallel or serial. A parallel cable used to connect a PC to a printer has a DB-25 connector on one end and normally contains a special "Centronics interface" connector at the opposite end. This connector is named after the firm that popularized this printer interface.

If you require a parallel cable, you will more than likely require a DB-25P cable connector, because it will probably be connected to a DB-25S connector on an adapter card. Although most vendors that manufacture adapter cards with parallel ports use a DB-25S connector, you should verify the connector, because some vendors have used a DB-25P connector that would then require a printer cable with a DB-25S connector to mate properly.

If you require a serial cable, there are four cable connector possibilities as indicated in Table 1.5. Normally, the serial port on an adapter card in your PC has a DB-25P connector, requiring one end of a cable to contain a DB-25S connector. Most modems contain a DB-25S connector, so the other end of the cable requires a DB-25P connector to provide cabling compatibility. Although a serial cable with DB-25P and DB-25S connectors is normally used to cable serial devices to a serial port, some vendors manufacture serial interfaced devices and adapter cards with opposite types of connectors.

Due to this incompatibility, you can use Table 1.5 to verify the types of connectors you should order for your serial cable. As you review the serial cable connector possibilities listed in Table 1.5, note that the second and third cables are equivalent; you can simply turn either cable to reverse the connectors on the cable ends.

**Table 1.5**  Serial Cable Connector Possibilities

| ADAPTER CONNECTOR | CABLE END | CABLE END | HARDWARE CONNECTOR |
|---|---|---|---|
| DB-25S | DB-25P | DB-25S | DB-25P |
| DB-25S | DB-25P | DB-25P | DB-25S |
| DB-25P | DB-25S | DB-25S | DB-25P |
| DP-25P | DB-25S | DB-25P | DB-25S |

## Intel 8088

The Intel 8088 microprocessor has 16-bit internal data paths, and for each memory operation generates a 20-bit address that can access $2^{20}$ (1,048,576) memory locations. However, the microprocessor has only eight pins for data, so it has to perform two memory operations to fetch or store a 16-bit data word, one byte at a time. Further, because it's desirable to be able to keep program code, data, and the stack in separate blocks of memory, the microprocessor computes every memory address in two parts, known as the *segment* and the *offset*.

The segment is a contiguous area of memory, and the offset is the number of bytes from the start of the segment. Because the segment is limited to 64K bytes in length, you can represent any offset by a 16-bit number. The segment must start on a 16-byte boundary within the physical memory. The 8088 has four 16-bit segment registers, each of which points to the base of one of the four possible segments (which may overlap each other). To calculate a physical address, the 8088 multiplies the value in a segment register by 16 and then adds the logical (offset) address; the result is always a 20-bit address. The upper four address bits appear on pins that are shared with the status bus (A19/S3 through A16/S0); the next eight bits appear on dedicated address pins (A15 through A8); and the least significant bits appear on pins that are shared with the data bus (AD7 through AD0). The ALE signal then loads the address into an external address register in order to free the status and data pins for their other functions.

Although the Intel 8088 can address up to 1024K of memory, only 640K of memory can be effectively used by the DOS. This limitation results from DOS requiring a contiguous memory area, of which 640K was always available based upon the assigned usage of different areas of memory.

Figure 1.10 illustrates the IBM PC and PC XT system memory maps. Note that some software products can use the extra 64K RAM above the 640K "barrier" if an IBM Enhanced Graphics Adapter is not installed. Later in the chapter you'll find detailed information covering the memory usage of the Enhanced Graphics Adapter operating in different graphics modes.

## Intel 8087

The empty 40-pin socket to the right of the Intel 8088 in Figure 1.5 accepts an Intel 8087 numeric coprocessor. This microprocessor extends the ca-

| Start Address | | Function |
| Decimal | Hex | |
|---|---|---|
| 0 | 00000 | 16-64Kb Read/Write Memory on original PC System Board |
| . | . | |
| 48K | 0C00 | |
| 64K | 10000 | Up to 256 Kb Read/Write Memory on newer PC and PC XT System Boards or Up to 640K via Memory Expansion Adapter cards or on new PC XT System Board |
| . | . | |
| . | . | |
| 640K | A0000 | Enhanced Graphics |
| . | . | |
| 704K | B0000 | Monochrome |
| 720K | B4000 | |
| 736K | B8000 | Color/Graphics |
| 752K | BC000 | |
| 768K | C0000 | Professional Graphics |
| 784K | C4000 | |
| 800K | C8000 | Fixed Disk Control |
| 816K | CC000 | 192K ROM Expansion and Control |
| . | . | |
| . | . | |
| 944K | EC000 | |
| 960K | F0000 | Reserved (Cartridge ROM Area) |
| 976K | F4000 | 48Kb Base System ROM contains BIOS, Cassette BASIC and POST |
| . | . | |
| 1008K | FC000 | |

(Rows from 640K through BC000 are bracketed as VIDEO)

**Figure 1.10** IBM PC and PC XT System Memory Maps.

pability of the 8088, because the 8087 can perform certain kinds of arithmetic operations much faster than the 8088. Essentially, the 8087 is designed to perform floating-point arithmetic in hardware, resulting in an increase in speed, range, and precision over arithmetic operations performed by the 8088.

Intel currently markets a family of math coprocessors, three of which are illustrated in Figure 1.11. Each coprocessor has a notch used to align the chip for insertion into a socket of the motherboard of the personal computer for which it is designed.

Make sure that you obtain the correct coprocessor for your computer. The 8087 operates with a standard 8088 processor that runs at 4.77 MHz— the standard speed adopted by IBM for the PC and PC XT. The 8087-1 works only with an 8086 microprocessor, which has a 16-bit external data

**28**  The PC Upgrader's Manual

**Figure 1.11**   Three Math Coprocessors. *Photograph courtesy of Intel Corporation.*

bus (the 8088's external data bus is only 8 bits wide). The 8087-2 works with an 8088-2 microprocessor that operates at 8 MHz, as found in many third party PC- and PC XI-compatible machines. If your machine runs at 4.77 MHz, the 8087-2 will work, but it costs $50 to $100 more than the slower version.

When you upgrade your machine with an 8087 math coprocessor, you should also check the copyright date(s) that appear(s) on the 8088 chip. If the date is "INTEL '78," only, you'll have to replace the 8088 with a more recent version that has dates such as "INTEL '78, 81, 83." An 8088 that carries any date more recent than 198 is compatible with the 8087, and you need not replace it.

## System Unit Rear

Figure 1.12 illustrates the rear of the system unit of an early model of the IBM PC, which is very similar to later versions of the rear panel of the PC and the PC XT. Both the PC and the PC XT rear panels include a

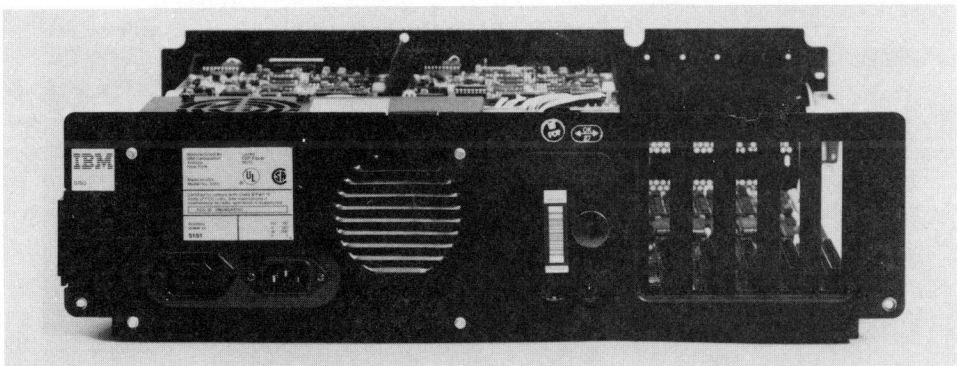

**Figure 1.12** Rear View of the IBM PC System Unit—The keyboard unit is connected to the left circular connector, and the right circular connector is used to interface a cassette recorder. This connector was removed from PCs manufactured after mid-1982 and was never included on the PC XT. *Photograph courtesy of IBM Corporation.*

receptacle you can use to provide power to the IBM Monochrome Display. This receptacle is located at the left of the panel, as illustrated in Figure 1.12.

The power cable connector located to the right of the receptacle connects to a cable that in turn is inserted into a 110VAC power outlet. The two circular connectors are used for the connection of the keyboard and an optional cassette recorder. The second connector for the cassette recorder was eliminated from all PCs manufactured from mid-1982 onward and was never included in the PC XT. You can remove the circular and oval covers above the circular connectors in order to run a cable from an existing adapter board through the circular or oval hole to an external device. Without these extra holes, you'd have to bring the cable out through the hole associated with an expansion slot, so that you could not use that slot.

## PC XT System Unit

Figure 1.13 shows the interior of a PC XT that has a full complement of adapter cards and two devices in its device housing areas. The interior layout of the PC XT system unit is very similar to that of the PC, the only difference being in the number of system expansion slots and con-

**Figure 1.13** Interior of the PC XT System Unit—The interior of the system unit of the PC XT is similar to the PC, with major changes in the number of expansion slots and configuration switches and the capacity of the power supply. *Photograph courtesy of IBM Corporation.*

figuration switches, the capacity of the power supply, and the population of the memory banks at the time the computer was manufactured.

## Expansion Slots

The system unit of the PC XT contains eight expansion slots; that of the PC has only five slots. Be careful when you change an adapter card for the PC XT; the diskette drive blocks some of the space behind slots 7 and 8, so you can't insert full-size cards into these slots. They will accept half-length cards (also known as *short cards*), but because of technical differences between the two slots, you have to be even more careful. An adapter card installed in slot 8 is required to return a "card select" signal when the card is addressed by the CPU. In addition, the timing requirements of slot 8 are more stringent that those of slots 1 through 7.

For these reasons, you should never install a card in slot 8 of a PC XT unless the card was specifically designed to operate there. Fortunately, several adapter cards (including the IBM Asynchronous Communications Adapter) contain a jumper that you can install if you want to insert the card into slot 8.

When the original PC XT was introduced, several adapter cards were included as a standard offering with this computer. One card was the asynchronous communications adapter, which is a half-length or short card and was inserted in system expansion slot number 8. A second adapter card included with the PC XT was the fixed-disk adapter card, because early versions of the PC XT included one 10M-byte fixed disk in the right device housing area, as well as a 5¼-inch diskette drive in the left device housing area. Since then IBM has marketed several versions of the PC XT, the key difference between versions being the number and types of storage devices (and their associated controller cards) included in the system unit.

## Configuration Switch

The system board of the PC XT has only one configuration DIP switch, located to the right of the eighth system expansion slot. The eight individual switches denote the amount of memory installed on the system board, the presence of an 8087 coprocessor, the type of display to be used at power-up, and the number of diskette drives installed. The top of Figure 1.14 illustrates the function of each of the positions on the configuration switch. The lower portion of Figure 1.14 indicates the DIP switch settings that denote the amount of random access memory installed on the system board of a PC XT that supported the use of 64K memory chips. Other versions of the PC XT support the use of both 64K- and 256K-bit chips, permitting up to 640K bytes of RAM to be installed on the system board.

## Power Supply

Because of the inclusion of a fixed disk in the PC XT, the capacity of its power supply was increased to 130 watts. In comparison, the power supply capacity of the PC is only 63.5 watts.

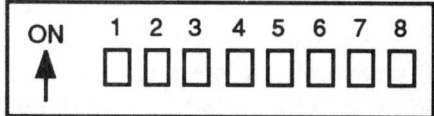

| Position | Function |
|---|---|
| 1 | Off for normal operation |
| 2 | Coprocessor |
| 3–4 | Amount of RAM on system board |
| 5–6 | Type of monitor used on power up |
| 7–8 | Number of 5¼-inch diskette drives installed |

DIP Switch Memory Settings Using 64K-bit Chips

| Total Memory | SW-3 | SW-4 |
|---|---|---|
| 128 K bytes | OFF | ON |
| 196 K bytes | ON | OFF |
| 256 K bytes | OFF | OFF |

**Figure 1.14** PC XT Configuration Switch.

## RAM

The system board of the PC XT, like that of the PC, contains four rows of sockets for the insertion of RAM. IBM originally offered the PC XT with 128K bytes of RAM, obtained by populating the first two rows of sockets with 64K-bit memory chips. You could add similar chips to expand the memory on the system board to 256K-bit chips in banks 0 and 1, yielding a total of 512K bytes; you could then add 64K-bit chips in banks 2 and 3, thereby expanding the system board memory to 640K bytes:

256K(0) + 256K(1) + 64K(2) + 64K(3) = 640K bytes

## Fixed Disk

The fixed disk that was originally supplied with the PC XT contained two rigid platters with two recording surfaces per platter. For each position of the heads, the four recording tracks under the heads are collectively called a *cylinder*. Although the disk has space for 345 cylinders, PC-DOS formatted only 306 cylinders, of which one was reserved for diagnostics. Thus, the total capacity of this disk, when formatted by PC-DOS, was

305 cylinders * 4 tracks/cylinder * 17 sectors/track * 512 bytes/sector = 10,618,880 bytes

Table 1.6 compares the major features of the IBM PC to several of the different models of the PC XT that have been marketed by IBM. Table 1.7 summarizes the initial or standard configuration of six IBM PC XT models as originally sold by IBM. Although the entries in Table 1.7 indicate the original hardware included with different PC XT models, you should verify the hardware of any computer you may consider purchasing. Many models of the IBM PC series were modified by the purchaser to include the addition of memory, replacement of storage devices, and the addition of one or more adapter cards.

**Table 1.6** Comparing PC and PC XTs

|  | **PC** | **PC XT** | **PC XT** | **PC XT** |
|---|---|---|---|---|
| Model Number | 5150 | 5160 | 5160 Model 68 | 5160 Model 78 |
| RAM M (K bytes) | 64/256 | 128/256 | 256 | 256 |
| Expansion Slots | 5 | 8 | 8 | 8 |
| Microprocessor | 8088 | 8088 | 8088 | 8088 |
| Addressable Memory (K bytes) | 576/640 | 640 | 640 | 640 |
| Standard Storage | 0, 1, or 2 diskette drives | 1 360K byte diskette 1 10M byte fixed disk | 1 360K byte diskette | 2 360K byte diskettes |
| Standard Adapters | None or diskette | Diskette; fixed disk asynchronous communications | Diskette | Diskette |
| Coprocessor Socket | Yes | Yes | Yes | Yes |
| Power Supply (W) | 63.5 | 135 | 135 | 135 |

**Table 1.7** 5160 Personal Computer XT Models

| MODEL NUMBER | FEATURES |
| --- | --- |
| Model 068 | System unit/keyboard; 256K-byte memory; one 5¼-inch double-sided diskette drive; diskette drive adapter. |
| Model 078 | System unit/keyboard; 256 K-byte memory; two 5¼-inch double-sided diskette drives; diskette drive adapter. |
| Model 086 | System unit/keyboard; 256K-byte memory; 10M-byte fixed disk drive; fixed disk drive adapter; one 5¼-inch double-sided diskette drive; diskette drive adapter; asynchronous communications adapter. |
| Model 087 | System unit/keyboard; 128K-byte memory; 10M-byte fixed disk drive; fixed disk drive adapter; one 5¼-inch double-sided diskette drive; diskette drive adapter; asynchronous communications adapter. |
| Model 470 | System Unit; 256K-byte memory; one 5¼-inch 320K-byte diskette drive and adapter; financial input adapter, and the finance 107-key administrative keyboard. |
| Model 589 | System unit/keyboard; 256K-byte memory; PC/370-M card (512K-byte memory); PC/370-P card (370 processor); 3278/79 emulation adapter; 10M-byte fixed disk drive; fixed disk drive adapter; one 5¼-inch double-sided diskette drive; diskette drive adapter; asynchronous communications adapter. |

Figure 1.15 illustrates three device housing area configuration options corresponding to several different PC XT versions. Only the Model 68 XT provides configuration flexibility, because it includes an empty device housing area. In the other models you first have to remove an existing full-height device to install one or more half-height devices if the configuration as purchased does not meet your requirements.

Table 1.8 lists the PC XT options introduced by IBM during 1986. The 3½-inch diskettes were introduced to provide data transfer between the IBM Convertible (a portable computer) and the PC XT, which, until the introduction of DOS 3.2, did not support those drives. The 3½-inch diskettes used with those drives are formatted with 80 tracks per side, using 9 sectors per track. This yields a total capacity of 720K bytes:

80 tracks/side * 2 sides * 9 sectors/track * 512 bytes/sector = 737,280 bytes

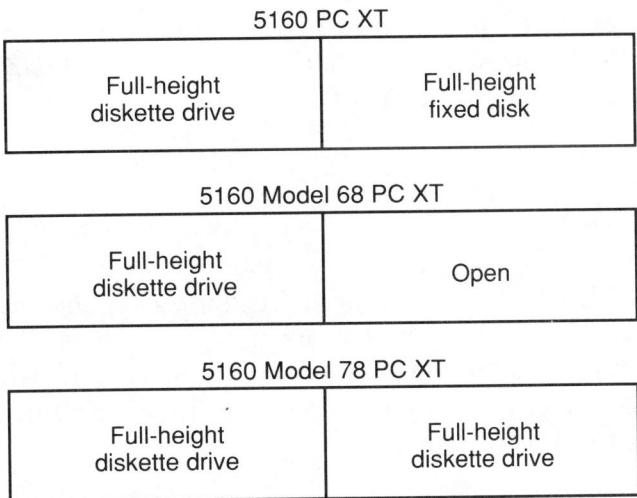

**Figure 1.15** PC XT Device Housing Area Configuration Options—Only the Model 68 PC XT provides configuration flexibility, because it includes an open device housing area.

**Table 1.8** Additional PC XT Options

| DRIVE | MEMORY |
|---|---|
| External 3½-inch diskette drive | 128K-byte memory module kit |
| Internal half-height 3½-inch diskette drive | 256K-byte memory module kit |
| 20M-byte fixed disk drive | |
| 20M-byte fixed disk drive adapter | |
| 5¼-inch half-height 360K-byte diskette | |

(Because all memory and disk capacities are powers of 2, 1K represents 1024, not 1000. Thus, 737,280/1024 = 720 K.)

The IBM Personal System/2 Model 30 computer introduced on April 2, 1987, uses the same 3½-inch diskette that is standard in the PC Convertible and is offered as an option for the PC XT. Other models of the Personal System/2 line use a 1.44M-byte diskette that can read the 720-byte, 3½-inch diskette. Although the 720K-byte disk drive cannot read a disk produced by a 1.44M-byte 3½-inch drive, you can format a disk in the 1.44M-byte drive for 720K-byte storage. Then you can easily transfer data between PC and PS/2 computers.

## The PC AT

The IBM PC AT (Advanced Technology) personal computer was introduced in mid-1984, three years after the original PC was announced. The structure of a PC AT computer system is similar to that of the PC and PC XT, consisting of a keyboard unit, system unit, and monitor as illustrated in Figure 1.16.

**Figure 1.16** IBM PC AT Computer System—The major components of a PC AT computer system include a keyboard, system unit, display, and a printer (not shown). *Photograph courtesy of IBM Corporation.*

## Keyboard

The keyboard supplied with the original PC AT has 84 keys and is a significant improvement over the earlier PC and PC XT keyboards, for several reasons. First the keyboards have a row of three green indicator lights to show you when the Caps Lock, Num Lock, and Scroll Lock keys are active. Second, the 10-foot, coiled cable is four feet longer than those of the earlier keyboards and gives you greater flexibility in arranging your work area—you can, for example, put the system unit on the floor. Later on, however, IBM introduced the Enhanced Keyboard (Figure 1.3), which replaced the original keyboard on all PC ATs manufactured after mid-1986.

## System Unit

The system unit of the PC AT can be considered the heart of that computer. Like the PC and PC XT system units, the AT's system unit includes ROM and RAM, system expansion slots for the installation of adapter boards, and a connector at the rear of the unit for the attachment of the keyboard.

When it is viewed from the front there are several small but significant differences between the system unit of the PC AT and those of the PC and the PC XT. To the right of the IBM label in the upper left corner of the unit is a keylock and two indicators. The keylock is designed to accept a hard-to-duplicate "tubular" key, similar to the keys used in many home and commercial security systems. You can lock the computer and remove the key, thereby preventing the system from recognizing commands or keystrokes entered from the keyboard. Thus, you can initiate an application and then leave the computer running without having to worry that someone might change, interrupt, or terminate the application. The first indicator to the right of the keylock position is a power-on indicator; the second is an LED that lights if a fixed disk is installed and active.

## Device Housing Area

Only one accessible device housing area is built into the system unit of the PC AT. Although one half-height 5¼-inch diskette drive is shown installed in Figure 1.16, this device housing area is capable of accepting two half-height diskette drives or one half-height diskette drive and one half-height fixed disk. To the left of the device housing area is an internal metal case that is only accessible when the cover of the system unit is removed. This metal case in effect can be considered as a second device housing area and was originally designed to accept either a 20M-byte or 30M-byte fixed disk.

## Basic and Enhanced Models

The storage devices installed in the system unit of the PC AT as well as the amount of RAM installed on the system board vary according to the particular PC AT model. When the computer was introduced in 1984, two models of the PC AT were marketed—a basic version and an enhanced version.

The basic PC AT includes 256K bytes of RAM and a single 5¼-inch half-height, double-sided diskette drive capable of storing 1.2M bytes on a diskette, which is installed in the upper portion of the device housing area, as illustrated in Figure 1.16. Also included in the basic PC AT is a dual-purpose diskette and fixed disk controller installed in a system expansion slot in the system unit.

Outwardly, the 5¼-inch diskette drive used in the basic PC AT model appears similar to the diskette drives used in the PC and PC XT. In actuality, the PC AT diskette drive is a high-capacity device capable of storing data on 80 tracks on a diskette, using 15 sectors per track. The separation between tracks is smaller than on a conventional 360K-byte diskette, so you should use special high-capacity diskettes in the PC AT's high-capacity diskette drive. The storage capacity of the PC/AT's diskette drive is

2 sides * 80 tracks/side * 15 sectors/track * 512 bytes/sector = 1,228,800 bytes

The enhanced PC AT includes 512K of RAM installed on the computer's system board, a 1.2M-byte diskette drive, a dual diskette and fixed disk controller, a serial/parallel adapter card, and a 20M-byte fixed disk.

The serial/parallel adapter card combines a serial and a parallel port onto one card. The serial port is similar in performance to the asynchronous communications adapter used with the PC and PC XT; the parallel port is equivalent in operation to the IBM parallel printer adapter and to the parallel port on the IBM Monochrome Display and Parallel Printer Adapter card. The one significant difference between the serial port on the serial/parallel adapter card and the serial port on cards designed for use in the PC and PC XT is the card's connector. Serial ports on cards designed for use in the PC and PC XT contain a DB-25 connector. In comparison, the serial port on the serial/parallel adapter card designed for use in the PC AT uses a DB-9 connector. Refer to Chapter 7 for additional information concerning the DB-9 connector on the serial/parallel adapter card.

Since the introduction of the PC AT, IBM increased its functionality and capability in several areas, which include the amount of RAM installed on the computer's system board, the capacity of the fixed disk, and the operating rate of the crystal installed on the computer's system board. PC ATs manufactured after mid-1986 have 640K of RAM installed on the computer's system board, and a 30M-byte fixed disk was introduced as an option. Although a 6-MHz crystal was initially installed in all PC ATs, later versions manufactured by IBM include an 8-MHz crystal, which increases the processing rate of the computer's microprocessor by one-third.

Options available for the PC AT include a conventional 360K half-height diskette drive, which is installed below the standard 1.2M-byte diskette drive; a second 20- or 30M-byte fixed disk (for an enhanced PC AT); and a variety of adapter cards that can be installed in system expansion slots to obtain additional functionality.

## System Unit Interior

Figure 1.17 shows, in diagrammatic form, the layout of the internal components of the PC AT. In the upper right corner of the interior of the system unit is the power supply, which is rated at 192 watts, as opposed to the 63.5 watts of the PC and 135 watts of the PC XT. Included in the power supply is a cooling fan that exhausts heat generated by the electrical operation of the components of the system to the rear of the system unit. A switch at the rear of the system unit sets the power supply for either 115- or 230-volt operation, so that you can use the PC AT anywhere in the world.

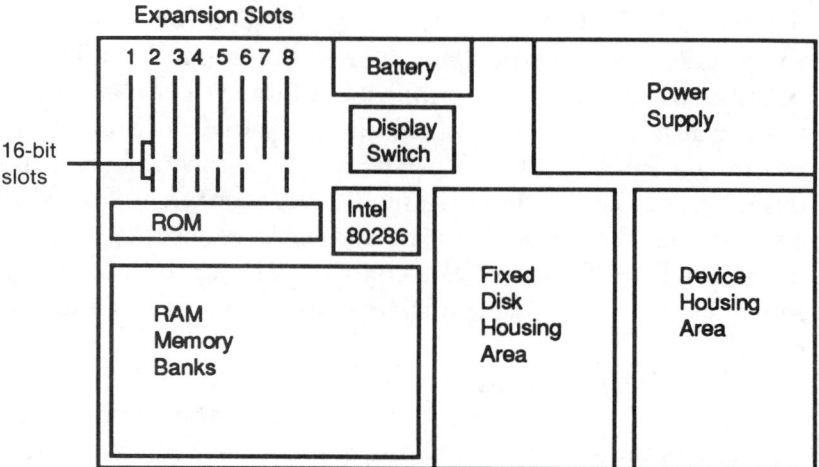

**Figure 1.17** IBM PC AT System Unit Interior—Expansion slots 2 through 6 and slot 8 can be used for either 16-bit or 8-bit data transfer adapter cards, containing either one or two edge connectors, as long as the card does not contain a skirt.

## Device Housing Area

The device housing area in the lower right corner of the system unit is designed to hold two half-height storage devices. A 1.2M-byte, high-capacity diskette drive is installed in the top portion of the device housing area in all PC ATs. The lower portion of the device housing area can be used to house a second 1.2M-byte diskette drive, a 360K-byte diskette drive, or a 20M- or 30M-byte fixed disk. Use care in the type of diskette used in the 1.2M-byte diskette drive as well as consider any other type of diskette drive you may use a high-intensity diskette in. The key problem associated with the use of the 1.2M-byte disk drive is the width of the tracks used for recording data. Standard double-density diskettes formatted in a standard diskette drive to store 360K bytes of data have 40 tracks equally spaced at a recording rate of 48 tracks per inch. The 1.2M-byte high-density drive records data onto 80 tracks using the same amount of space, because read/write heads are only half as wide as the read/write heads of a 360K-byte drive. Thus, if you record data onto a 360K-byte diskette in a 360K-byte drive and then write over it in a 1.2M-byte drive, the latter drive's smaller read/write head may not completely erase the old data. This should not affect your operations as long as the diskette is in a 1.2M-byte drive, but suppose you later attempt to use the diskette in a

360K-byte drive? The wider read/write heads of a 360K-byte drive may read portions of previously erased data.

To ensure proper operation of diskettes, you can record data onto 360K-byte disks in a 1.2M-byte drive as long as you only use those diskettes in 1.2M-byte drives or do not erase any data on the disk if you want to use it in a 360K-byte drive. Similarly, you can format 360K-byte disks in a 1.2M-byte drive and write to them using a 360K-byte drive as long as you restrict their use to 360K-byte drives. Only when you write and erase data on a 360K-byte formatted diskette in a 1.2M-byte drive and then use that disk in a 360K-byte drive do you run the risk of encountering problems. Due to the previously described potential problems, many PC AT users have installed a conventional 360K-byte diskette drive in the lower portion of the device housing area in order to create diskettes that can be read by the drives used in the PC and PC XT.

The area to the left of the device housing area accommodates either a 20M-byte fixed disk (standard on early models of the AT) or a 30M-byte drive (offered later as an option). You can't install diskette drives or tape backup units in this area, because you can't reach the area without removing the system unit cover.

## RAM

The lower left area of the PC AT's system unit is similar to that of the PC and PC XT. Four rows of sockets allow the insertion of nine memory chips per row; each row of memory is called a *bank*. When the PC AT was first introduced, IBM used a piggyback arrangement of two 64K-bit memory chips in each socket. In the basic model, only banks 0 and 1 were populated, yielding 256K bytes of RAM. In the enhanced model, all four rows were populated with piggybacked 64K-bit chips, to obtain a total of 512K bytes of RAM on the system board. As in the PC and PC XT, each bank consists of 9 chip sockets to enable memory parity checking. Later models of the PC AT used 256K-bit memory chips in banks 0 and 1 and 64K-bit chips in banks 2 and 3 to obtain a total of 640K bytes of on-board storage. The system memory map of the PC AT is similar to that previously illustrated for the IBM PC and PC XT.

## ROM

Located above RAM bank 0 is a row of ROM chips that contain the PC AT's POST, BIOS, and Cassette BASIC. Even though the AT has no cassette interface, Cassette BASIC is included in ROM, as it is a nucleus of the IBM's BASIC language. You add features to this nucleus by loading different BASIC interpreters from diskette into RAM.

### Intel 80286 Microprocessor

The Intel 80286 is a true 16-bit microprocessor that has both internal and external data buses that are 16 bits wide. This enables data to be manipulated in 16-bit units as well as sent to and received from expansion slots and memory in 16-bit units. The 8088 microprocessor used in the PC and PC XT manipulates data in 16-bit units but uses an 8-bit data bus to send and receive data in 8-bit units.

Other differences between the 80286 and 8088 concern the operating rate of each microprocessor, and the level of integration of auxiliary chips onto each device. The 80286 receives clocking directly from a crystal that can easily be replaced. Initial versions of the PC AT used a 6-MHz crystal that was faster than the 4.77-MHz operating rate of the 8088 used in the PC and PC XT. Later models of the PC AT use an 8-MHz crystal, which provides the 80286 with an operating rate almost twice that of the 8088.

The level of integration in the 80286 is approximately six times that of the 8088. The 80286 contains over 120,000 transistors on one chip, eliminating several separate chips that were required by the 8088. When taken together, the PC AT 80286's 16-bit data bus, its faster operating rate, and the higher level of chip integration permit software to operate between four and five times faster than on an 8088-based PC or PC XT.

### Bus

The 80286 bus consists of control, data, and address lines like the 8088 bus. The key differences between the 80286 and 8088 bus are in the physical number of data and address lines.

The 80286 data bus has 16 lines instead of the 8 lines used in the 8088-based PC and PC XT. The 80286 address bus consists of 24 lines, permitting the direct addressing of $2^{24}$ or 16M bytes of memory, although DOS 3.0 through DOS 4.0, which are primarily used with the PC AT and PS/2, only directly support 640K bytes of RAM. In comparison, the 8088 uses 20 address lines, permitting 1M byte of RAM to be addressed.

### Expansion Slots

To enable many of the large number of 8-bit adapter cards designed for operation in the PC and PC XT to work with the PC AT, IBM provided two control signals on the bus and structured the physical layout of the expansion slots to accommodate 8-bit adapter cards.

As indicated in Figure 1.17, there are eight system expansion slots in the PC AT. Expansion slots 2 through 6 and slot 8 have two edge connectors, whereas slots 1 and 7 each have only one edge connector. The edge connector closest to the rear of the system unit is the standard 62-pin IBM PC expansion slot connector used in the PC and PC XT. The second slot connector included in expansion slots 2 through 6 and slot 8 is a 36-pin connector designed to support the additional data and address lines used by the PC AT's 80286 microprocessor.

Cards specifically designed for 16-bit data transfers have two edge connectors and have to be inserted into expansion slots 2 through 6 or slot 8. Older adapter cards designed for use in the PC and PC XT can usually work in the PC AT; however, using them may significantly reduce the performance of the computer. One example of performance degradation is the use of an 8-bit memory adapter designed for use in the PC or PC XT. This adapter has a single 62-pin edge connector and lacks a skirt, enabling it to be installed in any PC AT expansion slot. If you install this 8-bit memory card in any of the expansion slots 2 through 6 or slot 8, its lack of a second 36-pin edge connector results in two control lines on the 36-pin expansion slot connector not being activated, in effect informing the AT that an 8-bit card is installed in that expansion slot. Thereafter, data transfers to and from that expansion slot occur 8 bits at a time. But because the PC AT can transfer data 16 bits at a time, using an 8-bit memory expansion card significantly reduces the performance of the computer.

If an 8-bit adapter card has a skirt, it is physically restricted to use in expansion slot 1 or 7. If you try to install it in any of the expansion slots 2 through 6 and slot 8 the skirt bumps against the second connector of these slots, and prevents the edge connector of the card from being inserted into the 62-pin connector, as illustrated in Figure 1.18. The color graphics card previously illustrated in Figure 1.9 is a prime example of an adapter card with a skirt that is physically restricted to installation in expansion slot 1 or 7 in the PC AT. Table 1.9 summarizes the AT compatibility, according to IBM, of adapter cards originally manufactured for use in the PC and PC XT. However, I have used many of the adapter cards "Not recommended for use in the PC AT" in my PC AT and have noted only a slight decrease in performance.

44  The PC Upgrader's Manual

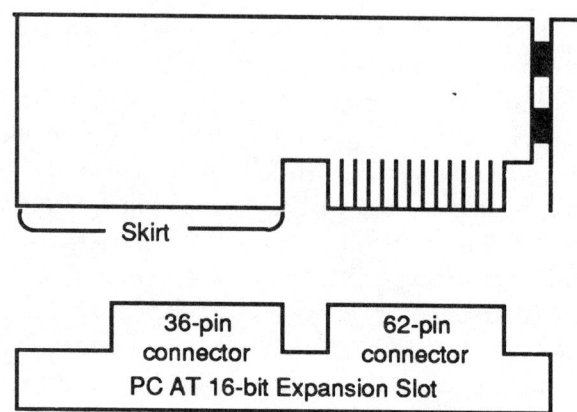

**Figure 1.18** Physical Incompatibility—The skirt on some 8-bit adapter cards physically precludes their insertion into a 16-bit expansion slot on the PC AT.

**Table 1.9** PC Adapter Compatability Guide

| ADAPTER CARDS | COMPATIBILITY WITH PC AT |
|---|---|
| Monochrome Display and Parallel Printer | Works in any expansion slot |
| Color Graphics | Works in expansion slot 1 or 7 |
| Enhanced Graphics | Works in any expansion slot |
| Parallel Printer | Not recommended for use in PC AT |
| 64K to 256K memory | Not recommended for use in PC AT |
| Asynchronous Communications | Not recommended for use in PC AT |
| 5¼-inch Diskette Drive | Not recommended for use in PC AT |

## Battery

Located between expansion slot 8 and the power supply is a lithium battery that is used to supply power to a clock/calendar and 64K bytes of complementary metallic oxide semiconductor (CMOS) RAM. The 64K-byte CMOS RAM is a low-power memory area that stores the system configuration data initially entered during the installation process. This memory area is set via software and replaces the inaccessible configuration switches found on the PC and PC XT.

Because the CMOS RAM contains information about the PC AT's configuration, if the battery should fail you not only lose the clock and calendar data but also such important information as the number of disk drives and amount of RAM memory installed. When this information is lost, you have to reconfigure the system every time it is turned on—a time-consuming and tedious task.

Figure 1.19 illustrates perhaps the most important replacement part you will require. The lithium battery illustrated is manufactured by Tadiran, which supplied over 80 percent of the batteries used in the IBM PC ATs. This battery is exclusively marketed by IBC of Reseda, Calif., as a replacement for the original battery supplied with the AT, which can be expected to last approximately 3 years. The Tadiran battery can be expected to last for about 10 years.

As previously noted, the loss of battery power will result in the loss of configuration information. To simplify selecting the appropriate options in the Setup program contained on the diagnostic diskette that is included with each PC AT, it is a good idea to use Setup to display and print your system's configuration prior to a battery failure. The following illustrates

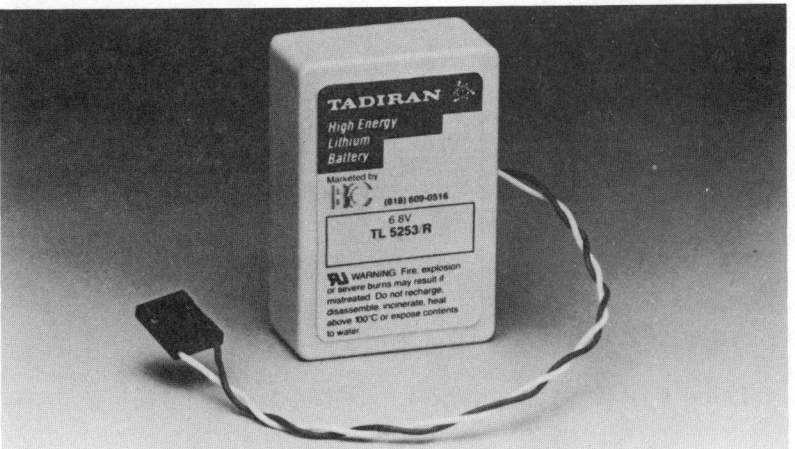

**Figure 1.19** IBM Replacement Battery—Because the life of the battery originally installed in the PC AT is approximately three years, many users will have to replace it one or more times during the life of their computer. *Photograph courtesy of IBC.*

the type of screen display you see as you use the Setup program. Once you save the program results, the replacement of a battery that results in the loss of configuration data becomes a simple procedure to correct by rerunning Setup.

```
Your system may have other options
installed.  They are not required for
Setup and are not displayed.

The following options have been set:
Diskette Drive A - High Capacity
Diskette Drive B - Double Sided
Fixed Disk Drive C - Type 2
Fixed Disk Drive D - Not Installed
Base memory size - 640KB
Expansion memory size - 1024KB
Primary display is:
- Color Display (80 columns)

Are these options correct (Y/N)?
```

## Display Switch

The only switch contained in the PC AT system unit is located slightly below the area where the battery is located. This switch sets the default for the type of display you want to use when the computer is powered on. When the switch is positioned toward the rear of the system unit, it selects the Monochrome Display as the primary display. If the switch is positioned toward the front of the system unit, a color graphics display becomes the default display. In essence, this switch is similar to one of the position elements of the configuration switch on the PC and PC XT. It enables you to install two display adapters in your PC AT and selects which adapter will become active when you turn on power.

## Adapter Cards and Options

Table 1.10 lists the adapter cards and options originally marketed by IBM for use with the PC AT. Adapter cards include memory expansion, serial and parallel ports, and monitor functions. Options include a memory expansion module to increase on-board system unit memory, as well as a special cable that converts a 9-pin connector on the serial portion of the serial/parallel adapter card to the more common 25-pin connector. Similar

**Table 1.10** IBM PC AT Adapter Cards and Options

| ADAPTER CARD/OPTION | FUNCTIONAL DESCRIPTION |
| --- | --- |
| Monochrome Display and Parallel Printer Adapter | Drives the IBM Monochrome Display and provides a parallel interface for connecting a printer |
| Color Graphics Adapter | Enables a variety of TV frequency monitors, composite video monitors, and TV sets to be connected; includes a light pen interface |
| Enhanced Graphics Adapter | Can be used with both the IBM Monochrome Display and IBM Color Display; provides improved resolution over the Color Graphics card when used with the IBM Enhanced Color Display |
| 128K Memory Adapter | Increases system unit memory by 128K bytes after on-board memory totals 512K bytes |
| 256K Memory Expansion Module | increases on-board system unit memory by 256K bytes |
| 512K Expansion Adapter | Increases system unit memory by 512K bytes after on-board memory totals 512K bytes |
| 1M Expansion Adapter | Increases system unit memory by 1M byte after on-board memory totals 512K bytes |
| Serial/Parallel Adapter | Contains the interface for one serial and one parallel device |
| Serial Adapter Connector | A short cable that converts the DB-9 (9-pin) connector on the serial interface of the card to a more common DB-25 (25-pin) connector |
| 1.2M Floppy Diskette Drive | Reads 5¼-inch diskettes in 160/180K-, 320/360K-, and 1.2M-byte modes; writes to diskettes in 1.2M-byte mode |
| Diskette Drive and Fixed Disk Adapter | Permits up to four diskette drives and fixed disks to be controlled; however, only three devices can be installed within the system unit |
| 320/360K Byte diskette Drive | Reads and writes 5¼-inch diskettes in 160/180K-byte and 320/360K-byte modes |
| 3½-Inch Diskette Drive | Reads and writes 3½-inch diskettes in 720K-byte mode |

to most adapter cards designed for use in the PC and PC XT, the PC AT adapter cards listed in Table 1.10 are no longer manufactured by IBM. However, many third party vendors continue to manufacture compatible adapter cards for use in the PC AT as well as in PC AT clones. This provides PC AT and PC AT clone owners with a viable source of personal computer components to build or expand their system.

If you want to expand the 256K-byte memory of a basic PC AT, you can obtain a 256K-byte memory-expansion kit that consists of 18 single 128K-bit chips. You insert these chips into the sockets of memory banks 2 and 3, bringing the total memory on the system board to 512K bytes. PC-DOS supports as many as 640K bytes of RAM, so you can bring the memory up to full capacity by adding a 128K-byte memory adaptor card in one of the expansion slots.

## Diskette Drives

The IBM PC AT supports the use of three types of diskette drives—the 1.2M-byte 5¼-inch high-capacity diskette drive, the 5¼-inch 360K-byte diskette drive, and the 3½-inch 720K-byte diskette drive.

Although the 1.2M-byte high-capacity diskette drive can read 5¼-inch diskettes created on the PC and PC XT as previously discussed, when it writes onto a diskette using a 360K-byte format, the data are placed on tracks closer together than on conventional 5¼-inch diskettes. This means that most PC and PC XT diskette drives will more often than not be unable to read diskettes created on the 1.2M-byte high-capacity diskette.

To provide a data interchange capability with PCs and PC XTs, IBM recommends the installation of a conventional 360K-byte 5¼-inch diskette in the lower portion of the device housing area. When purchased from IBM, this diskette drive has a star in its lower right corner to distinguish it from the high-capacity diskette drive.

Since the announcement of the two original PC ATs in mid-1984, IBM added several PC AT models to its product line. Table 1.11 compares the features of the IBM PC AT models 319 and 339 with the original basic and enhanced PC ATs introduced in mid-1984. As indicated, the primary difference between the original and later introduced PC AT models is in the crystal rate, types of memory chips used, total RAM supported, and the type of keyboard included with the system.

Table 1.12 summarizes the standard hardware configuration for 14 different models of the IBM PC AT. The data in Table 1.12 represents the original IBM hardware configuration of different PC AT models and, as such, may have been modified by the purchaser through the use of IBM and/or third party hardware products. Thus, it is a good idea to verify all

**Table 1.11** PC AT Model Comparison

|  | BASIC | ENHANCED | MODEL 319 | MODEL 339 |
|---|---|---|---|---|
| RAM in bytes | 256K | 512K | 640K | 640K |
| Crystal rate | 6 MHz | 6 MHz | 8 MHz | 8 MHz |
| Chips used | 64K bit | 64K/128K bit | 64K/256K bit | 64K/256K bit |
| Maximum RAM | 3Mb | 3Mb | 3Mb | 10.5Mb |
| Standard diskette | 1.2Mb | 1.2Mb | 1.2Mb | 1.2Mb |
| Standard fixed disk | None | 20/30Mb | 20/30Mb | 20/30Mb |
| Serial/parallel adapter | No | Yes | Yes | Yes |
| Fixed disk/diskette drive adapter | Yes | Yes | Yes | Yes |
| Keyboard | Standard | Standard | Standard | Enhanced |

hardware components of the computer if you anticipate purchasing a PC AT from one of the numerous dealers that sell restored personal computers.

# The PC XT Model 286

Encased in the system unit of a PC XT, the Model 286 is considered by many as a clone of the PC AT because of the inclusion of an 80286 microprocessor, 1.2M-byte floppy disk, and five of eight expansion slots designed to support a 16-bit data bus.

The interior of the system unit of the XT 286 is illustrated in Figure 1.20. Included in the XT 286 are a 20M-byte fixed disk and 1.2 M-byte diskette drive, leaving room for one additional half-height storage device to be installed in the lower portion of the left device housing area. Standard adapter cards included in this computer are a serial/parallel card and a dual-purpose diskette and fixed-disk controller. This is an improvement over the PC XT, which requires separate adapters for controlling the diskette and the fixed disk.

Five of the eight system expansion slots are designed for 16-bit data paths. Unfortunately, because the height of the XT system unit is slightly less than the height of the AT system unit, many adapter cards marketed by third party vendors for use in the AT will not fit into the XT 286. In

**Table 1.12**  5170 Personal Computer AT Models

| MODEL NUMBER | FEATURES |
| --- | --- |
| Model 068 | System unit/keyboard; 256K-byte memory; high-capacity 1.2M-byte diskette drive; ROM-based BASIC language; clock/calendar with battery backup; keylock. |
| Model 099 | System unit/keyboard; 512K-byte memory; high-capacity 1.2M-byte diskette drive; 20M-byte fixed disk drive; serial/parallel adapter; ROM-based BASIC language; clock/calendar with battery backup; keylock. |
| Model 239 | System unit/keyboard; 512K-byte memory; high-capacity 1.2M-byte diskette drive; 30M-byte fixed disk drive; serial/parallel adapter; ROM-based BASIC language; clock/calendar with battery backup; keylock. |
| Model 319 | Same as model 239 except Intel 80286 microprocessor with 8-MHz clock is standard. |
| Model 339 | Same as model 319 except 101-key Enhanced Personal Computer keyboard is standard. |
| Model 495 | System unit and Series/1 microprocessor with 256K-byte memory integrated with Personal Computer AT with 512K-byte memory; 20M-byte fixed disk drive; fixed-disk/diskette drive adapter; 1M-byte double-sided diskette drive; six-port terminal/host attachment card; Personal Computer AT keyboard; serial/parallel adapter. |
| Model 496 | System unit and Series/1 microprocessor with 1M-byte memory integrated with a Personal Computer AT (Model 339) with a 512K-byte memory; 30M-byte fixed disk drive; fixed disk/diskette drive adapter; 1M-byte high-capacity diskette drive; six-port terminal/host attachment card; 101-key Enhanced Personal Computer keyboard; serial/parallel adapter. |
| Model 599 | AT/370. This model is a preconfigured system unit/keyboard (Model 099) with an AT/370 option kit and an IBM 3278/79 Emulation Adapter. |
| Model 739 | AT/370. System unit/keyboard (Model 239) with an AT/370 option kit and an IBM 3278/79 Emulation Adapter. |
| Model 839 | AT/Store Controller. This model of the Personal Computer AT is a preconfigured system unit/keyboard (Model 239) with an IBM Store Loop Adapter. |

**Table 1.12**  5170 Personal Computer AT Models (continued)

| MODEL NUMBER | FEATURES |
|---|---|
| Model 849 | System unit/keyboard; Intel 80286 microprocessor at 8 MHz; 512K-byte memory; high-capacity 1.2M-byte diskette drive; fixed disk/diskette drive adapter; serial/parallel adapter; 30M-byte fixed disk drive; ROM-based BASIC language; keylock; clock/calendar with battery backup; 101-key enhanced personal computer keyboard; store loop adapter. |
| Model 899 | AT/Store Controller. This model of the Personal Computer AT is a preconfigured system unit/keyboard (Model 099) with an IBM Store Loop Adapter. |
| Model 919 | AT/370. System unit/keyboard (Model 319) with an AT/370 option kit and a 3278/79 emulation adapter. |
| Model 939 | AT/370. System unit/keyboard (Model 339) with an AT/370 option kit and a 3278/79 emulation adapter. |

addition, of the three 8-bit expansion slots, two are half-size because they are blocked by the 1.2M-byte diskette. In fact, the eighth slot next to the power supply is probably too short for use by most half-length adapters, and thus may present a problem to many users.

Included on the system board of the XT 286 are 640K bytes of RAM and a battery used to power a clock/calendar and CMOS RAM for storing configuration information similar to that of the AT. Options offered for the XT 286's three half-height device housing area include a 3½-inch, 720K-byte diskette drive; a 5¼-inch, 360K-byte diskette drive; and a second 5¼-inch, 1.2M-byte diskette drive.

One unusual feature of the 80286 microprocessor is the absence of wait states. On the PC AT, wait states are used to slow down the 80286 so the rest of the system can keep up with that microprocessor. On the XT 286 IBM removed the wait states, resulting in very fast bus cycles. Even though the 80286 microprocessor in the XT 286 operates at 6 MHz, its processing speed is almost two and a half times that of a conventional XT. In fact, the lack of wait states makes it faster than a 6-MHz PC AT.

The standard keyboard shipped with the XT 286 is the 101-key IBM Enhanced Keyboard Unit. The fixed disk marketed with the XT 286 uses a very slow head-positioning technique, which results in an average access

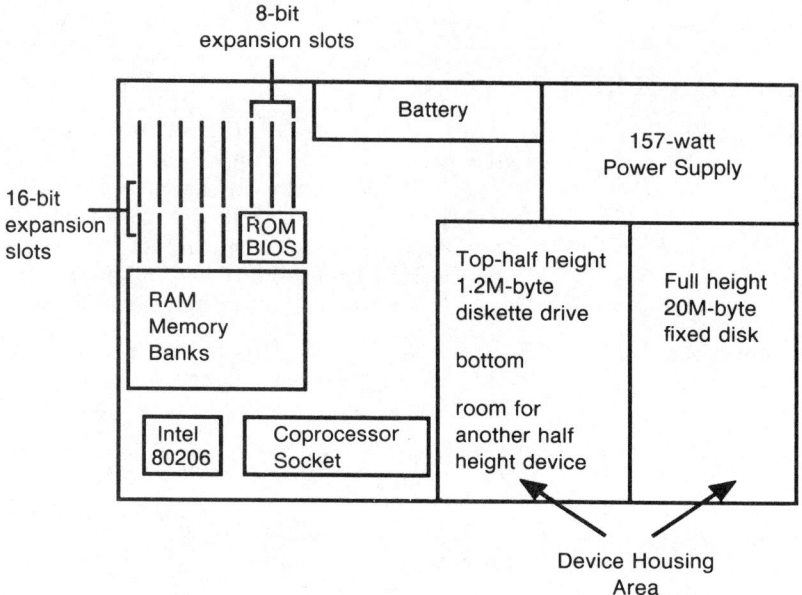

**Figure 1.20**  IBM PC XT Model 286 System Unit Interior.

time of 85 milliseconds in the under-40-millisecond access time of the fixed disks used in the AT. Unfortunately, the XT 286 does not support the 20M- and 30M-byte fixed disks used in the AT.

# Monitors and Display Adapters

IBM originally marketed seven types of displays that can be used with the PC, PC XT, PC AT, and XT 286, the successful operation of the display being dependent on the type of adapter card installed in the computer's system unit. Displays originally marketed by IBM for the PC series include the 5151 Monochrome Display, the 5153 Color Display, the 5154 Enhanced Color Display, and the 5175 PC Professional Graphics Display. Adapters marketed by IBM include the Monochrome Display and Parallel Printer Adapter (MDA), the Color Graphics Adapter (CGA), the Enhanced Graphics Adapter (EGA), and the Professional Graphics Adapter (PGA).

When IBM announced its PS/2 series of personal computers, it introduced several monitors and one adapter card for PCs. The adapter card provides the older series of computers with the Video Graphics Array

(VGA) capability included as standard with most members of the PS/2 family, whereas the new monitors enable the full capability of the adapter card to be displayed.

## Monochrome Display and Adapter

The IBM 5151 Monochrome Display (Figure 1.2) is a high-resolution, green phosphor display that has an 11½-inch wide surface that is coated with an antiglare material. The monochrome display supports upper- and lowercase text using 25 lines of 80 characters. Each character is displayed as a 7 by 9 dot text image within a 9 by 14 dot box, and the total resolution in graphics mode is 720 horizontal by 350 vertical pixels.

The IBM Monochrome Display requires the installation of either the Monochrome Display and Parallel Printer Adapter (MDA) or the Enhanced Graphics Adapter (EGA) into one of the system expansion slots in the system unit. Figure 1.21 illustrates the Monochrome Display and Parallel Printer adapter card. Like all adapters, this card is inserted in the system unit so its connectors are accessible from the rear of the unit. At the top right of the illustration is a 9-pin video connector that attaches to the cable, which has one end built into the Monochrome Display. The

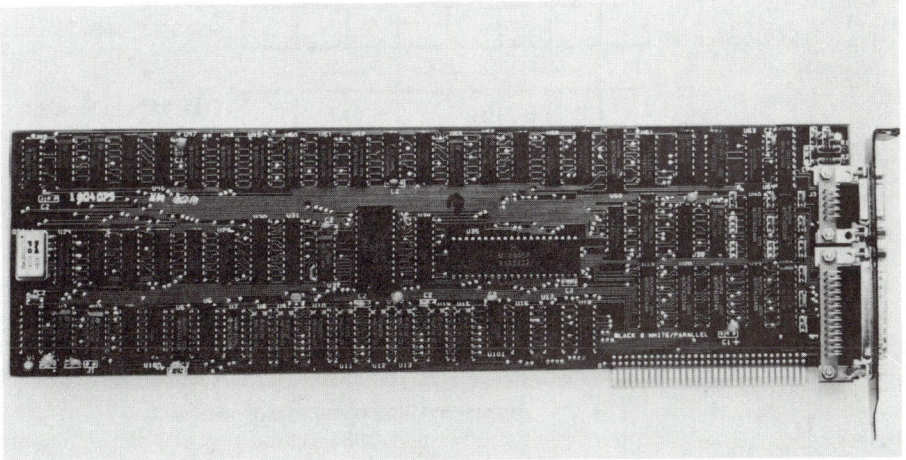

**Figure 1.21** IBM Monochrome Display and Parallel Printer Adapter—This adapter card permits a parallel printer to be connected to the system in addition to supporting the monochrome display. *Photograph courtesy of IBM Corporation.*

lower 25-pin connector enables you to connect a parallel printer to the system and uses the device address LPT1.

Two key components built into the MDA, as well as into other display adapters, are RAM and ROM. The Monochrome Display Adapter contains 4K bytes of RAM that uses addresses B0000–B0FFF, as illustrated later in Figure 1.25. Multiplying 25 lines by 80 characters per line seems to indicate a total storage requirement of 2K bytes of RAM. In actuality, each character requires a pair of bytes; the byte located at an even address contains the ASCII value of the character to be displayed; the second byte, at the adjacent odd address, contains the character's attribute code. Figure 1.22 illustrates how characters are stored in the IBM Monochrome Display Adapter.

In addition to RAM, the Monochrome Display Adapter contains 8K bytes of ROM, which stores the patterns used to generate characters. These character patterns define the display of 256 ASCII characters.

Another key component of a display adapter is its raster generator, which produces the video and synchronizing signals required to drive a display monitor or a TV set. The Monochrome Display Adapter's horizontal scan rate is 18.432 KHz, and its vertical scan rate is 50 KHz. To display data generated by this adapter, a monitor must be compatible with those two scan rates.

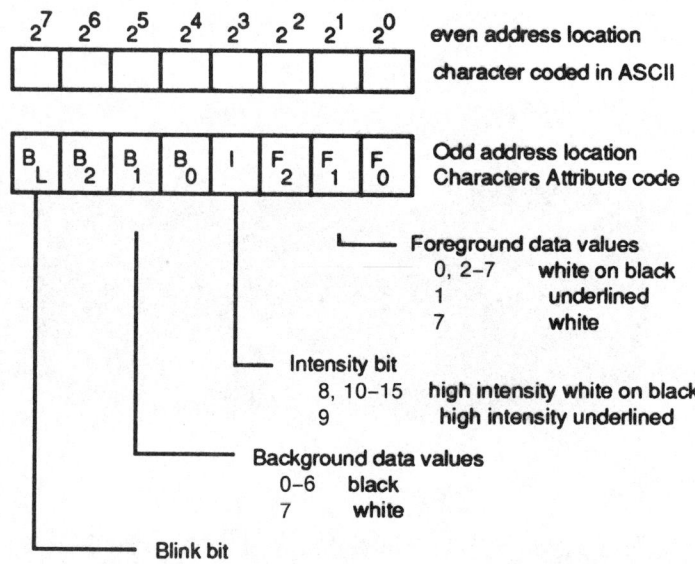

**Figure 1.22** IBM Monochrome Display Adapter Character Storage.

## Color Displays and Adapters

Four color displays and four adapter cards were marketed by IBM for use with the PC, PC XT, AT, and XT 286.

### 5153 Color Display and CGA Card

The first color display marketed by IBM was the 5153. This display can generate both text and graphics output, with text displayed using 25 lines of 80 characters. The 5153 has a 13-inch diagonal screen and permits 16 colors to be displayed at one time.

The use of the 5153 color display requires the installation of either the CGA or the EGA card into a system expansion unit slot in the system unit of the PC, PC XT, PC AT, or XT 286.

The CGA card was previously illustrated in Fig. 1.9. The lower protrusion of the card in front of its edge connector, the skirt, precludes the adapter from being used in 16-bit system expansion slots in the PC AT and XT 286 computers.

The CGA card supports several video interfaces, including an RGB (red, green, blue) connector; an RCA composite jack; and a 4-pin Berg strip that can be used to connect the adapter to a radio frequency (RF) modulator. The RF modulator can be cabled to a standard TV, enabling you to obtain a low-cost color graphics display capability.

The CGA can be used with the IBM 5153 Color Display and the IBM 5154 Enhanced Color Display. When used with the latter, the Enhanced Color Display's resolution is exactly the same as when that monitor is used with the 5153 color display. The 5154's attributes are discussed later in this section.

The CGA board contains 16K bytes of memory, which reside in the 8088 address space beginning at location Hex B8000. In the graphics mode, the 16K bytes hold the bit map of the images to be displayed. This adapter supports two graphics modes—medium resolution of 320 by 200 pixels, and high resolution, which is 640 by 200 pixels. In medium-resolution mode, two bits are used to define the color of each pixel, so that it can display up to four different colors at any one time. In high-resolution graphics mode, 640 by 200 pixels requires the full 16K bytes of storage on the CGA. Hence, each pixel can only be on or off, to indicate black or white. Figure 1.23 illustrates medium-resolution and high-resolution graphics storage in the Color Graphics Adapter.

**Medium Resolution (320 Pixels/line)**

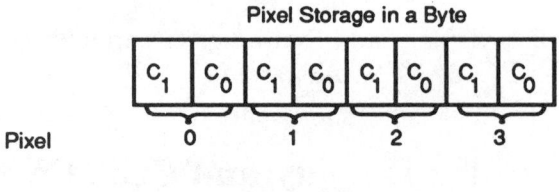

**Color Assignment to Pixels**

| $c_1$ | $c_0$ | Color |
|---|---|---|
| 0 | 0 | 0 |
| 0 | 1 | 1 |
| 1 | 0 | 2 |
| 1 | 1 | 3 |

**High Resolution (640 Pixels/line)**

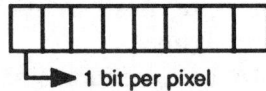

1 bit per pixel

**Figure 1.23** Medium- and High-Resolution Graphics Storage in the Color Graphics Adapter.

The horizontal and vertical scan rates of the Color Graphics Adapter are 15.750 KHz and 60 KHz, respectively. These scan rates are the rate at which video information changes on the display and govern the number of pixels per scan line and the number of lines on the display.

In text mode, the CGA stores characters in the same way that the MDA does, using two bytes per character. The first byte (even address) contains the ASCII code value of the character. The second byte (odd address) contains the attributes of the character—that is, information that defines the foreground color, background color, and whether the character is to blink. Figure 1.24 shows how these attributes are stored in the byte.

The use of three bits and an intensity bit to define the foreground color lets you select one of 16 colors. The use of three bits to define the background enables you to choose one of eight background colors.

However, text displayed by the CGA appears much coarser than when the Monochrome Display Adapter is used with a Monochrome Display.

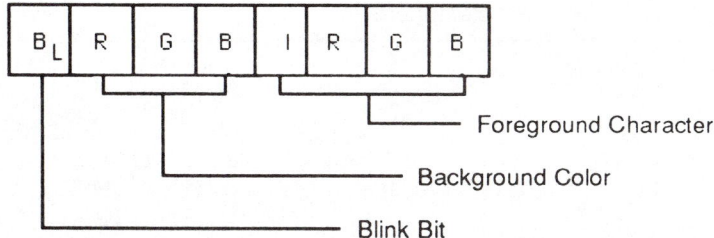

**Figure 1.24** Color Graphics Adapter Attribute Byte Format.

This is because the Color Graphics Adapter displays text as a 7 by 7 matrix set in an 8 by 8 box.

## 5154 Enhanced Color Display and EGA Card

The IBM 5154 Enhanced Color Display is similar in size to the 5153 monitor but includes circuitry that allows a greater resolution. The 5154 can display data with a resolution of 640 by 350 pixels as well as operate in the lower resolutions of 320 by 200 and 640 by 200 of the 5153 display. When the unit is operating in the enhanced color display mode, it can display 16 colors at one time from a palette of 64 colors. To operate in this mode, you must install an EGA adapter in an expansion slot in the system unit of a PC, PC XT, PC AT, or XT 286. When used with a CGA card, the 5154 functions as if it were a 5153 display. Table 1.13 compares the major parameters of the three IBM monitors previously discussed.

## EGA Card

The Enhanced Graphics Adapter can be considered as three display adapters on one card, because it can be used with the IBM Monochrome Display, the 5153 Color Display, and the 5154 Enhanced Color Display. Unlike the CGA adapter, the EGA does not support television receivers or composite monitors. Like the CGA, the EGA does not include a built-in parallel printer adapter such as that of the IBM Monochrome Display and Parallel Printer Adapter card.

The IBM EGA card consists of three modules that were originally sold separately. The EGA full-slot board included 64K bytes of RAM. A

**Table 1.13**   IBM Monitor Parameters

| PARAMETER | MONITOR | | |
|---|---|---|---|
| | MONOCHROME | COLOR/ENHANCED (TV FREQUENCY) | ENHANCED (HIGH RESOLUTION) |
| Horizontal Scan Rate | 18.43 KHz | 15.75 KHz | 21.85 KHz |
| Vertical Scan Rate | 50 Hz | 60 Hz | 60 Hz |
| Displayable Colors | 4 | 16 | 64 |
| Normal Character Size | 7 by 9 pixels | 7 by 7 pixels | 7 by 9 pixels |
| Character Box Size | 9 by 14 pixels | 8 by 8 pixels | 8 by 14 pixels |
| Maximum Resolution (scan lines) | 720 by 350 | 640 by 200 | 640 by 350 |

Graphics Memory Expansion Card (GMEC) piggybacks onto the EGA, adding 64 K. A Graphics Memory Module Kit consists of 128K of memory chips that fill out the GMEC for a total of 256K bytes of memory.

The EGA not only provides all of the display modes of the MDA and CGA, but adds several new modes. If you have a 5154 display unit (or equivalent), the EGA will provide a 16-color, 320-by-200-pixel image; and on a Monochrome Display unit, the EGA will provide 640-by-350-pixel, 4-color graphics, and a 43-line upper/lowercase text display with 40 or 80 characters per line.

You may wonder how a monochrome monitor can provide four colors. In fact, blinking and high intensity are each considered as a "color," and these, together with black and white, provide four distinct ways of representing any part of an image. A 43-row text display is also unusual. If you generate characters in a 9-by-14-pixel box, dividing the 350 scan lines by the 14-pixel box height yields 25 rows of characters. However, if you reduce the size of the character box to 8 by 8 pixels, which is the standard size for the color-graphics mode, you get 350/8 = 43.75 rows—of course, you can't use three-quarters of a row, so you end up with 43 rows. Figure 1.25 shows the memory requirements of the EGA board for each of its display modes, and compares these to the requirements of the MDA and CGA boards.

## Professional Display and Controller

The IBM 5175 graphics display and professional graphics controller permits up to 256 colors to be simultaneously displayed from a palette of 4096 colors with a bit-mapped resolution of 640 by 480 pixels.

The display controller consists of two boards that must be installed in two adjacent expansion slots in the system unit of a PC, PC XT, PC AT, or XT 286. This controller includes an Intel 8088 microprocessor, 320K bytes of memory, and 64K bytes of ROM. It permits such graphics functions as two- and three-dimensional drawing, rotating and scaling, a user-redefinable color selection, user-selectable character sizes, and moving and drawing with absolute or relative coordinates. Unfortunately, because the cost of the display and controller are almost equivalent to the cost of a PC AT, very few people can afford it.

## VGA Card and Analog Monitors

With the introduction of the PS/2 series, IBM incorporated a new video standard into all systems except the PS/2 Model 25 and Model 30. Known as the Video Graphics Array (VGA), in actuality, the video circuits are

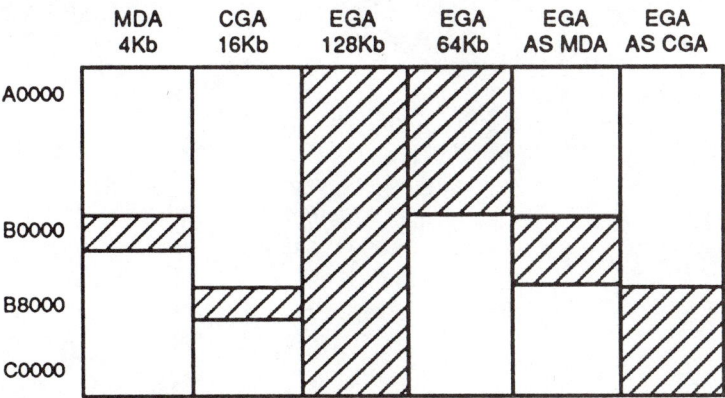

**Figure 1.25**   IBM Display Adapter Memory Usage.

built into the PS/2 system board and do not require the use of a separate adapter card. To provide an upgrade path for PC series users, IBM marketed a VGA adapter board for use in that series of personal computers.

Unlike earlier adapter cards that generate discrete digital signals, the VGA adapter generates analog output signals and cannot be used with earlier monitors that were designed to accept digital signals. Using analog signals, the intensity information required to drive the red, green, and blue color guns of a display is encoded as variable- rather than fixed-level signal amplitudes. This enables a VGA adapter to display a much wider range of colors than an EGA or other digital video cards.

In its maximum color mode of operation, the VGA uses three color registers, each 6 bits wide. Since each color register can produce 64 intensity levels for each primary color, a total of 64 * 64 * 64 or 262,144 different color combinations are selectable. See Chapter 2 for a more detailed description of the VGA video standard, as well as for information concerning the different analog monitors IBM markets for use with its PS/2 family of computers. Each of the monitors discussed in that chapter can be used with the VGA adapter card sold for use with members of the PS/2 series.

CHAPTER 2

# PS/2 Hardware Overview

The IBM Personal System/2 is a family of personal computers that represent IBM's second generation of small computer technology. Unveiled approximately six years after the introduction of the IBM PC, members of the PS/2 family were designed to provide users with enhanced performance while retaining a high degree of compatibility with programs developed for operation on the earlier series of personal computers.

When the IBM PS/2 family was introduced in April 1987, four distinct models were announced. Each of these models—30, 50, 60, and 80—could have its level of performance equated to its model number, with the Model 80 representing the highest level of performance. Subsequent to the April 1987 introduction, IBM added five additional models to the PS/2 family: the Models 25, 50Z, 55, 70, and P70. The Model 25 presently represents the entry-level member of the PS/2 family. The Model 50Z and Model 55 can provide a higher level of performance than the Model 60, whereas the Model 70 can provide a higher level of performance than the Model 80. The Model P70 is IBM's first portable member of the PS/2 family.

Because there can be substantial confusion in comparing the performance levels of different members of the PS/2 family, I will first examine the basic components of each computer in this chapter. Then I focus on the system unit, because this component is designed to contain the microprocessor, memory and circuitry and to house on-line storage devices that govern the functionality and level of performance of each computer. Using this information as a base, I then examine each member of the PS/2 series to describe its level of performance as well as its ability to operate under the control of IBM's two major operating systems—DOS and OS/2.

# Major PS/2 Components

Although there will probably never be a "typical" PS/2 system, each PS/2 is similar to members of the PC series, because they include a minimum of four major components—a keyboard unit; a system unit containing space for the installation of memory, a variety of adapter boards, and storage devices; a monitor; and a printer. For all members of the PS/2 family except the Model 25, each of the four major components is a modular, stand-alone device with the keyboard, monitor, and printer capable of being connected via individual cables to the system unit. The Model 25 consists of a system unit and a monitor in one common housing, eliminating the requirement to cable a monitor to the system unit of that computer.

Figure 2.1 illustrates the four members of the PS/2 family that were announced in April 1987. The Model 30 and Model 50 are desktop units, each having a system unit that can be placed horizontally on a desktop above which your monitor can be added. Both the Model 60 and Model 80 have a vertically constructed system unit designed to be placed on a floor. Then your keyboard and monitor can be placed on a desktop and cabled to the floor-standing system unit.

Although each member of the IBM PS/2 family has a keyboard and system unit, the wide variety of equipment marketed by IBM and other manufacturers may cause your system to appear slightly different from any of those shown in Figure 2.1. Among the major differences that can occur are the type of monitor used and the number and type of on-line storage devices either inserted into your system unit or cabled to that component. The remaining portions of this section examine two components that are common to all PS/2s—the keyboard and system unit. The system unit, however, varies among different models of the PS/2.

## Keyboard

Each member of the IBM PS/2 family uses the Enhanced PC Keyboard, which was previously illustrated in Figure 1.3. This 101-key keyboard is

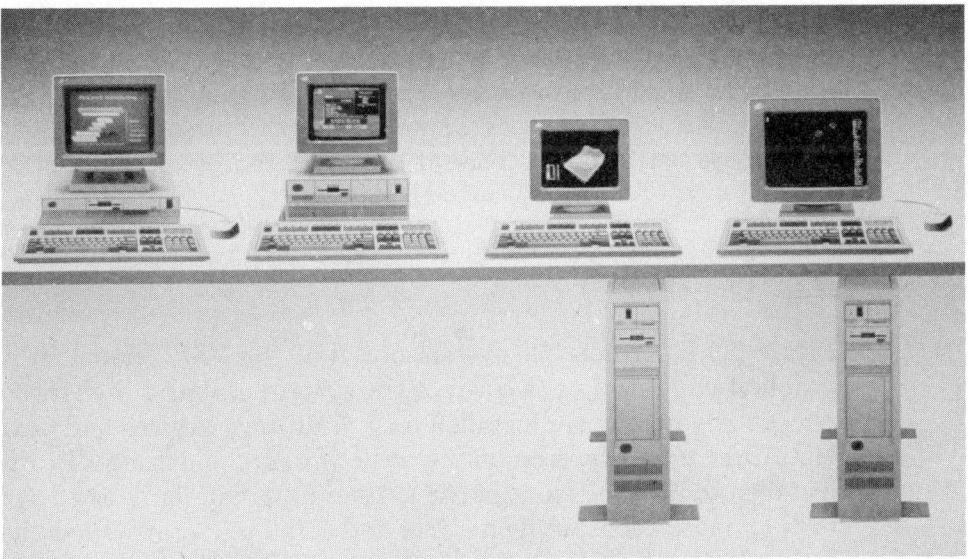

**Figure 2.1** The Original Members of the PS/2 Family. The IBM PS/2 family introduced in April of 1987 consisted of the Model 30, Model 50, Model 60, and Model 80, shown from left to right in this picture. *Photograph courtesy of IBM Corporation.*

attached via a coiled cable to the rear of the system unit of the computer. The keyboard contains all of the keys found on a conventional typewriter, as well as many special keys whose operations were previously described in Chapter 1. As an option, you can obtain an 84-key Space-Saving Keyboard for the Model 25. This keyboard is essentially the same as the Enhanced Keyboard, except that it does not have the numeric keypad.

## System Unit

The heart of each member of the IBM PS/2 family is its system unit. When viewed from the front, each desktop unit has the IBM logo in the upper left corner and at least one 3½-inch diskette drive located to the right of the section containing the logo. Depending upon the storage devices you obtain with your computer, you can have another 3½-inch diskette drive or a fixed disk installed in the housing area to the right of the first diskette. At the extreme right of the front of the system unit is a power-

**64** The PC Upgrader's Manual

on light and the power switch. Figure 2.2 illustrates the front of the system unit of the PS/2 Model 50, highlighting its exterior parts.

In examining the interior of a PS/2's system unit, I will use the Model 50 for illustrative purposes, as well as for referencing the similarities and differences between members of the PS/2 family of personal computers.

## System Board

Figure 2.3 illustrates the system board of the PS/2 Model 50. It becomes visible if you remove the cover of the system unit and then disconnect and remove any previously installed on-line storage devices and adapter cards. Note that the right side of the system board illustrated in Figure 2.3 is installed to face the front of the system unit. Similarly, the left side of the system board—containing parallel and serial ports, as well as the keyboard and pointing device connectors—is installed facing the rear of the system unit. This layout explains why you must cable the monitor, keyboard, and other peripheral devices to connectors located at the rear of the system unit.

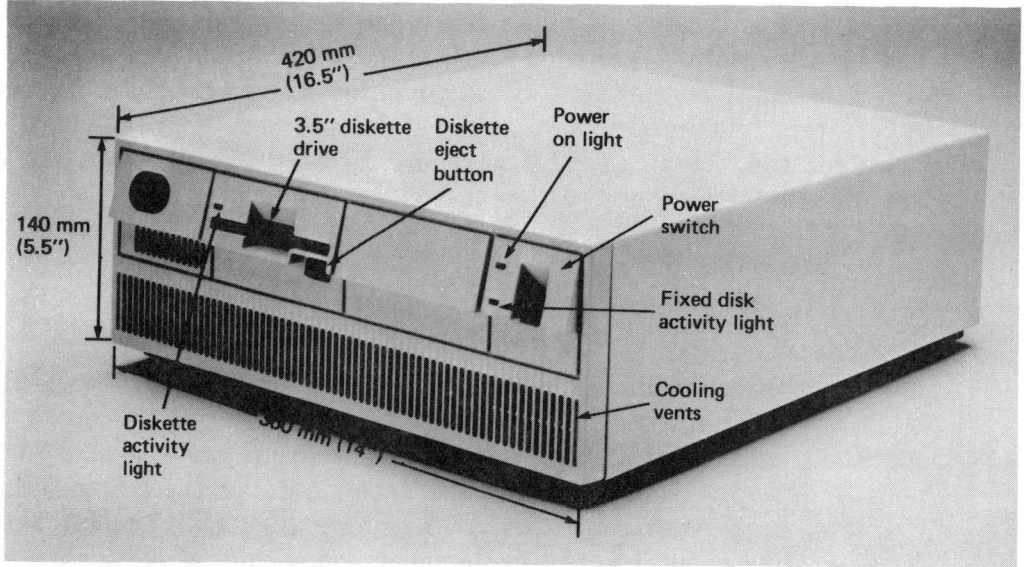

**Figure 2.2** Front of the PS/2 Model 50 System Unit.

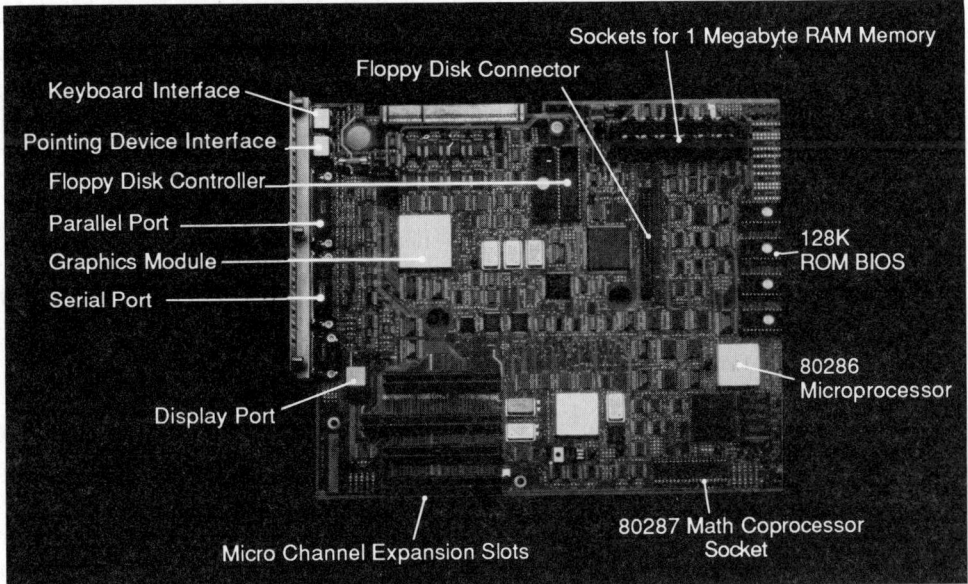

**Figure 2.3**  Model 50 System Board.

The square and rectangular areas located in the lower right portion of Figure 2.3 are for the microprocessor and optional math coprocessor, respectively.

## Microprocessor

Depending on the PS/2 model you have, the system unit contains one of three microprocessors manufactured by the Intel Corporation. The Model 25 and Model 30 use the Intel 8086; the Model 50 and Model 60 use the Intel 80286; and the Models 55, 70, P70, and 80 use the Intel 80386 microprocessor.

Although the PS/2 family was introduced as the successor to the IBM PC series, in actuality the microprocessors used in some PS/2 models either predate (as with the 8086) or are the same chip (notably the 80286) used in some members of the original IBM PC series of personal computers.

When IBM was designing its first personal computer, Intel marketed two similar microprocessors, the 8086 and the 8088. The Intel 8086 was first manufactured in 1978, a year before the 8088. Both microprocessors manipulate data in 16-bit increments; however, the 8086 exchanges data with memory and many peripherals in 16-bit segments, whereas the 8088, as previously discussed in Chapter 1, is limited by its 8-bit data bus to performing I/O operations in 8-bit segments. Another key difference between the 8086 and the 8088 is their operating rates.

## Operating Rate Versus Clock Rate

The operating rate of a microprocessor is a function of a quartz crystal included on the system board. This crystal can be thought of as similar to a metronome. It provides a steady beat in increments of time that are used by different electrical elements on the system board to operate correctly in tandem with one another. The crystal generates pulses used to synchronize the flow of electronic pulses between the computer circuits and components in the system unit. The rate at which the crystal oscillates, or beats, is known as its *clock rate* and is the governing factor in how fast information can flow in the computer. Thus, the faster the clock, the quicker data bits can be recognized and processed.

Although it would appear that simply increasing the clock rate could make a computer more powerful, many design constraints limit the speed of the clock used in a particular computer. First, a faster clock operates at a higher frequency (more oscillations per unit of time) than a more slowly operating clock. High frequencies are more likely to leak than low frequencies, so at some crystal operating rate errors will occur due to leaks being interpreted as false pulses.

A second limit to the clock rate is imposed by the memory chips used in a computer. These chips are rated to operate at a defined clock rate, so a clock that's too fast for the chips to handle eventually causes data stored or read from memory to be lost. Although both of these limitations to clock rate can be circumvented to a degree—by shielding connectors and using faster memory chips—these solutions are costly. Thus, personal computers are designed to operate at a specific clock speed or, in some cases, at one of two clock speeds.

Clock speed is measured in megahertz (MHz), which stands for millions of cycles or pulses per second. The rate at which the crystal oscillates differs from the rate at which the microprocessor operates, because circuitry in all personal computers derives fractions of the crystal oscillation rate to operate different components mounted on the system board. Thus, one measurement of the amount of information a microprocessor can process is its operating rate and not the system clock rate. Fortunately, all personal computer manufacturers specify the actual operating rate of the microprocessor they use in their computer.

## 8086 Versus 8088

The Intel 8086 operates at 8 MHz, whereas the 8088 (used in the IBM PC and PC XT) operates at 4.77 MHz. Even though the wider data path and higher operating rate of the 8086 boosts its performance to approximately twice that of an 8088, IBM selected the 8088 for its first personal computer. The reason for its selection was probably economics, because it would have been more expensive for IBM to develop adapter cards and other parts that could take advantage of the 8086's 16-bit bus structure. Thus, the selection of the 8088 enabled IBM to take advantage of the 16-bit processing capability of the microprocessor as well as the lower costs associated with the use of an 8-bit bus architecture.

Although several vendors incorporated 8086 microprocessors into their personal computers both before and after the IBM PC was introduced in 1981, it took IBM until 1987 to incorporate that chip into its computers—the PS/2 Model 25 and Model 30. Even then, IBM did not take full advantage of the 8086, because the bus used in the PS/2 Model 25 and Model 30 computers was constructed using an 8-bit data path. Although this design precludes taking full advantage of the 8086, it permits adapter cards designed for use in 8088-based IBM PC and PC XT personal computers to be used in the PS/2 Model 25 and Model 30 computers.

## 80286

The Intel 80286 was first manufactured in 1982 and used by IBM in its PC AT, which was introduced in 1984. The 80286 is similar to the 8086 in that both are true 16-bit microprocessors, each with a 16-bit data bus. Although similar to the 8086, the 80286 has several significant differences, including the ability to operate in two different modes and the capability to address much more memory. In addition, IBM used Intel 80286 microprocessors that operated at 6 MHz and 8 MHz in its PC AT. In comparison, the original PC's 8088 microprocessor operated at 4.77 MHz, and the 8086 used in different PS/2s operates at 8 MHz.

The 80286 can operate in either real or protected mode. When the microprocessor operates in its real mode, in essence, it functions as an 8088 or 8086 with respect to its memory address capability. In this mode the 80286, like the earlier 8086 and 8088, can only address 1024K of memory directly. This limit is because it uses a 20-bit address to access memory. The 80286 uses a 20-bit address to provide compatibility with the IBM PC and PC XT, both of which use the 8088 microprocessor. The design of the 80286's real mode addressing is related to the design of the 8088. The Intel 8088 has 16-bit internal data paths and for each memory operation generates a 20-bit address that can access $2^{20}$ (1,048,576) memory locations. However, as explained in Chapter 1, the 8088 microprocessor has only eight pins for data, so it has to perform two memory operations to fetch or store a 16-bit data word, one byte at a time.

Further, because it's desirable to be able to keep program code, data, and the stack in separate blocks of memory, the microprocessor computes every memory address in two parts, known as the *segment* and the *offset*. To calculate a physical address, the 8088 multiplies the value in a segment register by 16 and then adds the logical (offset) address; the result is always a 20-bit address. Thus, the 20-bit address that is used by the 80286 in its real mode provides address compatibility with both the 8088 and the 8086 microprocessors.

The second operational mode of the 80286 is the *protected mode*. In this mode the microprocessor uses a 24-bit address bus, permitting the direct addressing of 16M bytes of memory. In addition, in the protected mode the microprocessor becomes capable of running several applications at one time, a process more formally known as *multitasking*.

## 80386

In 1985, Intel released the 80386, which is a 32-bit microprocessor. The 80386 contains approximately 275,000 transistors and can directly address 4 gigabytes of memory, which is 250 times more than the 80286 can address. In addition to processing data in 32-bit increments, the 80386 also operates at higher clock rates than the 80286, permitting software to execute three to four times faster than on an 80286-based personal computer. Like the 80286, the 80386 can be operated in both real and protected modes.

## Coprocessor

A mathematical coprocessor similar to the Intel 80287 shown installed in a system in Figure 2.3 is one of the few options available across the entire PS/2 product line. Each member of the PS/2 family is manufactured with a socket designed to accept a particular math coprocessor that operates in tandem with the installed microprocessor. The coprocessor extends the capability of the microprocessor, because the coprocessor can perform certain kinds of arithmetic operations much faster than the microprocessor. The coprocessor is designed to perform floating-point arithmetic in hardware, resulting in increased speed, range, and precision compared with arithmetic operations performed by the microprocessor.

The Intel 8087 coprocessor is used with 8086 and 8088 microprocessors. The 80287 coprocessor is used with the 80286 microprocessor, and the 80387 coprocessor is used with the 80386 microprocessor.

## ROM BIOS

The four chips aligned vertically above and to the right of the microprocessor illustrated in Figure 2.3 are the read only memory (ROM) chips. Similar to the ROM chips used in the PC series, these chips also contain instructions or program statements that can only be read and are non-alterable. The four ROM chips illustrated in Figure 2.3 contain approximately 128K bytes of code divided into BIOS (Basic Input/Output System) and a set of BIOS routines called POST (power-on self test). System boards used in the Model 25 and Model 30 computers contain 64K bytes of code, similarly subdivided into different routines.

## POST

The PS/2 POST in ROM is similar to the POST in the PC series, containing a set of routines designed to test the keyboard, memory, and other critical elements of the computer. During POST, the computer writes data into each memory location, computing the proper parity-bit state, and compares this with the parity bit read from memory. If they differ, a parity error has occurred and the memory chip is considered to be defective. The computer displays a code in the upper left corner of the monitor to denote that a parity error occurred as well as to define the chip location that caused the error. This information can then be used to replace the failed chip.

If no fatal errors are encountered during POST, a routine is initiated that activates the computer's disk drives. This routine searches for a drive that contains the operating system and, on finding one, loads a small program from the disk or diskette and executes it. This program, in turn, loads the remainder of the operating system. When the operating system is completely loaded, control of the computer passes from the BIOS to the operating system. Thereafter, the BIOS functions as an intermediary through which the operating system and application programs can control system devices.

## RAM

In Figure 2.3, the rectangular box located at the top right of the illustration denotes the area into which RAM chips are inserted on an IBM PS/2 Model 50. A similar location on the system board is used by other members of the PS/2 family for the installation of RAM. Because this memory is installed directly on the system board at the time of manufacture, it is also commonly referred to as *on-board memory* or *system RAM*.

Most members of the PS/2 series are manufactured with 1M byte of RAM installed on the system board. The two exceptions to this are the Model 25 and Model 30, which are manufactured with either 512K or 640K bytes of RAM. The Model 25 is manufactured with 512K bytes of RAM; however, you can order this computer with a 128K-byte expansion kit, which consists of RAM chips that plug into the system board, resulting in a total of 640K bytes of memory. The Model 30 is manufactured with 640K bytes of RAM on its system board.

## Bus

The lines that are visible between system expansion slots in Figure 2.3 are known as *trace lines* and are part of the bus. These lines are similar to the trace lines in a PC computer in that they contain three types of data paths or circuits—addressing, control, and data. The control circuits direct the flow of information to and from the expansion slots; the addressing circuits enable data to reach its appropriate destination or to be read from a specific destination; and the data circuits carry information to or from the CPU.

PS/2s that use the 8086 microprocessor were designed with 8 data lines from the microprocessor to the system expansion slots in order to maintain compatibility with the IBM PC and PC XT. This enabled IBM to design the system expansion slots of the Model 25 and Model 30 computers to accept adapter cards manufactured for use in the PC and PC XT computers.

For 80286- and 80386-based PS/2 computers, with the exception of the PS/2 Model 30 286, IBM designed a new bus structure called the *Micro Channel.* The Micro Channel architecture required a complete redesign of the system expansion slots, resulting in the development of Micro Channel expansion slots that are incompatible with the original PC expansion slots. As a result of this incompatibility, adapter boards that can be used in the Model 25 and Model 30 computers cannot be used in the other members of the PS/2 series and vice versa. For the PS/2 Model 30 286, IBM used 16 data lines to maintain compatibility with the PC AT. This design permits adapter cards designed for the PC AT to be used in the PS/2 Model 30 286.

The Micro Channel offers several key advantages over the PC bus structure. First, and perhaps most obvious to persons familiar with the older PC series, is the elimination of DIP (dual in-line package) switches on adapter boards designed for insertion into a Micro Channel expansion slot. This omission of DIP switches results from the Micro Channel's support for automatic configuration of the system and all add-in cards—a feature IBM calls "Programmable Option Select (POS)." In comparison, add-in cards designed for use in a PC bus normally require the user to set tiny DIP switches when a card is installed, as well as to set or reset one or more positions on a DIP switch housing on the system board of the computer. If you set a DIP switch incorrectly, you might easily disable your computer. Because the POS feature permits adapter boards designed for the Micro Channel to be automatically configured when the computer is turned on and reconfigured, if necessary, by software, it simplifies the hardware installation process while eliminating the possibility of DIP switch setting errors.

The second major advantage of the Micro Channel over the PC bus is that the Micro Channel supports bus arbitration. This technique enables processors on expansion cards, called *masters,* to take temporary control of the computer system. Arbitration allows different devices to gain access to the system's data bus; if two or more devices attempt to control the Micro Channel at the same time, an algorithm built into hardware resolves the conflict. Through hardware arbitration, it becomes possible for the microprocessor on the system board to delegate special computing tasks to an adapter card designed specifically for that task. Then, after delegating the task, the main microprocessor can perform other functions, resulting in a higher level of performance.

The Micro Channel is designed to support a total of 16 intelligent processors, including the microprocessor on the system board. This means that the Micro Channel can support up to 15 additional processors that perform such independent functions as communications, graphics, encryption, and intelligent disk control. In fact, microprocessors included on adapter cards for installation into a Micro Channel expansion slot do not have to be compatible with the microprocessor on the system board. This is because the arbitration scheme governs access to the bus to pass data between devices, providing board manufacturers flexibility in designing their products.

Other benefits of the Micro Channel architecture include its acceptance of a new card format and pin pattern, the latter significantly reducing the possibility of the computer generating electromagnetic interference (EMI). The new card format of adapter boards designed to fit in a Micro Channel expansion slot is optimized for dense-logic design. This permits Micro Channel adapter cards to have more very large scale integration (VLSI) chips mounted on such cards than on cards designed for use in an older IBM PC bus.

Concerning pin patterns, Micro Channel requires adapter cards to have ground pins spaced every fourth pin on both sides of the card connector. This pattern is offset by two pins on opposite sides of the connector, resulting in each signal pin being adjacent to a radio-frequency (RF) ground. Due to this design, EMI is significantly reduced.

## Disks and Storage Media

Members of the IBM PS/2 family primarily use 3½-inch diskettes and fixed disks for storing information. Each member of the PS/2 family has one or more 3½-inch diskettes and/or fixed disks installed in its system unit. To provide data-transfer compatibility with members of the IBM PC series that use 5¼-inch diskettes, IBM markets an external 5¼-inch diskette drive that can be cabled to the PS/2 system unit.

Figure 2.4 illustrates the components of a 3½-inch diskette whose magnetic material used for recording information is encased in a shell of hard plastic, which provides handling protection. Access to the magnetic material is obtained via a sliding metal cover that is retracted only when the diskette is placed inside a disk drive. The write-protect switch located at the bottom of the diskette provides the ability to prevent data from being recorded onto a disk. When the switch is positioned so that the square hole in the disk is open, the diskette is write-protected. When the

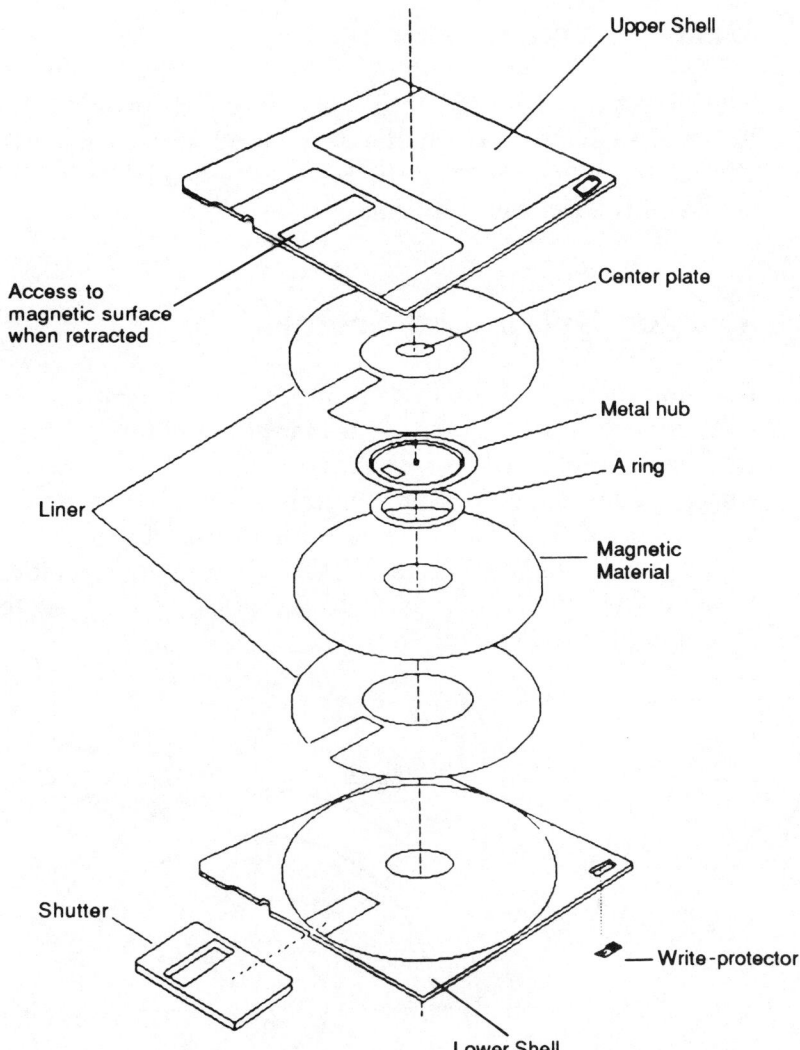

**Figure 2.4** Components of a 3½-Inch Diskette.

switch is positioned to remove a visible square hole when looking down from the top of a disk, information can be written onto the diskette. Some diskettes, such as the IBM Reference Disk shipped with each PS/2 and some operating system diskettes, do not have this switch and are permanently write-protected.

## Diskette Operation

The diskette is inserted into the diskette drive with the shutter on the upper shell facing toward the computer. As the diskette is inserted, its shutter retracts, providing the read/write heads of the diskette drive with access to the magnetic media.

## Tracks, Bytes, and Sectors

Information in the form of data or programs is written onto and read from a 3½-inch diskette similar to the manner used for 5¼-inch diskettes, using concentric circles called *tracks,* as illustrated in Figure 2.5. There are 80 tracks on a 3½-inch diskette, numbered from 0 to 79. Depending on the diskette used, the type of diskette drive used to format the diskette, and the personal computer user's FORMAT command specification, each track is subdivided into either 9 or 18 sectors, and each sector can store 512 eight-bit bytes of information.

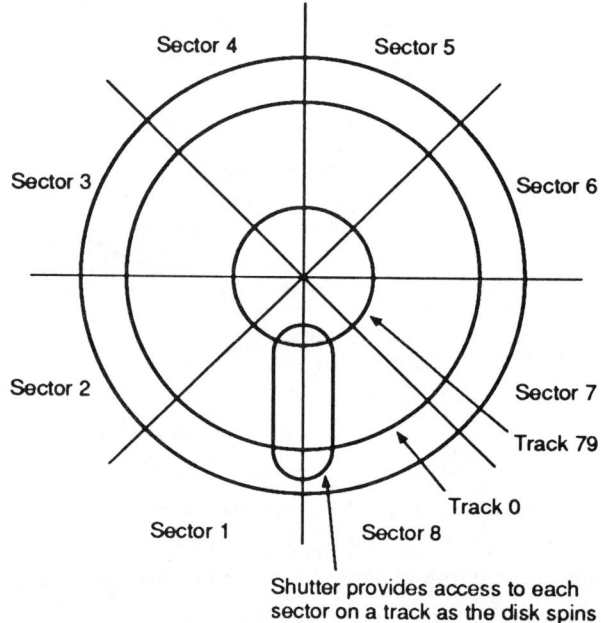

**Figure 2.5** Track and Sector Relationship.

## Storage Capacity

The IBM PS/2 family supports two types of 3½-inch diskette drives—standard and high-capacity. The IBM PS/2 Model 25 and Model 30 use standard 3½-inch diskette drives. Diskettes used in these drives are formatted with 80 tracks per side, using 9 sectors per track. Thus, 2 sides times 80 tracks per side times 9 sectors per track times 512 bytes per sector yields 737,280 bytes of information, or 720K bytes of data storage capability.

Other members of the PS/2 series are manufactured with 3½-inch high-capacity diskette drives. You can use standard 3½-inch diskettes in this drive and FORMAT the diskette to store 720K bytes of data or you can use high-capacity diskettes to double the data-storage capacity. If you use 3½-inch high-capacity diskettes, you can format the diskette to store 18 sectors per track. The storage capacity of this diskette then becomes 2 sides times 80 tracks per side times 18 sectors per side times 512 bytes per sector, yielding 1,474,560 bytes (1.44M bytes) of data storage.

## Fixed Disks

The fixed disks used with members of the IBM PS/2 family vary in capacity from 20 to 144M bytes of storage. Unlike the PC series, which requires a disk controller to be installed in an expansion slot to control the operation of the disk, several PS/2 computers have equivalent circuitry installed in a special socket on their system board. Those PS/2 computers need fewer expansion slots than members of the PC series and therefore occupy less desktop space.

## Video Display Support

Unlike the earlier PC series, in which video display support is in the form of adapter boards installed in expansion slots, members of the PS/2 family have built-in graphics chips on the system board of each computer. The graphics chips used in the PS/2 computers provide two new standards of video display capability over the original PC series, as well as downward video standard compatibility with the video standards supported by IBM's first generation of personal computers.

The IBM PS/2 Model 25 and Model 30 include a built-in graphics chip that provides Multicolor Graphics Array (MCGA) display support. MCGA supports the 320-by-200-pixel graphics resolution of the IBM Color Graphics Adapter (CGA), which was IBM's first product to display color and graphics, enabling up to four colors to be simultaneously displayed from a palette of 16 colors. In addition to CGA support, MCGA adds three additional video modes—320 by 200 pixels with up to 256 simultaneous colors from a palette of 256,000 colors; a 640-by-480-pixel mode in two colors; and a monochrome mode that supports up to 64 simultaneous shades of gray.

The PS/2 Model 30 286, the PS/2 Model 50, and all higher models use the Video Graphics Array (VGA) chip, which is a superset of the MCGA. The VGA adds a 640-by-480-pixel mode that can display 16 colors simultaneously from a palette of 256,000 colors.

The VGA standard incorporates 17 different video modes on a single chip. To give you an appreciation for the capabilities of the VGA and MCGA chips, a review of the earlier video standards previously presented in Chapter 1 is warranted.

For PS/2 users not satisfied with the MCGA or VGA, several upgrade possibilities exist. For MCGA computers, you can upgrade to VGA capability by the installation of an adapter card in the system unit of a Model 25 or Model 30. For PS/2 computers that support the Micro Channel, you can install IBM's 8514/A display adapter, which must be used in conjunction with the firm's 8514 color display to achieve its maximum resolution capability.

## Monitors

Unlike IBM's previous monitors, which were strictly digital, only analog monitors can be used with members of the PS/2 family. The older digital monitors were controlled by four or six lines that were used by the adapter board in the system unit to inform the monitor which color to display. Thus, CGA monitors with 4 lines were limited to $16(2^4)$ total colors, whereas EGA monitors with 6 lines were limited to a total of $64(2^6)$ colors.

In comparison, the video chips for the MCGA and VGA standards describe the amount of color by varying the voltage on an analog line between 0V and 1V, with a higher voltage resulting in a brighter color. The VGA monitor uses three analog inputs, one for each of the red, green, and blue primary colors. By having the ability to generate 64 values for each of the primary colors, a total of 262,144 (64 * 64 * 64) colors becomes available for display, of which 256 can be displayed simultaneously.

## Monitor Selection Considerations

In selecting an appropriate monitor for your PS/2, you should examine its dot pitch, horizontal and vertical scan frequency, and adapter or video chip compatibility. The dot pitch is measured in millimeters and indicates the spacing of the pixels from one another. In general, the smaller the dot pitch, the sharper the characters appear on a display.

The display capability of a monitor results from an electron beam that is passed from right to left over each line of the screen. This beam's intensity is varied in proportion to the intensity of the image to be displayed on the screen; a memory buffer in the video display adapter or video chip stores a bit pattern of the image to be displayed. Thus, the data in the buffer is used to tell the monitor when to turn the electron beam on or off.

The rate at which the video adapter reads the content of the display buffer and translates it into a screen display corresponds to the scan rate of the adapter. This scan rate actually consists of horizontal and vertical scan components. The rate at which the electron beam sweeps from right to left across the screen is known as the *horizontal scan frequency,* and the rate at which the beam moves from the top to the bottom of the screen is known as its *vertical scan rate.* In general, the faster the scan rate, the lower the amount of screen flicker, because a high scan rate allows a screen to be redrawn in a shorter amount of time.

The VGA's horizontal scanning frequency is 31.5 KHz, which is approximately double the CGA's 15.75 KHz rate, almost double the MDA's 18.4 KHz rate, and almost 50 percent above the EGA's 21.85 KHz rate. The VGA's vertical scan rate is 70 Hz, in comparison to the 60 Hz rate of the CGA and EGA adapters and the 50 Hz rate of the MDA adapter.

PS/2 computers operate only with analog monitors, because of the design of the graphics chips used in each computer. Because the video adapters originally manufactured for use with the PC series were designed to support digital displays, you cannot normally use monitors designed for the MDA, CGA, or EGA video modes with a PS/2 computer. The primary exception to this is multiscan monitors that can operate up to the 70 Hz rate of the VGA adapter and can be reset to support analog input. Similarly, if you use a VGA adapter card in a PC series computer, you must connect that card to an analog monitor.

## IBM Monitors

IBM offers four types of monitors for use with its PS/2 series of computers. All four monitors share a number of attributes, including the ability to accept analog input at the scan rate associated with VGA.

### 8503 Monochrome Display

The IBM 8503 Monochrome Display has a 12-inch diagonal screen. This display is capable of generating up to 64 shades of gray on a paper-white background. The 8503 weighs 19 pounds and is encased in a pearl-white housing that matches the color of the PS/2's system unit. The monitor case measures approximately 12 inches square, resulting in a 144-square-inch footprint, and it supports a maximum resolution of 640 by 480 pixels.

### 8512 Color Display

The IBM 8512 Color Display has a 14-inch diagonal screen. This display weighs approximately 33 pounds, including a tilt-and-swivel base. Like the 8503 monochrome display, the maximum resolution of the 8512 is 640 by 480 pixels. The 8512 has a coarse dot pitch of 0.41 mm that produces only marginally legible characters. Because of this, the 8512 should probably be restricted to moderate daily use.

### 8513 Color Display

The IBM 8513 Color Display uses a 0.28-mm dot pitch, resulting in a clearer image than that obtainable with the 8512. The 8513 has the same maximum resolution as the 8503 and 8512 monitors; however, it has a better dot pitch than the 8512 for a retail-price difference of less than $100, making it more suitable for heavy daily use.

### 8514 Color Display

At the top of the line of IBM monitors is the firm's 40-pound 8514. Unlike the other IBM monitors, which are compatible only with the MCGA and

VGA scan rates, the 8514 is a multiscan monitor that you can use with MDA, CGA, and EGA adapters in addition to the PS/2 video adapters. The maximum resolution of the 8514 is 1024 by 768 pixels. This resolution is only obtainable, however, when the IBM 8514/A Display Adapter is installed in a Micro Channel expansion slot on a PS/2 Model 50 or higher computer.

Having examined the major components of the PS/2 family, you are now ready to examine each computer in detail.

# Model 25

The PS/2 Model 25 illustrated in Figure 2.6 represents an entry-level computing capability whose marketing target is the educational and home

**Figure 2.6**   The PS/2 Model 25. *Photograph courtesy of IBM Corporation.*

professional user. This computer, like the Model 30 that was actually introduced approximately six months before the Model 25, uses the 16-bit Intel 8086 microprocessor with an 8-bit bus design operating at 8 MHz. Unlike other members of the PS/2 family that have separate system units and monitors, the Model 25 combines both into one compact housing.

You can purchase the Model 25 in several configurations. A basic Model 25 comes with one 720K-byte 3½-inch diskette drive, as well as a disk controller, serial and parallel ports, and an MCGA video controller mounted on the system board. The computer comes with 512K bytes of memory, which can be expanded to 640K bytes.

Both the Model 25 and Model 30 are manufactured with IBM PC type expansion slots. The Model 25 contains two PC type expansion slots—one for a full board and one for a three-quarter-length card that can be up to eight inches in length. Included on the system board is a pointing device (also known as *mouse*), port and a socket for an optional 8087 math coprocessor.

Initially, the Model 25 was available in two configurations. The Model 25-001 has a 12-inch analog monochrome monitor, and the Model 25-004 incorporates a 12-inch analog color monitor in its housing. In 1988, IBM added a new Model 25 with a Token Ring adapter for use on local area networks. Similar to the initially announced Model 25, the Model 25LS, which includes a Token Ring adapter, can be obtained with a monochrome or a color display.

Both the Model 25 and Model 25LS support either an optional second 3½-inch diskette or a 20M-byte fixed disk. The key differences between the Model 25 and Model 25LS are in the area of standard memory and available expansion slots. The Model 25LS comes with 640K bytes of RAM, while the Model 25 has 512K bytes, expandable to 640K bytes. Because the Token Ring adapter uses one expansion slot, the Model 25LS has only one free expansion slot. In comparison, the Model 25 has two free expansion slots.

Two keyboards are offered for both versions of the Model 25. One is a space-saving 84-key model, which has a cursor control pad but no numeric keypad. The alternative is the enhanced 101-key keyboard that is standard with other members of the PS/2 series.

# Model 30

Similar to the Model 25, the Model 30 is a desktop computer system that uses the Intel 8086 16-bit microprocessor with an 8-bit bus. Due to this design, the Model 30 can accept adapter cards manufactured for use in the original IBM PC series. Unlike the Model 25, which incorporates the system unit and monitor in one housing, the Model 30 was designed so that its system unit can be cabled to any analog monitor; thus, you can purchase a monitor from a third party vendor for this computer.

## Features

When announced by IBM, the Model 30 was marketed in two configurations. The Model 30-002 includes two 720K-byte 3½-inch diskette drives; the Model 30-021 has one 720K-byte diskette drive and one 20M-byte fixed disk. Both configurations come with 640K bytes of RAM, which, according to IBM, is the maximum system memory supported by the Model 30. Memory on each Model 30 configuration consists of 128K bytes of RAM soldered to the system board and two 256K-byte banks of IBM's Single Inline Package (SIP) memory modules that can slide out. Although IBM does not currently offer memory beyond 640K bytes, RAM expansion is possible by removing the SIP memory and installing memory manufactured by a third party.

The key to the functionality of the Model 30, as well as other members of the PS/2 family, is the system unit of the computer. Both versions of the Model 30 include built-in serial, parallel, and pointing device (mouse) ports, as well as built-in MCGA graphics and a built-in diskette controller. Because so much functionality was added to the system board, only three expansion slots were included in the Model 30. These expansion slots are placed horizontally, parallel to the system board to save space. This reduces the system unit's footprint to 16 inches wide by 15.6 inches deep.

The expansion slots are formed on the Model 30 by the use of a card that contains three sockets and attaches to the system board at a 90-degree angle. This card is held in an upright position by a plastic bracket. To install an expansion board, you must first pry off a strip of plastic on the rear panel of the system unit, enabling the board to be slid into the expansion bus connector card.

Figure 2.7 illustrates the back panel of the system unit of the Model 30. The figure illustrates the relationship between the connectors on the system unit and the location of the three horizontal expansion slots.

Like all PS/2 computers, the appearance of the Model 30 system unit (shown on the left of Figure 2.1) differs in two respects from the system unit of the members of the original PC series. First, and probably most

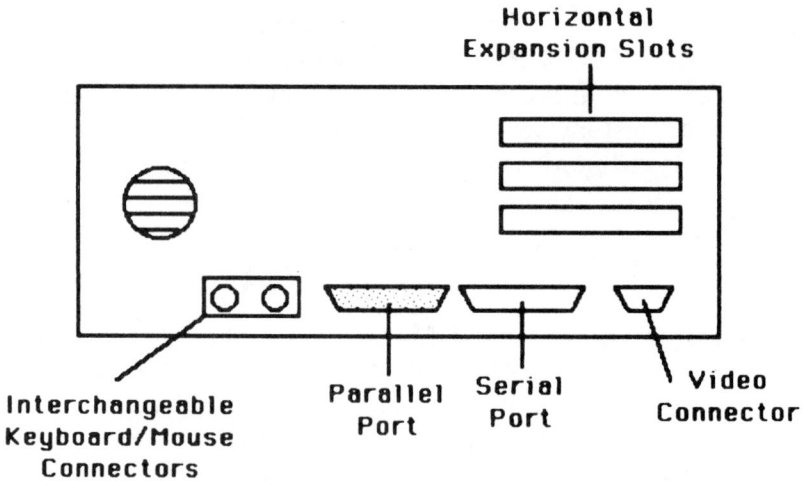
**Figure 2.7** PS/2 Model 30 System Unit Back Panel.

practical, is the placement of the power switch on the front right corner of the system unit. Second, because the device housing areas for 3½-inch storage devices are smaller, you can't install 5¼-inch drives in the system unit of any member of the Personal System/2 computer family. Users who require 5¼-inch diskettes can obtain an external diskette drive that can be cabled to the rear of the system unit.

Other standard features of the Model 30 include 640K bytes of memory, a 70-watt power supply and battery-powered clock. The dimensions of the system unit are 16 inches wide by 4 inches high and 15.6 inches deep; thus, the desktop footprint is approximately 25 percent smaller than that of a PC or PC XT.

## Limitations

Although considered by IBM to be a member of the PS/2 family, in actuality the Model 30, as well as the Model 25, can be considered to be an enhanced member of the PC series. The use of the 8086 microprocessor, which does not support protected-memory operations, precludes running OS/2 on either model. In addition, both models use an 8-bit PC expansion slot architecture instead of the Micro Channel bus. This architecture precludes the development of adapter boards with separate processors that can communicate with one another using a bus arbitration scheme, which is possible with PS/2 Models 50 and above. In spite of these limitations, the 8-MHz operating rate of the 8086 boosts the overall performance of the Model 30 to more than twice that of the 8088-based IBM PC and PC XT for performing computations.

## Model 30 286

In late 1988, IBM supplemented its PS/2 product line with the addition of two 80286 microprocessor-based computers. Both Model 30s include three dual-8 and 16-bit bus PC AT style system expansion slots in place of the 8-bit bus expansion slots built into the Model 30s. This enables each Model 30 286 to use the large number of 8- and 16-bit adapter cards originally designed for use in the PC, PC XT, and PC AT.

### Features

Like the Model 30s, each Model 30 286 includes many standard features built into its system board. These standard features include a diskette controller, serial and parallel ports, mouse and keyboard ports, and time-of-day clock. The Intel 80286 microprocessor operates at 10 MHz, providing a system throughput approximately twice that of the Model 30.

Other standard features of the Model 30 286-E01 include 512K bytes of memory, expandable to 1M byte, 2M bytes, or 4M bytes on the system board; one 3½-inch 1.44M-byte diskette drive; VGA display capability; expansion slots that accept most IBM PC, PC XT, and PC AT adapter cards. The Model 30 286-E21 adds a 20M-byte fixed disk drive with integrated controller to the standard features previously described.

The Model 30 286 is marketed in two versions: one with a 20M-byte fixed disk drive and one without. Both versions include one high-density 3½-inch 1.44M-byte diskette drive and can support up to 4M bytes of memory on the system board and up to 16M bytes of total system memory.

The Video Graphics Array (VGA) chip used by the Model 30 286 is a superset of the MCGA. The VGA adds a 640-by-480-pixel mode that can display 16 colors simultaneously.

## Model 50

The Model 50, illustrated as the second from the left in Figure 2.1, is a desktop system. This model has only one configuration—the 50-021—which includes one 1.44M-byte, 3½-inch floppy diskette drive and a 20M-byte fixed disk. The floppy disk drive, as you shall see later, can have serious compatibility problems both with the PS/2 Model 25 and Model 30 and with members of the original PC family that use this type of drive.

## Features

The Model 50 comes with 1M byte of RAM, and you can expand the memory to 8M bytes. The microprocessor is an 80286, which has a 16-bit external data path. For upward compatibility, the Model 50 uses a 16-bit subset of IBM's 32-bit Micro Channel. The Micro Channel bus is physically and electrically incompatible with that of the IBM PC series, so you can't use 8-bit adapter cards designed for the PC series in any PS/2 computer except the Model 25 and Model 30. Like the Model 30 286, the Model 50 and all higher models use the Video Graphics Array (VGA) chip, which is a superset of the MCGA. The VGA adds a 640-by-480-pixel mode that can display 16 colors simultaneously.

The Model 50's system unit contains four 16-bit Micro Channel expansion slots. Because one is used by the standard equipment hard disk controller, only three are actually available for use. Because of the use of 3½-inch disk technology, and proprietary integrated circuit chips on the system board that replaced many separate chips on earlier computers, the Model 50's system unit was shrunk to 5½ inches high by 14 inches wide by 18½ inches deep.

## Limitations

Although the PS/2 Model 50 is more powerful than the PC AT it was designed to replace, its 20M-byte fixed disk storage capacity—as well as the slow 80-millisecond drive access time—was considered by many persons to be a serious limitation. The slow access time made the Model 50 impractical as a server on a local area network as well as for use as a stand-alone system for disk-intensive applications. The paltry 20M bytes of on-line storage do not leave much space for application programs once OS/2 is installed. Probably because of these limitations, IBM introduced the Model 50Z.

## Model 50Z

The outward appearance of the Model 50Z is the same as the Model 50. Internally, there are several significant differences between these two members of the PS/2 family.

The first significant difference between the Model 50 and the Model 50Z is in the number of wait states. The Z in the Model 50Z's name denotes that this member of the PS/2 family operates using zero wait states. IBM used RAM chips designed for 85-nanosecond access in the Model 50Z, instead of the 125-nanosecond chips used in the Model 50. This permitted IBM to redesign the system board to remove the wait state from memory reads and writes.

The second significant difference between the Model 50Z and the Model 50 is in disk drive access time and storage capacity. The Model 50Z can be obtained with either a 30M-byte or a 60M-byte fixed disk, both disks having a relatively fast access time of 39 milliseconds. Other changes between the Model 50 and Model 50Z include the increased use of integrated chips, which reduced the size of the Model 50Z's system board, and a choice of either 1M byte or 2M bytes of RAM on the system board of that computer, as opposed to 1M byte on the Model 50.

## Model 55 SX

In May 1989, IBM extended its PS/2 family with the introduction of the Model 55 SX. This personal computer uses the Intel 80386SX microprocessor, a less powerful version of the 80386. The 80386SX can perform up to approximately 40 percent faster than the fastest IBM 80286-based PS/2, although the microprocessor costs considerably less than an 80386. Thus, at its introduction many computer analysts touted both the aggressive price of the PS/2 Model 55 SX, as well as its perceived significant price/performance. It provides end-users with the power, performance, and functionality of an 80386 desktop computer at a price approaching that of an 80286 system.

The PS/2 Model 55 SX is housed in a system unit identical to that of a PS/2 Model 30. The Model 55 SX comes standard with one 3½-inch high-capacity diskette drive and can be obtained with either a 30M-byte or 60M-byte fixed disk drive. Similar to the Model 50 and Model 70, the Model 55 SX contains three Micro Channel expansion slots. The Model

55 SX includes 2M bytes of RAM on the system board and the computer can support a total of 16M bytes. Like all members of the PS/2 family above the Model 30, the Model 55 SX comes standard with VGA graphics capability; built-in mouse; serial, parallel, and keyboard ports; and a diskette controller.

# Model 60

Like the Model 50, the Model 60 uses an 80286 microprocessor and the 16-bit subset of the Micro Channel bus. Unlike the smaller models, however, the Model 60 is a floor-standing system (illustrated second from the right in Figure 2.1) that comes in two configurations. The 60-041 includes a 1.44M-byte, 3½-inch floppy disk drive and a 40-millisecond average access time, 44M-byte fixed disk; the 60-071 uses the same floppy disk drive but comes with a 70M-byte, 30-millisecond access time fixed disk.

The Model 60 shares many of the basic design and performance features of the Model 50, including the 10-MHz operating rate of the 80286; 1M byte of RAM on the system board; and built-in serial, parallel, keyboard, and mouse connectors. Unlike a desktop system, the Model 60's system unit is constructed as a vertical tower that is 23 inches tall by 6½ inches wide by 19 inches deep. Optional mass-storage expansion includes a second 1.44M-byte, 3½-inch disk drive, a second 44M-byte fixed disk on the Model 60-041, and either a second 70M-byte or 115M-byte fixed disk on the Model 60-071.

The Model 60 has seven available expansion slots, whereas the Model 50 and Model 50Z have only three. Another significant difference between the Model 50 and Model 60 is in maximum on-line storage supported. The Model 60 can support up to 185M bytes of on-line storage, whereas the Model 50 is limited to 80M bytes and the Model 50Z to 120M bytes. The Model 60 is therefore more suitable as a file server on a local area network, because a server requires a substantial amount of shared storage capacity.

# Model 70

The Model 70 is IBM's first desktop PS/2 to use the Intel 80386 microprocessor. Figure 2.8 illustrates the Model 70, which as you can see resembles other desktop members of the PS/2 family. Three versions of the Model 70 were introduced by IBM approximately a year after the PS/2

**Figure 2.8** IBM PS/2 Model 70. The Model 70 was the first desktop PS/2 to use the Intel 80386 microprocessor. *Photograph courtesy of IBM Corporation.*

was announced. The chief difference between each version is in the operating rate of the 80386 microprocessor and the disk storage capacity contained in the computer's system unit.

Like earlier members of the PS/2 series, each version of the Model 70 includes built-in serial, parallel, keyboard, and mouse ports. Like the Model 50, 50Z, and 60, each Model 70 comes with one 1.44M-byte, 3½-inch disk drive as standard equipment.

The Model 70-E61 uses a 16-MHz Intel 80386 and has a 60M-byte fixed disk with a 29-millisecond average access time. The Model 70-121 runs at 20 MHz and uses a 120M-byte fixed disk that has an average access time of 23 milliseconds. The Model 70-A21 is the fastest desktop machine marketed by IBM; its 80386 microprocessor operates at 25 MHz.

From the outside, each Model 70 appears similar to the Model 50 and 50Z, occupying the same footprint of 14 inches wide by 16½ inches deep. Like the Model 50 and Model 50Z, each version of the Model 70 has three available Micro Channel expansion slots and 2M bytes of 80-nanosecond RAM on the system board, expandable to 8M bytes. Another 8M bytes of 32-bit memory can be added, providing a total of 16M bytes of RAM.

Comparing the Model 60 and Model 70 is similar in many respects to comparing the Model 50Z to the Model 60. Both the Model 50Z and Model 70 operate faster than the Model 60. However, the Model 60 has seven expansion slots, in comparison to the three expansion slots available on the Models 50Z and 70. Thus, selection of a Model 50Z or Model 70 in comparison to a Model 60 is primarily a choice between processor speed and expandability.

# Model P70 386

The Model P70 386 is IBM's first Micro Channel portable computer. This computer is designed for the traveling executive, scientist, or business professional who requires the power, the performance, and the functionality of a portable personal computer that incorporates the Intel 80386 microprocessor.

One of the most distinguishing features of the P70 386 is its 10-inch gas plasma display, which provides exceptional visibility for a portable computer. Unfortunately, the gas plasma display, diskette and fixed disk drives, and 4M bytes of standard memory contribute to the portable's hefty weight—21 pounds.

The PS/2 Model P70 386 is available with either a 60M-byte or 120M-byte fixed disk. Like the Model 55 SX, the P70 386 comes with 4M bytes of system board memory that is expandable up to 16M bytes. With the computer's built-in VGA capability, the gas plasma display provides 640-by-480-pixel graphics resolution with 16 shades of gray.

Two Micro Channel expansion slots are built into the Model P70 386. One expansion slot is half the length of a conventional slot. This half-length slot is primarily designed for an internal modem card. When the system is used in that configuration, one full-length Micro Channel expansion slot is available to support the use of other options.

## Model 80

The flagship of the PS/2 family is the Model 80; the processor is an 80386 that can perform both 16- and 32-bit data transfers. Three configurations are offered: the 80-041, which runs at 16 MHz and comes with 1M byte of RAM, a 1.44M-byte floppy disk drive, and a 44M-byte fixed disk; the 80-071, which also runs at 16 MHz and uses the same floppy disk drive, but has 2M bytes of RAM and a 70M-byte fixed disk; and the 80-111, which runs at 20 MHz and comes with 2M bytes of RAM and a 115-byte fixed disk. At the time of its introduction, the Model 80-141 cost approximately $11,000 and provided users with as much processing power as an IBM System/370 mainframe that in 1975 sold for $3.4 million.

Like the Model 60, the system unit of the Model 80 is a vertically constructed, floor-standing unit. The system board can hold up to 4M bytes of RAM and has three 32-bit and four 16-bit Micro Channel expansion slots. As in all PS/2 computers, the system board includes built-in serial and parallel ports, as well as keyboard and mouse connectors.

Table 2.1 presents a comparison of the major features of the different members of the PS/2 family.

## Comparison to PC Series

Only the Model 25, Model 30, and Model 30 286 of the PS/2 family can be directly compared to the earlier PC family, because only those models have a bus structure that accepts cards meant for use with the PC series. Further, many of the older adapter boards perform functions that are built into the motherboard of the previously mentioned PS/2 models. You don't need any adapter boards for conventional memory up to 640K bytes, one serial and one parallel port, a mouse port, graphics, because these functions are already built into the motherboard of each member of the PS/2 family. On the other hand, you need adapter boards if you want to add a second serial and/or parallel port, expanded memory, or additional support storage devices.

If you want data-storage compatibility with other machines, you have to install one or both of two separate options. For compatibility with members of the IBM PC family, you need to connect an external 5¼-inch, 360K-byte floppy disk drive and power supply. You'll also need an adapter board containing the controller for the external drive.

Table 2.1  IBM PS/2 Family Comparison

| | MODEL 25 | MODEL 30 | MODEL 30 286 | MODEL 50 | MODEL 50Z | MODEL 55 SX | MODEL 60 | MODEL 70 | MODEL P70 386 | MODEL 80 |
|---|---|---|---|---|---|---|---|---|---|---|
| Microprocessor | 8086 | 8086 | 80286 | 80286 | 80286 | 80386SX | 80286 | 80386 | 80386 | 80386 |
| Clock Speed | 8 MHz | 8 MHz | 10 MHz | 10 MHz | 10 MHz (Zero Wait State) | 16 MHz | 10 MHz | 16, 20, 25 MHz | 20 MHz | 16, 20 MHz |
| Keyboard Keys | 84,101 | 101 | 101 | 101 | 101 | 101 | 101 | 101 | 101 | 101 |
| Standard Memory | 512, 640 Kb | 640 Kb | 512 Kb | 1 Mb | up to 2 Mb | 4 Mb | 1 Mb | up to 2 Mb | 4 Mb | up to 2 Mb |
| Expandable to | 640 Kb | | 16 Mb | 16 Mb | 16 Mb | 16 Mb | 16 Mb | 16 Mb | 16 Mb | 16 Mb |
| Video Support | MCGA | MCGA | VGA | VGA | VGA | VGA | VGA | VGA | VGA | VGA |
| Diskette Size and Capacity | 3½ inch 720 Kb | 3½ inch 720 Kb | 3½ inch 1.44 Mb | 3½ inch 1.44 Mb | 3½ inch 1.44 Mb | 3½ inch 1.44 Mb | 3½ inch 1.44 Mb | 3½ inch 1.44 Mb | 3½ inch 1.44 Mb | 3½ inch 1.44 Mb |
| Fixed Disk[1] | | 20 Mb | 20 Mb[6] | 20 Mb | 30 Mb, 60 Mb | 30 Mb, 60 Mb | 44 Mb, 70 Mb | 60 Mb, 120 Mb | 60 Mb, 120 Mb | 44 Mb, 70 Mb, 115 Mb, 314 Mb |

Notes:
[1] Model 30 comes in two diskette and 1 diskette plus fixed disk configurations.

**Table 2.1** IBM PS/2 Family Comparison (continued)

| | MODEL 25 | MODEL 30 | MODEL 30 286 | MODEL 50 | MODEL 50Z | MODEL 55 SX | MODEL 60 | MODEL 70 | MODEL P70 386 | MODEL 80 |
|---|---|---|---|---|---|---|---|---|---|---|
| Additional Options[2] | 3½ inch 720 Kb drive or 20 Mb fixed disk | | 20 Mb for E01 version | 60 Mb | 60 Mb for 031 version | | 44 Mb, 70 Mb, 115 Mb | | | 44 Mb, 70 Mb, 115 Mb, 314 Mb |
| Maximum Configuration[3] w/option | 20 Mb | 20 Mb | 20 Mb | 60 Mb | 60 Mb | 30 Mb, 60 Mb | 185 Mb | 120 Mb | 60 Mb, 120 Mb | 628 Mb |
| Expansion Slots[4] | 2[5] | 3 | 3 | 3 | 3 | 3 | 7 | 3 | 2[7] | 7 |
| Operating System(s) | DOS | DOS | DOS, OS/2 | DOS, OS/2 | DOS, OS/2 | DOS, OS/2, AIX PS/2 | DOS, OS/2 | DOS, OS/2, AIX PS/2 | DOS, OS/2 | DOS, OS/2, AIX PS/2 |

Notes:
[2] Model 25 version with IBM Token Ring Network Adapter card is also available.
[3] The IBM 3363 Optical Disk Drive can provide an additional 200 Mb to 1.6 Gb of on-line storage, depending on the model.
[4] Models 25 and 30 use IBM PC expansion slots, Model 30 286 uses IBM PC/AT expansion slots, others include Micro Channel slots.
[5] One slot is 8 inches in length.
[6] The Model 30 286-E21 includes a 20 Mb fixed disk. The Model 30 286-E01 is a diskette-based system.
[7] One is half-length.

For data transfer compatibility between PS/2 Models 25 and 30 and other members of the PS/2 family, be very careful in formatting diskettes. The Models 25 and 30 only support the use of 720K-byte floppy disks, whereas the other members of the PS/2 family use 1.44M-byte drives. To ensure data transfer compatibility, format diskettes in the 1.44M-byte drive for 720K-byte storage. To accomplish this, you must use the /N:9/T:80 optional parameters in the FORMAT command to instruct DOS to format a 720K-byte diskette in a 1.44M-byte drive. Once you format the diskette for low density, data recorded to diskette in a 1.44M-byte drive can be read in a 720K-byte drive.

CHAPTER 3

# PC Series Third Party Hardware Overview

The acceptance of the IBM PC in both business and home environments stimulated hundreds of manufacturers to develop hardware products that add functionality to PCs, often at much lower prices than equivalent IBM products. Each member of the IBM PC series inherently provided a computational power greater than that of any 8-bit microcomputer; however, it was the introduction of third party hardware devices that gave potential PC purchasers the ability to configure a system in many different ways so that it could meet a wide variety of requirements.

This chapter begins with a discussion of the input/output (I/O) addressing scheme by means of which the processor selects a particular external device and transfers data to or from the device. You need to know something about this topic, because some third party products don't allow much flexibility in selecting their addresses and can cause addressing conflicts with another product. As a result, neither product works properly, because they are both present in the same system.

We'll then describe major categories of third party products from a functional perspective and show just how they enhance the performance and capabilities of PC systems. Finally, the chapter looks at some representative products in the various categories and reviews their capabilities and limitations. The information in this chapter will help you to select products that will not only give you the extra features you want but will do so without degrading the performance of your existing system.

# I/O Address Space

One of the trade-offs involved in computer design is determining how the microprocessor will communicate with peripheral devices and add-in hardware. Devices such as printers, keyboards, and video display units operate much more slowly than the CPU and its memory. Therefore, the CPU does not communicate directly with these devices, but rather with interface circuits. The circuits accept data and device-control commands at the CPU's speed and pass them on to the device at whatever speed the device can handle. Some microprocessors, such as the 68000, treat the registers in the interface as if they were memory locations. The disadvantage of this scheme is that the addresses reserved for I/O interfaces reduce the amount of RAM available for programs and data. The Intel microprocessor family can use this memory-mapped I/O scheme, but Intel-based systems more often use a port I/O scheme that distinguishes between memory addresses and I/O device addresses.

The Intel microprocessors provide special instructions for port input (IN) and output (OUT). These instructions generate a control signal that informs the data-bus controller that the accompanying address is to select an I/O port, not a memory location. Of the 20 address leads (which can address up to 1M byte of memory), the IN and OUT instructions activate only the lower 10, yielding an I/O address space of up to 1024 individual I/O ports. Figure 3.1 illustrates memory and port addressing on the 8088 and 80286 microprocessors.

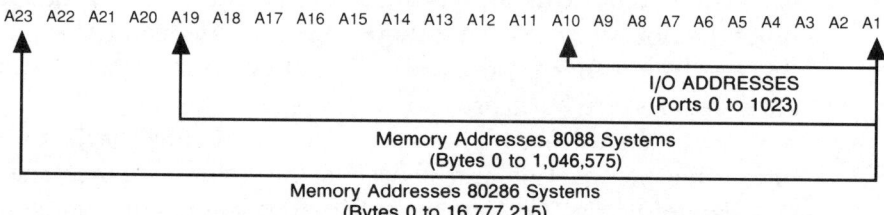

**Figure 3.1**  PC Addressing.

## Port Categories and Addresses

The PC has two categories of I/O ports: system-board ports, which are reserved for devices such as timers and counters that are integral components of the mother board, and I/O channel ports, which are reserved for adapter cards plugged into the expansion slots.

Both 8088- and 80286-based PC systems reserve port addresses X'000 through X'0FF (X' denotes hexadecimal notation) for devices on the system board. The I/O channel port addresses are X'200 through X'3FF on 8088-based PCs, and X'100 through X'3FF on 80286-based PCs.

The fact that an 8088 system has 512 I/O channel port addresses and an 80286 system has 786 does not imply that you could add that number of expansion products. First, most peripheral devices require several ports, each of which is assigned to a separate function of the device. Second, IBM originally reserved many port addresses for future use, and third party vendors avoid these in order to prevent the possibility of addressing conflicts in the future. Last, IBM assigned blocks of port I/O addresses to different types of hardware options. These addresses are searched at system initialization time. As an example, upon power-on or system reset, a block of port I/O addresses starting at location X'378 is searched to determine if they are in use. If an IBM monochrome display and parallel printer adapter, or compatible third party hardware, is installed, the parallel printer port on the card will be assigned device address LPT1. Because the available port I/O addresses differ slightly between 8088 and 80286 systems, you may wish to examine the use of I/O channel ports for both systems. If you think that you may eventually need to move a card from an 8088 to an 80286 system, this information will help you to select a card that has enough addressing flexibility to allow the move. Figure 3.2 illustrates the channel I/O port usage of available, reserved, and assigned I/O addresses for the IBM PC series of personal computers.

## Addressing Conflicts

As indicated in Figure 3.2, a small subset of port I/O addresses is available for third party vendors that manufacture such devices as a clock/calendar, digital-to-analog converter, and other "unofficial" non-IBM-manufactured hardware. Like any I/O device, this hardware requires ports. However, unlike IBM-sanctioned hardware such as asynchronous communications

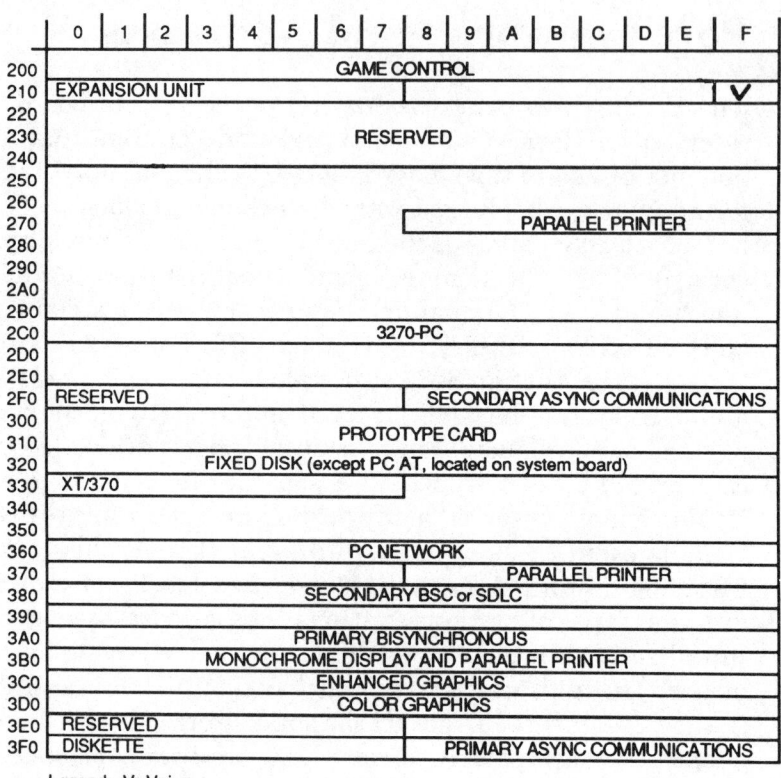

**Figure 3.2** I/O Channel Address Map.

adapter cards and printer ports, no official address space was allocated by IBM for the previously mentioned hardware functions. This means that you cannot rely on the operation of a clock/calendar or similar nonsanctioned hardware, because the I/O ports assigned to the hardware could be in conflict with other third party products that were designed independently to use the same I/O port addresses. To prevent addressing conflicts from occurring, you should investigate how third party products use I/O address space, verifying that they are using an unassigned area. Next, you should examine the port I/O addresses used by other third party products previously installed in your computer, because an attempt by two devices to share an address almost always ensures that something will go wrong.

If two add-in products use the same address space for one or more features, you should then check to determine whether you can disable the feature on one or both cards by the setting of a jumper or a DIP switch element on the adapter card. As an example, you might consider purchasing two multifunction cards to obtain the memory and ports needed for a specific application. If each multifunction board contained a clock/calendar, an addressing conflict would arise when the software attempted to access this function. However, if you could disable the clock/calendar on one card, the clock/calendar would work correctly on the second multifunction board.

Assigned address space represents a second area where addressing conflicts can occur. As an example, installing two asynchronous communications adapters, two multifunction boards with serial ports, or a combination of the two adapters that use I/O ports X'3F8 through X'3FF could cause an addressing conflict. This conflict would occur when software attempted to use the first communications adapter or serial port whose port I/O address is X'3F8 through X'3FF and whose device address is COM1. To prevent an addressing conflict from occurring, you should determine if the serial port on one device can be disabled or reassigned to device address COM2.

By carefully examining the port I/O address in conjunction with the device address assigned to different functions on adapter boards, you can identify potential addressing conflicts before they occur. If you take care to select only equipment that allows you to change its I/O address by means of jumpers or switches, you'll obtain a high degree of flexibility that will allow a board not only to be compatible with your current system but to remain compatible with your future upgrades and additions.

# Representative Hardware

The remainder of this chapter examines a variety of third party hardware that is representative of many other popular expansion products that are available for use with members of the IBM PC family. There would be no room here to describe all of the hundreds of devices on the market, so the discussion is confined to devices that will be useful to a majority of PC users. Reading the various sections may give you an understanding of the operating characteristics from a system viewpoint and help you develop a set of criteria for selecting future enhancements and additions to your system.

Note that representative third party hardware products described in this chapter were included for illustrative purposes and should not be construed as an endorsement of such products. Similarly, the omission of a vendor's product that operates and provides similar functionality to a described product should not be construed as a negative endorsement.

## AC Power Protector

Although devices that protect a personal computer from spikes, surges, noise, and brownouts are not necessary for the operation of the computer, they are one of the first accessories you should consider.

AC power protector products include surge suppressors, isolation transformers, and voltage regulators. Some devices perform just one of these functions; others may perform two or all three of the functions.

The surge suppressor rejects high-amplitude spikes and, depending on manufacturer, may or may not reject radio frequency interference (RFI) noise. An isolation transformer provides a higher degree of spike filtration than a surge suppressor and also rejects RFI noise. The most sophisticated AC power protector is a voltage regulator. This device includes a transformer that maintains a constant output voltage over a wide range of input voltages; it works fast enough to eliminate sudden as well as gradual surges and sags; and it suppresses short spikes as well as RFI that is carried by the house wiring. The independent windings isolate the load equipment from the house wiring, and provide a high degree of protection against electrical shock in the event of a catastrophic malfunction in the load equipment's own power supplies.

Figure 3.3 illustrates the SSB Design Pure Power Plus, which is a combined multiple outlet, surge suppressor and isolation transformer. The SSB Design Pure Power Plus provides six 115 VAC electrical outlets at the rear of the device whose power activity is controlled by individual switches at the front of the unit. Although several manufacturers make similar devices, the current indicator at the front of the unit is probably unique and provides you with a visual indication of how much current your equipment is using. The voltage indicator tells you the condition of the line voltage, which can be especially valuable during the summer months when electric utilities sometimes reduce voltages during periods of peak consumer demand.

In addition to protecting against spikes and surges, the SSB Design Pure Power Plus includes EMI and RFI filtration. Because noise in the form of electromagnetic interference (EMI) or RFI can result in memory

**Figure 3.3** The SSB Design Pure Power Plus—The SSB Design Pure Power Plus is a combined surge suppressor and EMI/RFI filter. With six outlets at the rear of the unit this device can be used to distribute up to 15 amps of power to a personal computer and five peripheral devices. *Photograph courtesy of SSB Design.*

errors, this feature may be valuable for personal computers located in an industrial area.

# Keyboards

Because of the controversy surrounding the design of the keyboard offered with the IBM PC and most versions of the PC XT, several third party vendors entered the keyboard replacement market. Most of these third party keyboards include features that were conspicuous by their absence on equivalent IBM devices, such as the placement of the Shift and Enter keys in the same location as they exist on the IBM Selectric typewriter and the inclusion of light emitting diodes (LEDs) to indicate the status of dual state keys such as Caps Lock and Num Lock.

## Popular PC and PC XT Replacements

Figure 3.4 illustrates the KeyTronic KB5150 keyboard, which is a very popular replacement for the keyboards originally bundled with the IBM PC and most PC XT systems. In comparing this keyboard to that originally offered by IBM you'll note several differences. First, many special keys such as the Tab, Shift, and Enter keys are labeled, whereas on IBM PC and PC XT keyboards they are denoted by symbols. Secondly, the Shift and Enter keys on the KB5150 are placed in their equivalent IBM Selectric typewriter locations, which, according to some experts, increases the productivity of touch typists. Third, and perhaps most significant, is the inclusion of LEDs on the Caps Lock and Num Lock keys. These LEDs tell you at a glance what modes are active, thereby eliminating a very frequent source of typing errors. Finally, in the extreme right corner of

**Figure 3.4** KeyTronic KB5150 Keyboard—This IBM PC and PC XT replacement keyboard includes legends on the Tab, Shift, and Enter keys; light emitting diodes on the Caps Lock and Num Lock keys; the relocation of the Shift and Enter keys to their Selectric typewriter locations; and the inclusion of an Enter key on the numeric keypad. *Photograph courtesy of KeyTronic.*

the keyboard, you'll see that the numeric keypad has an Enter key, which makes it much easier to enter sequences of numeric data.

A second KeyTronic keyboard (the 5151) that can be used with the PC and PC XT is illustrated in Fig. 3.5. This keyboard is notable because the function keys were relocated to the top row across the keyboard to match the layout adopted by IBM in the Enhanced Keyboard. Note, however, that the KeyTronic 5151 contains 10 function keys, whereas the IBM Enhanced Keyboard contains 12.

The KeyTronic 5151 keyboard is similar to that vendor's 5150 in its use of legends rather than symbols, LED indicators for Caps Lock and Num Lock, placement of the Shift and Enter keys in the familiar Selectric typewriter locations, and the inclusion of an Enter key on the numeric keypad. This keyboard additionally differs from the original IBM keyboards for the PC and PC XT as well as from the vendor's 5150 keyboard in its placement of the function keys across the top of the keyboard and the inclusion of several special keys on the top row to the right of the function keys. These special keys include Pause, Cursr Pad, Prt Sc, and Reset.

The Pause key generates the scan codes associated with the simultaneous depression of Ctrl and Num Lock on a conventional keyboard, reducing a two-key operation to one. Similarly, the Prt Sc key generates

**Figure 3.5** KeyTronic Keypad—The KeyTronic 5151 keyboard includes function keys relocated to the top of the keyboard, a separate cursor and editing keypad, as well as several keys whose depression generates two and three key sequences. *Photograph courtesy of KeyTronic.*

the Shift plus Prt Sc key combination on a conventional PC or PC XT keyboard, and the Reset key generates the Ctrl + Alt + Del three-key sequence normally required to perform a system reset. Finally, the Cursr Pad key activates a separate cursor and editing key keypad, which is located between the typewriter keys and the numeric keypad. Although the IBM Enhanced Keyboard includes a Prt Sc key labeled PrintScreen and a Pause key similar to the KeyTronic 5151 keyboard, it does not include a Reset key, so users must generate a reset by pressing Ctrl + Alt + Del.

One interesting feature of the KeyTronic 5151 is a low-cost conversion kit that enables you to use this keyboard with an IBM PC AT. By contrast, IBM PC and PC XT keyboards cannot be used with that vendor's AT personal computer, whereas the IBM Enhanced Keyboard cannot be used with the IBM PC and PC XT computers.

## Bar Code Input

Although several vendors market bar code readers that you can connect to a serial port located on an adapter card that is installed in your system unit, KeyTronic offers a novel approach to providing bar code capability. As you can see in Figure 3.6, you can plug a bar code wand directly into the 5151B keyboard. The 5151B keyboard contains circuitry that handles the electrical connections to the wand, and the 8048 microcontroller has firmware routines that translate bar code signals into the corresponding ASCII characters. Thus, you do not need to install or use a separate serial port for the bar code wand, nor do you need any extra software. You can use the 5151B keyboard with a PC or PC XT, but unfortunately the vendor does not market a conversion kit that would let you use this keyboard with a PC AT.

## Touch Pad Keyboard

One of the most interesting keyboards on the market can be considered a cross between a pointing device and a conventional keyboard. Marketed by KeyTronic as the 5153 Touch Pad Keyboard, this device includes a built-in Touch Pad that you can use either to generate predefined function key messages or cursor-key movements, or as a mouse or direct pointing device for graphics applications.

**Figure 3.6** KeyTronic 5151B Keyboard—The KeyTronic 5151B keyboard permits bar code data to be input to the computer through the keyboard, eliminating the need for utility software and the use of a serial port. *Photograph courtesy of KeyTronic.*

The KeyTronic 5153 keyboard illustrated in Figure 3.7 is bundled with utility software and snap-in templates that fit into the rectangular touch pad area. In the cursor-key mode of operation, the movement of the operator's fingers or a stylus across the Touch Pad is converted into equivalent keystrokes that can be useful for operating several types of electronic spreadsheet programs. In the mouse mode with appropriate driver software, the Touch Pad serves as an alternative to a mouse. By moving your fingers or a stylus on the Touch Pad, you can use the 5153 to perform mouse operations without a mouse.

The 5153 also provides a graphics mode and a function-key mode. In the graphics mode, you can use the touch screen as a digitizing tablet. In the function-key mode, up to 36 keys can be preassigned messages of up to 70 characters in length. Then, pressing a predefined area on the Touch Pad denoted by a template initiates a preassigned message. Included with the 5153 are templates for DOS, Lotus 1-2-3, and WordStar. In addition, you can create custom templates with a ruled paper pad and clear plastic that are supplied with the keyboard.

**Figure 3.7** KeyTronic 5153 Keyboard—The Touch Pad in this keyboard supports cursor, mouse, graphic, and function key modes. Up to 36 areas on the Touch Pad can be programmed to reduce key sequences to a single touch on the Touch Pad. *Photograph courtesy of KeyTronic.*

# Multifunction Boards

One of the earliest criticisms of the IBM PC was directed at its limited number of system expansion slots and at the adapter boards offered by IBM, which for the most part supported only a single hardware function. An early model IBM PC with 64K bytes of memory on its system board could easily have all its expansion slots filled. As an example, installing an IBM Color Graphics Adapter, Parallel Printer Adapter, Diskette Drive Controller, Asynchronous Communications Controller, and a 64K-byte memory card would fill the computer, eliminating the potential to add further functionality unless a previously installed adapter was removed. Fortunately, this situation did not persist for long, because third party vendors recognized this product void and rapidly introduced multifunction boards to satisfy user requirements.

## Card Structure

By definition, a multifunction board contains two or more hardware functions built onto one adapter card. Multifunction boards generally provide some combination of expansion RAM, one or more serial and/or parallel ports, a clock/calendar, and a game port. Although there is no such item as a typical multifunction board—because of the diversity of functions that can be incorporated onto an adapter card—Figure 3.8 illustrates a common multifunction adapter card structure that will be used as a point of reference in discussing this hardware.

## RAM

The early IBM PCs could hold no more than 64K bytes of RAM on the system board and could address no more than 576K bytes in all. Until mid-1982, therefore, many multifunction boards contained space for the addition of as many as 512K bytes of RAM in eight banks on nine chips per bank (including the parity bit). However, when IBM introduced the PC XT, the company's designers changed the system board of both the PC XT and the PC to accommodate 256K bytes of RAM; a new version of the BIOS increased the total memory of both machines to 640K bytes. Because PC-DOS requires contiguous memory, you must fully populate the system board before you add any further memory on adapter cards. Thus, to expand a PC or PC XT to the full 640K bytes of memory, you

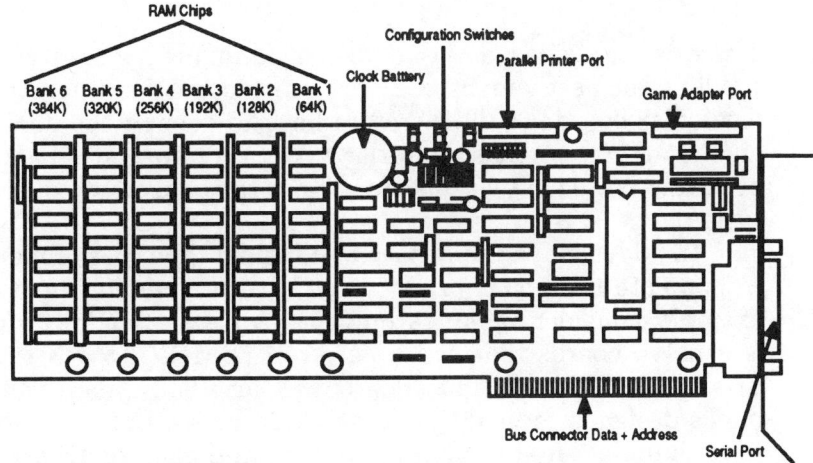

**Figure 3.8** Common Multifunction Adapter Card Structure—A multifunction adapter card normally includes up to six RAM chip banks, a clock/calendar, one or more parallel and serial ports, and a set of configuration switches that are used to set the address of ports and starting memory.

would need 640K bytes less 256K bytes (384K bytes) additional RAM. This figure is now the standard memory capacity of most multifunction boards.

Although the RAM banks are labeled 1 through 6 in Figure 3.8, they are addressed as banks 4 through 9, because the system board contains memory banks 0 through 3. If the computer detects a memory error, it reports it in the form xxyy 201, where xx is the bank and yy is the chip in the bank that failed. When a chip on an adapter card fails, you can identify its bank location by subtracting 3 from the bank number reported. Thus, a memory error message indicating a failure of a chip in bank 4 actually refers to the first bank on the expansion card.

To provide complete flexibility in allowing the memory on an expansion board to operate with any memory already installed, either on the system board or on another adapter board, most vendors include one or more configuration switches. Figure 3.9 shows how the elements of a configuration switch might be used to set the starting address and the total memory available on a multifunction card. Assume, for example, that the system board has 256K bytes of memory and the multifunction card has 384K bytes. You would set the switches of Figure 3.9 as follows:

| 1 | 2 | 3 | 4 | 5 | 6 | 7 | 8 |
|---|---|---|---|---|---|---|---|
| ON | OFF | ON | ON | OFF | ON | ON | OFF |

There is no standard way of using configuration switch elements; each vendor assigns them in the way most convenient for the layout of the particular board. You'll therefore have to consult the hardware manual of any board you purchase in order to obtain information about the function performed by each switch element and the proper way of setting it for your system.

In addition, you may have to consider the types of memory chips used to populate the board prior to setting the configuration switches. As an example, consider one of several types of AST SixPak Plus multifunction expansion boards that can be used in IBM PC, PC XT, and compatible personal computers. This board was originally manufactured with nine banks designed to hold 64K-byte RAM chips. Later versions of the board were manufactured with three banks, and each bank could be populated with either 64K-byte or 256K-byte memory chips. In 1989, AST introduced a new memory expansion board specifically designed for PC AT 80286 16-bit bus systems. Called the SixPak 286, this board accepts either 256K-bit memory chips or 1M-byte single in-line memory modules (SIMMs),

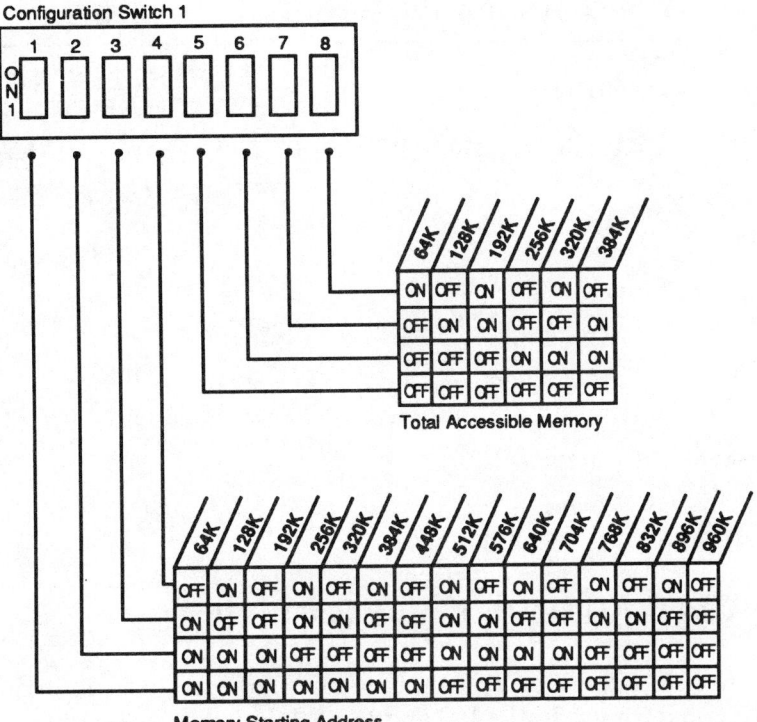

**Figure 3.9** Multifunction Board Configuration Switch—The configuration switch on a multifunction board enables the user to set the starting memory address and total accessible memory to be used on the board.

which can be expanded in increments of 512K or 2M bytes to as much as 4M bytes per card. Table 3.1 indicates the AST Research SixPak Plus configuration switch setting required to denote the total memory installed on the board, which is based both on the type of memory chips used to populate this multifunction board and on the total memory resulting from populating each of the banks.

In examining Table 3.1 you might be puzzled about why a person might purchase and install a multifunction board that can support up to 576K bytes of memory without adding any memory chips to the board. Upon occasion, the use of a multifunction board without additional memory may be an economical and expedient method to add a clock/calendar and one or more serial, parallel, and game ports to your computer using just one system expansion slot. Each of these multifunction board features is discussed later in this chapter.

**Table 3.1** AST Research SixPak Plus Configuration Switch Settings

| MEMORY CHIP USAGE | | | CONFIGURATION SWITCH SETTINGS | | | TOTAL RAM |
|---|---|---|---|---|---|---|
| BANK 0 | BANK 1 | BANK 2 | SW1-4 | SW1-5 | SW1-6 | |
| – | – | – | OFF | OFF | OFF | 0K bytes |
| 64K bytes | – | – | OFF | OFF | ON | 64K bytes |
| 64K bytes | 64K bytes | – | OFF | ON | OFF | 128K bytes |
| 256K bytes | – | – | OFF | ON | ON | 256K bytes |
| 64K bytes | 256K bytes | – | ON | OFF | OFF | 320K bytes |
| 64K bytes | 64K bytes | 256K bytes | ON | OFF | ON | 384K bytes |
| 256K bytes | 256K bytes | – | ON | ON | OFF | 512K bytes |
| 64K bytes | 256K bytes | 256K bytes | ON | ON | ON | 576K bytes |

## Clock/Calendar and Battery

Another common feature incorporated into most multifunction boards designed for use in the PC and PC XT is a clock/calendar. The clock/calendar is set by software provided by the multifunction board vendor and its operation is normally controlled by a configuration switch element; one position of the switch enables the clock and the opposite position disables it. Some multifunction boards, such as the previously discussed AST Research SixPak Plus, contain a jumper block onto which you either insert or remove shorting plugs to enable or disable many board features including the clock/calendar and serial and parallel ports.

Figure 3.10 illustrates one of three jumper blocks incorporated onto the AST Research SixPak Plus multifunction board. This jumper block contains two rows of pins formed into six columns. By placing a shorting plug over two pins in a column, you enable the option. Similarly, removing a shorting plug disables the option. Because the shorting block's presence or absence either enables or disables specific ports on the multifunction board, this jumper block is referred to as the *port enable jumper block* by AST Research.

If two or more adapters in a PC have clock/calendars, it is important to be able to disable all except one of the clocks. Otherwise, an addressing conflict will occur when the clock/calendar is addressed, with the result that none of the clocks will operate correctly.

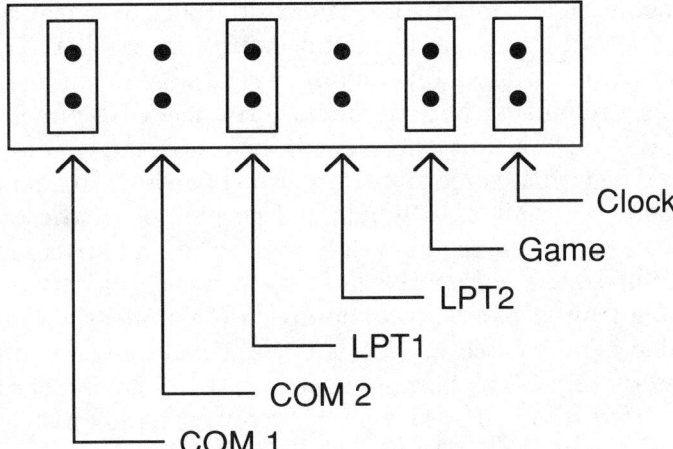

**Figure 3.10** AST Research SixPak Plus Port Enable Jumper Block—The factory configuration for the port enable jumper block contains shorting plugs covering the COM1, LPT1, game, and clock jumpers. The remaining jumpers are not covered with shorting plugs and are disabled when the board is received from the factory.

The battery on the adapter card provides power to the clock/calendar and can be an important consideration in selecting a multifunction board. Some batteries are soldered to the card, whereas others are easily removable, fastened to the adapter by a metal clip. Another consideration is the rated life of the clock battery, which can range from one to five or more years.

## Ports

The PC supports three logical printer devices that are designated LPT1, LPT2, and LPT3. It's important to select adapter boards that can assign the on-board parallel-port hardware to one of these logical addresses or disable the board altogether. If you don't, you could end up with graphics cards, data-acquisition cards, and memory-expansion cards, all of which have parallel ports that are unusable because of addressing conflicts.

Another hardware consideration is the fact that there is a fixed amount of space on a mounting bracket. Thus, vendors whose boards have more than one port normally use a flat ribbon cable, wiring the port interface directly mounted on the card to a connector. The other end of the ribbon cable contains a standard parallel or serial connector that can be connected to a separate metal mounting bracket. This mounting bracket in turn is mounted on the upper rear edge of the back of the system unit. Other mounting options include the use of a punch-out area at the rear of the system unit and the use of a special system expansion slot cover provided with some multifunction boards. This expansion slot cover includes a cutout onto which the connector of the cable can be fastened. However, its use requires that an unused system expansion slot is available, as illustrated in Figure 3.11. This figure shows the routing of a flat ribbon cable from a parallel port jumper on a multifunction board to which the cable is connected on one end via a rectangular connector. The opposite end of the flat ribbon cable contains a DB-25S connector that is shown inserted into a special type of system expansion slot cover. Both the connector and the expansion slot cover can be inserted and secured into a system expansion slot cover mounting area. In this way the DB-25S connector appears to be affixed to an adapter card. Figure 3.12 shows the connection of two flat ribbon cables to an Expanded Quadboard manufactured by Quadram Corporation.

## Software

Most multifunction boards include a diskette containing several enhancement programs. Typical programs furnished include a printer spooler, a

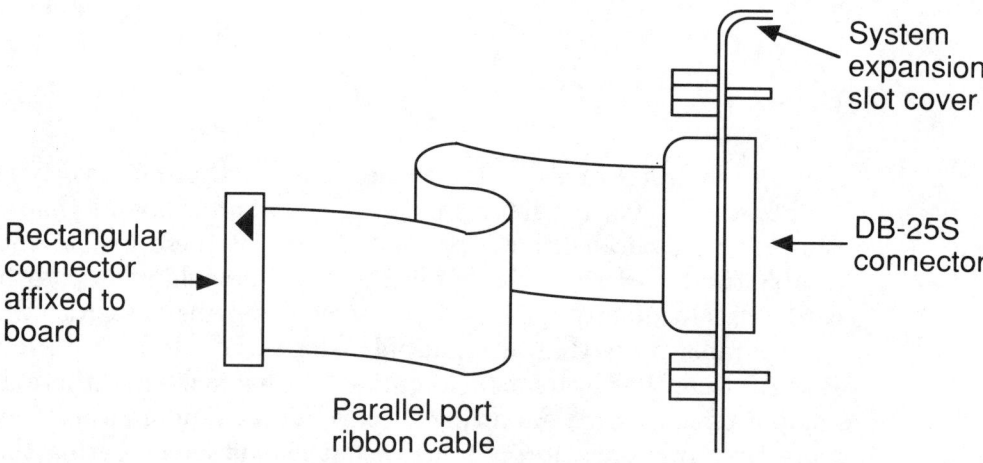

**Figure 3.11** Mounting the Flat Ribbon Connector.

PC Series Third Party Hardware Overview  **111**

**Figure 3.12** Expanded Quadboard. *Photograph courtesy of Quadram Corporation.*

RAM-disk driver, and programs to read and set the clock/calendar time and day.

When loaded, the printer spooler directs printer output from an application program into a buffer area of memory. The spooler then responds to interrupt requests that indicate the printer is in its background operation, leaving you free to initiate another function before the print job is complete. The spooler program usually enables you to choose the size of the print buffer to suit your needs.

Using the RAM-disk driver, you assign a block of memory to act as an electronic disk drive. The program treats this memory block as if it were another diskette or fixed disk drive and gives it the next free disk letter. That is, if you have two diskette drives designated A: and B:, the RAM disk becomes drive C:. You can copy programs from magnetic disks to the RAM disk, as well as the data on which the programs will operate. You'll find that disk-intensive programs (such as database managers or word processors) run very fast, because data transfers between the RAM disk and the program's working memory take place at full memory speed; when the data has to be fetched from a magnetic disk, it's delayed by the electromechanical characteristics of the drive (rotation speed, track-seek times, and so on). Another advantage is that on machines with only one diskette drive (such as the original PC XT), you obtain an extra drive at minimal cost. Table 3.2 lists some of the features that you'll find on various multifunction cards and may help you decide which features to look for when you purchase a multifunction board.

## Representative Hardware

The Expanded Quadboard manufactured by Quadram Corporation is illustrated in Figure 3.12. The Quadboard and AST Research's SixPak Plus are two of the most popular multifunction boards used with the IBM PC and PC XT. However, a large number of other vendors have developed similar products.

The Expanded Quadboard illustrated in Figure 3.12 is shown with 384K bytes of memory installed. In the lower right portion of the card is

**Table 3.2** Multifunction Board Selection Features

| FEATURE | DETAILS |
| --- | --- |
| Memory | On-board minimum and maximum<br>Configuration switch starting address<br>Configuration switch accessible memory<br>Type<br>    Conventional<br>    Extended<br>    Expanded |
| Ports | Type and Number<br>    Serial<br>    Parallel<br>Settings<br>    Address settings<br>    Port enable and disable |
| Clock Battery | Removable<br>Permanently attached |
| Mounting Bracket | System expansion slot cover<br>Bracket that attaches to rear of system unit |
| Software Bundled | Printer spooler<br>Clock/calendar |

a serial port. Two flat ribbon cables are shown connected to parallel and serial ports; the card's battery is located at the top of the card between the two flat ribbons. To the left of the leftmost ribbon is an eight-element configuration switch that sets the starting memory address and total memory residing on the board.

## Memory Cards

When the IBM PC was introduced, a 32K-byte memory expansion board was marketed by the computer manufacturer. This card could be added after the system board was fully populated with four banks of 16K-byte chips, resulting in one obtaining a total of 96K bytes of RAM. Since then, the amount of memory contained on many cards has increased by a factor of 100 or more. Prior to an examination of memory cards, a discussion of the types of memory is warranted.

## Extended and Expanded Memory

Until now, this chapter has basically discussed only conventional memory—physical memory within the contiguous 1M-byte address space that can be directly addressed by an 8088 microprocessor, or by an 80286 or 80386 microprocessor operating in its real mode (that is, when it is emulating an 8088). The rest of this chapter discusses extended memory.

*Extended memory* is the contiguous address space from 1M byte to 16M bytes. The 8086 and 8088 microprocessors, which have only 20 address lines, cannot directly address memory above 1M byte, nor can they operate in protected mode and run an operating system such as OS/2. However, when operating in real mode as an 8088, the 80286 and 80386 are limited to memory use of 640K bytes, because the various versions of PC-DOS through 3.3 don't support more than 640K bytes of memory.

*Expanded memory* is defined by the LIM 4.0 specification as any 64K-byte segment of memory above the 1M-byte boundary. An 8088, or an 80286 or 80386 in real mode, can access segments of expanded memory by means of paging, or bank switching. *Bank switching* is the process of electronically repositioning expanded memory into the microprocessor's address range. The expanded memory is divided into 16K-byte blocks called *pages,* and these are swapped into or out of an area of main storage called the page frame. This page frame effectively becomes a window that can look into various blocks of expanded memory, as shown in Figure 3.13.

To use expanded memory, programs must be designed to operate with a switching scheme, taking into consideration such factors as the location of the page frame and page register as well as the size of the page. Fortunately, two specifications that are basically compatible with each other have attracted the widespread support of software developers.

The first specification to gain wide support was jointly introduced by Lotus Development Corporation, Intel Corporation, and Microsoft Corporation. Known as LIM EMS, this expanded memory specification uses up to four 16K-byte windows between memory locations 768K and 896K for bank switching to obtain a 64K-byte window to expanded memory. This window is known as the page frame. The LIM EMS supports up to 8M bytes of addressable memory and requires the use of a device driver to act as an interface between an applications program and expanded memory.

Unfortunately, programs sold prior to the introduction of the LIM EMS, or programs not developed to use this standard, cannot take advantage of expanded memory. To do so you must obtain a new release of the program that supports the expanded memory specification or a multitasking shell program under which the application program can operate.

A second extended memory specification was introduced with backing from AST Research, Quadram Corporation, and Ashton-Tate. Known as

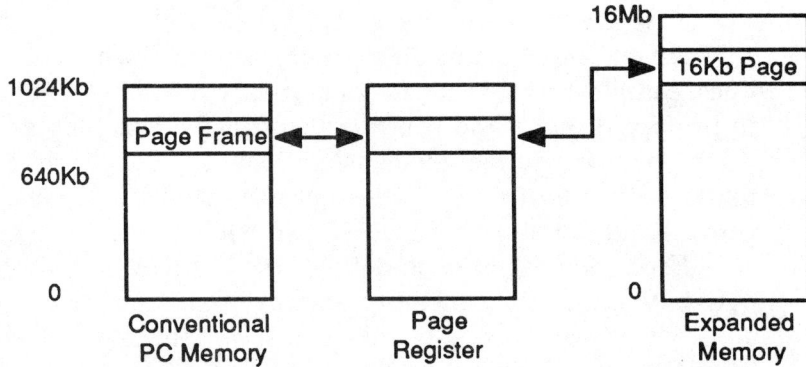

**Figure 3.13** Expanded Memory Operation—When expanded memory is used, a page frame in conventional memory serves as a sliding window for using expanded memory. A location in memory, the page register, maintains the status of the associated page frame.

the AQA Enhanced Extended Memory Specification (AQA EEMS), this specification can be considered as a superset of LIM. The EEMS specification initially uses 4-page frames that are the same as the LIM specification, which makes the two compatible. Where the EEMS specification differs from LIM is in its support of up to 64-page frames, although in actuality only a subset can be used at one time due to the physical constraints of conventional memory.

## Selecting Memory

Before you can use expanded memory, you must install 640K bytes of conventional memory in your computer. Some expanded memory cards permit memory on the card to be partitioned between conventional and expanded. Thus, say you have 512K bytes of memory installed on your system board. You would select 128K bytes on a card with partitioning capability in order to make up your conventional memory to the full 640K bytes. If the expanded memory card cannot be partitioned, you'll have to add a 128K-byte memory card before you can use expanded memory.

## Representative Hardware

The Quadram Corporation Liberty board is illustrated in Figure 3.14. This adapter card can be populated with up to 2M bytes of memory that conforms to both the LIM EMS and AQA EEMS specifications. Configuration switches on the card set the location of the page frame, paging register, and the amount of memory on the card.

Under the Above Board trademark Intel markets a variety of adapter boards, including the Above Board PS, Above Board PS/AT, Above Board/PC, Above Board/AT, and the Above Board Plus 8 I/O.

The Above Board PS and the Above Board PS/AT are multifunction boards, because they include a parallel and serial port as well as a clock/calendar on the card and are bundled with several software programs. Either adapter can be populated with 64K-bit or 256K-bit chips. The 64K-bit chips provide a maximum of 384K bytes of memory, which can be used as either conventional or expanded memory. The 256K-bit chips increase the capacity of the board to 1.5M bytes, of which up to 384K bytes can be used as conventional memory and the remainder (or all the memory on the board) as expanded memory.

**Figure 3.14** Quadram Liberty Board—The Quadram Liberty expanded memory card can be populated with up to 2M bytes of RAM and supports both the LIM EMS and AQA EEMS specifications. *Photograph courtesy of Quadram Corporation.*

The Above Board/PC and Above Board/AT are similar to the Above Board PS and Above Board PS/AT in their ability to use either 64K-bit or 256K-bit memory chips. You can install as many as 2048K bytes of memory on the Above Board/PC or Above Board/AT, assigning up to 640K bytes as conventional memory, and the remainder as expanded memory. A configuration switch on the board specifies the type of memory chips used to populate the card's sockets, the assignment of conventional and expanded memory, and the port address of the board. Because you can install as many as four Above Board/PC cards in the system unit of a PC, the last four elements on the board's configuration switch determine the card's I/O port address. Although this addressing capability was designed primarily to prevent addressing conflicts between four Above Board/PC cards, it can also prevent any addressing conflict with other adapter cards previously installed in the computer.

Another interesting Intel Above Board product is that vendor's Above Board Plus 8 I/O adapter card. This board is manufactured with 2M bytes of memory and contains sockets that accept an additional 6M bytes of RAM. A piggyback board that holds another 6M bytes of RAM can be snapped onto this Above Board Plus 8 I/O, resulting in a total of 14M bytes of RAM available in one expansion slot. In addition to the RAM, this board includes one serial and one parallel port.

Memory on the Above Board Plus 8 I/O can be configured via software as conventional, expanded, and extended. Expanded memory conforms to the previously discussed LIM specification, so you can use this board to fill out the 640K of conventional RAM if your computer has less memory or to set the remaining memory on the board as expanded memory. If you are using the board in an 80286- or 80386-based computer, you can set all or a portion of the board's memory as extended to enable it to be used with OS/2.

Another interesting and potentially valuable feature of the Above Board 8 I/O card is its ability to be used with PCs, XTs, and ATs. Although the card contains two connectors similar to other cards designed for use in the PC AT, a chip on the board controls its use of an 8-bit or 16-bit bus for memory transfer. Thus, you can use the Above Board Plus 8 I/O in an 8-bit bus IBM PC or PC XT and by the replacement of a chip on the board use it in a 16-bit bus PC AT.

Although the Intel Above Board/PC, as well as extended memory products from other vendors, is designed to work with the IBM PC, PC XT, and compatibles, you should check the total power consumption of all hardware installed in a PC. The IBM PC's power supply provides 7 amps at 5 volts, and each Above Board can consume up to 1.3 amps at 5.0 volts. If the cumulative power consumption of all options exceeds 7 amps, the power supply will simply shut itself off to prevent damage. If this situation arises, you can either remove some of the existing hardware in your PC or install a more robust power supply, such as one equivalent to that used in the PC XT, which supplies 15 amps at +5 volts and has a total wattage of 135.

When you install one or more Above Board/AT cards in a PC AT, the 192-watt power supply is usually sufficient to run any combination of boards in that computer.

## Software Installation

New versions of Intel Above Board add-in memory cards, as well as smaller third party products, are software-installable. Marketed by Intel Corporation as the Above Board 286, Above Board PS/286, and Above Board Plus 8 I/O, these cards are packaged with an installation program you use to initialize or modify the memory configuration. This feature eliminates the use of configuration switches, so you don't have to open the system unit of a PC to change a previously set configuration.

Table 3.3 contains a list of key features that should influence your selection of a memory card. Consider how each one will affect your current

**Table 3.3** Memory Card Selection Features

| FEATURE | DETAILS |
|---|---|
| Type of Memory | Conventional<br>Extended<br>Expanded |
| Expanded Memory Specification Support | LIM EMS<br>AQA EEMS |
| Memory Partition Capability/Capacity | Conventional<br>Expanded |
| Ports Included/Options | Serial<br>Parallel |
| Clock/Calendar | |
| Memory Chip Usage | 64K bit<br>256K bit |
| Configuration | By switches<br>By software |
| Compatibility | PC<br>PC XT<br>PC AT |

system usage and your plans for future expansion, as well as the cost of the hardware.

# Accelerator Cards

As application programs increase in complexity, the processing speed at which a personal computer executes tasks becomes more noticeable. Sorting large databases, recalculating spreadsheets, and computing a statistical analysis on a data set are but a few examples of applications whose task duration can be decreased by increasing the computer's processing speed. These applications are commonly referred to as "compute-bound," in comparison to other applications, such as the printing of a mailing list, which are called "I/O bound."

There are three basic ways of speeding up compute-bound programs. First, if you're developing the programs yourself, for your own use or for distribution, you can optimize the program structure and the computational algorithms for fastest execution. Second, if the programs run under an interpreter (such as BASIC), you may be able to substitute a compiled version that will run 10 to 50 times faster than the interpreted version. Both of these methods depend on your programming ability and are time consuming.

If you're not a programmer and can't modify the programs you use, your only course is to use a faster computer. In the mainframe and minicomputer worlds, you'd have to replace the central processing unit with a faster, more powerful unit in the same family as your present system. The personal computer market, however, offers add-in cards that make your PC or compatible run faster. These adapter cards are commonly known as *accelerator cards*; their complexity ranges from a small card that contains a faster version of the original microprocessor and a matched systemclock generator, to other cards containing a more powerful microprocessor and a block of fast memory.

## Types of Accelerator Cards

There are two types of accelerator cards—those designed to make an IBM PC or PC XT approach or exceed the operating rate of a PC AT, and those designed to enable a PC AT or XT 286 to approach or exceed the operating rate of an 80386-based computer. The first type of accelerator card normally includes an Intel 8086, 80186, or 80286; the second type of card has an Intel 80386 or 80386SX microprocessor installed. The 80386SX can be considered a hybrid 80386 microprocessor. Although the 80386SX has all the processing and multitasking capability of a 32-bit 80386, the former microprocessor was designed to use the 16-bit data bus of an 80286. This bus reduction significantly reduced the cost of the microprocessor and can result in the cost of accelerator cards using an 80386SX being several hundred dollars less than similar cards that use an 80386.

The use of accelerator cards should not be confused with two other methods that can be used to accelerate the processing capacity of a personal computer—changing a speed-related component such as the crystal or microprocessor and adding a coprocessor card to operate in tandem with the microprocessor installed in the personal computer. Replacing speed-related components is a relatively inexpensive process that can boost the performance of certain computers. As an example, the 6-MHz crystal on the original PC AT was replaced by many users with an 8-MHz crystal, increasing its processing performance by one-third for an investment of a few dollars. Unfortunately, only certain 6-MHz PC ATs can be upgraded in this manner, because IBM changed the BIOS in the original PC AT to prevent this upgrade, and then marketed an improved PC AT that included a crystal operating at 8 MHz!

The use of a coprocessor results in two microprocessors operating at the same time in one computer. The second microprocessor is a self-contained computer with its own bus, clock, and system memory mounted on a plug-in card. Because the coprocessor operates faster than the normal computer processor, a special program is employed to shift processing to the coprocessor, and the original processor is used only for input/output operations. This division of effort, and the greater processing power of the coprocessor, can double or triple the performance of one's personal computer.

The key to the increased processing capability obtained through the use of accelerator cards lies in their operating rate and data-bus width. The 8086, 80186, 80286, and 80386SX microprocessors each use a 16-bit data bus instead of the 8-bit data bus of the Intel 8088 that is standard in the PC and PC XT. The 80386 uses a 32-bit data bus that is twice as wide as the data path used by the 80286 in the PC AT and PC XT 286. This means that an 80386 can move twice as much data in one instruction as the 80286, and four times as much data as an 8088 I/O operation. The 8088 used in the PC and PC XT operates at 4.77 MHz; the other microprocessors operate at clock speeds from 8 MHz to 20 MHz. Taken together, the increased clock rate and extended data-bus width enable accelerator boards to increase the operating rate of a PC by two to eight times when performing compute-bound operations such as recalculating a large spreadsheet or solving an extensive mathematical formula. See Processor Performance in Chapter 4 for additional information concerning the relationship between the operation of the crystal, microprocessor, coprocessor, and memory.

## Cache Memory

One addition to accelerator boards offered by many vendors is cache memory. *Cache memory* is essentially a temporary buffer area that allows data transfers between the processor and the cache to take place at maximum speed. In the microcomputer world, a cache is most often used as an interface between the processor and disk storage devices, which are relatively slow. It works on the principle that when the CPU requests one particular sector from disk, the next request is likely to be for a sector that is logically adjacent (or at least close) to the one previously requested. Thus, by filling the cache memory, the CPU will be able to access of number of data sectors without further physical (slow) disk accesses. Similarly, when writing data, the CPU writes first to the cache, and only when the cache is full does the I/O processor transfer data to the electromechanical devices.

An alternative to cache memory is obtained by the inclusion of a full complement of RAM on the accelerator board. This RAM enables the 16-bit or 32-bit microprocessor on the adapter card to access memory via a 16-bit or 32-bit data bus and replaces the use of other memory previously installed on the system board and on other adapter cards. Although other memory adapter cards can be removed, system board memory cannot because a PC cannot be initialized without memory on the system board.

Some accelerator cards include additional RAM for the copying of BIOS and Cassette BASIC into the card's on-board memory, permitting true 16-bit or 32-bit access for all operations. Note that accelerator cards are usually designed to operate in a particular type of host environment. Thus, an accelerator designed for the PC or PC XT probably will not operate correctly in a PC AT. In addition, an 80386-based accelerator designed for use in a PC XT may not run software correctly in a PC AT, unless there is an option on the card that enables it to duplicate the environment of a PC AT.

## Other Features to Consider

In addition to conventional and cache memory, some accelerator boards include many of the hardware elements normally found on multifunction boards—serial ports, parallel ports, and a clock/calendar. Some vendors include sockets for the addition of chips to provide the previously mentioned hardware, and other vendors include the additional hardware as a standard feature.

## Installation

Accelerator boards include a flat ribbon cable with a connector at the end of the cable. After you have installed the board in a system expansion slot, you have to remove the existing microprocessor from the system board. You then plug the connector on the cable attached to the accelerator board into the socket vacated by the removal of the original microprocessor.

## Representative Hardware

Two representative accelerator cards are the Intel Inboard 386/AT and the Quadram Quad386 XT.

### Intel Inboard 386/AT

Intel's Inboard 386/AT is an adapter card that includes the company's 80386 microprocessor designed for an operating rate twice that of the 80286 chip that it replaces in the PC AT.

In addition to containing an 80386, the Inboard 386/AT can be configured with up to 3M bytes of memory, of which 2M bytes are obtained by the addition of an optional piggyback memory board. A socket is included on the board for the installation of an optional 10-MHz 80287 mathematical coprocessor, which can significantly increase the speed of numeric calculations.

### Quadram Quad386 XT

The Quad386 XT can be considered more than a simple accelerator board due to its variety of standard and optional features. Designed specifically for upgrading PC XTs, this board features a 16-MHz 80386 processor, 1M byte of true 32-bit memory, and the support for either the 80287 or 80387 math coprocessor or a Weitek math coprocessor chipset.

One of the more interesting features of the Quad386 XT is an optional daughter card. The daughter card can be populated with 2M bytes of RAM, increasing the total Quad386 XT storage to 3M bytes. Figure 3.15 illustrates the Quad386 XT with its optional daughter board. Like other accelerator cards, the cable and pin connector must be fastened to the socket obtained from the removal of the microprocessor on the personal computer's system board it is designed to operate with. In the case of the Quad386 XT, the 8088 microprocessor on the system board of the PC XT must be removed so the adapter can be cabled to the system board.

In Figure 3.15 you'll note the absence of switches and jumpers. This omission is intentional, because the adapter's configuration is set by answers to a software prompt. This switchless installation process, because it's so easy, is being incorporated into the adapter cards manufactured by several vendors, and can be expected to gain in popularity.

Table 3.4 lists key selection features to consider when you acquire an accelerator card. During the selection process the features of each product

**Figure 3.15** Quad386 XT—Shown with its optional daughter board the Quadram Quad386 XT is designed to provide an 80386 level of performance for IBM PC XT and compatible computers. *Photograph courtesy of Quadram Corporation.*

under consideration should be compared to your specific requirements. Then, if you don't need a particular feature, its inclusion on one vendor's product and omission on another vendor's product should be considered neutral during the evaluation process. As an example, consider two accelerator cards, one that includes a serial port and the second with no serial ports. If you don't need another serial port, its inclusion on one vendor's product and omission from another product is of no importance and should not affect your choice.

## Fixed Disks

Fixed disk technology predates the personal computer by several decades. In 1953, legend has it that IBM's code name for the project to develop a fixed or nonremovable disk (designated 3030) was Winchester (after the

**Table 3.4** Accelerator Card Selection Features

| FEATURE | DETAILS |
|---|---|
| Processor Used | |
| Clock Rate | |
| System Compatibility—PC, XT, AT, XT 286 | |
| On-Board Memory | |
| Cache Memory | Minimum Memory<br>Maximum Memory |
| Options | Serial Port(s)<br>Parallel Port(s)<br>Clock/Calendar |
| Installation Configuration | By Switches<br>By Software |

.303 rifle); that name became synonymous with the terms fixed disk and hard disk.

In 1980 when the first 5¼-inch Winchester disk drive was shipped, its capacity was limited to 5M bytes. Today, drives of the same or smaller physical size can store hundreds of megabytes of data, and more recently introduced 3½-inch drives are already approaching the 200M-byte barrier.

## Operation

The fixed disk operates in a very similar way to a diskette drive. Inside a hermetically sealed housing is a read/write head and one or more platters. Figure 3.16 illustrates the inside of a Seagate Technology ST212 fixed disk, consisting of one platter and a read/write head. The read/write head is an electromagnet capable of detecting and producing a switchable magnetic field to read and write bit streams. The read/write heads are positioned by an arm known as an *actuator* from track to track, without the heads actually touching the disk surface as they float on an air cushion several millionths of an inch in height. Data is stored on each track in a group of 512 bytes known as a *sector*. Many disks are formatted for 17 sectors per track, so that each track stores 8.5K bytes.

To read information previously stored on disk or to write information requires the read/write heads located at the ends of the moving head arms

**Figure 3.16** Interior of a Fixed Disk—The Seagate Technology ST212, shown with its cover removed, is a half-height Winchester disk drive that consists of a single platter rated at 13M bytes of storage (unformatted). *Photograph courtesy of Seagate Technology.*

to be positioned to a specific location above a platter. This positioning is required to place the read/write head over a specific track.

To position the read/write heads, a head actuator either pushes or pulls the read/write head based on control information. The control information originates as a read or write program request that DOS translates to a specific disk location access request based on the structure of the file allocation table (FAT) of the disk. Once DOS determines where the data will be recorded to or read from, it sends a movement request through the disk controller to position the read/write heads at the location on the disk where data is to be recorded or read. The controller is cabled to a printed circuit or logic board that is usually found beneath the mechanical components of the disk. This board translates the disk controller's commands initiated by DOS into voltage fluctuations that cause the head actuator to push or pull the read/write heads across the surface of the platter. By aligning magnetic particles on the platter's surface, data is written to disk, whereas data is read from disk by the read head detecting the state of particles previously aligned.

Tracks on a fixed disk are numbered from 0 near the circumference in ascending order toward the center of the platter, the actual number of tracks depending on the storage capacity of the disk. Figure 3.17(A) illustrates a schematic diagram of the track layout on a fixed disk.

To increase the capacity of a fixed disk, data bits can be recorded closer together, additional platters of data storage can be added to the device, or a combination of both techniques can be employed. When mul-

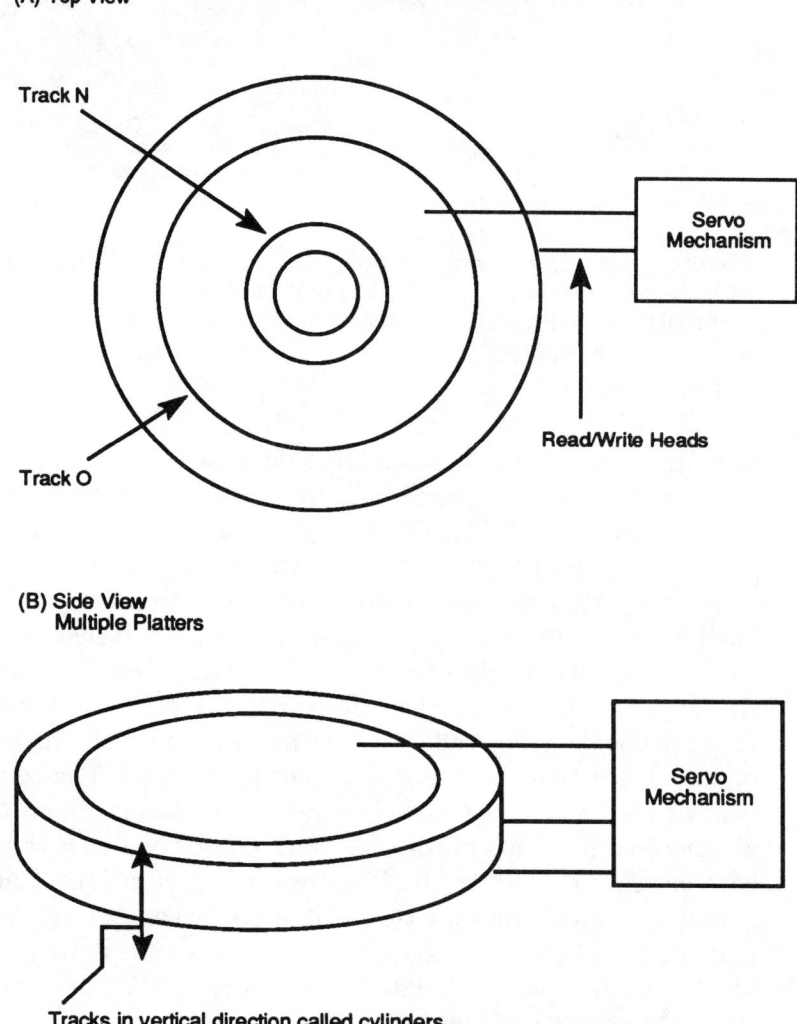

**Figure 3.17** Fixed Disk Track Layout and Platter Operation—By placing more tracks on a platter and/or more platters into a disk, storage capacity is increased.

tiple platters are used in a fixed disk, multiple read/write heads are used to read and record data onto the corresponding track of each surface at the same time. The assembly of vertically corresponding tracks of each surface is known as a *cylinder,* illustrated in Figure 3.17(B).

During a read or write operation, the head is first moved to the appropriate track. The time required to position the head is known as the disk's *seek time* and varies depending on the number of tracks across which the head must be moved to reach the desired track. For a single track movement, a seek time of a few milliseconds may be required, whereas a movement from the outermost to the innermost track end of the disk could require 100 milliseconds or more. The average time to position the read/write head across one-third of the disk to a random sector is known as the *average access time,* and is usually published by disk manufacturers. Other times published by some manufacturers include track-to-track access and random reads based upon defined seek widths.

Once the read/write head is positioned on the appropriate track another delay occurs until data can be read from or written onto the disk. This time is known as the *rotation time* and is the delay until the platter rotates to position the first of the sectors to be accessed under the read/write head. For a disk spinning at 3600 rpm the average rotation time is 8 milliseconds.

## Interleave Factor

The fixed disk normally rotates at 3600 rpm (or some rate between 2400 and 3600 rpm). As the disk rotates, the first sector to be read or recorded onto passes under the head and the data transfer begins. Because the gap between sectors is small, the next sector will arrive very quickly—too quickly in fact for most disk controllers, because they usually require some time to get ready for the transfer to or from the next sector. If the controller is not ready when the second sector passes under the head, the controller must wait for an entire revolution of the disk for the appropriate sector to be correctly positioned.

To eliminate this waste of time, most disks are formatted to separate logically consecutive sectors by one or more physical sectors. This separation is called *interleaving,* and provides the controller with additional time to read or record data onto consecutive sectors without requiring additional disk rotations.

Figure 3.18 shows two single platter disks, one formatted without sector interleaving and the second formatted with an interleave factor of three—meaning that logically consecutive sectors are separated by two physical sectors. Normally, the interleave factor can be considered as an important parameter in comparing the performance of two fixed disk drives.

As an example of the differences between interleave factors, consider two disks, one with an interleave factor of two, and another with an interleave factor of four. To retrieve all of the data on a track requires two disk revolutions when the interleave factor is two, but four disk revolutions if the interleave factor is four. Thus, a fixed disk with a low interleave factor is normally more efficient in storing and retrieving data than a disk with a higher interleave factor.

## Drive Motors

A fixed disk drive may use either a stepper-motor or a voice-coil motor to position the read/write heads. A stepper motor moves the heads a fixed

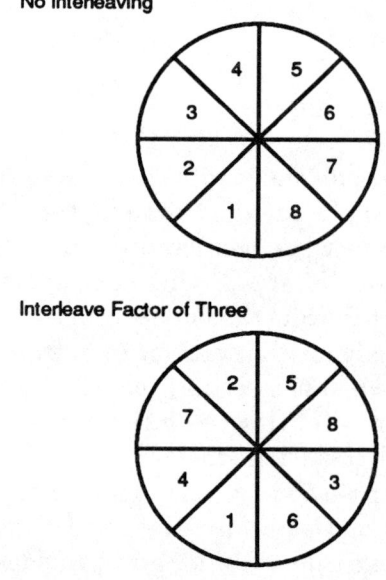

**Figure 3.18** Sector Interleaving—Each logical sector is separated by two physical sectors, resulting in the logical separators spaced three physical sectors apart.

distance and relies on the mechanical accuracy of the motor to position the heads to the correct location. Because the motor cannot adjust for media expansion or contraction, there are constraints on how closely tracks of information may be spaced in order to be recorded and retrieved correctly. These constraints limit the storage capacity of a stepper motor system.

In a fixed disk using a voice coil, the motor controls the read/write head movement electronically, based upon reference data stored on the disk surface. The capability to alter the reference data enables a greater number of tracks to be formatted onto a disk. In addition, many voice-coil drives are so designed that when primary power is lost or turned off, the remaining power stored in the power supply's capacitors is applied to the voice coil in such a way as to retract the heads quickly to a parking position outside the data-storage area of the platter.

Stepper-motor drives are normally two to three times slower than voice-coil drives. In addition, stepper-motor drives usually have less storage capacity than voice-coil drives; however, they are also less expensive. If you do not require a large capacity drive with fast access time, such as might be necessary for a personal computer functioning as a local area network server, a stepper-motor drive will normally suffice. If large capacity storage and quick access are of primary importance, consider purchasing the voice-coil motor drive.

## Cluster

Although a cluster is a logical rather than a physical parameter and is controlled by software, the concept of a cluster is important to understanding the efficiency of fixed disk operations. The cluster is the smallest addressable unit of storage space used by DOS. This unit of storage corresponds to an entry in the DOS file allocation table (FAT), which can be considered as a map of available space on a storage medium.

Under DOS 2.X, FAT entries are 12 bits in length, permitting 4096 ($2^{12}$) unique numbers. If each number denoted a 512-byte sector, the maximum capacity of the disk would be 4096 * 512 = 2,097,152 bytes. To increase the available storage, DOS 2.X assigns each FAT entry to a cluster of 8 logically consecutive sectors. There's a trade off, of course. The total storage on the disk is now 4096 * 4096 = 16,777,216 bytes, but the smallest amount of storage that you can allocate to a file is 4096 bytes. Thus, saving a file that contains only one character results in wasting 4095 bytes of disk storage. You can, of course, read or write a single 512-byte sector, because each sector is physically identified on the disk, and the operating system can translate a logical sector number within a file to a physical track and sector number that the disk controller hardware can use.

Under DOS 3.X, the FAT was changed so each entry could be either 12 or 16 bits in length. When 16-bit entries are used, the number of clusters supported increases to 65,535, permitting a cluster size of 4 sectors or 2048 bytes to be used. Thus, fixed disks formatted under DOS 3.X store data more efficiently than fixed disks formatted under DOS 2.X.

## Landing Zone

To prevent data from being damaged due to vibrations or a bump to the computer system, many manufacturers incorporate what is known as a *landing zone* into their drive. The landing zone is a fixed location that does not contain data, onto which the read/write heads are positioned whenever power to the system turns off or is lost. Although the use of a landing zone alleviates potential damage to data due to vibrations or small bumps, if you want to move a PC, first use the IBM Diagnostic Diskette and select the "Preparing to Move" option. This option parks the heads in a fixed position and is a much better protection mechanism than a reliance upon the automatic landing zone. Some fixed disks, such as the IBM 30M byte used with the AT model 239, have retractable heads that move to a safe landing zone whenever power is turned off, obviating the necessity of using the Diagnostic Diskette "Preparing to Move" option.

## Increased Storage Capacity

Essentially, there are three ways to increase the capacity of a fixed disk drive. First, the number of platters and read/write heads can be increased. A second method involves increasing the number of tracks per inch, which requires improvements in both magnetic media and servo mechanism technology. A third method used to increase disk capacity is to increase the data-bit density recorded on a track.

From a cost effective perspective, increasing the data-bit density recorded on a track is the most favored method of increasing disk capacity. Although several methods to accomplish this have been introduced, the Run Length Limited (RLL) 2,7 encoding scheme is being adopted by many manufacturers. Developed originally by IBM for use in mainframe disk technology, this technique has been used to boost the storage capacity of PC fixed disks by 50 percent. The term 2,7 in the RLL code signifies that a minimum of two and a maximum of seven logical 0's are allowed between any two consecutive 1's based upon the definition of the code. Although RLL 2,7 requires more encoding bits to represent data than the modified frequency modulation (MFM) technique normally used for recording data onto fixed and floppy disks, each flux reversal under RLL 2,7 represents a greater number of bits. Because flux reversals are used to encode data on the disk, this enables RLL 2,7 to achieve a 50 percent increase in bit density.

Since the introduction of RLL 2,7 for use with personal computer fixed disk drives, several derivatives of this coding technique have been announced. One of the more prominent derivatives is the Enhanced Run Length Limited (ERLL) coding technique, which incorporates a compression algorithm to boost data-encoding densities beyond those of RLL.

Table 3.5 indicates how different encoding methods affect the storage capacity of a fixed disk. The key to RLL and ERLL is their ability to pack more sectors onto each track than the original MFM encoding technique can do. The table provides a data-storage comparison for a 4-head, 305-track fixed disk that is compatible with both RLL and ERLL controllers. The number of sectors per track was selected for illustrative purposes. In actuality, MFM controllers typically support 17 or 18 sectors per track, whereas RLL and ERLL controllers support 25 to 27 and 33 to 35 sectors per track, respectively.

The following list shows nine fixed disk features that you should consider when selecting hardware in this category:

Disk controller compatibility
Internal or external unit

**Table 3.5** Fixed Disk Storage Comparison

| RECORDING METHOD | HEADS | TRACKS | SECTORS PER TRACK | BYTES PER SECTOR | STORAGE (M BYTES) |
|---|---|---|---|---|---|
| MFM | 4 | 305 | 18 | 512 | 11.2 |
| RLL | 4 | 305 | 26 | 512 | 16.2 |
| ERLL | 4 | 305 | 34 | 512 | 21.2 |

Formatted capacity in M bytes
Average access time in milliseconds
Half or full height
Power consumption
Dedicated landing zone
Interleave factor
Motor control

Although most fixed disks are sold bundled with a controller, mail-order discount wholesalers may sell fixed disk drives without a controller. In such cases, it is advisable to verify that a commonly available controller can be used with the fixed disk.

The primary advantage of an external fixed disk over an internal device is the inclusion of a built-in power supply in the cabinet housing the external disk. Because the external disk is powered separately from the computer, you avoid the replacement of the computer power supply that may be necessary when you install some internal fixed disks. Unfortunately, the external fixed disk requires additional desk space, which is sometimes at a premium.

When you're looking at fixed drive data sheets or advertisements, make sure that they specify the formatted capacity of the drive. If you see a drive specified as "12M bytes unformatted," you have to remember that the track and sector identifiers and intersector gaps account for many bytes each, so that the formatted capacity of the drive (that is, the space available for your data) will probably be no more than 10M bytes. Depending upon devices previously installed in the computer's device housing areas, you may be able to install full- or half-height disk drives without removing an existing device.

Although power consumption is normally not an important consideration for external devices, it is very important for an internal fixed disk. Some internal fixed disks have a very low power requirement and may be operable in an IBM PC without requiring the replacement of the computer's 63.5-watt power supply. Other internal disks draw a high amperage when they are turned on and cannot be used in an IBM PC unless the computer's power supply is replaced.

To obtain RLL capability requires a controller capable of supporting the RLL recording technology. Unfortunately, RLL controllers do not work with all fixed disks, and you must carefully consider the compatibility of the controller with your disk before you install the controller, because a large data loss can result if the controller and disk are incompatible.

## Fixed Disk Card

In late 1985 Plus Development Corporation introduced a low-powered 10M-byte hard disk combined with controller circuitry mounted on an expansion card. Since then, approximately twenty vendors have introduced fixed disk cards of varying capacity and their popularity has increased. This is due to several key factors. First, these disk cards can be installed in a system expansion slot without requiring the removal of a diskette drive or another device previously installed in a device housing area as is required when a conventional fixed disk is installed. Second, the low power requirements of many disk cards enables them to be installed in an IBM PC without requiring the 63.5-watt power supply to be replaced.

Figure 3.19 illustrates the Rodime R-Card 35. Note the edge connector on the card, which is inserted into the system expansion slot of a PC similar to the installation of any type of adapter card. In addition to having storage capacity of 35M bytes this plug-in fixed disk has an average seek time of 28 milliseconds, which is approximately one-third that of the full height fixed disk marketed by IBM for use in the PC XT. Because of

**Figure 3.19** Rodime R-Card 35—The Rodime R-Card plugs into a single PC system expansion slot. *Photograph courtesy of Rodime Inc.*

its fast seek time, the Rodime disk card is well suited for use in a PC or PC XT that is to be used as a server on a local area network.

## Features to Consider

The following list shows some of the features you may wish to examine when comparing fixed disk cards:

Formatted capacity in M bytes
Average access time in milliseconds
Power consumption in watts
Power connection—bus or direct connect to power supply
Number of expansion slots required
8- or 16-bit slot support
Automatic head park when powered off
Automatic configuration to highest drive
Maximum partition size
Preformatted
Activity indicator
Works with 2nd fixed disk card

Although many of the features are self-explanatory, several require some elaboration.

## The Y Cable

Some fixed disk cards are powered directly from the bus, and others require a direct connection to the power supply of the personal computer. Because the power supply cables may already be in use, most vendors include a "Y" cable. To use this cable you first disconnect an existing power cable from a diskette drive or other device. Then you plug the long end of the "Y" cable into the power connector and connect the two ends at the top of the "Y" cable to the fixed disk card and the device to which the power supply was previously connected.

## Expansion Slot Usage

All fixed disk cards have a single edge connector that plugs into one expansion slot. The phrase "number of expansion slots required" refers to the fact that the card may be thick enough to block off another expansion slot and thus prevent you from using that slot. Some fixed disk cards are narrow and occupy only the area normally reserved for one adapter card. Other fixed disk cards may be thick enough to occupy the space of 1½ adapter cards, or even of two adapter cards. When the disk card occupies 1½ slots, the extra thickness of the drive unit may be either on the left of the card (solder side) or on the right of the card (component side). Because the drive unit is at the end of the card remote from the connector, you can sometimes insert a short card in the adjacent expansion slot that is partially blocked by the drive. However, unless you plan in advance, you may find that you have to shift all your existing cards around, and you may even find that one of them is unusable. (See Figure 3.20.)

Consider an IBM PC XT in which you have already installed full-size cards in slots 1 through 5 and short cards in slots 7 and 8. If you want to install a fixed disk card in this machine, you must select one that occupies only one slot width, so that you can install it in slot 6. If you are willing to sacrifice one of your other adapters, you could install a fixed disk card that occupies 1½ slots, but only if the extra width is on the left (partially blocks slot 5). If the extra width is on the right, you could not put the card in slot 6, because the drive unit would bump against the drive

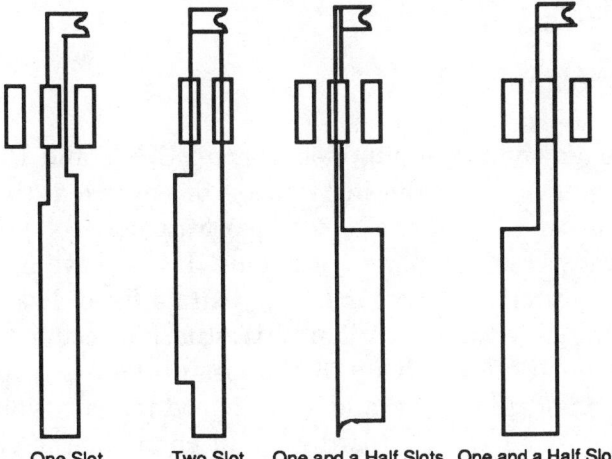

One Slot    Two Slot    One and a Half Slots    One and a Half Slots

**Figure 3.20**  Fixed Disk Card Expansion Slot Requirements—The number of expansion slots required by a fixed disk card actually refers to the width of the card and whether the width occupies space that could be used by other expansion cards.

already installed in the left device housing area. You could put that card in slot 5, but you'd still lose the use of slot 6.

Most fixed disk cards are preformatted by the vendor, relieving you of the necessity of performing a time-consuming formatting operation. Because the fixed disk card is installed inside the case, there is no visual indicator to denote when the disk is in use. To provide you with an activity indicator similar in scope to the red LED on most conventional fixed disks, many vendors include an optional visual indicator. This option displays a special character (such as a plus sign) in the upper right corner of the screen whenever the fixed disk is reading or writing.

## 8- or 16-Bit Slot Support

Some fixed disk cards are manufactured with an 8-bit expansion slot connector and only provide a satisfactory level of performance when they are used in an IBM PC or PC XT. Other fixed disk cards are manufactured with a 16-bit expansion slot connector, enabling those devices to be effectively used in a 16-bit expansion slot contained in a PC AT. Data can then be written to and read from the fixed disk card in 16-bit increments.

## Power Supply

Although the power supplies of the PC XT and PC AT are usually more than sufficient for the installation of any fixed disk card in combination with other adapter cards, the 63.5-watt power supply of the IBM PC can normally result in power problems. If you have a full complement of expansion products in your PC and add a fixed disk card, the power supply will probably overload. When this situation occurs, the power supply simply turns itself off, resulting in the loss of data. If you have a memory card, diskette adapter card, and a low-speed modem, you will normally be able to operate a fixed disk card without changing the power supply of an IBM PC. Due to the high power consumption of internal 1200 bps and 2400 bps modems, a fixed disk card installed in a system with one of those devices will result in a power requirement beyond the capacity of the PC's power supply.

## Tape Backup Units

The BACKUP and RESTORE commands included in DOS can be considered two of the most formidable obstacles to fixed disk backup on a regular basis. To understand the problems associated with using diskettes to back up data from a fixed disk, let us assume you have a 20M-byte fixed disk installed in your personal computer. Assuming that one or more standard 360K-byte diskette drives is installed in the computer, a total of 56 diskettes would be required to completely back up 20M bytes of data. In comparison, a single tape or at most a few tapes can normally store the contents of a fixed disk.

Until the introduction of DOS 3.3, several deficiencies in the BACKUP command made life rather frustrating to users who lacked a tape backup unit. One example of potential frustration occurs during a BACKUP procedure when you don't have enough previously formatted diskettes to hold the backed-up data. When this situation occurs, you must either use another PC to format additional diskettes or terminate the BACKUP procedure in order to format the additional diskettes required. Unfortunately, invoking BACKUP a second time under most versions of DOS requires you to restart the process from the beginning. Under DOS 3.3 and later versions of the operating system, unformatted diskettes will be formatted by the BACKUP command. While DOS 3.3 and later versions of the operating system eliminate the formatting problem, they do not reduce the large number of diskettes required to back up fixed disks with storage capacities of 20M bytes or more. Thus, the storage capacity of the fixed disk presents both an obstacle to good backup habits and a strong incentive to obtain a tape backup system.

## Types of Systems

Most tape backup units use industry standard quarter-inch tapes that are similar in appearance to audio cassettes. Other tape backup units are constructed to use 5¼-inch cartridges or ½-inch cartridge tapes. Figure 3.21 illustrates the Mountain Computer 5¼-inch disk cartridge system installed in the lower portion of the device housing area of an IBM PC AT. Each 5¼-inch disk cartridge has the capacity to store 20M bytes of data, making the backup process of a fixed disk faster as well as requiring less storage space in comparison to the use of diskettes.

**Figure 3.21** Mountain Computer Micro Bernoulli—The Mountain Computer Micro Bernoulli internal tape backup unit is capable of storing 20M bytes of data on a removable disk cartridge. *Photograph courtesy of Mountain Computer.*

Figure 3.22 illustrates an external tape backup unit combined with a fixed disk installed in one device housing area. The system illustrated in Figure 3.22 is designed to be placed on top of the computer's system unit, next to the monitor, thereby requiring no additional desk space.

## Method of Operation

In addition to internal and external systems, tape backup units can be classified according to their method of operation and interface. The two prevalent methods of operation are "start/stop" and "streamer." In a start/stop method of operation the tape moves only one record at a time during transfers from a fixed disk. Although a start/stop tape backup unit is preferable for applications such as selective backup due to its search and record capability, the extra precision for its tape movement makes it the more expensive backup device.

**Figure 3.22** Mountain Computer Series 7000 Combo System—The Mountain Computer Series 7000 Combo System consists of a fixed disk and tape backup unit in one external housing. Designed to be placed on top of the system unit of a PC XT or AT next to the monitor, the unit requires no additional desk space. *Photograph courtesy of Mountain Computer.*

The streamer type of tape backup unit is, as its name implies, designed for continuous recording. Streamer backup units are typically used to record the entire contents of a disk drive in a single session.

Typically, streamer tape backup units employ a microprocessor to control their servo mechanism. Although they have faster throughput and cost less than start/stop systems, they cannot perform selective retrievals.

## Interface Considerations

The interface required to operate a tape backup unit varies considerably among vendor products. Many tape backup units require a separate controller, and require a system expansion slot to be available for its installation. Some tape backup units can be cabled to the rear connector of the diskette controller, permitting one external tape backup unit to serve several personal computers. Although tape backup units connected to a diskette controller have a lower data transfer rate than obtainable through the use of a separate controller, the portability afforded by the use of this interface and its ability to enable one unit to serve many computers usually outweighs the few extra minutes a full backup procedure may require.

## Controller Card Considerations

When a separate controller card is required to operate a tape backup unit, you should check both its ability to change configuration settings and the expansion slots where it can be used. Most, but not all, controller cards have DIP switches or jumpers similar to those illustrated on the AST Research SixPak Plus by which the assignment of the use of a specific direct memory access (DMA) channel, interrupt number, and input/output (I/O) port starting address can be set. Concerning system expansion slot use, controller cards are manufactured with 8-bit and 16-bit bus connectors, the former designed for use with PC and PC XT systems and the latter designed for use with PC AT systems. When using an 8-bit bus connector controller card, you should also determine whether the card is full-length or half-length. The full-length type of card cannot be used in several expansion slots in a PC or PC XT where equipment you previously installed in the left device housing area precludes the installation of a full-length card.

Concerning configuration change capability, most controller cards are manufactured to work in PCs that may house other types of devices that could interfere with controller operation. To alleviate potential interference from other adapter cards, ensure that the tape backup controller you are considering permits you to change the DMA channel assignment, interrupt number used by the card to request microprocessor processing, and the I/O port starting address.

The DMA is a specialized chip on the system board that enables data to flow from memory to a specific device, such as a fixed disk or tape backup unit, without having to first pass through the microprocessor. PC and PC XT computers have four DMA channels through which data can flow, whereas ATs have eight DMA channels.

DMA channels on PCs and PC XTs are numbered 0-3, whereas DMA channels on the PC AT are numbered 0-7. Normally, channel 0 is used for memory refreshing, leaving channels 1-3 or 1-7 available for use to send data to and receive data from devices that support high-speed data transfer.

A fixed disk normally uses DMA channel 3, requiring you to set the jumper or DIP switch on the tape backup controller card that controls DMA channel assignments to select channel 1 or 2. If you are using a PC AT, select channel 4, 5, 6, or 7. If you have other high-speed data transfer devices installed in your computer, check their controller card setting to prevent a DMA conflict. If a DMA conflict should occur, usually your computer will fail to boot. You can alleviate the DMA conflict by resetting the DIP switch or jumper plugs to select a different DMA channel for your tape backup unit controller card.

The interrupt number selected on the controller card assigns the interrupt by which the card requests microprocessor processing cycles. Because different hardware devices use different interrupts, take care in selecting the appropriate interrupt number for the controller to use. If two devices use the same interrupt number, both devices will not operate even though your computer will boot correctly. Table 3.6 contains a list of commonly used interrupts you will probably want to avoid when configuring your controller card. If you do not have a COM2 port installed or you previously disabled a COM2 port on a multifunction board, use interrupt 3 to configure your controller card.

Because I/O ports provide the actual path by which peripherals communicate with the microprocessor, take care also to eliminate I/O port conflicts. As noted in Chapter 1, many port addresses are available for use by nonstandard devices. Although you can use any port address not used by equipment previously installed in your computer, you should first check the manual accompanying the controller card to determine its default set-

**Table 3.6** Commonly Used Interrupts

| INTERRUPT NUMBER | EQUIPMENT USING INTERRUPT |
|---|---|
| 2 | PC Network Adapter, EGA adapter |
| 3 | Second serial port (COM2) |
| 4 | First serial port (COM1) |
| 5 | Fixed disk drive |
| 6 | Diskette drive |
| 7 | Printer |

ting. Most tape backup controller cards are assigned a default I/O starting address that avoids a conflict with any standard IBM equipment, usually eliminating the necessity of reconfiguring this option. A port addressing conflict can usually be recognized by this symptom: Your system boots correctly but freezes each time you attempt to use the tape backup unit or the other device that uses the same I/O ports assigned to the tape backup controller. If this situation occurs, reconfigure the starting port I/O address on the controller card by the use of a jumper shorting plug or DIP switch to select a different port I/O starting address.

## Software

The software provided by most tape backup unit manufacturers typically permits three types of backup—file by file, image, and by entire subdirectory. The file-by-file backup method can be used with either a start/stop or streamer unit. If a start/stop unit is used, the interrecord gaps waste tape. Normally, a file-by-file backup is used to selectively safeguard small amounts of data.

In an image backup, all data on a disk is recorded to tape. Many streamer units can operate at 90 inches per second, resulting in the backup of a full 20M-byte disk in approximately 5 minutes.

## Representative Software

One of the more popular programs for tape backup units is Mountain Computer's FileSafe Tape Software. This menu-driven program permits personal computer users to perform a backup or restore operation by the use of a few keystrokes.

Figure 3.23 illustrates the FileSafe command menu that is displayed when you enter the command TAPE once the vendor's software is loaded onto your system. Note that in addition to performing a backup or restore, you can request a directory of FileSafe tape files. Although the FileSafe menu system is easy to use, its features can be accessed directly from the DOS command level by entering a command name consisting of the word TAPE, followed by the underline character and a mnemonic indicator for the command option you want. Thus, you can enter TAPE_BK from DOS to initiate the Backup DOS Partition option, equivalent to its se-

```
FileSafe Tape Backup System for MS-DOS
MS-DOS Version-3.XX (M.XX) -DMA Channel 2
Copyright (C) 1985, Mountain Computer, Inc.

            ┌─────────────────────────────┐
            │     Tape Command Menu       │
            └─────────────────────────────┘

B - Backup DOS Partition to FileSafe Tape
R - Restore DOS Partition from FileSafe Tape
F - Restore Individual Files to DOS Partition from FileSafe Tape
D - Directory of FileSafe Tape Files

E - Exit to DOS

Enter Selection:
```

**Figure 3.23** FileSafe Tape Software Command Menu—FileSafe software enables you to perform most tape backup functions with a minimum of keystrokes.

```
            ┌─────────────────────────────┐
            │     Tape Backup Options     │
            └─────────────────────────────┘

A - Append this DOS Partition at end of tape
C - Continue backup at present tape position without rewinding
H - Halt tape at end of this Partition
L - Specify search Label for this Partition
S - Subdirectory backup
B - Bypass concurrent Direct Memory Access
M - Limit buffer memory to below 256K
V - Post backup byte-for-byte verify of entire tape image

Toggle desired option (Press ENTER to proceed, Q to quit) :
```

**Figure 3.24** FileSafe Backup Option Menu—Using the FileSafe Backup Option Menu you can assign a partition to the file you are backing up.

lection from the command menu, whereas a similar two-part command can be used to directly access the other menu options.

As an example of the backup process, assume the Backup option was selected from the FileSafe command menu. Its selection results in the display of a Backup Option Menu as illustrated in Figure 3.24.

Multiple selections can be made from the Backup option menu, which governs such functions as the assignment of a label to the partition on the tape (option L), comparing the data backed up to tape with the data on the fixed disk (option V), as well as determining where the backup image should be placed on the tape (options A and C) and other selections.

Once you complete your selection from the Tape Backup Options menu, you can begin the backup. After you press the Enter key, the prompt illustrated in Figure 3.25 is displayed. FileSafe uses drive C as the default drive to backup; however, users can enter another disk drive letter if appropriate.

Once you have entered the default drive or a specific drive letter, FileSafe asks you to enter a descriptive title of up to 59 characters that is used for identifying the tape. The description should not be confused with what is known as the *partition label*, which can be used to store a description of the partition backed up to tape, permitting multiple partitions to be recorded and retrieved from one tape. FileSafe software enables you to use the parameters $D and/or $T to place the current date/time on the label.

After the backup begins, the message Searching directories. . . is displayed for a short period of time. This message is then replaced by a message that updates the progress of the backup, indicating the time to completion of the backup operation, as well as two inverse video bars that visually indicate the amount of data on the disk to be backed up and how much data has been backed up. If you selected the verification operation, FileSafe software will automatically rewind the tape and verify the recorded data by comparing the contents of the disk data to the data previously recorded to tape. After the verification process is completed, FileSafe displays a screen of statistics concerning the backup operation similar to that illustrated in Figure 3.26. At this point, you can press any key to return to the main menu and then select E to exit the program and return to DOS.

```
┌─────────────────────────────────┐
│    Backup DOS Partition to Tape │
└─────────────────────────────────┘
```

Enter backup drive (press ENTER for C) :

**Figure 3.25** Selecting the Drive to Back Up—FileSafe uses drive C as the default drive for disk backup; however, you can enter any appropriate drive designator.

```
DOS Partition backup successfully completed.

Performance statistics:

Total Data Backed up    >>>        2803712 bytes
Elapsed Time            >>>           1:58 minutes: seconds
Averaged Data Rate      >>>        1425600 bytes/minute

Reverify time           >>>           1:49

(press any key to return to main menu)
```

**Figure 3.26** Backup Operation Statistics—FileSafe software provides the user with statistics concerning the backup operation.

**Table 3.7** Tape Backup Unit Selection Features

| FEATURE | DETAILS |
|---|---|
| Type of Unit | Internal<br>External |
| Data Storage Capacity | M Bytes |
| Recording Mechanism | Start/stop<br>Streamer |
| Interface | Separate controller<br>Floppy disk controller |
| Controller Configuration Settings | None—Defaults used<br>DMA<br>Interrupt number<br>Port I/O address |
| Software | File by file<br>Image<br>By subdirectory |

In Table 3.7 you will find a list of tape backup unit selection features that you may wish to consider when acquiring tape backup unit hardware.

# Mouse

The pointing and selecting device first popularized by the Apple Macintosh has gained acceptance by IBM PC users. This acceptance is due to the development of a variety of programs ranging in scope from desktop publishing to drawing and drafting that are enhanced by the use of a mouse.

## Connection Types

Two types of mouse connections can be used with PC systems. The serial mouse, as its name implies, is connected to a serial port, which can be on the asynchronous communications adapter or on a multifunction card. The second type of mouse, a bus mouse, connects to a bus board inserted into a system expansion slot. Figure 3.27 illustrates a Logitech Bus Mouse and the bus board to which it is connected.

## Operation

Most mice incorporate a ball bearing in the mouse body, with a small portion of the ball protruding through a circular hole at the bottom of the housing. As you move the mouse on the desktop the ball inside the housing moves. This ball movement is converted into a series of movement signals transmitted through the mouse cable to the computer. The mouse is not included with PCs, so a device driver must be used to operate the device. This device driver activates software supplied by the mouse vendor, which moves a pointer on the screen to correspond with the movement of the mouse on the desktop.

## Optical Mouse

A second type of operation is obtained by using an optical mouse. In place of a ball, the optical mouse uses a set of LEDs and optical receivers in conjunction with a reflective pad that contains grid lines. As the mouse is moved over the pad, the LEDs focus light on the pad and the receivers measure the reflectivity of the light. Because the reflectivity changes as the mouse passes over a grid line, its position on the pad can be determined. The advantage of an optical mouse is its lack of moving parts. This can be especially advantageous in an industrial environment, where dirt can cause a ball based mouse to stick to its housing.

**Figure 3.27** Logitech Bus Mouse—The operation of the Logitech Bus Mouse requires the installation of an adapter card into a system expansion slot. *Photograph courtesy of Logitech.*

## Software Compatibility

Most mice are bundled with a diskette containing one or more utility programs and a mouse driver for installation in DOS. Some application programs are designed to work directly with the mouse driver; others include drivers that were developed to work with specific mice. On the other hand, some application programs (such as Lotus 1-2-3) were not designed to work with a mouse. For this reason, many mouse vendors include "shell" programs that make a nonmouse application program behave just like a program that was developed specifically for use with a mouse. Some of the bundled utilities are preconfigured to handle the mouse settings required by popular application programs.

## Display Adapters

Here we will first examine several display adapters that can be used with the IBM Monochrome Display. Then we will examine the features of several interesting display adapters that offer important features unavailable with equivalent IBM products, concluding with a list of display adapter features to consider before you obtain a display adapter for your system.

### Hercules Graphics Card

The Hercules Graphics Card is a high-resolution display adapter that adds a graphics resolution of 720 by 348 pixels to the IBM Monochrome Display. This card is designed to replace the IBM Monochrome Display and Parallel Printer Adapter card and is supplied with a diskette containing several programs to assist you in the operation of your PC and in graphics programming.

Physically, the Hercules Graphics Card is similar in appearance to the IBM Monochrome Display and Parallel Printer card. As illustrated in Figure 3.28, the Hercules Graphics Card contains a 9-pin connector at the top rear of the adapter for connection to the IBM Monochrome Display cable and a 25-pin connector for the attachment of a cable to a parallel printer. The parallel printer address is fixed as LPT1, which requires you to adjust the address of any other cards in your system that contain a parallel printer port previously set to that device address.

Through software the Hercules Graphics Card can be placed into one of three configurations—FULL, HALF, or DIAG. FULL is the normal operating configuration of the card and results in unrestricted access to the 64K bytes of memory contained on the card. The HALF configuration limits access to the first 32K bytes of memory on the card, enabling an IBM Color Graphics card to remain in your PC when the Hercules Graphic Card is installed. The DIAG configuration permits the IBM Diagnostic program to be run, converting the Hercules Graphics Card into an IBM

**Figure 3.28** Hercules Graphics Card—The Hercules Graphics Card permits graphic images to be displayed on the IBM or an equivalent monochrome display. *Photograph courtesy of Hercules Computer Technology.*

Monochrome Display emulation mode that limits access to 4K bytes of memory, which is the amount of memory on the IBM card. When a PC system containing a Hercules Graphics Card is powered on, the card enters the DIAG configuration automatically. Thereafter, you must load vendor supplied software to switch to the card's FULL or HALF configuration.

Three interesting programs supplied with the Hercules Graphics Card are SAVE, HPRINT, and HBASIC. The SAVE program automatically blanks the PC screen after five minutes of keyboard inactivity. Thereafter, pressing the Shift key restores the screen. The HPRINT program permits graphic images to be printed on an IBM Graphics printer. HBASIC is a graphics library of subroutines that permit BASICA, with all its graphics commands, to be run on the Hercules Graphics Card.

One of the problems associated with using HBASIC is its use of a character size of 9 by 14 pixels, whereas BASICA uses a character size of

8 by 8 pixels. Because of this, you must note the difference when converting screen positions from rows and columns to X,Y coordinates. Another change from BASICA is HBASIC's range of screen coordinates, which is from 0 to 719 horizontally and 0 to 347 vertically in HBASIC. BASICA uses 0 to 319 or 0 to 639 horizontally and 0 to 199 vertically; the horizontal range depends upon which color graphics mode you selected for BASICA. Note, too, that HBASIC does not support the COLOR, SCREEN 0, SCREEN 1, and WIDTH 40 statements in BASICA.

## STB Chauffeur HT

The STB Chauffeur HT can be considered a five-in-one display adapter, because it combines the technology of five video display adapters onto one adapter card. This card supports IBM Color Graphics, IBM Monochrome Display, Hercules Graphics Card, The Tseng Labs UltraPAK-S, and the STB Chauffeur. Figure 3.29 shows a photograph of the STB Chauffeur HT card denoting the major components and options on the board.

The switch box on the Chauffeur HT is a 10-position configuration switch. Switches 1 through 5 are used to indicate the type of monitor the adapter will be connected to. Switches 6 and 7 control the operation of the card's parallel port, whereas switches 9 and 10 can be used to control the operation of an optional serial port. Switch 8 controls the size of the display memory buffer.

By setting switches 6 and 7, the parallel port on the card can be assigned device address LPT1, LPT2, LPT3, or disabled. Similarly, switches 9 and 10 permit the optional serial port to be assigned device address COM1, COM2, COM3, or disabled.

The key advantage of the Chauffeur HT is its ability to support the monochrome display, standard color display, enhanced color display, and a high-resolution color display without requiring software drivers. When this adapter is configured for use with a monochrome display, colors are converted to 16 shades of green, and the IBM CGA 200-line graphics is expanded to a full screen format. In comparison, it should be noted that some adapter cards that produce graphics on a monochrome display map the 200-line graphics onto 200 scan lines, leaving a gap of 75 lines at the top and bottom of the display. Other characteristics of the Chauffeur HT include the ability to display 132 columns when it emulates the Tseng Labs UltraPAK-S and to display data in a 720 by 348 pixel resolution when it is driven by Hercules compatible software.

**Figure 3.29** STB Chauffeur HT—The STB Chauffeur HT display adapter can be considered as a five-in-one display adapter. It supports the IBM MDA and CGA, Hercules Graphics, Tseng Labs UltraPAK-S, and the STB Chauffeur display modes. *Photograph courtesy of STB Inc.*

Although the Chauffeur HT does not include an EGA mode, it runs CGA software on EGA monitors as well as on high-resolution color displays.

Recognizing that many PC users may already have a clock/calendar, this capability is offered as an option with the Chauffeur HT. You can purchase a clock option kit, which includes a clock chip that is inserted into a socket on the adapter card, a battery holder that mounts on the rear of the system unit, a battery, and a cable from the battery to the clock chip.

## Hercules Color Card

The Hercules Color Card is a substantial improvement over the IBM Color Graphics adapter in two areas—card length and the inclusion of a printer port.

Whereas the IBM Color Graphics Card is a full-length adapter with a skirt, the Hercules Color Card is a half-length adapter. This enables the Hercules Color Card to be used in short expansion slots 7 and 8 of a PC XT or in any expansion slot of a PC AT, including expansion slots 2 through 6 and slot 8, into which the IBM card cannot fit due to its skirt. The second significant improvement over the IBM Color Graphics Adapter is the inclusion of a parallel printer port on the Hercules Color Card. This port is automatically assigned address LPT1 or LPT2, depending upon the presence or absence of other cards in the PC containing a parallel port. If the Hercules Color Card is the only adapter containing a parallel port in your system, it is assigned device address LPT1. If a Hercules Graphics Card is also in your system, its parallel port is assigned device address LPT1, whereas the color card's parallel port is assigned device address LPT2. Any other adapter cards with a parallel port must be configured to be either LPT1 or LPT3, or must be disabled because the color card's parallel port will automatically be assigned address LPT2 under such circumstances.

## AST-3G

The AST-3G display adapter can be considered as a four-in-one video card, because it is compatible with software written for the IBM Enhanced Graphics Adapter, the IBM Color Graphics Adapter, the IBM Monochrome Display and Parallel Printer Adapter, and the Hercules Graphics Card. Illustrated in Figure 3.30, the AST-3G includes a parallel printer port, located in the lower right portion of the card.

The AST-3G is designed to work with the IBM 5151 monochrome monitor as well as the 5153 and 5154 color monitors, similar to the capability of the IBM EGA adapter. Where the two cards diverge in capability is the inclusion of a parallel printer port and support of the Hercules Graphics Card mode of operation on the AST-3G.

## QuadEGA ProSync

The QuadEGA ProSync graphics adapter marked by Quadram Corporation differs from most EGA products in its inclusion of two additional high-resolution display modes. These two modes—640 by 480 and 752 by 410 pixels—are only available when the adapter is used with a multiscan

**Figure 3.30** AST Research AST-3G Display Adapter—The AST-3G display adapter can be considered a four-in-one video card. This adapter supports the IBM MDA, CGA, and EGA display modes as well as the Hercules graphics display mode. *Photograph courtesy of AST Research Inc.*

type monitor. When operating in these modes up to 37 percent more data can be displayed on a multiscan monitor than that obtainable with a conventional EGA adapter.

Figure 3.31 illustrates the Quadram QuadEGA ProSync graphics adapter. Since the adapter was designed as a compact half-card, it is available for use in the short slots of a PC XT or PC AT. In comparison, the IBM EGA graphics adapter is a full-size card that cannot be used in the short slots of the PC XT and PC AT.

Shortly after IBM introduced the PS/2 family of computers, Quadram and STB as well as several other vendors began to market inexpensive ROM BIOS upgrades for their EGA adapter cards. These BIOS upgrades added support for the VGA 640 by 480 display in 2 and 16 color modes when used with multiscan monitors. However, they did not provide complete VGA compatibility for all 17 VGA display modes. To obtain complete VGA compatibility for your PC, you will have to purchase a VGA compatible display adapter and analog monitor.

## Genoa Systems SuperVGA

The Genoa Systems series of SuperVGA graphics adapters provides a mechanism for IBM PC series equipment to obtain the display capability of the PS/2 series. In addition to obtaining full IBM VGA compatibility, two models of the SuperVGA series can be used in either 8- or 16-bit expansion slots. This means your PC can be upgraded to a PC AT compatible without sacrificing its VGA card.

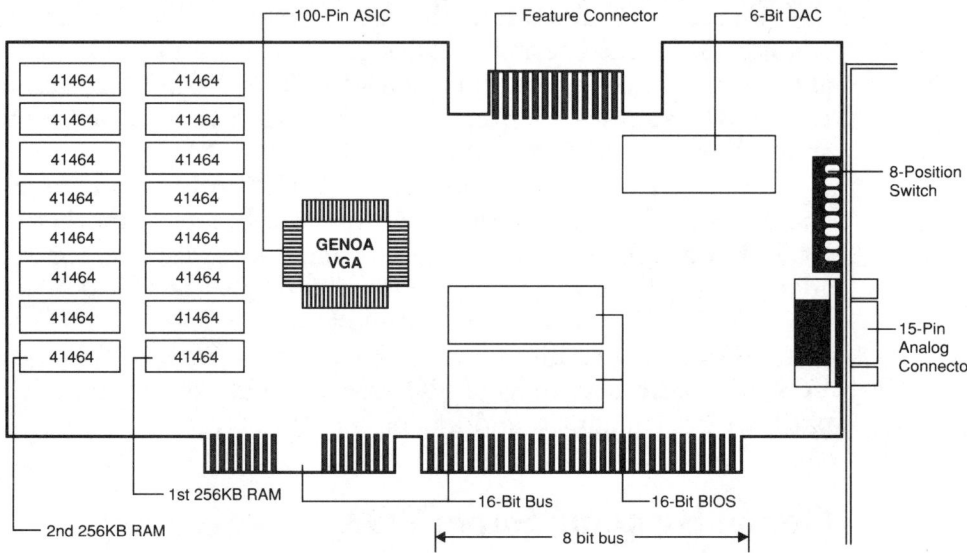

**Figure 3.31** Genoa SuperVGA Graphics Adapter—The Genoa SuperVGA Model 6400 provides a display resolution of 1024 by 768 pixels in 16 colors as well as 800 by 600, 640 by 480, and 512 by 512 in 256 colors. *Photograph and schematic diagram courtesy of Genoa Systems Corporation.*

The top portion of Figure 3.31 illustrates the actual Genoa SuperVGA Model 6400 graphics adapter with a full complement of 512K bytes of RAM. In the lower portion of Figure 3.31, a schematic diagram of the SuperVGA graphics adapter denotes the major components of the adapter.

The 8-position switch block mounted on the right of the adapter controls the monitor type selection, method of RAM access, Auto Display setting, and card BIOS. The switches that control the monitor type selection permit a full range of monitors from IBM analog to NEC MultiSync and Sony 1300 series displays to be supported. The AutoDisplay switch permits the automatic support of CGA, MDA, and Hercules programs and is normally left in the ON position. The switches that control RAM and BIOS can be set to support 8- or 16-bit memory access, permitting such display functions as text scrolling to appear smoother when performed on a PC AT or PC AT compatible computer.

The connection of the SuperVGA card to a monitor is via a 15-pin analog connector. The card's connector is located in the lower right corner of the schematic in Figure 3.31. Underneath the analog connector is the 16-bit bus edge connector, which runs along the lower edge of the card. Actually consisting of two edge connectors, this card can be installed in either an 8-bit or a 16-bit bus, making it usable in both PC and AT type computers. When you install the SuperVGA card in a 16-bit bus PC AT with the appropriate switch setting on the adapter card to support 16-bit access, information will flow twice as fast between the personal computer's microprocessor and the VGA, allowing scrolling to appear to be nearly instantaneous.

The two columns of 4164 chips located along the left portion of the graphics adapter are fully populated for the SuperVGA Model 6400. The SuperVGA Model 6300 comes with 256K bytes of RAM and can be upgraded to a Model 6400 by the addition of 256K bytes of RAM. All VGA graphics cards contain a minimum of 256K bytes of RAM, because that amount of memory is sufficient to support the display of all IBM VGA screen modes. The SuperVGA Model 6400, as well as several other third party VGA display adapters, requires an additional 256K bytes to support higher-resolution graphics modes.

The Genoa VGA chip mounted in the middle of the card is the key to its graphics capability. This chip contains a proprietary application specific integrated circuit (ASIC) that adds 1024 by 768 and 800 by 600 pixel display capability as well as 132-column by 25-, 29-, 32-, 44-, and 60-row text display compatibility beyond standard VGA support. To use this extended display capability, Genoa includes a series of software drivers that support the use of many popular spreadsheets, word processing, and desktop publishing applications, as well as several window environments. Because most VGA manufacturers develop their software to work directly with extended VGA modes based on their hardware design, a driver provided with one vendor's card should not normally be used with another vendor's graphics adapter. Doing so could result in either a poor display or no display, depending on the differences in hardware design between vendor products. Table 3.8 lists the Genoa SuperVGA display modes obtainable through the use of the Model 6300 and Model 6400 graphics adapters. The numerous advanced graphics modes supported by this adapter should be used for comparison purposes if you require a graphics display ability beyond the normal VGA modes.

## Display Adapter Selection

Table 3.9 lists nine categories of display adapter features you should consider prior to selecting equipment in this category. Most of the categories are self-explanatory, but several warrant additional discussion.

The resolution element of the graphics on the IBM monochrome display category refers to the formation of individual text characters from a row and column of pixels as well as the mapping of a graphics screen onto the monochrome display. For the former, the resolution of characters is governed by the number of vertical and horizontal pixels used to form a character and the size of the pixel box. For graphics screen mapping, resolution of mapping references whether a graphics screen of 200 vertical scan lines is mapped directly onto the monochrome display that contains 350 scan lines, leaving a blank band of 75 lines at the top and bottom of the screen, or if the mapping results in a full screen display. Obviously, the latter situation is preferred.

The port address and selectability element under the printer port category refers to the address the parallel printer port included on many cards is initially assigned to and whether the address can be changed. If the adapter card's parallel port address is fixed, addressing conflicts can occur if an existing card has a parallel port with the same address or at a later date an adapter card with a parallel port containing the same address is added to the computer. Thus, the ability to select a port address via configuration switches or jumpers on the card or via software is normally preferable to fixed port addresses.

Table 3.8  Genoa SuperVGA Display Modes

| MODEL | | _____ DISPLAY MODE CHARACTERISTICS _____ | | | | |
|---|---|---|---|---|---|---|
| 6300 | 6400 | MODE TYPE | COLOR | FORMAT | CHARACTER CELL | RESOLUTION |
| X | X | A | mono | 80 × 29 | 9 × 12 | 720 × 348 |
| X | X | A | mono | 80 × 32 | 9 × 12 | 720 × 384 |
| X | X | A | mono | 80 × 44 | 9 × 8 | 720 × 352 |
| X | X | A | mono | 132 × 25 | 8 × 14 | 1056 × 350 |
| X | X | A | mono | 132 × 29 | 8 × 12 | 1056 × 348 |
| X | X | A | mono | 132 × 32 | 8 × 12 | 1056 × 384 |
| X | X | A | mono | 132 × 44 | 8 × 8 | 1056 × 352 |
| X | X | A | 16 | 132 × 25 | 8 × 14 | 1056 × 350 |
| X | X | A | 16 | 132 × 29 | 8 × 12 | 1056 × 348 |
| X | X | A | 16 | 132 × 32 | 8 × 12 | 1056 × 384 |
| X | X | A | 16 | 132 × 44 | 8 × 8 | 1056 × 352 |
| X | X | A | 16 | 132 × 60 | 8 × 8 | 1056 × 480 |
| X | X | A | 16 | 80 × 60 | 8 × 8 | 640 × 480 |
| X | X | G | 16 | 80 × 30 | 8 × 16 | 640 × 480 |
| X | X | A | 16 | 80 × 66 | 8 × 8 | 640 × 528 |
| X | X | A | 16 | 100 × 37 | 8 × 16 | 800 × 592 |
| X | X | G | 16 | 100 × 75 | 8 × 8 | 800 × 600 |
| X | X | G | 16 | 64 × 32 | 8 × 16 | 512 × 512 |
| X | X | G | 256 | 64 × 32 | 8 × 16 | 512 × 512 |
| X | X | A | 16 | 80 × 32 | 9 × 16 | 720 × 512 |
| X | X | G | 16 | 90 × 32 | 8 × 16 | 720 × 512 |
| X | X | A | 16 | 100 × 42 | 8 × 14 | 800 × 588 |
| - | X | G | 256 | 80 × 25 | 8 × 14 | 640 × 350 |
| - | X | G | 256 | 80 × 30 | 8 × 16 | 640 × 480 |
| - | X | G | 256 | 90 × 32 | 8 × 16 | 720 × 512 |
| - | X | G | 256 | 100 × 75 | 8 × 8 | 800 × 600 |
| - | X | G | 16 | 128 × 48 | 8 × 16 | 1024 × 768 |
| X | X | G | 4 | 128 × 48 | 8 × 16 | 1024 × 768 |

**Table 3.9** Display Adapter Selection Features

| FEATURE | DETAILS |
|---|---|
| Monitor Compatibility | Monochrome Display<br>Color Display<br>Enhanced Color Display<br>Professional Display<br>Analog Display<br>Other |
| Adapter Compatibility | Hercules Graphics Card<br>Color Graphics<br>Enhanced Graphics<br>Professional Graphics<br>Monochrome<br>VGA<br>Other |
| Graphics on IBM Monochrome Display | Resolution<br>Use of Gray Scale for Color |
| Printer Port | Inclusion<br>Port Address and Selectability |
| Bus Support | 8-bit<br>16-bit<br>8- and 16-bit |
| Options | RAM<br>Clock/Calendar |
| Software Driver Requirements | |
| Software Capability | |
| Configuration Switches | |

Software drivers refer to a special program or programs that must be used with the adapter to enable a specific operating mode. An example is the Hercules HBASIC program, which is required to run BASIC graphics on the monochrome display when you are using the Hercules Graphics Card. Software compatibility refers to the ability of application programs to work in one or more display adapter video modes. Examples include Lotus version 1A, which when used with an EGA card can operate in CGA or monochrome mode but was not written to operate in the EGA mode.

Many EGA boards include a configuration switch accessible from the rear of the system unit. The switch protrudes through the rear of the system expansion slot cover. One or more switch elements normally are employed to define the type of monitor used, whereas other switch elements are used to define a default graphics mode and a secondary mode if software is not compatible with the default mode. Other EGA boards permit keyboard entries to be used to select the video mode, and some boards can automatically adjust to the user's software, alleviating the setting of switches.

There are three key questions that you should ask before purchasing a display adapter:

- Will the video mode or modes of the display adapter work with the monitor you intend to use?
- Are the video mode or modes of the display adapter you want to use compatible with your software?
- Does the selection of display modes require the setting of switches or can it be accomplished via the keyboard or automatically?

## Monitors

Until a few years ago, the selection of a monitor for use with a personal computer was limited to a monochrome display or a few color displays capable of graphics operation. Originally, display adapters had to be carefully paired with a monitor. With the introduction of IBM's EGA and VGA adapters and compatible third party hardware as well as monitors with variable scan rates, the barriers of the former relationship have been broken.

### Monitor Features

Table 3.10 lists eight major categories of monitor features you can analyze prior to obtaining this type of equipment.

Although many monitors can only operate with one display adapter or an EGA or VGA adapter operating in one mode, other monitors can operate with several adapters and provide the ability to add a new display adapter at a later date without replacing the monitor. Devices in this category are called *multiscan monitors,* because they are capable of adjusting to the scan rate of different display adapters. As an example of the

**Table 3.10** Monitor Selection Factors

| FEATURE | DETAILS |
|---|---|
| Type of Monitor | Analog<br>Digital<br>Selectable |
| Compatibility with Adapter | Monochrome<br>Color Graphics<br>Enhanced Graphics<br>Professional Graphics<br>Video Graphics Array<br>MultiColor Graphics Array<br>Multiscan |
| Physical Dimensions | Screen Size Diagonal in Inches<br>Height<br>Width<br>Depth |
| Cable Length | Power Cable Connector |
| Scan Resolution | 320 × 200<br>640 × 350<br>640 × 480<br>720 × 350<br>800 × 600<br>900 × 560<br>1024 × 768<br>Other |
| Dot Pitch in Millimeters | |
| Video Input | RGB<br>Composite<br>Analog |

capabilities and limitations of multiscan monitors, consider the horizontal scan rates of the CGA, EGA, and PGC adapters.

If you anticipate connecting a monitor to a member of the Personal System/2 family or an adapter board that supports either of the two IBM PS/2 graphics modes, the type of monitor as well as its scan rate must be considered. The two IBM graphics modes introduced with the Personal System/2 computers—MultiColor Graphics Array (MCGA) on the PS/2 Model 25 and Model 30 and the Video Graphics Array (VGA) on the other members of the PS/2 family—produce analog signals at a vertical scan rate of 70 Hz. In addition, the monitor pin connector used with the PS/2 series contains 15 pins, whereas adapters designed for the original IBM PC series contain a 9-pin monitor connector. Based upon the preceding, incompatibilities can exist between MCGA and VGA display adapters and IBM PC series monitors in the areas of monitor type, monitor scan rate, and the monitor connector.

Because many multiscan monitors are designed to accept both analog and digital signals, IBM's switch to analog may not present a problem in selecting a monitor that can support the display modes of the original PC series as well as the Personal System/2 if you need the capability for both machines. What may be more difficult is obtaining a monitor that can handle the 70-Hz speed of the VGA. As the popularity of this display increased, additional monitors supporting its operation reached the market. Many vendors offer a 9-pin to 15-pin connector adapter that enables the PS/2 display output to be used with existing analog monitors that support a 70-Hz scan rate.

In general, all adapters operating at or below the scan rate supported by a monitor can work with the monitor. Thus, an EGA monitor that operates at 21.85 KHz is capable of working with a CGA adapter. However, only a subset of the monitor's colors will be displayed due to the lower display capability of the CGA. Table 3.11 compares the scan rate, resolution, and number of displayable colors of different monitors, including two well-known vendor products used as a frame of reference.

The cable length is normally not an important consideration unless you want to place the monitor at a location distant from the system unit

**Table 3.11** Monitor Comparison

| TYPE | SCAN RATE (KHz) | RESOLUTION | NUMBER OF COLORS |
|---|---|---|---|
| CGA | 15.75 | 640 × 200 | 4 |
|  |  | 320 × 200 | 16 |
| EGA | 21.85 | 640 × 350 | 16 |
| PGC | 30.48 | 640 × 480 | 256 |
| NEC Multiscan | 35.0 | 800 × 560 | depends on adapter |
| Sony Multiscan | 35.0 | 900 × 560 | depends on adapter |
| VGA | 70.0 | 640 × 480 | 256 |

of the computer. Similarly, the power cable connector is normally not considered by many monitor purchasers, even though monitors that can be directly connected to the power source at the rear of the computer's system unit can alleviate long cable runs or the use of a power strip when you use many peripheral devices.

The dot pitch actually refers to the screen mask hole diameters inside the cathode ray tube of the monitor. The smaller the holes, the finer the resulting display. A few years ago, 0.60 millimeter was considered acceptable, while current high quality monitors have a dot pitch of 0.28 mm. To put this size in perspective, 0.15 mm is the dot pitch associated with *picture postcards*.

## Sony Multiscan

Sony's Multiscan monitor is representative of displays that adjust to any type of adapter that produces a scan rate between 15 and 35 KHz. This monitor can work with any color card from the CGA to the PGC, as well as with cards on the drawing board as long as such cards operate within the monitor's scan range.

One of the key attributes to the quality of the Sony display is its dot pitch of 0.26 mm, which is finer than that of most monitors.

CHAPTER 4

# *PC Hardware Upgrade Strategies*

There are two basic methods you can consider to obtain the latest in available personal computer technology. The first method involves the purchase of a new system to obtain one or more key features included with a recently announced product. As an alternative, you can consider upgrading existing hardware to achieve a desired level of functionality and capability equivalent to a new computer system. Because the hardware upgrade strategy can be viewed as prolonging the initial personal computer hardware investment, that option is usually preferable to replacing an existing system.

    This chapter examines a variety of strategies you can consider to increase the capability and functionality of existing hardware, including members of the IBM PC Series as well as compatible personal computers. The upgrading process is based upon knowledge of performance constraints of existing hardware, so we will first review the general characteristics of components in the system units of the IBM PC series with respect to the constraints they impose upon computer performance. This examination focuses on the key areas of RAM, processor performance, on-line storage capacity, and system expansion slot availability and usage. With this information as a base, we can then examine specific hardware upgrade strategies that allow your PC to obtain the performance level of a more advanced computer.

## Performance Constraints

There are four interrelated areas that constrain the performance of a personal computer—RAM, processor speed, on-line storage, and expansion slot availability. In this section we will examine each of these interrelated areas as well as discuss methods that can be used to overcome each constraint.

## RAM

The amount of random access memory (RAM) supported by DOS versions through 4.0 is limited to 576K or 640K bytes. IBM PCs whose serial numbers are below 300,000 are also known as PC1's in comparison to PCs manufactured after mid-1982, which in some instances are also referred to as the PC2. Early PCs must have their BIOS replaced to support 640K bytes of RAM, effectively converting a PC1 into a PC2.

The RAM chips used on the system board of PC1's were 16K-bit memory chips. Thus, the four banks of memory that must be filled to populate the system board of the original IBM PC result in a maximum of 64K bytes of on-board RAM. Later versions of the IBM PC as well as early versions of the IBM PC XT used 64K-bit memory chips. When the system board of these computers is fully populated, the result is a total of 256K bytes of on-board RAM. Later versions of the PC XT used 256K-bit memory chips, which resulted in a total of 1M byte of on-board RAM when all four memory banks were fully populated. Toward the end of their manufacturing cycle, IBM produced PC XTs with 640K bytes of RAM installed on the system board, accomplishing this by using 256K-bit chips in banks 0 and 1 and 64K-bit chips in banks 2 and 3.

The PC AT was marketed using 64K-, 256K-, and a combination of 64K- and 256K-bit chips. As a result of the different use of memory chips, PC AT users can have 256K, 512K, or 640K bytes of storage on their system board. If 256K bytes of memory was installed, an additional 256K bytes could be added, resulting in a total of 512K bytes of storage. If the PC AT already had 512K bytes of storage on its system board, a memory card or multifunction board with 128K bytes could then be used to expand memory to the limit supported by DOS.

Thus, the amount of memory that must be included on a memory or multifunction card to obtain a total of 640K bytes of RAM depends upon the type and version of the personal computer. This is because different members of the IBM PC series, as well as different versions of some members of that series, differ in their maximum on-board RAM. Because DOS requires a contiguous area of memory, the system board must be fully populated prior to adding memory in the form of an adapter card. Table 4.1 lists the required RAM that must be obtained through the use of an adapter card or cards to obtain a total of 640K bytes of RAM based upon the maximum memory that can be installed on the computer's system board.

Because the maximum amount of RAM on conventional memory adapter cards and multifunction cards is typically limited to 384K bytes, upon occasion you may have to install two boards to obtain the 640K-byte DOS support limit. If this situation occurs, carefully examine the ability of the card to set the starting address of its memory. Some memory boards are designed on the premise that they will be the only memory board installed in the system unit and the on-board RAM is fully populated to a specific level. This type of adapter card is very inflexible, because it can only be used with PCs that have a predefined amount of RAM on the system board.

Another area of inflexibility of this type of memory card occurs when a second memory card is installed in the system unit of a personal computer. When this situation occurs, the starting address of memory on the second card must be selectable, because the starting address of the first card is fixed. Otherwise, memory address conflicts will occur and the system will probably freeze.

A second type of address that should be included on a memory card for optimum flexibility enables the total amount of memory on the card to be set. Because a card may not be fully populated, this capability enables you to populate only the amount of RAM actually required. In some situations, you may wish to purchase a multifunction board to obtain the

Table 4.1  Reaching the DOS Limit RAM Required by Adapter Card Usage

| MAXIMUM ON-BOARD COMPUTER MEMORY | MEMORY REQUIRED VIA ADAPTER CARD(S) |
|---|---|
| 64K bytes | 576K bytes |
| 256K bytes | 384K bytes |
| 512K bytes | 128K bytes |
| 640K bytes | 0K bytes |

additional serial and parallel ports and/or clock/calendar capability, but may not require the use of any additional memory. For this type of situation the ability to disable any memory installed on the board is an important consideration.

The means of setting starting memory address, amount of memory on the adapter card, and whether memory is enabled varies among different vendor products. Some cards have these configuration parameters set via DIP switches; other adapters may use a combination of DIP switches and jumpers. In addition, some memory adapter cards that support the Expanded Memory Specification (EMS) and Enhanced Expanded Memory Specification (EEMS) have their configurations set via software, enabling you to reconfigure your adapter cards without having to open your system unit and reset DIP switches or jumpers.

## Expanded Memory

The use of expanded memory requires a minimum of 640K bytes of RAM to be previously installed. Recognizing the fact that many personal computers were manufactured with the capability to support a maximum of 256K or 512K bytes of storage on their system board, most expanded memory card manufacturers enable you to partition RAM on their expanded memory cards. As an example, consider a personal computer with 256K bytes of storage installed on its system board. If the personal computer user desires to add expanded memory, he first must increase the amount of conventional RAM to 640K bytes. This could be accomplished by the installation of a memory or multifunction card containing 384K bytes of RAM; however, the installation of that card would require the use of one system expansion slot. Then, when the user obtains an expanded memory card, there may not be another system expansion slot available for its use.

If the expanded memory adapter includes a memory partition capability, you can use one system expansion slot to both populate the system to 640K bytes of RAM and to add expanded memory. Assuming an expanded memory card containing 1.5M bytes was obtained with a memory partition capability, the user could configure 384K bytes of RAM as conventional memory and the remainder as expanded memory. This would permit one system expansion slot to be used to add enough RAM to "top off" conventional memory at the 640K-byte DOS support limit as well as to add expanded memory.

## Processor Performance

For compute-bound applications such as spreadsheet recalculations, numerical analysis, and similar number crunching, the processing capability of the personal computer's microprocessor directly affects the duration of the activity. Parameters that govern the processing capability of the computer's microprocessor include its operating rate expressed in megahertz, its data-bus width, and its level of chip integration. The system clock speed, which is crystal controlled, governs how fast the microprocessor performs operations such as add, subtract, and multiply, as well as left shift by bit, input data from a port, and so on. The data-bus width governs the rate at which data is read from or written to memory. Finally, the level of chip integration affects the overall performance of the microprocessor, because time delays associated in accessing separate chips are reduced when many chips are integrated together with the microprocessor.

As an example of the use of the three previously discussed parameters, consider the performance of an 80286-based PC AT in comparison to an 8088 PC or PC XT. If the clock rate of the PC AT is 8 MHz and the clock rate of the PC or XT is 4.77 MHz, you might initially surmise that the performance of a PC AT system is less than twice that of an 8088-based system. In actuality, the performance of the PC AT is approximately 3.5 times that of a PC or PC XT, because it accesses memory in 16-bit words instead of 8-bit bytes and has a much higher level of chip integration.

Perhaps the easiest way to increase the performance of an existing microprocessor is to replace the crystal on the system board with a faster device. Unfortunately, with the exception of the IBM PC AT, other members of the IBM PC series use the crystal to obtain common clocking or timing signals for other chips on the system board. This precludes the simple replacement of one crystal with a faster operating device, because other components on the system board are affected. As previously mentioned in Chapter 3, early versions of the PC AT that used 6 MHz crystals can be replaced by 8-MHz devices; however, later 6-MHz versions of the PC AT were manufactured with a version of BIOS that precluded the use of a faster crystal.

Table 4.2 lists the ROM BIOS dates of three models in the IBM PC AT series. Only the PC AT with a ROM BIOS date of 01/10/84 can have its 6-MHz crystal replaced by an 8-MHz crystal. The reader is referred to Chapter 1 for the explanation of the use of a BASIC program to read the ROM BIOS date of his or her computer.

Table 4.2  IBM PC AT Models

| PC AT MODEL | CRYSTAL | ROM BIOS DATE |
|---|---|---|
| AT with 20M-byte disk | 6 MHz | 01/10/84 |
| AT with 30M-byte disk | 6 MHz | 06/10/85 |
| AT with 30M-byte disk | 8 MHz | 11/15/85 |

Due to the problems associated with replacing crystals, several third party vendors have designed low-cost "accelerator boards" that in effect replace the existing crystal and microprocessor with faster operating devices. Included on these cards are circuits that derive the required clocking rates necessary to drive other chips on the system board. With a retail price of approximately $200 to $300, these adapter cards can be used to obtain a 30 to 50 percent system throughput gain. These accelerator boards only attack the processor speed constraint, so their effect upon overall performance is much less in comparison to true accelerator boards that contain a microprocessor with a wider data bus and memory designed to support the new bus structure. As a result of this, replacing the original 4.77-MHz 8088 of an IBM PC or PC XT with an accelerator card containing an 8-MHz or 10-MHz 80286 will result in an overall performance level considerably below that of an 8-MHz 80286.

To obtain a much higher performance increase, you must use a true accelerator board that contains a microprocessor with a wider data bus than that of the microprocessor presently installed on the computer's system board. Other features of this type of accelerator board can include a bus structure that permits on-board memory to be addressed in 16-bit or 32-bit increments and/or the use of cache memory, as previously discussed in Chapter 3. This type of adapter card can increase the processing capability of the computer by a factor of two to four.

# On-Line Storage

The constraints associated with on-line storage fall into three broad categories—floppy diskettes, fixed disks, and removable mass storage. Table 4.3 lists some of the major constraints for each category of on-line storage.

**Table 4.3** On-Line Storage Constraints

| STORAGE TYPE | CONSTRAINTS |
|---|---|
| Diskette | Controller |
|  | Media |
|  | Drive Type |
| Fixed Disk | Controller |
|  | Power Requirements |
|  | Performance |
| Removable Mass Storage | Controller |
|  | Media |
|  | Access Time |
|  | Power Requirements |

## Diskette

The controller required to operate diskettes varies according to the drive it is to control. The standard diskette controller used with the PC and PC XT is capable of supporting both the 5¼-inch 360K-byte and 3½-inch 720K-byte diskette drives. However, DOS 3.2 or a later version of the operating system is required to support 3½-inch diskette drive operations. The dual purpose diskette and fixed disk controller marked for the PC AT supports the 5¼-inch 360K-byte, 5¼-inch 1.2M-byte and 3½-inch 720K-byte drives, with the latter also requiring the use of DOS 3.2 or a later version of the operating system. The number of devices that can be installed into the device housing area of members of the PC series depends on the current configuration of previously installed devices, so you may have to consider acquiring external drives if space is not available for the addition of an internal drive. Other constraints to consider if you are adding internal mounted storage devices include the compatibility between the existing controller and the drive to be added, the power cable connector requirements, and the power requirements of the total system in comparison to that provided by the power supply.

In general, there are two types of controllers used in the PC series. The first type of controller was designed for use with PC and PC XT computers and can control up to four low-density diskette drives, such as the 360K-byte 5¼-inch and 720K-byte 3½-inch drives. Although other controllers are marketed that are limited to supporting two low-density drives, both types of controllers share the common capability of transferring data at the low speed required to support low-density drives.

A second type of controller usually supports a combination of fixed disks and diskettes. This type of controller is commonly referred to as an AT controller, because it was first used in the PC AT. In comparison to PC and PC XT diskette controllers, the PC AT controller can support both low- and high-density drives (1.2M-byte 5¼-inch and 1.44M-byte 3½-inch drives). Unfortunately, AT type controllers and their normal BIOS do not have the ability to set high-density mode and transfer rate correctly for a 1.44M-byte 3½-inch drive.

To alleviate this problem, many 1.44M-byte diskette drives include the ability to sense the type of diskette inserted in the drive. You can then use the DOS FORMAT command. However, this type of drive typically formats the diskette at its normal density, which introduces a new problem if you want to format a 1.44M-byte diskette for 720K-byte compatibility with a laptop or IBM PS/2 Model 25 or Model 30 usage.

To overcome these problems you can consider acquiring a "system" consisting of a controller adapter card and an internal or external 3½-inch diskette drive. Here the controller mounted on an adapter card includes its own BIOS that directly supports both low- and high-density data transfers, permitting you to read and write data on 720K-byte and 1.44M-byte 3½-inch diskettes.

The existence of two IBM personal computer series that were manufactured with four different primary storage capacities on two different types of diskette drives makes media transfer capability an important constraint. The 5¼-inch drives used with the IBM PC series have storage capacities of 360K and 1.2M bytes, whereas the 3½-inch diskette drive has a storage capacity of 720K bytes. The 3½-inch diskette drives offered with the IBM Personal System/2 family have storage capacities of 720K and 1.44M bytes, resulting in a total of four distinct recording densities on two different types of diskette media. Unfortunately, both the older 5¼-inch and newer 3½-inch diskette drives have a degree of incompatibility between similar size diskette drives. That is, data recorded onto a 360K-byte 5¼-inch drive can be read in a high capacity 1.2M-byte 5¼-inch drive, but due to recording density differences data written onto a 5¼-inch disk in a 360K-byte format in a high-capacity drive often is unreadable by a conventional 360K-byte drive. Similarly, 720K-byte 3½-inch diskettes can be read when inserted into a 1.44M-byte 3½-inch drive; however, a 1.44M-byte diskette created in a 1.44M-byte drive cannot be read by a 720K-byte drive.

## Media Transfer

There are four primary methods by which programs and data recorded on 5¼-inch media can be transferred to 3½-inch media and three methods for the reverse transfer of data. First, IBM and third party vendors market internal and external 3½-inch drives that can be used with the IBM PC series and external 5¼-inch drives that can be used with the IBM Personal System/2 series.

Several constraints must be considered when adding a 3½-inch drive to a member of the PC series or a 5¼-inch drive to a member of the PS/2 series. First, DOS version 3.2 or a later version of the operating system must be used with the PC series to obtain support of a 3½-inch diskette. Secondly, DOS only permits the copying of "allowable" files, which IBM defines as programs that can be backed up in accordance with the software vendor's operating instructions. This constraint precludes the copying of copy-protected software. As just discussed, you must also consider the compatibility between the disk controller and drive, including the controller's support of low- and high-density drives.

## With Diskettes

Since many available hardware products do not support the direct transfer of data between 1.2M-byte 5¼-inch and 3½-inch diskette drives, many users must use a 360K-byte 5¼-inch drive as intermediate storage for this type of media transfer. That is, users must first transfer data from a 1.2M-byte 5¼-inch diskette to a 360K-byte 5¼-inch diskette prior to transferring the data to a 3½-inch diskette. Similarly, data required to be transferred from a 3½-inch diskette to a 1.2M-byte 5¼-inch diskette must first be transferred to a 360K-byte 5¼-inch diskette. Over the past few years, several third party vendors have introduced 1.2M-byte 5¼-inch external diskette drives that can be connected to most PS/2 computers. Doing so provides organizations with a mixture of PC AT and PS/2 computer systems with the capability to directly transfer data between 1.2M-byte 5¼-inch and 3½-inch diskettes.

Figure 4.1 illustrates the installation of a Toshiba 3½-inch half height internal diskette drive into the system unit of an IBM PC. This disk drive is marketed with a kit that permits the 3½-inch drive to be installed in the device housing areas of IBM PC, XT, AT, and compatible computers that were designed for 5¼-inch devices.

**172** The PC Upgrader's Manual

**Figure 4.1** Installing the Toshiba 3½-inch Internal Disk Drive—The Toshiba 3½-inch internal disk drive includes a kit that enables it to be mounted in the device housing area of an IBM PC, XT, AT, or compatible computer. *Photograph courtesy of Toshiba.*

## With Data Migration Facility

A second method for the transfer of data between different media involves the use of a special cable and software designed to permit data transfer from 5¼-inch drives to 3½-inch drives. Marketed by IBM as the Data Migration Facility (DMF), the cable is used to connect the parallel port of a member of the IBM PC series to the parallel port of a PS/2 computer. The two biggest problems with DMF are the fact that it only permits data transfer in one direction and can only be used by computers that are close to one another physically.

## With Communications Software

The third method of media transfer involves the use of communications software on two personal computers. Under this method of media transfer, programs and information in the form of files can be transferred between computers. If the two computers are within 50 feet of one another, a special null modem cable can be used to connect the serial port of each computer.

Otherwise, modems are required and one computer user has to call the telephone number of the business line connected to the modem of the second computer to transfer data via a communications facility. Just as copy-protection schemes prevent you from using an additional drive for data transfers, copy-protected programs normally cannot be transferred between computer systems over a data communications link.

### With File Transfer Program and Cable

The fourth method of media transfer is based upon the use of a third party file transfer program including the use of one or more multiheaded cables that cable two personal computers together. Typically, commercial file transfer programs include both 5¼- and 3½-inch diskettes, which enable the software to operate on both PCs and PS/2s. When this series of software originally reached the market, the multiheaded cable was designed to connect two computers together via their serial ports. Typically, one or both ends of the cable have DB-25 and DB-9 connectors. Sometimes, one end has both connectors and the opposite end has one DB-25 connector. By providing both DB-25 and DB-9 connectors, if your computer has a 25-pin connector serial port it can connect to the DB-25 connector, whereas if your computer has a 9-pin connector serial port, it can connect the cable using the DB-9 connector. Once the two computers are connected, the software programs operated on each computer enable one operator to control both systems, including copying files from a diskette on one computer to a diskette on the other computer.

Because the use of a serial port results in data transfer occurring one bit after another in a serial manner, the data transfer rate is typically limited to approximately 38.4 Kbps or less. Recognizing this limitation, a few file transfer programs now use the parallel ports of each personal computer for data transfers. This technique permits eight data bits to be transferred simultaneously, significantly reducing the time required to transfer large files between two personal computers. Table 4.4 summarizes the major constraints in transferring information from 5¼-inch to 3½-inch diskette drives.

## Fixed Disk

Three key constraints associated with fixed disks are the type of controller required to be used with the device, its power requirement and resulting

**Table 4.4** Diskette Drive Data Transfer Constraints

| METHOD | CONSTRAINTS |
|---|---|
| Additional Internal/External Drive | Requires additional hardware investment<br>Requires DOS 3.2 or DOS 3.3 to support 3½-inch drive<br>Precludes transfer of copy-protected software |
| Data Migration Facility | Requires use of parallel port on each computer<br>Requires computers to be positioned close to one another<br>One-way data transfer from 5¼-inch to 3½-inch diskettes<br>Precludes transfer of copy-protected software |
| Data Communications | Requires a modem or null cable to link computers<br>Requires communications software on each computer<br>Precludes transfer of copy-protected software |
| File Transfer Program and Cable | Some require use of serial port<br>Some require use of parallel port<br>Software must operate on both PCs<br>Cable distance between PCs limited<br>Precludes transfer of copy-protected software |

effect upon the power supply of the computer, and its level of performance. The performance level normally references the average access time to retrieve data and its interleave factor.

Fixed disk controllers are designed to work with certain types of fixed disk drives. Many fixed disk controller manufacturers specify a limited number of fixed disk drives that they support. Normally, in examining fixed disk advertisements you will probably see the expression "works with XXX controller," indicating the type of controller required to operate the fixed disk.

In most cases, the addition of a fixed disk to an IBM PC requires the replacement of the computer's 63.5-watt power supply. Although replacing a power supply may appear complex, in actuality it simply involves removal of four screws and unfastening the connectors from the power supply to the system board and to previously installed storage devices located in the device housing areas of the system unit. Once the power supply of an IBM PC is upgraded to 135 watts or more, it is capable of supporting just about any type of storage device—including those used with the PC XT and PC AT as long as appropriate controllers are installed.

One fixed disk performance area that can significantly increase the storage capacity of the disk is the addition of a Run Length Limited (RLL) or Enhanced Run Length Limited (ERLL) controller. Designed to pack data more efficiently on fixed disks, either controller may boost the storage capacity and access speed by 50 to 100 percent or more with an existing disk drive. Due to the controller's sophisticated circuitry it can usually support 25 to 30 sectors per track instead of the 17 sectors per track supported by conventional controllers. In addition, RLL and ERLL controllers may enable the interleave factor of the fixed disk to be lowered, resulting in a higher data transfer rate.

Prior to purchasing an RLL or ERLL controller, verify its compatibility with the fixed disk currently used. To do this, simply remove the cover of the system unit and note the vendor's name and model number, which usually appears on a rectangular metal plate affixed to the top of the disk. Then, after confirming that the RLL or ERLL controller supports the fixed disk by calling the manufacturer, an increase in the storage capacity of a 10M-byte drive to 15M bytes or a 20M-byte to 30M bytes can be expected. To accomplish this storage capacity increase, the existing controller must be replaced with a new controller and the fixed disk must be reformatted. Thus, prior to installing the new controller, you should back up all files on the fixed disk.

## Removable Mass Storage

Removable mass storage devices can be considered as a hybrid between a diskette and a fixed disk, providing some of the best features of each. Although many removable mass storage devices provide the storage capacity and access times associated with the use of fixed disks, they resemble diskettes with respect to the ease with which the media can be removed. Due to this, they are excellent for applications that require data security and/or portability of large quantities of data. In addition, they provide a virtually unlimited amount of data storage capacity; when one cartridge or tape is full, you can simply remove it and insert a new one into the removable storage device.

The most popular type of removable mass storage devices is based on the use of special types of floppy diskettes encased in cartridges. Other common types of removable mass storage currently being marketed incorporate removable sealed fixed disks, special servo positioning mechanisms to obtain the ability to record data at a very high density on 3½-inch diskettes, or VHS video type cartridges.

The use of diskettes encased in cartridges was pioneered by Iomega Corporation in its Bernoulli Box, in which the read/write head of the device rests upon a cushion of air as the diskette rapidly spins in the cartridge. The Bernoulli Box, which was originally marketed in the early 1980s, used 5¼-inch disk technology and was mounted in a large chassis that was equivalent in deskspace requirements and weight to the system unit of an IBM PC. Since then, several vendors have introduced smaller external chassis as well as a chassis designed for installation into the device housing area of a PC, PC XT, or PC AT. Externally housed chassis include their own power supply, making the primary constraint for their use the availability of a system expansion slot for the installation of a controller card. Although a PC XT or PC AT power supply is normally more than sufficient to power an internally installed drive, the 63.5-watt power supply of an IBM PC must be replaced by at least a 135-watt power supply for any type of removable mass storage device to operate correctly when installed in a device housing area.

Manufacturers marketing removable fixed disks base their products on the use of a sealed Winchester drive inserted into an assembly or chassis that contains the control mechanism for reading and writing data. Because the removable media is a fixed disk, including the platter and read/write heads, this type of media is the most expensive of all removable mass storage. Similar to other removable mass storage, key constraints governing its use include system expansion slot availability for a controller, power supply wattage for internally housed devices, and the cost of the removable media. In addition, because the removable media is an encased Winchester disk, it is the most fragile of all categories of removable media and should not be dropped or bumped harshly, obviously limiting its handling.

In the area of high-capacity, diskette-based removable mass storage, several vendors offer data-storage capacity ranging up to 50M bytes per 3½-inch diskette. The key to obtaining this high level of storage capacity is the use of special servo positioning equipment that enables data to be stored on tracks minutely separated from one another. Vendors require the use of special preformatted 3½-inch diskettes, so you cannot use conventional diskettes in these devices. Although most vendors use a modified conventional magnetic encoding process where tracks are magnetically encoded very close to one another on the diskette, one vendor supplements magnetic encoding by employing optical technology to obtain the high storage capacity on the diskette. This is accomplished by the vendor preformatting diskettes with optical and magnetic tracks and using an optical sensing mechanism on top of the drive's read/write head for positioning. An infrared beam from an LED or a beam of light generated from a low-power laser is focused through a hole in the read/write head and reflects the image of the optical tracks previously embedded on the diskette. The reflected information is received by a photodetector similar to those used in compact disc players and provides the information required to position the read/write heads over the magnetically encoded data tracks.

For very large removable data storage, a few vendors have introduced storage devices based upon the use of VHS video cartridges. Due to the relatively poor quality of VHS tape in comparison to magnetic media designed for data storage, manufacturers have incorporated powerful error correction algorithms into their equipment. These algorithms minimize the possibility of a data error to less than that associated with conventional magnetic media. Typical VHS video cartridge systems provide up to five gigabytes of storage on a single T-120 Super VHS video cartridge. This storage capacity, while many magnitudes beyond what is required to back up the largest capacity fixed disk, can be useful for data acquisition-based personal computer systems that must record a continuous process over an extended period of time. Unlike other types of removable mass storage, systems based upon the use of VHS video cartridges are only available as external units.

Table 4.5 lists key selection parameters to consider when you evaluate removable mass storage systems. Although both the capability and price per cartridge or tape are listed as selection parameters, upon occasion vendor literature will express both parameters as one by indicating the media cost per 1M byte of data storage capacity.

**Table 4.5** Removable Mass Storage Selection Parameters

| FEATURE | DETAILS |
|---|---|
| Drive Type | Internal |
| | External |
| Controller Requirement | Uses existing controller |
| | Requires new controller |
| Drive Price | |
| Media | Capacity in Mb |
| | Price per cartridge or tape |
| | Access time |
| | Durability |

## Expansion Slot Availability

There are several methods readers can consider to alleviate the constraint associated with a fixed number of expansion slots included in the system unit of each personal computer. The most expensive method, and in comparison to alternatives perhaps the most impractical, is the use of an expansion unit. Other methods you can consider include the use of external devices to obtain a desired level of functionality, the use of multifunction cards to satisfy new requirements, and the replacement of single-function adapter cards with multifunction cards to free up expansion slots to permit the use of other adapter cards.

## Expansion Unit

The expansion unit was originally manufactured by IBM to extend the capacity of the five-expansion-slot IBM PC. Later, other expansion units were marketed by IBM and third party vendors to increase the number of system expansion slots that could be used with the PC XT and PC AT. An expansion unit is very similar in external appearance to the system unit of an IBM PC or PC XT. Inside the expansion unit are a power supply, a number of system expansion slots, and one or more device housing areas. To connect the system unit of the personal computer to the expansion unit requires the installation of a special adapter card in each device. These cards are connected to one another by a cable as illustrated in Figure 4.2.

The adapter card installed in the system unit is more formally known as a *driver card,* and the adapter card installed in the expansion unit is called a *receiver card.* The shielded cable that connects the cards carries all bus signals except the clock. Each adapter card requires the use of a

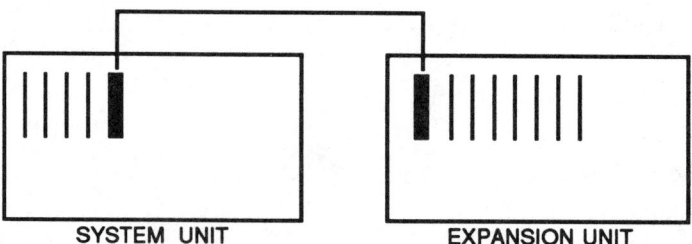

**Figure 4.2** Connecting the Expansion Unit—Two adapter cards and expansion slots are required to connect a system unit to an expansion unit.

system expansion slot, so cabling an IBM PC to an 8-slot expansion unit results in an increase in usable slots from 5 to 11. The power supply installed in expansion units is normally rated between 135 and 200 watts, permitting an IBM PC to use a full-height fixed disk and high-speed internal modems without requiring the power supply in the system unit to be replaced. Although the additional expansion slots and the ability to use high-power consumption devices are most beneficial, the cost of an expansion unit that can equal the cost of a clone computer makes alternatives to obtaining additional expansion slots more economically attractive to consider.

One alternative to using a full-size expansion unit is to obtain one of the smaller expansion chassis manufactured by several third party vendors. Such expansion chassis are manufactured in a variety of configurations, ranging from devices that simply include space for one half-height on-line storage device and include a low wattage power supply to chassis that may contain up to 8 or 12 expansion slots; a 100-, 150-, or 200-watt power supply; and room for four half-height storage devices. The following lists expansion unit/chassis constraints to examine prior to selecting a device in this hardware category:

Number of expansion slots
Space for half-height storage devices
Power supply wattage
Physical dimensions

## External Devices

Another alternative to the expansion unit is the use of external devices, such as modems and storage units. Although the number of system expansion slots obviously remains the same, this technique may permit better use of existing ports and interfaces. As an example, consider the difference between using an internal and external modem. An internal modem is a combination communications adapter and modem mounted on one board which is installed into an empty system expansion slot. In comparison, an external modem is cabled to a serial port on a communications adapter card or it can be cabled to a serial port on a multifunction card. If the serial port on a multifunction card is used, the requirement for a separate communications adapter is alleviated. This technique then frees one expansion slot, enabling it to be used by a different adapter.

## Multifunction Card

A third method that can be used to alleviate the constraint of a fixed number of expansion slots is to replace two or more existing adapter cards by a multifunction card. While the first use of multifunction cards that comes to mind is the combination of memory, clock/calendar, and serial and parallel ports, there are other types of multifunction cards that should also be considered. Table 4.6 lists a few of the capabilities of multifunction cards by card feature and the separate adapter cards they may replace.

Two representatives of nonstandard multifunction cards that can economize the use of expansion slots are the AST Research SixPak Premium/EGA and Rampage/EGA. The SixPak Premium/EGA is a single slot, expanded memory multifunction and EGA graphics board designed for use in the IBM PC, PC XT, and compatible computers. Illustrated in Figure 4.3, this card incorporates the Chips & Technology EGA chipset and enables you to select from the EGA, CGA, MDA, and Hercules graphics modes. The graphics display capability of the card is compatible with such IBM PC monitors as the 5151 Monochrome Display, the 5153 Color Display, and the 5154 Enhanced Color Display, as well as compatible displays. Up to 2M bytes of expanded memory can be added to the board and a split memory addressing capability is included, enabling you to use a portion of the card's memory to fill the computer's conventional memory to 640K bytes. Additional features included on this card are a serial port, parallel port, and clock/calendar with battery backup.

The utility of this card is best judged by comparing it to the number of separate IBM adapter cards that would be required to obtain a similar level of functionality. The IBM Monochrome Display and Parallel Printer adapter combines a parallel port with the MDA display capability, but the IBM CGA and EGA cards do not include a parallel port. Thus, three IBM

Table 4.6  Multifunction Card Capabilities

| CARD FEATURES | CARDS THEY MAY REPLACE |
| --- | --- |
| Standard Multifunction | Memory and serial and/or parallel ports |
| Video and Memory | Display, memory, and serial and/or parallel ports |
| Diskette and Disk Controller | Diskette drive controller and fixed disk controller |

PC Hardware Upgrade Strategies    **181**

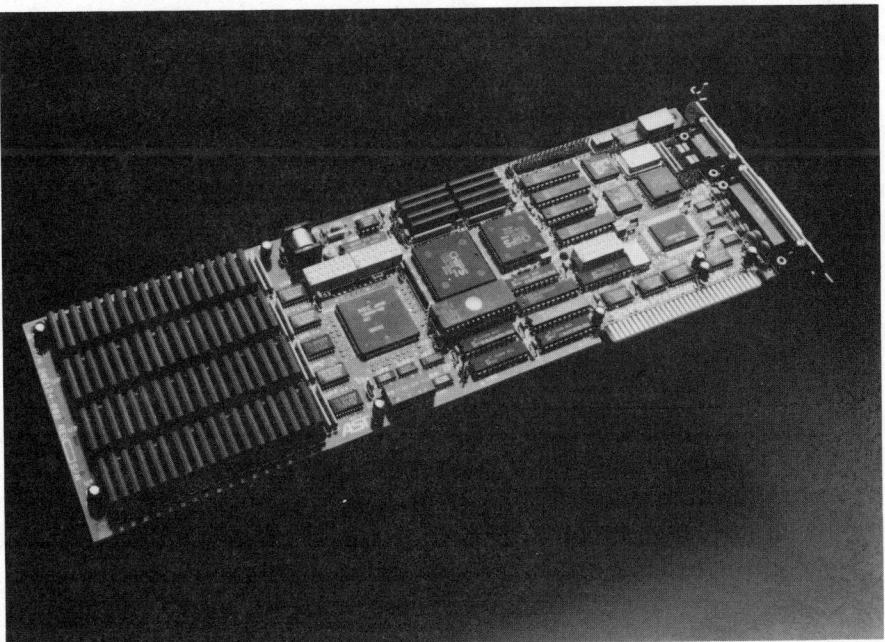

**Figure 4.3**  AST Research SixPak Premium/EGA—This adapter card combines expanded memory with four graphics display modes and includes a serial port, parallel port, and clock/calendar with battery backup. *Photograph courtesy of AST Research, Inc.*

graphics adapters as well as an asynchronous communications adapter would be required to obtain just a portion of the functionality of this card. Because IBM does not market an extended memory board and clock/calendar for use with the PC or PC XT, you could purchase four IBM adapters and still require one or more third party hardware products to obtain the functionality that the SixPak Premium/EGA provides.

The AST Research Rampage/EGA is a combined expanded memory and/or extended memory and graphics board that is designed for use with 6-MHz and 8-MHz IBM PC ATs and compatible computers. Although this card is similar to the SixPak Premium/EGA card previously discussed, there are several notable differences between the two. First, the memory on the Rampage/EGA can be used as conventional, expanded, and/or extended memory. Extended memory is capable of supporting a protected mode operating system such as OS/2 or XENIX. Second, the Rampage/EGA does not include serial and parallel ports that are included with the

SixPak Premium/EGA. Finally, because the PC AT includes a built-in clock/calendar capability, this feature is also omitted from the Rampage/EGA card.

## Upgrade Strategies

This section reviews some of the upgrade strategies you can consider to increase the capability and functionality of your existing computer system. The hardware required to effect an upgrade strategy depends upon two main factors—the existing computer system configuration and your future processing requirements. Taking these factors into consideration, we will examine three specific hardware upgrade strategies. First, we will discuss methods to increase the performance and capability of an IBM PC without changing the power supply of the computer. Next, we will examine how an IBM PC can be upgraded to meet or exceed the performance level of a PC XT system. Last but not least, we will discuss the hardware upgrade strategies you can consider to obtain a level of performance associated with the PC AT through upgrading your PC or PC XT.

## IBM PC Upgrade

There are numerous devices that can be added to the IBM PC without requiring the replacement of the computer's 63.5-watt power supply. The following lists nine IBM PC upgrade possibilities that can be considered without requiring a replacement of the 63.5-watt power supply:

Keyboard replacement
Combined graphics display adapter
EMS/EEMS memory board
Multifunction board
Selective internal/external storage devices
Accelerator card
Diskette and fixed disk controller card
External modem
Expansion unit/chassis

## Keyboard Replacement

The replacement of the IBM PC keyboard by an "AT style" device containing indicators to denote the state of Caps Lock, Num Lock, and Scroll Lock is normally done to obtain a small increase in typing productivity. If the computer is primarily used for programming in a language that is case insensitive, the replacement of the PC keyboard will have a negligible effect upon productivity.

## Combined Graphics Mode Display Adapter

Using a combined or multigraphics mode display adapter, you can obtain the display capabilities of several IBM video adapters on one card. In addition to reducing the number of system expansion slots required to support multiple display modes to one, you may obtain the capability to support such nonstandard IBM display modes as Hercules Graphics, Tsang Ultra Pak, and others.

## EMS/EEMS Memory

By installing an EMS or EEMS memory board, you can populate conventional memory to the 640K bytes supported by DOS as well as obtain virtual disk capability through the board's extended memory. For user applications that require sorting, the use of one or more virtual disks can significantly reduce storing times. This reduction is due to the electronic speed of the operation of the virtual disk in comparison to the electromechanical speed of a diskette or fixed disk. Other requirements that may justify the installation of extended memory include the support of software that requires the use of this memory to operate more efficiently and operating systems that in the future may support this memory beyond the use of virtual disk usage.

## Multifunction Board

A combined graphics display adapter, like a multifunction board, reduces expansion slot usage by including one or more serial and/or parallel ports and a clock/calendar and battery backup with additional memory on a single card. For the ultimate conservation of system expansion slots, consider the use of a multifunction board that includes a combined graphics display, such as the AST Research SixPak Premium/EGA previously described.

## Internal/External Storage Devices

By the appropriate selection of internal and external on-line storage devices, you can obtain a storage capability that exceeds that offered with the PC AT while you obtain a backup mechanism far superior to that provided by the DOS BACKUP and RESTORE commands.

The key to using the computer's existing power supply is employing low-power consumption internal storage devices and employing external higher-power consumption devices. If you require fixed disk storage capacity, consider the installation of a half-height, low-power fixed disk or the use of a disk card. The latter requires 1, 1½, or 2 available expansion slots, but another option to consider is the installation of a diskette and fixed disk controller. By replacing the IBM diskette controller with a dual-purpose controller, no additional system expansion slots are required. Unfortunately, due to the high power consumption of internal modems that operate at data rates at or above 2400 bps, simultaneous use of this type of modem and an internal fixed disk or disk card is usually mutually exclusive. Thus, if a high-speed internal modem was previously installed, an external fixed disk should normally be used to obtain the large capacity on-line storage users may require.

## Accelerator Cards

If processing power is the bottleneck to computer operations due to frequent spreadsheet recalculations or other compute-bound applications, consider the addition of a mathematical coprocessor, accelerator card, or an accelerator card with a coprocessor. If the program most frequently used with the personal computer supports the use of an 8087 coprocessor, its installation is probably the most economical method for reducing processing time. Otherwise, the use of an accelerator card—whose cost is typically three times that of an 8087—should be considered.

## Expansion Unit/Chassis

Upon occasion, the five expansion slots of an IBM PC will not be sufficient to satisfy your full range of requirements. As an example, consider a PC with 256K bytes of RAM installed on its system board. If you operate large spreadsheets, additional memory in the form of an adapter board will be required. Further assume that you require the use of an accelerator board and that the computer is to be connected to a local area network and requires full screen access to a corporate mainframe via a coaxial connection to an IBM 3274 controller. Because memory board, accelerator cards, local area network cards, and coaxial connector cards have yet to have their functions combined, four separate cards requiring four system expansion slots would be required. This would leave only one available expansion slot for driving a display and any on-line storage devices, which would be an impossible task in a five-expansion-slot IBM PC. Under such circumstances the lack of a sufficient number of expansion slots can only be alleviated by acquiring a PC XT with eight expansion slots or by obtaining an expansion unit or chassis.

## PC to PC XT

There are several methods you can consider to obtain the capacity and functionality of an IBM PC XT with an IBM PC. The selection of one method over another depends upon a variety of factors: the type of IBM PC, the number of on-line storage devices currently installed in the PC's device housing areas, the presence or absence of high-power-consumption adapter boards in the computer's system expansion slots, and the number of available system expansion slots in the computer.

## RAM

The original version of the IBM PC used 16K-bit chips on the system board, resulting in a maximum of 64K bytes of on-board memory. Later versions were manufactured with 256K bytes of RAM. Because PC XTs were originally manufactured with 128K or 256K bytes on their system board, whereas later versions contained 512K or 640K bytes of RAM, many

PC users will have to expand their RAM by the addition of an adapter card to obtain an equivalent level of memory associated with the PC XT.

## Storage Devices

The type and number of on-line storage devices previously installed in a PC may result in the preference of one type of fixed disk over another. If both device housing areas are filled and you do not want to consider replacing full-height diskette drives with half-height devices, a fixed disk card should be considered. If a system expansion slot is not available for the fixed disk card, consider the acquisition of an adapter card that combines the functions of two previously installed cards to free up a slot. Alternatively, consider the replacement of one full-height storage device by an equivalent half-height device to free up a portion of a device housing area. For either situation, the power consumption of presently installed equipment as well as the power consumption of the disk card or the internal fixed disk must be compared to the capacity of the computer's power supply.

## Components Required

Converting an IBM PC into the equivalent of an IBM PC XT can require the addition of up to four major hardware components—memory, a fixed disk and fixed disk controller or a fixed disk card, a power supply, and a ROM BIOS chip. As previously discussed, early IBM PCs require the installation of either a multifunction or memory card to obtain the amount of memory installed on a minimum RAM PC XT. Any additional memory beyond 128K or 256K bytes will be based upon the requirements of the application programs used with the computer. Because memory is relatively inexpensive, it is a good idea to fully populate adapter cards to their maximum memory capacity.

When the IBM PC XT was announced, it included a 10M-byte fixed disk and a fixed disk controller whose BIOS supported four types of disk drives. The controller BIOS used in the PC XT is initiated by the BIOS on the computer's system board. IBM PCs with 64K bytes of RAM on their system board have an older version of BIOS, so a ROM BIOS upgrade kit must be obtained from IBM and a new BIOS chip installed to permit this personal computer to support fixed disk operations. Later versions of the IBM PC with 256K bytes of RAM on the system board have the updated ROM BIOS already installed. If you are in doubt as to what version of BIOS your computer has, refer to Chapter 1, which explains the use of a short BASIC program that can check the version of BIOS installed.

As previously mentioned, the IBM fixed disk controller included with the original PC XT supports four types of fixed disks. The characteristics of each type of disk supported are listed in Table 4.7 and can be used as a guide in selecting hardware that is compatible with the BIOS on the IBM controller.

The drive initially marketed with the PC XT was a Type 3 device. This fixed disk has two platters resulting in four heads used to record or retrieve information. The disk is formatted into 512-byte sectors and there are 17 sectors per track, so the total formatted storage capacity of this disk becomes:

512 bytes/sector * 17 sectors/track * 306 tracks/side * 4 sides = 10,653,696 bytes.

Several years after the introduction of the PC XT, IBM began to market a 20M-byte disk that was a Type 1 drive. Between 1981 and 1985 advertisements in magazines sold 5.3M-byte disks at very economical prices. Rumor has it that these drives were originally to be used in the PC XT; however, IBM decided to offer a 10M-byte drive, which resulted in a large surplus of the former types of fixed disks becoming available. By 1990 many of these drives were still being sold by computer resellers.

## Power Supply Replacement

In matching the fixed disk to a controller, the rectangular metal plate on the disk drive should be read to accurately obtain the vendor's model

**Table 4.7** Types of PC XT Fixed Disks Supported by BIOS

| DRIVE TYPE | CYLINDERS | HEADS | CAPACITY (M BYTES) |
|---|---|---|---|
| 0 | 306 | 2 | 5.3 |
| 1 | 375 | 8 | 26.1 |
| 2 | 306 | 6 | 15.9 |
| 3 | 306 | 4 | 10.6 |

number. Most drives conform to the Seagate Technology (ST) 412/506 interface, which is an industry standard. The initial operation of the disk motor results in a power surge that can consume a majority of the available power from an IBM PC power supply, so the use of most internal fixed disks requires a replacement of the PC's power supply.

By reading the classified advertising section of any one of numerous trade publications, you can select among a number of advertisements for replacement power supplies. You may select a 130-watt PC XT power supply as well as consider devices rated as high as 250 watts. In contemplating a replacement power supply for the IBM PC, the most important considerations are the dimensions of the power supply and its power cables. Any wattage above 135 should be sufficient for all but extreme power sensitive applications.

Figure 4.4 illustrates the dimensions of the power supply of the IBM PC, which is the same size as the power supply used in the PC XT. Note that both devices have a height of approximately five inches. Replacement power supplies should be either the same as or have slightly less length, width, and height than the dimensions illustrated in Figure 4.4 to fit correctly into the IBM PC. One important convenience is to ensure that the power supply includes an AC socket for the monochrome monitor.

IBM PC power supply replacements normally include between four and six cables with power connectors at the end of each cable. Two of the power connectors each contain 12 pins and are connected to the system board. The remaining power connectors contain 4 pins and are used to power internal storage devices. Each diskette and fixed disk requires a

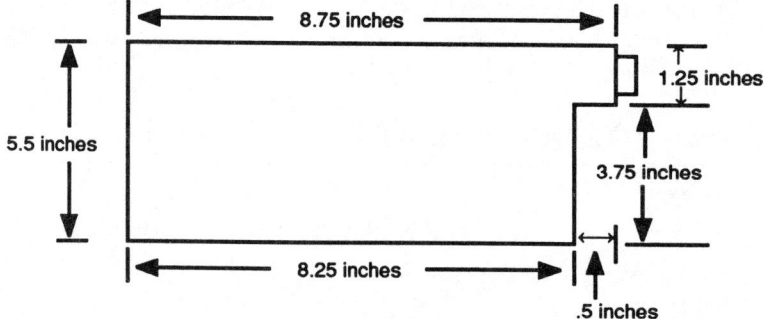

**Figure 4.4** IBM PC and PC XT Power Supplies Dimension Viewed from the Top—The dimensions of replacement power supplies should be reviewed to ensure they can be correctly installed into the system unit of an IBM PC.

separate connection to the power supply; thus, two 4-pin connector cables may be insufficient for some computer configurations. In such circumstances a "Y" power cable connector should be ordered with the replacement power supply. When attached to one power cable connector, the "Y" connector permits two devices to obtain power. Thus, if three storage devices are to be installed in the computer's device housing areas and the power supply has two 4-pin connector power cables, one "Y" connector should be ordered. Similarly, if four storage devices are to be installed using a power supply with two 4-pin connector power cables, two "Y" connectors will be required.

## PC or PC XT to PC AT

The major differences between the IBM PC or PC XT and the PC AT involve the keyboard, on-line storage capacity, processor performance, and operating modes of the computers.

### Keyboard

When IBM replaced the original keyboard marketed with the PC AT with the IBM Enhanced Keyboard, this device was also marketed with newer models of the PC XT. IBM PC and early versions of the PC XT cannot use the IBM Enhanced Keyboard due to differences in the BIOS included on the system board of the computers that do not support some of the additional keys included with the new keyboard. To obtain an equivalent PC AT keyboard for the IBM PC and most versions of the PC XT, you can select from a variety of third party devices marketed by many vendors. Although these keyboards only contain 10 function keys, they normally include the three key-state indicators that boost typing productivity.

### On-Line Storage

The PC AT differs from the IBM PC and the PC XT in the use of a 5¼-inch high-capacity (1.2M-byte) diskette drive and the availability of a 30M-byte fixed disk. Although a 5¼-inch high-capacity diskette drive is not marketed by IBM for use in the PC or PC XT, several third party vendors offer this product for use in those computers. Because the standard diskette controller does not support the 1.2M-byte diskette drive, if you require this drive you must replace your existing diskette controller with a controller that supports both 360K-byte and 1.2M-byte diskette drives.

Although IBM markets only 20M- and 30M-byte fixed disks for use with the PC AT, 14 disk drives are supported, ranging in capacity from 10.6M bytes to 117.5M bytes. Table 4.8 lists the fixed disk drives supported by the ROM BIOS located on the system board of the PC AT. As you compare the PC XT to the PC AT, note that DOS 2.X uses an interleave factor of 6 for PC XT fixed disks; DOS 3.X uses an interleave factor of 3 for PC AT fixed disks. This difference results in long data transfers taking twice as long on a PC XT as on a PC AT.

Because the constraint concerning the types of PC XT fixed disks supported resides in the BIOS on the controller used in the XT computer, if you want larger storage capacity, faster disk access, or both, you can obtain a third party disk controller that will support the desired fixed disk. Doing so will require an upgrade to DOS 3.X to format the fixed disk with

**Table 4.8** Fixed Disks Supported by PC AT BIOS

| DISK TYPE | CYLINDERS | HEADS | LANDING ZONE | STORAGE CAPACITY |
|---|---|---|---|---|
| 1 | 306 | 4 | 305 | 10.6 |
| 2 | 615 | 4 | 615 | 21.4 |
| 3 | 615 | 6 | 615 | 32.1 |
| 4 | 940 | 8 | 940 | 65.4 |
| 5 | 940 | 6 | 940 | 49.0 |
| 6 | 615 | 4 | 615 | 21.4 |
| 7 | 462 | 8 | 511 | 32.1 |
| 8 | 733 | 5 | 733 | 31.9 |
| 9 | 900 | 15 | 901 | 117.5 |
| 10 | 820 | 3 | 820 | 21.4 |
| 11 | 855 | 5 | 855 | 37.2 |
| 12 | 855 | 7 | 855 | 52.0 |
| 13 | 306 | 8 | 319 | 21.3 |
| 14 | 733 | 7 | 733 | 44.6 |

a lower interleave factor to obtain a higher level of performance. Although a similar strategy can be followed for the PC, as previously discussed, its 63.5-watt power supply will more likely than not require replacement.

## Processor Performance

Several factors enable the 80286 in the PC AT to exceed the performance of the 8088 microprocessor used in the PC and PC XT: the clock rate of the AT, its 16-bit data bus, and the level of chip integration into the 80286 in comparison to the 8088. Options available to increase the processing performance of PC and PC XT computers are

Crystal replacement
Mathematical coprocessor
Accelerator board
Virtual disk

Although the first three methods listed were previously discussed, an additional elaboration concerning accelerator boards is warranted. The variety of accelerator boards currently marketed for use in the IBM PC and PC XT ranges in scope from the 8086 and 80286 microprocessors to the 80386. Although the use of accelerator boards can significantly improve processing performance, other computer operations such as disk I/O will be limited to 8-bit data transfers, whereas the PC AT uses 16-bit data transfers. If you have a disk-intensive application, the use of a virtual disk in conjunction with an accelerator board may actually result in a level of performance that exceeds that of a PC AT. Obviously, if you have a PC AT, a virtual disk could also be used to boost the processing capacity of that computer.

## Operating Mode

The last major difference between the PC or PC XT and the PC AT is in the operating modes each computer system supports. The 80286 used in the PC AT is capable of operating in either real mode or protected mode. In its real mode of operation, the 80286 emulates the 8088 and has the same 1M-byte memory limit as the 8088. When the 80286 is operated in its protected mode, it is capable of addressing 16M bytes of RAM. In addition, this mode of operation supports multitasking, which is the ability to run more than one task at the same time.

Because DOS supports only real mode operations, PC and PC XT users who will not require the functions of IBM's OS/2 do not have to consider this difference between 8088-based PC and PC XTs and the 80286-based PC AT. Users who simply require a multitasking capability without the other features of OS/2 can consider the acquisition of a multi-tasking shell program under which their applications will operate. Multi-tasking on an 8088 is sluggish due to its level of performance; an accelerator board will be required to improve performance to an acceptable level. Although IBM has publicly stated that OS/2 will not operate on 8088-based personal computers, it is very probable that several third party vendors will introduce adapters that will enable OS/2 to operate on the PC and PC XT.

CHAPTER 5

# PS/2 Hardware Enhancements

This chapter focuses on hardware options you can consider from both IBM and third party sources to increase the performance and capability of your PS/2 computer system. We will first examine several on-line storage devices you can use with PS/2s, such as 5¼-inch disk drives and tape backup units. Because members of the PS/2 family can be categorized based upon the type of bus incorporated into their system unit, this chapter will also examine the use of adapter cards based on the type of expansion slot they are designed to operate in. In doing so, we will first examine adapter cards designed for use in the PC bus of the Model 25 and Model 30 computers. This will be followed by an examination of the use of adapter cards designed for use in PS/2 computers that incorporate Micro Channel architecture.

## On-Line Storage Devices

Two of the more popular types of on-line storage devices used to supplement the capability of PS/2 computers are 5¼-inch disk drives and tape backup units. Both IBM and several third party vendors currently market both categories of on-line storage devices for use with different members of the PS/2 family. The key differences between products are normally in the areas of price, performance, and specific PS/2 model support. Due to the dynamic nature of the personal computer market, we will focus on key performance characteristics potential purchasers of these devices should consider and leave it to you to compare prices between competitive products when you are ready to purchase a specific type of device as well as to ascertain its compatibility with a specific member of the PS/2 series.

## 5¼-inch Diskette Drive

The IBM 5¼-inch external diskette drive as previously noted in Chapter 3 is one of the longest, if not the longest, diskette drive ever built. To operate this drive, you must first install IBM's PS/2 5¼-inch external diskette drive adapter in an available system expansion slot. A flat ribbon cable supplied with this option is used to cable a connector on the adapter to a drive connector assembly. The latter is actually a modified expansion slot cover that contains a connector onto which a cable protruding from the IBM 5¼-inch diskette drive is fastened.

Figure 5.1 illustrates the connection of the IBM 5¼-inch diskette drive to the drive connector assembly mounted in a PS/2. A second cable from the IBM drive is a power cable and must be inserted into an electrical outlet for the drive to operate. Once the drive is connected and powered on, it is always recognized as drive B. Another limitation associated with the IBM 5¼-inch external drive is the fact that it is limited to reading and writing 360K-byte diskettes. This precludes its use with high-capacity 1.2M-byte diskettes that are commonly used with IBM PC AT and compatible personal computers. Thus, transferring data from a PC AT to a PS/2 via diskette when using an IBM 5¼-inch external diskette drive requires PC AT users to have a 360K-byte drive in their computer system. Then, they would first write the data files to the PC AT's 360K-byte disk and use the resulting diskette in the IBM external drive attached to a PS/2.

One third party external 5¼-inch diskette drive that warrants discussion due to several technical capabilities is Sysgen Corporation's Bridge-File. In actuality, the term Bridge-File references a series of 3½- and 5¼-inch diskette drives. The vendor's 3½-inch Bridge-File is designed for use with IBM PC series computers, whereas the 5¼-inch Bridge-File is designed for use with PS/2 products. Due to this, we focus on the 5¼-inch Bridge-File in this chapter.

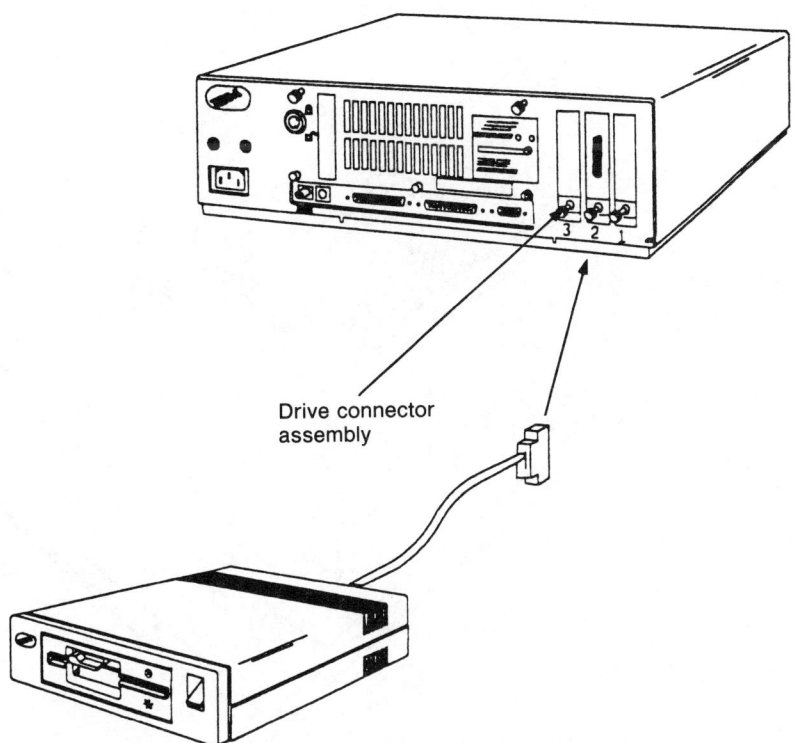

**Figure 5.1** IBM External 5¼-inch Disk Drive Connection—The IBM 5¼-inch external disk drive is connected to the rear of the system unit of a PS/2 computer through a drive connector assembly mounted as an expansion slot cover.

Similar to IBM, to use a Bridge-File 5¼-inch external diskette drive you must install an adapter board. However, use of an expansion card slot is restricted to the PS/2 Model 30. For Micro Channel bus PS/2s, Sysgen provides a most interesting adapter whose use alleviates the necessity of using a Micro Channel expansion slot.

For Micro Channel bus PS/2s, Sysgen provides a three-connection adapter board that replaces the IBM installed Diskette Drive Bus Adapter to which IBM diskette drives are normally connected. Figure 5.2 shows the position of the IBM Diskette Drive Bus Adapter inside a PS/2 Model 50 computer. Note that this adapter has an edge connector pushed into a slot on the system board and two rectangular connectors into which the edge connectors on the rear of 3½-inch diskette drives are connected.

The IBM Diskette Drive Bus Adapter is only capable of supporting two drives. Thus, its removal and replacement by a Sysgen supplied adapter

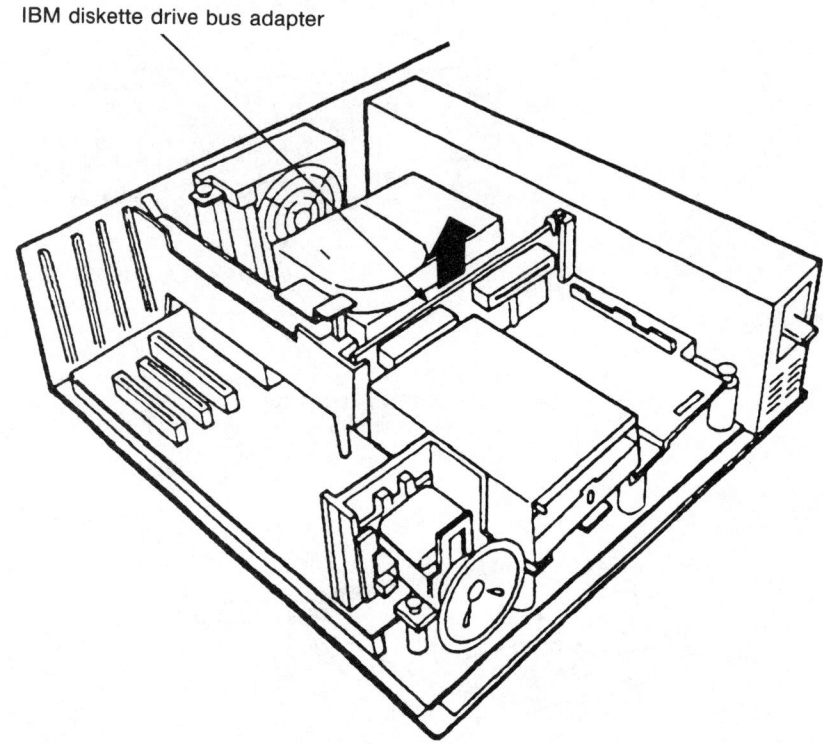

**Figure 5.2** The IBM Diskette Drive Bus Adapter—The IBM diskette drive bus adapter contains two rectangular connectors into which the edge connectors of diskette drives are inserted.

that has three connectors will enable an external drive to be supported without using a Micro Channel expansion slot.

Figure 5.3 illustrates the insertion of a Sysgen-supplied adapter board that contains three rectangular edge connectors. The two connectors facing the front of the system unit are exactly the same as those on the IBM adapter it replaces. The key difference between the Sysgen and IBM drive bus adapters is that the former includes a third 40-position connector mounted on the side opposite the dual drive connectors. A Sysgen-supplied flat ribbon cable is fastened to the third connector. The other end of the Sysgen-supplied cable contains a bracket that is mounted on an expansion slot cover. Once the bracket is installed, you connect the Sysgen 5¼-inch diskette drive via a cable to the new expansion slot cover, which contains the cable bracket.

PS/2 Hardware Enhancements    **197**

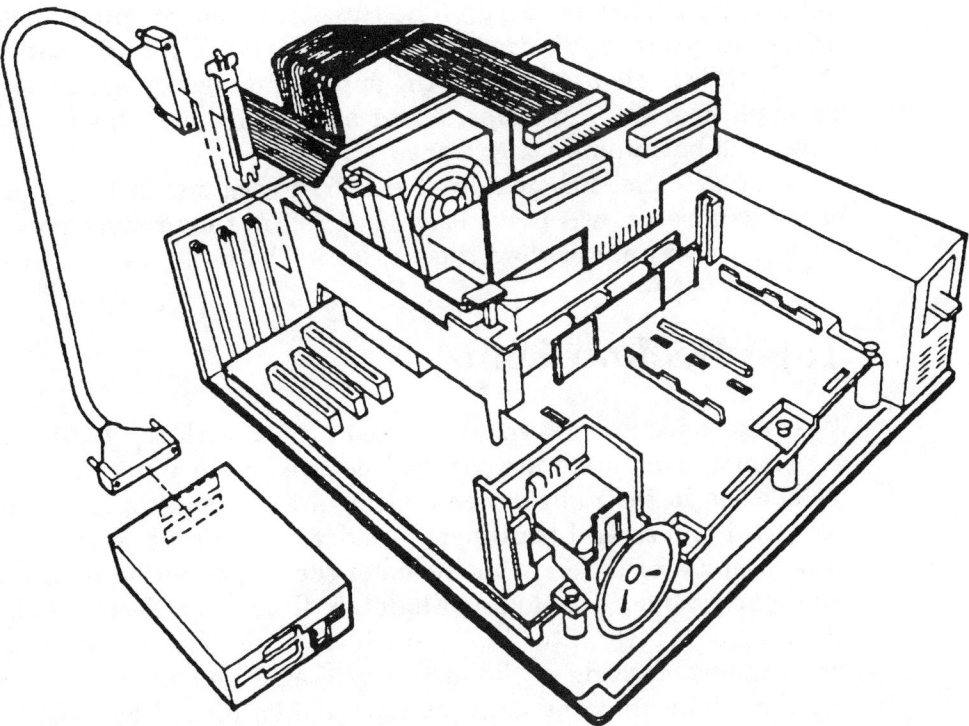

**Figure 5.3** Installing Sysgen Bridge-File Hardware—The key to using the Sysgen Bridge-File disk drive is the vendor's disk drive adapter bus, used as a replacement for the adapter bus provided by IBM.

In addition to permitting the use of an external diskette drive without sacrificing the use of an expansion slot the Sysgen Bridge-File offers two other features that can be important selection criteria to many users. First, the drive obtains its power from the PS/2 via the cable connection to the newly installed adapter. This alleviates the necessity of obtaining a power strip or adding an electrical receptacle for many persons. Second, the Sysgen Bridge-File, unlike IBM's external 5¼-inch drive, supports both 1.2Mbyte and 360K-byte diskettes, enabling PC AT users to transfer data directly between the high-capacity diskette drive in a PC AT and a PS/2. Unlike the IBM external drive that does not require special software, to use the Bridge-File you must install and use a utility program supplied by Sysgen with its hardware. This program enables you to install the Bridge-File as drive B or D (you cannot use drive designator B if your PS/2 already has a second diskette drive). The Sysgen install program adds a device driver to your boot disk (normally drive C) and modifies your CONFIG.SYS file to reference the appropriate device driver. Once this is accomplished, you can simply power on your PC and the required service driver will be automatically loaded.

Table 5.1 lists PS/2 external disk drive selection factors. Because each of the parameters was previously discussed in the product reviews in this section, we will not explore the entries in the table.

## Tape Backup Unit

Most tape backup units manufactured for use with the IBM PS/2 family of personal computers are internal devices. Such units are designed for installation in the right device housing area on desktop PS/2 models.

IBM and several third party vendors currently market internal tape backup units for different members of the PS/2 family. IBM and several third party vendors, including Mountain Computer, design their drives to be plugged directly into the 3½-inch diskette drive slot inside a PS/2's system unit, resulting in the insertion of an edge connector at the rear of the tape drive into the connector on IBM's disk drive adapter bus, as illustrated in Figure 5.4.

The key differences between IBM and third party internal tape backup units are in the areas of data storage capacity and the rate of data

**Table 5.1** PS/2 External Disk Drive Selection Parameters

| FACTOR | DETAILS |
|---|---|
| Drive capacity | 360K bytes<br>1.2M bytes<br>360K/1.2M bytes |
| Operating drive designator | B<br>D<br>B or D<br>Other |
| Power source | Requires separate outlet<br>Obtains from PS/2 |
| Expansion slot requirement | None<br>One |

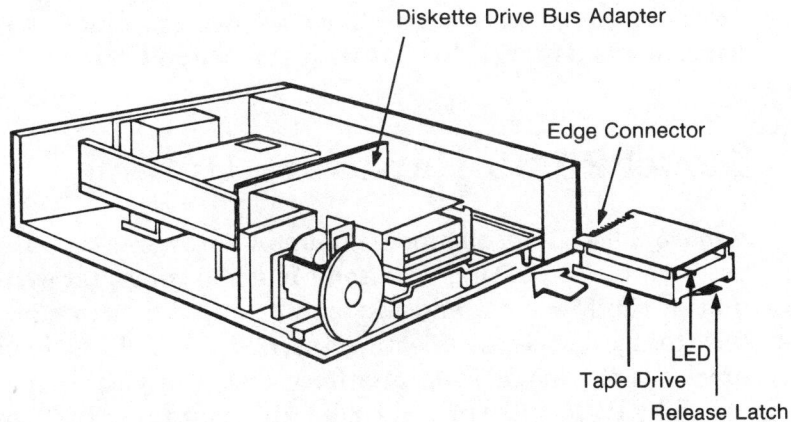

**Figure 5.4** Internal Tape Drive Installation—Internal tape drives used with PS/2s are plug replacements for the second diskette drive. The edge connector at the rear of the tape drive is designed for insertion into the connector mounted on the IBM diskette drive bus adapter.

transfer. IBM currently markets an internal tape backup unit that can hold up to 80M bytes of data. This tape records data at 2M bytes per minute, permitting the full backup of a 60M-byte fixed disk to occur in 30 minutes. In comparison, most third party vendors market 40M-byte capacity drives, requiring the use of two tapes to fully back up a 60M-byte fixed disk. This difference between drives is basically meaningless for PS/2 users with fixed disk drives having a storage capacity of 40M bytes or less, so let the data-storage capacity of your fixed disk be a governing factor in determining the minimum capacity of a tape backup unit unless you are willing to use multiple tapes during a backup procedure. Concerning the tape recording rate, unless you frequently use the tape unit, the additional cost associated with some high speed units may make them very expensive on an hourly usage basis if you periodically perform selective backups.

## Other Internal Enhancement Products

This section examines a variety of hardware enhancement products that can be installed inside the system unit of a PS/2. Members of the PS/2 family are categorized by the bus structure they support, so we will examine internal enhancements similarly. That is, we will first examine internal enhancements designed for use in the PC bus-based PS/2 Model 25 and

Model 30 computer systems. Then we will examine internal hardware enhancements designed for use with the Micro Channel PS/2 computers.

## Model 25/30 Hardware Options

Table 5.2 lists 13 of the more common hardware options IBM markets for use with the PS/2 Model 25 and Model 30 computer systems. The system unit of the Model 25 and Model 30 computers can contain only two on-line storage devices, so selecting a second 3½-inch 720K-byte diskette drive precludes the installation of a fixed disk and vice versa.

The IBM 3363 Optical Disk Drive contains a built-in laser that burns tiny spots on specially coated media contained in removable cartridges that are inserted into the drive. This technology provides you with the ability to *w*rite *o*nce on the medium but to *r*ead it *m*any times; hence, another term used to describe this technology is WORM. The storage capacity of the disk cartridge used in the IBM 3363 Optical Disk Drive is 200M bytes, which is equivalent to over two hundred fifty 720K-byte diskettes.

Figure 5.5 illustrates the stand-alone IBM 3363 Optical Disk Drive and a 5¼-inch optical disk cartridge. This disk drive is controlled by an adapter board inserted into a system expansion slot of a PS/2 computer.

**Table 5.2** Common PS/2 Model 25/30 Internal Options

| OPTION TYPE | PRODUCTS AVAILABLE |
|---|---|
| Drives | IBM 3½-inch 720 K-byte diskette drive |
| | IBM 3½-inch 20M-byte fixed disk drive with adapter |
| | IBM 3½-inch 20M-byte fixed disk drive |
| | IBM 3363 Model A1 Optical Disk Drive |
| Adapters | IBM 2MB Expanded Memory Adapter |
| | IBM 3117 Scanner Adapter |
| | IBM PS/2 Display Adapter |
| Communications | IBM PC 1200 bps Internal Modem |
| | IBM PC 2400 bps Internal Modem |
| | IBM Binary Synchronous Communications Adapter |
| | IBM SDLC Communications Adapter |
| Networks | IBM PC Network Adapter II |
| | IBM Token-Ring Network Adapter |

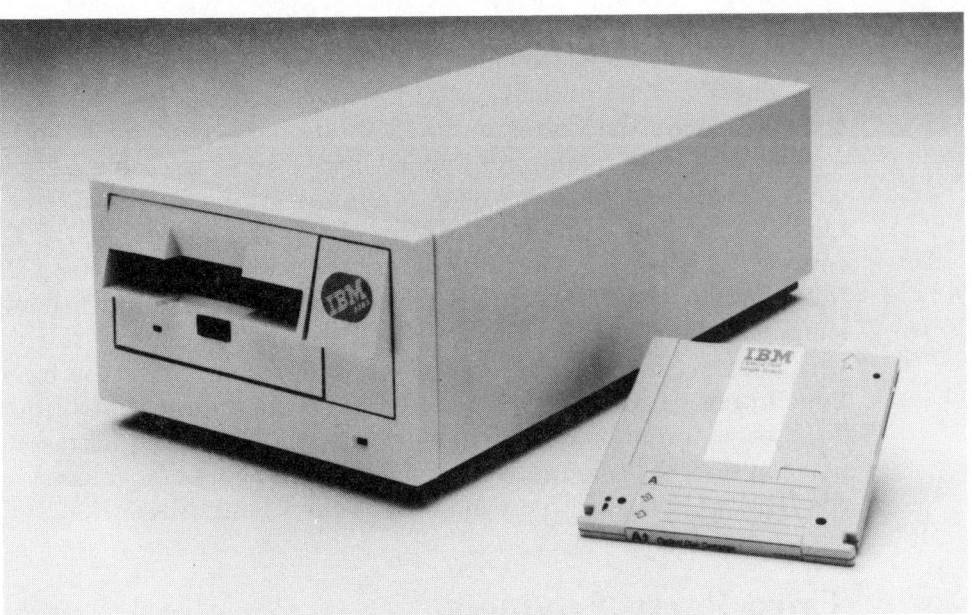

**Figure 5.5** IBM 3363 Optical Disk Drive—The IBM 3363 Optical Disk Drive incorporates a low-power laser that burns tiny holes in specially prepared 5¼-inch media to provide a storage capacity of 200M bytes per cartridge. *Photograph courtesy of IBM Corporation.*

Two different types of external optical disk drive systems are marketed by IBM, the difference being the type of adapter card used in the PS/2 computer. The Model A01 Optical Disk Drive system includes an adapter designed for insertion into PC bus systems, whereas the Model A11 is designed for use in Micro Channel-based systems.

The IBM 2MB Expanded Memory Adapter contains 2M bytes of expanded memory and a standard parallel printer port. This adapter can be used in PC bus computers to expand memory above the 640K bytes of maximum RAM installed on the system board of a Model 25 or Model 30 computer.

The IBM 3117 adapter permits you to attach an IBM 3117 Scanner to a PC bus PS/2 computer. To obtain the same Video Graphics Array (VGA) function built into Micro Channel-based PS/2s, you can install the IBM PS/2 Display Adapter in a PC expansion slot of a PS/2 Model 30.

The remaining six internal options listed in Table 5.2, including two internal modems, are all constructed on adapter cards designed for insertion into PC type expansion slots. IBM also markets similar adapter cards for installation in Micro Channel-based PS/2 computers.

The PC 1200 and PC 2400 internal modems provide asynchronous transmission at data rates up to 1200 bits per second (bps) and 2400 bps, respectively. The remaining four adapters listed in Table 5.2 enable your computer to perform specialized communications functions. The IBM Binary Synchronous Communications Adapter and the SDLC Communications Adapter permit your computer to communicate with an IBM mainframe computer. The Binary Synchronous Communications Adapter supports IBM's older binary synchronous communications protocol, whereas the SDLC Communications Adapter supports the more modern Synchronous Data Link Control (SDLC) communications protocol. The last two adapters listed in Table 5.2 enable PS/2 computers with PC expansion slots to be connected to two different types of local area networks—the IBM PC Network and the IBM Token Ring Network.

## Third Party Products

The PS/2 Model 25 and Model 30 computers use the original PC bus architecture incorporated in the IBM PC and PC XT. Thus, literally hundreds of PC-compatible third party products were also compatible with the Model 25 and Model 30 when these were introduced. Two of the more popular third party products that users of PC bus-based PS/2 computers may wish to consider are fixed disk cards and VGA adapter cards.

### Fixed Disk Card

As noted in Chapter 3, Plus Development Corporation's introduction, in 1985, of a low-powered 10M-byte hard disk combined with controller circuitry mounted on an expansion card resulted in approximately 20 vendors introducing fixed disk cards of varying capacity. Disk cards can be installed in a system expansion slot without requiring the removal of a diskette drive or another device previously installed in a device housing area. Thus, a fixed disk card provides the ability to install two diskette drives and two fixed disks in the system unit of your PS/2, because a fixed disk card can be used as either drive C or, if a fixed disk was previously installed, as drive D. In addition, the low power requirements of disk cards with respect to the wattage of PS/2 power supplies enables them to be installed in most computers without upgrading the power supply.

At the time this book was published, disk cards were only available for use in PC bus PS/2s, such as the Model 25, Model 30, and Model 30 286. Although the Model 30 286 uses the 16-bit PC AT bus structure, several 8-bit disk cards are capable of operating in that computer in addition to disk cards specifically manufactured for use in a 16-bit PC bus. The key difference between the two types of disk cards with respect to their use in a PC AT or PS/2 Model 30 286 is the fact that read/write operations are slightly extended in duration when an 8-bit data path disk card is used in a 16-bit bus computer, because the computer must then transfer data 8 bits at a time instead of 16 bits at a time.

## VGA Adapter

Many VGA adapters designed for use with the IBM PC series can also be used with the PS/2 Model 30 to upgrade its MCCA video display capability. Although those adapters can be installed in a Model 25, due to the inclusion of an MCCA display built into the case of that computer, which also houses its system unit, the addition of a VGA card would not be useful with the built-in display. Similarly, the PS/2 Model 30 286 includes a VGA chip set built into its system board, so you would normally not consider upgrading the video display capability of that computer.

The selection process for an appropriate VGA adapter should examine the functions previously listed in Chapter 3. Although you can eliminate a 16-bit bus from consideration when the adapter is to be used in a PS/2 Model 30, you may want to consider the other features, including adapter (emulation) compatibility and the inclusion of a printer port on the card.

## Multifunction Boards

Due to the limited number of expansion slots included in the PC bus-based members of the PS/2 family, it is quite easy to run out of expansion cards. To alleviate this situation you can consider the use of many third-party vendor multifunction boards that contain several functions on one card and only require the use of a single expansion slot. Some multifunction boards combine a mixture of serial and parallel ports, whereas other boards combine memory and serial and/or parallel ports. Refer to Chapter 3; the multifunction boards discussed in that chapter can be used in PC bus PS/2 computers.

## Micro Channel Hardware Options

Table 5.3 lists 20 of the more common IBM hardware options designed for use in PS/2 computers that have a Micro Channel bus architecture.

The 3½-inch 1.44M-byte diskette drive provides 1.44M bytes of formatted storage capacity when high-capacity diskettes are used. In the drive's low-density recording mode, it is compatible with the 720K-byte 3½-inch drive used in the Model 25 and Model 30 computers.

**Table 5.3** Common PS/2 Micro Channel Computer Internal Options

| OPTION TYPE | PRODUCTS AVAILABLE |
|---|---|
| Drives | IBM 3½-inch 1.44M-byte Diskette Drive<br>IBM PS/2 5¼-inch External Disk Drive<br>IBM PS/2 Fixed Disk Drive<br>  30M byte<br>  44M byte<br>  60M byte<br>  70M byte<br>  115M byte<br>  314M byte<br>IBM 3363 Model A11 Optical Disk Drive<br>IBM Internal Optical Disk Drive |
| Adapters, Coprocessors, and Expansion Kits | IBM 3117 Scanner Adapter/A<br>IBM PS/2 80287 Math Coprocessor<br>IBM PS/2 80387 Math Coprocessor<br>IBM PS/2 80286 Expanded Memory Adapter/A<br>IBM PS/2 80286 Memory Expansion Option<br>IBM PS/2 80286 Memory Expansion Kit<br>IBM PS/2 80386 Memory Expansion Option<br>IBM PS/2 80386 System Board Memory Expansion Kit<br>IBM PS/2 80386 Memory Expansion Kit |
| Communications and Networks | IBM PS/2 300/1200 Internal Modem/A<br>  3270 Connection Adapter<br>  Token-Ring Network Adapter/A<br>  PC Network Broadband Adapter II/A<br>  Dual Asynchronous Adapter/A<br>  Multi-Protocol Adapter/A |

## IBM Hardware

As indicated in Table 5.3, IBM markets a variety of fixed disks that can be installed in the system unit of a PS/2 that uses the Micro Channel bus architecture. One fixed disk, the 60M-byte drive, is designed as a replacement for the original fixed disk drive included with the PS/2 Models 50-021 and 50-031. Some fixed disks, such as the 44M-byte and 70M-byte drives, are designed to work with specific controllers either built into the system board or constructed on an adapter card that was installed in a Micro Channel system expansion slot as standard equipment. Thus, if you want to add more fixed disk storage capacity to your PS/2 computer, verify that the fixed disk drive you are purchasing is supported by the fixed disk controller in your computer.

Two types of optical disk drives are marketed for use with Micro Channel based PS/2 computers—internal and external units. The external drive is similar to that used with PC bus-based PS/2s and requires a controller constructed for use in a Micro Channel system expansion slot. The internal version of the stand-alone IBM Optical Disk Drive is only available for use in the PS/2 Models 60 and 80.

The IBM 3117 Scanner Adapter/A is designed specifically to be installed in a Micro Channel system expansion slot. Similar to the 3117 adapter for PC bus computers, the 3117 Scanner Adapter/A provides the ability to attach an IBM 3117 Scanner to your Micro Channel PS/2 computer.

The 80287 math coprocessor is designed for insertion into the coprocessor socket of the system board of PS/2 computers that use the Intel 80286 microprocessor. The 80287 performs floating-point, extended-integer and binary-coded decimal (BCD) operations. When installed, the coprocessor works in parallel with the 80286 microprocessor and enables your computer system to perform high-speed arithmetic, logarithmic functions, and trigonometric operations. The 80387 math coprocessor performs the same functions as the 80287, but works only with the Intel 80386 microprocessor.

The six memory products listed in Table 5.3 can be classified by their use in 80286 or 80386 computer systems. The 80286 Expanded Memory Adapter/A adds 2M bytes of usable memory to the system board memory of PS/2 computers using the 80286 processor, such as the Models 50 and 60. The 80286 Memory Expansion Option is an adapter card designed for use with PS/2 computers that use the Intel 80286 microprocessor. This adapter card contains 512K bytes of RAM and can be expanded in 512K-byte increments through the use of the 80286 Memory Expansion Kit, up to a total of 2M bytes of RAM. The 80386 Memory Expansion Option is a single full-length card designed for use in the PS/2 Model 70 and Model 80 computers. This card contains 2M bytes of 80-nanosecond RAM and can be expanded to hold a total of 6M bytes of RAM. This expansion is accomplished by the use of the 80386 Memory Expansion Kit, which contains 2M bytes of RAM. The 80386 system board memory expansion kit, as its name implies, is used to expand RAM on the system board. This kit provides 1M byte of 80-nanosecond RAM for the system board of the PS/2 Model 8580-041 computer, bringing total RAM on the system board to 2M bytes.

In addition to the previously mentioned memory products, IBM markets an 80286 Expanded Memory Adapter/A that can hold up to 8M bytes of 16-bit RAM. This board can be populated with several types of memory module kits of varying capacity. Available memory kits for the 80286 Expanded Memory Adapter/A contain 0.5M, 1M, and 2M bytes of 120-nanosecond RAM. Using these memory kits and the Expanded Memory Adapter/A, you can add a total of 8M bytes of RAM into one Micro Channel expansion slot of a PS/2 Model 50, Model 50Z, or Model 60. Up to two adapters can be installed in each computer, for a total memory of up to 16M bytes.

The next four adapter cards listed at the bottom of Table 5.3 perform, in a Micro Channel PS/2, communications functions similar to those performed by the PC bus adapter cards previously described in this chapter. Only the last two adapter cards listed in Table 5.3 perform communications functions that are unique to Micro Channel bus PS/2 computers.

The PS/2 Dual Asynchronous Adapter/A provides two independent serial communications ports on one card. Each port supports asynchronous communications at data rates from 50 to 19,200 bps and can be used to control such devices as an external modem, serial printer, serial plotter, or serial mouse.

The PS/2 Multi-Protocol Adapter/A provides the capability to communicate with a variety of devices that support different communications protocols, one device at a time. Instead of having to install separate adapter cards, you can use the Multi-Protocol Adapter/A card to transmit data using asynchronous, bisynchronous, and HDLC protocols.

## Third Party Hardware

Each PS/2 computer contains one serial and one parallel port built into the system board. Thus, if you wish to attach multiple serial or multiple parallel devices to your computer, you must install an appropriate adapter card that contains circuitry for an additional port or ports.

Although IBM markets an adapter card with dual ports, both ports on the card are asynchronous serial ports. To conserve system expansion slots, if you require an additional serial and parallel port, as well as an expansion of RAM, consider the use of the Quadram Quadboard PS/Q Multifunction Board or a similar third party product. This board is illustrated in Figure 5.6 and is Micro Channel bus compatible, providing the ability to add one parallel and one serial port as well as up to 4M bytes of RAM using one system expansion slot. Similar to IBM memory adapter cards, you can populate the Quadboard PS/Q Multifunction Board using 0.5M-byte or 1M-byte memory kits. Unlike some IBM memory adapter cards whose use is restricted to extended memory, the Quadboard PS/Q's memory is switch-selectable between extended memory and LIM specification expanded memory. This means that you can use the memory on the board under OS/2, or you can use software that supports LIM bank switching to access memory above the DOS 640K-byte barrier.

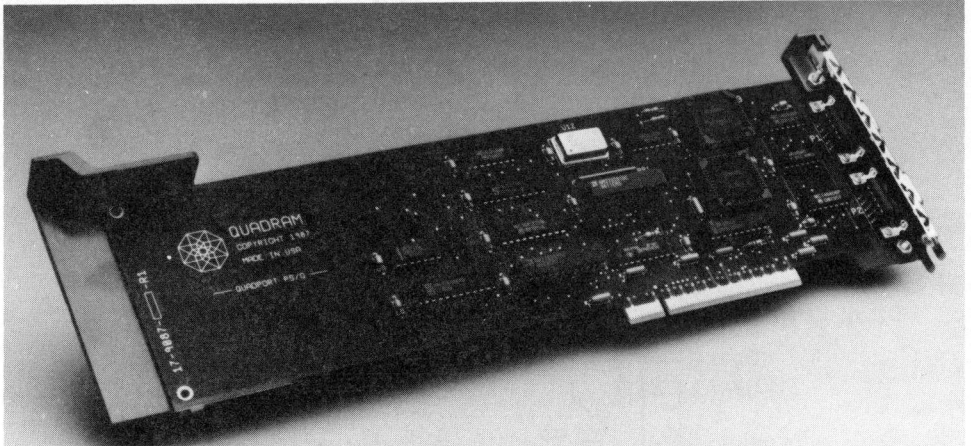

**Figure 5.6** Quadboard PS/Q Multifunction Board—The Quadboard PS/Q Multifunction Board combines one serial and one parallel port and up to 4M bytes of extended or expanded memory using only one Micro Channel expansion slot. *Photograph courtesy of Quadram Corporation.*

For PS/2 users unsure of future requirements, Cumulus Corporation markets a memory adapter that can be upgraded into a multifunction adapter. This vendor's CuRAM 32 can be populated with either 256K-byte or 1M-byte chips to provide 1, 2, 4, or 8M bytes of memory for PS/2 Models 70 and 80 computers. At a later date, PS/2 users can install the vendor's CuRAM Module-SP, a piggyback option module that adds a serial and parallel port to a previously installed CuRAM adapter. In this manner you can use the vendor's CuRAM Module-SP to turn the CuRAM 32 adapter into a multifunction card, adding memory and serial and parallel ports while using only one PS/2 expansion slot.

Two additional PS/2 memory cards that warrant discussion due to their wealth of features are the Tecmar MicroRAM 386 and the AST Research Rampage Plus/MC. The Tecmar MicroRAM 386 can add up to 32M bytes of extended memory and two serial and one parallel port to an IBM PS/2 Model 70 or Model 80. The AST Research Rampage Plus/MC can support up to 8M bytes of memory configured as expanded and extended as well as a variety of optional I/O modules to add one parallel and one serial port or two serial ports in a piggyback arrangement that eliminates the necessity of using another Micro Channel expansion slot.

For power users with large memory requirements, the Tecmar MicroRAM 386 offers a number of expansion options. This board can be populated using 256K-byte, 1M-byte, or 4M-byte Single On-Line Memory Modules (SIMMs), resulting in a total memory board capacity of 2M bytes, 8M bytes, and 32M bytes, respectively.

Figure 5.7 illustrates in schematic diagram format the Tecmar MicroRAM 386 board. This board has two banks that each contain four

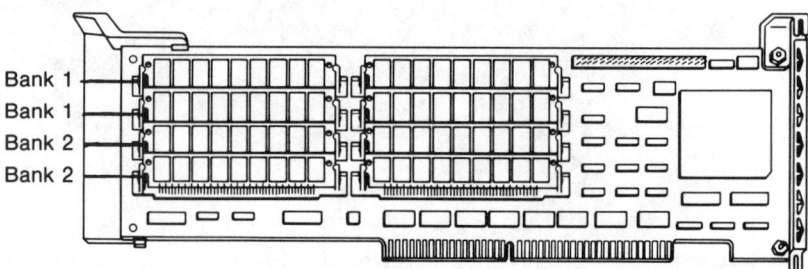

**Figure 5.7** Tecmar MicroRAM 386. *Diagram courtesy of Tecmar, Inc.*

SIMMs. The SIMMs must be installed in sets of four matched types to fill one bank at a time. Note that the configuration of the MicroRAM 386 is such that Bank 1 consists of the top two rows, and Bank 2 consists of the bottom 2 rows of the board. On other memory boards from Tecmar and other vendors that support a lesser amount of memory four individual banks were assigned, with SIMMs being required to be installed in sets of two to fill one bank at a time.

One of the major advantages associated with PS/2 memory boards in comparison to earlier PC computer products is the ease in expanding memory through the use of SIMMs. Unlike conventional memory modules that must be individually installed nine times (8 bits plus parity) to populate a bank, a SIMM module consists of nine prefabricated memory modules grouped into a common housing, as illustrated in Figure 5.8. To install a SIMM, which, in effect, is a grouping of nine memory modules, you first position it so that the metal fingers on the SIMM line up with the wires in the slot on the board and then press the module until it slides into the slot. Once the SIMM is in the board slot, you can simply tilt it toward the rear until chips on each side of the SIMM snap into place.

If our expansion requirements are limited to serial and/or parallel ports, you can consider using one or more of the third party port adapter boards listed in Table 5.4. The parallel and serial port adapter boards each add a single port to your computer and represent a low-cost mechanism to fulfill a single port expansion requirement. The parallel and serial port

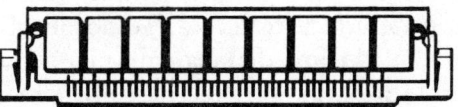

**Figure 5.8** Single In-Line Memory Module—A SIMM is a grouping of nine memory chips in a common housing, which simplifies memory expansion. *Diagram courtesy of Tecmar, Inc.*

**Table 5.4** PS/2 Third Party Port Adapter Boards

| PARALLEL | SERIAL | PARALLEL AND SERIAL |
|---|---|---|
| Parallel Port | Serial Port | Parallel and Serial Port |
| Dual Parallel Port | Quad Serial Port | |

adapter enables you to add both a parallel and a serial port to your Micro Channel PS/2 through the use of one expansion slot. Similarly, the dual parallel port adapter and the quad serial port adapter enable you to add two parallel ports or four serial ports via the use of one expansion slot per adapter.

Because there is a limited amount of mounting space on the rear of an adapter board, you may be curious about how a vendor can manufacture a quad serial port adapter board. Instead of attempting to mount four RS-232 connectors on the bracket at the rear of the board, which would be a physical impossibility, vendors manufacturing a quad serial port adapter install one large connector on the rear of the adapter. Then, a special cable is employed that has a single connector on one end and that terminates four short "pig-tail" cables with individual RS-232 connectors at the end of each pig-tail cable. After connecting one end of the cable to the rear of the adapter board, you can connect each of the four short cables that are terminated with RS-232 connectors to serial devices, in effect obtaining the same capability as if four RS-232 connectors were mounted on the rear of the adapter.

Unlike PC computers that require the use of switches and jumpers to set port addresses, the PS/2 Micro Channel architecture is designed to permit configurations to occur through the use of software. Thus, once you have installed a Micro Channel adapter, you can reconfigure your system by using the IBM Reference Diskette provided with the PS/2 computer and a diskette provided by the manufacturer of the adapter.

Each time a hardware option is added or removed from a PS/2, its configuration must be updated. To accomplish this you normally copy the contents of an option diskette provided by the manufacturer of a PS/2 option onto a backup copy of the IBM Reference Diskette and then select a Set Configuration option when you execute IBM's configuration program. This procedure eliminates the possible occurrence of addressing conflicts as well as setting DIP switches and jumpers.

Anther interesting third party product designed for use with the IBM PS/2 family is the Princeton Graphic Systems MAX-15 autoasynchronous monochrome monitor. This monitor, illustrated in Figure 5.9, has the widest autoasynchronous horizontal and vertical scan range available, which makes it compatible with the IBM PS/2 family, the PC/XT/AT computers, and the Apple Macintosh II. The resolution of the MAX-15 is 1024 by 670 pixels, which provides an outstanding display resolution that can be used to display large "landscape" images when used in conjunction with appropriate software.

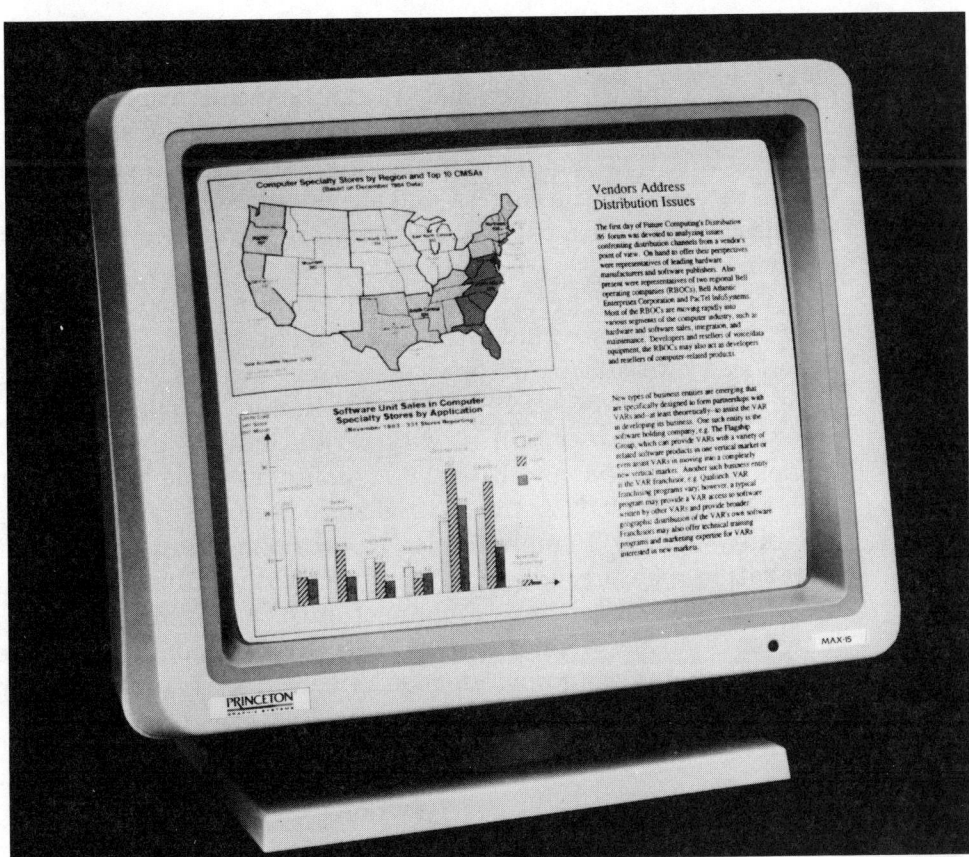

**Figure 5.9** The Princeton Graphics MAX-15 Monitor—This monitor has a resolution of 1024 by 670 pixels, which permits "landscape" images to be displayed. *Photograph courtesy of Princeton Graphics Systems.*

# PS/2 Upgrading

As previously indicated, PS/2 owners have a large variety of IBM and third party products to select from to upgrade their personal computers. Upgrade possibilities include adding memory, installing a tape backup unit, increasing the number of serial and/or parallel ports, or replacing an existing storage device with a larger capacity device. In replacing your fixed disk, take care to examine the controller requirements of the fixed disk you are considering as a replacement. In manufacturing the PS/2, IBM built the disk controller onto the system board of several models, while other models require the use of a fixed disk controller mounted on an adapter card. Each controller is designed to support a specific type or series of disks. Thus, the replacement of one fixed disk by another could result in incompatibility between the disk and the controller unless you verify their compatibility. In situations that require the installation of a disk controller card, you should review both the current and the potential Micro Channel expansion slot usage, because most PS/2 computers have a limited number of expansion slots.

In the area of performance, you may wish to consider the use of a replacement processor mounted on an adapter card. Several vendors have introduced Intel 80386 microprocessors mounted on adapter cards designed to upgrade 80286-based PS/2 Micro Channel computers. Through such processors you can obtain a workstation level of performance on PS/2 Model 50, Model 55, and Model 60 computers while being able to execute both DOS and OS/2 software. Because the only replacement processor capability for PS/2 computers is based upon the use of an adapter, its installation may preclude obtaining some other function based upon the use of an adapter—such as a connection to a Token Ring network or an increase in memory. Thus, review your current and anticipated expansion slot usage against your upgrade requirements that require the use of adapter cards. In some situations you may have to sacrifice one upgrade to obtain another.

CHAPTER 6

## *Printers*

Because a majority of personal computer operations result in the generation of printed output, a printer is one of the most popular hardware options marketed for use with personal computers. The number of types of printers, as well as the differences in the operating characteristics of these devices, provides you with a wide selection of products to consider. Fortunately, the two standard types of printer interfaces are supported by both PC series and PS/2 personal computers, enabling a device purchased for use with one computer series to be easily used with other members of that series or with a machine from a different series.

This chapter focuses on the operational characteristics of several types of popular printers: impact, dot matrix, and laser printers. It also examines several IBM products marketed for use with PCs and PS/2s. Prior to this examination, we will review the methods used to interface printers to a personal computer, including the hardware options you may have to acquire to enable a printer to be connected to your computer. After each printer category is examined, we focus on the key to printer operation—printer control codes. Once we investigate the use of those codes and their use to control two popular printers, we conclude this chapter by creating a BASIC language program to help use a printer more effectively.

## Types of Interface

Most printers are constructed with a parallel interface. This type of interface is designed to accept at the same time all of the bits that form a character. Hence the lines used to transmit data bits from the computer to the printer are routed in parallel in a cable connecting the two devices. The second type of printer interface is designed to accept data bits on one line, in a serial sequence. Thus, this type of interface is called a *serial interface*.

To use a parallel interface printer with a member of the PC series, you make a cable connection from the printer to a parallel port on the computer. The parallel port is obtained by installing a parallel printer adapter card or another type of card, such as a video display or multifunction card that includes a parallel port. Similarly, to use a serial interface printer you cable that printer to a serial port. The most common types of serial ports are obtained through the use of an asynchronous communications adapter and the serial port included on many multifunction cards. Like the parallel port, to use a serial port you install an adapter card in a PC series computer.

If you are connecting a printer to a member of the PS/2 family, the installation of an adapter card in your computer may not be required to operate a printer. This is because each member of the PS/2 family contains a built-in serial and parallel port whose connectors are located at the rear of the system unit. Only if you previously used a port for another serial or parallel device must you use an adapter card or a multifunction card to obtain the necessary port for your printer.

## Printer Type Formation

The most common method of printer categorization is by the method used for type formation. The three most popular methods of type formation are impact, dot matrix, and toner bonding.

### Impact Printers

An impact printer uses a rotating wheel or a similar functioning mechanism to position a character between a hammer and the printer's ribbon. The hammer strikes the wheel's character, which is pressed onto the ribbon, resulting in a solid image of the character being printed. Because the use of an impact printer results in the generation of a solid, preformed image, type quality is dependent on the clarity of the symbols on the printwheel or another print mechanism. In general, impact printers produce superior character images to most dot matrix and many laser printers. However, because the output of an impact printer is based on preformed symbols, its graphics capability is limited to block graphics, such as half-squares, triangles, and similar symbols that may be included on a printwheel.

Key selection characteristics for impact printers include their interface, the character set supported, the availability of a sheet feeder, the character set available for printwheels, and their carriage width. Some printwheels may include both pica and a second type, enabling you to send a code to the printer to select the appropriate type to be used for printing a letter. Other printers may require you to physically change a printwheel.

If you plan to use a sheet feeder, prior to purchasing one you should ensure that the software you intend to use—such as a word processing program—supports its use. Similarly, the support of different printwheels should be verified, because some vendors manufacture a large variety of printwheels that your software does not support.

Due to the relatively slow printing speed of impact printers and their inability to generate graphics, their use is primarily relegated to banks, law firms, and other organizations that require high-quality correspondence.

## Dot Matrix Printers

In a dot matrix printer, a printhead consisting of a matrix of pins is used to form characters. A microprocessor in the printer "fires" individual pins that hit the ribbon to form each character, normally resulting in a slight space between pin imprints. Because individual pins can be fired, a dot matrix printer is capable of printing graphic images.

Dot matrix printers are commonly manufactured with 9-, 18-, and 24-wire printheads, with most printers manufactured after 1985 designed to provide a near letter quality (NLQ) print mode of operation. Printers with a 9-wire printhead typically perform NLQ printing by moving the printhead across the paper in one direction as it fires its pins, then moving the paper a fraction of an inch prior to the printhead firing pins across the paper in the opposite direction to repeat the row of characters. By printing in this manner, the spaces between the dots formed by the pins in the printhead are either reduced or eliminated.

Printers with 18- or 24-wire printheads either rely on the higher density of pins to achieve NLQ printing or print each line twice, similar to the method 9-pin printers use for NLQ printing. As you might infer, a 24-wire printhead normally produces a superior NLQ type to that obtainable through an 18- or 9-wire printhead. This is because the pins in a 24-wire printhead are finer than those on a 9- or 18-wire printhead, with less space between pins. Due to improvements in NLQ printing technology, dot matrix printer sales significantly exceed the sale of impact printers.

## IBM Printers

IBM manufactures numerous dot matrix printers that can be used with personal computers. Here we examine two of that firm's more popular printers—the Proprinter and Quietwriter.

### The Proprinter Series

The IBM Proprinter II illustrated in Figure 6.1 is a low-priced printer intended for low to medium printing volumes. This printer has a 9-wire printhead and can print acceptable quality characters in its NLQ print mode.

The Proprinter II can be set to print at one of four speeds. In its "Fastfont" mode, it can print as many as 240 characters per second (cps). In its DP mode, it can print as many as 200 cps, and in its emphasized print mode, the printing rate drops to 120 cps. Finally, when placed in its NLQ print mode of operation, the Proprinter II's maximum print rate is 40 cps.

Perhaps the most interesting feature of IBM Proprinters is their ability to accept envelopes or single-sheet paper without requiring you to remove continuous form paper. This is accomplished by inserting an envelope or a single sheet of paper end-up into the front slot in the printer. Then, by pressing the line feed button you can align the envelope or single sheet of paper properly.

There are several other members of the IBM Proprinter series that warrant discussion. The Proprinter XL is similar to the Proprinter II but has a wide carriage that enables you to print spreadsheets or charts as

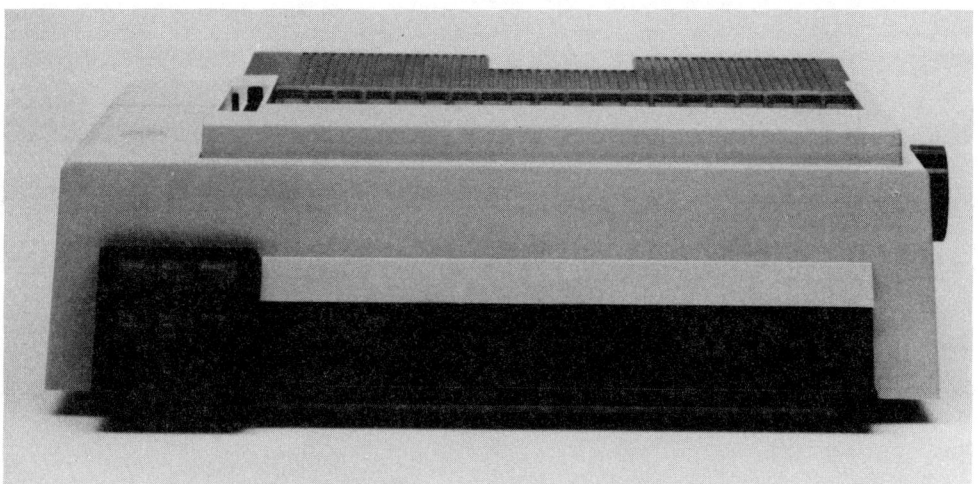

**Figure 6.1** IBM Proprinter II. *Photograph courtesy of IBM Corporation.*

wide as 13.6 inches, in comparison to the 11-inch-paper width limitation of the Proprinter II. Three other members of the Proprinter series are the Proprinter X24, the Proprinter XL24, and the Proprinter X24E. Each of these printers uses a 24-wire printhead, which results in a crisper, sharper NLQ print.

Two of the more interesting features of most Proprinters are their control panel and ability to support an optional sheet feeder. Figure 6.2 illustrates an IBM Proprinter X24 with a sheet feeder installed. Note the control panel at the left of the printer, which contains the button labeled Ltr Q. Pressing this button places the printer into its NLQ print mode, alleviating the necessity of transmitting a control code to the printer to perform the same operation. Newer Proprinters, such as the X24E, contain a button labeled Propark, which can be used to automatically position envelopes and letterhead paper inserted into the front slot of the printer.

## IBM Quietwriter

The IBM Quietwriter series of printers is designed for use in an office environment where a requirement exists for executive letter quality production in a quiet environment.

The key to the silence and print quality of the Quietwriter is the use of resistive ribbon thermal transfer technology in each printer. Unlike the

**Figure 6.2** IBM Proprinter X24 with Sheet Feeder—The IBM Proprinter X24 supports the use of an optional sheet feeder. *Photograph courtesy of IBM Corporation.*

impact of pins hitting a ribbon in a dot matrix printer, the resistive ribbon thermal transfer technology uses an electric current applied to selective pins in a dot matrix to melt portions of the ribbon onto the paper. As a result of using electricity instead of the physical impact of pins on a ribbon, the Quietwriter's noise level is significantly less than a conventional dot matrix printer, and its print image is improved.

Figure 6.3 illustrates the IBM Quietwriter III printer, the third IBM printer to use resistive ribbon thermal transfer technology. Similar to a Proprinter, the Quietwriter III has an all points addressable (APA) graphics printing capability. The APA resolution of the Quietwriter is 240 by 240 dots per inch, in comparison to a maximum resolution of 180 vertical by 360 horizontal dots per inch on the Proprinter X24 and XL24. For

**Figure 6.3** IBM Quietwriter III Printer. *Photograph courtesy of IBM Corporation.*

comparison purposes, note that the maximum resolution of the most common type of laser printer is 300 by 300 dots per inch.

## Dot Matrix Printer Selection Factors

Due to the immense popularity of dot matrix printers, a summary of key selection factors is presented in Table 6.1. Here you would enter the character-per-second (cps) print rates applicable to your requirements. Although many of the entries in this table are self-explanatory, several entries deserve a more detailed discussion of the operational characteristics of dot matrix printers.

Although a comparison of print speeds between devices measured in characters per second may appear to be an easy task to perform, be aware that some vendors cite their highest rate when, as an example, the speed of proportional and pica printing differ. Thus, for a meaningful comparison you should compare the print rates for both the same print modes and print types. Concerning printer emulation, the IBM Graphics printer originally marketed with the IBM PC series was manufactured by Epson. This printer was built to respond to predefined printer control codes in order to generate bold, underlined, and italic characters as well as to print graphics. Because many word processing programs were originally developed to support printing on that printer, many vendors included an IBM Graphics

**Table 6.1** Dot Matrix Printer Selection Factors

| FEATURE | DETAILS |
|---|---|
| Print speed | Draft print speed rate _____ cps<br>NLQ print speed rate _____ cps |
| Printer emulation | IBM graphics printer<br>Other |
| Print head and print matrix | Print head 9-, 18-, or 24-wire<br>Print matrix: nlq, graphics, proportional |
| Characters per line | |
| Graphics resolution in dots per inch | |
| Character font support | Built-in<br>Obtainable via cartridge |
| Character type support | Bold<br>Underline<br>Super/subscript<br>Italics<br>Overscore<br>Double width<br>Double strike |
| Line spacing | 1/6, 1/8, n/x inches |
| Front panel controls | Pitch<br>Font selection<br>Line spacing<br>Page length<br>Margins |
| Paper entry/parking method | Top, bottom, rear |
| Paper feed method | Friction<br>Push tractor |
| Number of printable copies | |
| Character set support | |
| Buffer size in K bytes | |
| Interface | Parallel or serial |
| Dimensions | |

printer emulation capability in their printers. Although this feature used to be very important, most major programs include a variety of printer drivers that may support the full capability of a hundred or more printers. Thus, this feature may be more important when you are purchasing a printer for use with an existing system than when you purchase a new system. Refer to the last section of this chapter for a detailed discussion of printer control codes.

Although a greater number of wires on the printhead normally provides a better print quality, you should also examine the print matrix used for different printing, such as draft, NLQ, and proportional. As an example, some printers use a 7 by 9 print matrix for draft printing, whereas other printers use a 9 by 9 print matrix.

The number of characters per line depends on the carriage width of the printer as well as the type of printing. As an example, an 80-column printer normally prints 80 characters using Pica type and 96 characters using Elite, whereas 136 or 137 characters might be printed in the printer's condensed print mode. Similarly, a 136-column printer that normally supports printing of 136 characters per line using Pica type will probably support 163 characters in Elite and 233 characters in a condensed or compressed print mode.

One of the more important dot matrix printer features unfortunately not considered by many users is the printer's page entry method. Many printers now incorporate a mechanism that allows envelopes and single sheet stationery to be printed without first having to remove continuous form paper. Many printer manufacturers reference this capability as *paper parking*. To accomplish paper parking, a variety of paper entry mechanisms are used by printer manufacturers, including slots in the front, top, and rear of their printers.

The buffers built into most dot matrix printers range in size from 2K bytes or less to 64K bytes or more. With a printer buffer, you can issue a print command and have the data to be printed first sent electronically into the buffer. Data in the buffer is then printed at the printer's lower mechanical speed. If the size of the printer buffer exceeds the size of the file to be printed, you can perform another function or operate a different program while the printer is operating, because all the data to be printed has been transmitted into the buffer. Even when the file size exceeds the size of the printer buffer, the size of the buffer may accommodate a significant portion of the file, permitting you to resume the use of your computer for other activities sooner than if your printer had no buffer or a smaller size buffer.

## Laser Printers

A laser printer can be considered a close relative of the photocopier. Both devices use a toner powder to form an image on paper. Two key components of a laser printer include its print engine and controller. The print engine contains a series of evenly spaced parallel lines contained on a photosensitive drum. A light source—which is usually a laser but can also be a light emitting diode—is used to charge areas on the drum. This electrical charge attracts toner grains as the drum rotates past a toner compartment. As the drum continues to rotate, an electrically charged wire attracts the toner from the drum onto paper that is fed through the laser while a heated roller brush is used to fuse the toner onto the paper. A second wire in the engine neutralizes the drum's electrical charge, enabling it to be written to as it rotates back under the light source.

The resolution of a laser depends on the spacing of the parallel lines in its engine, with a smaller spacing providing a higher resolution. Most laser printers have a 300 dot per inch resolution; however, a few printers available for use with personal computers have a resolution of 400 dots per inch.

The controller of a laser printer, unlike the controllers used with most on-line storage devices, is housed within the printer instead of manufactured as an adapter for installation in the system unit of a personal computer. This design enables you to simply cable the serial or parallel port of your computer to the laser printer, depending on whether the printer has a serial or parallel interface. The key function of the controller is to generate print, which includes building the fonts and print sizes supported by the printer. Some controllers generate fonts based on bitmap images, in which each font is described as a series of bits. Other controllers are capable of generating fonts based on mathematical formulas that describe the fonts as a series of lines and curves. The latter type of font is scalable and is referred to as an *outline*, because it can be filled with a variety of patterns or printed using different graphic effects.

Printers that use bitmapped fonts, in effect, design each character on a bit-by-bit basis by arranging the bits or dots into patterns. Unfortunately, when you enlarge or shrink a bitmapped character its edges become ragged. Thus, the only method to obtain smoothly formed characters is to purchase a different font for each font size you intend to use.

Laser printers that support outline fonts store characters as mathematical formulas. This enables the outline for each character to be expanded or contracted without ragged edges. As you can imagine, a scalable font provides you, in effect, with an infinite number of sizes, whereas you can only obtain one typeface in one size when you use a bitmapped font.

Adobe was among the first companies to develop scalable fonts for laser printers. The firm's scalable fonts are marketed under the term *PostScript,* with the term *PostScript printer* referencing the fact that a laser printer manufacturer includes a variety of Adobe's typescripts that enable you to print any size character from each typescript.

Because each laser printer supports a limited number of fonts, you must acquire cartridges, adapter cards that you install in the printer, or software to obtain the capability of printing different fonts.

Table 6.2 lists some of the factors you may wish to consider prior to selecting a laser printer. Although most of the entries in that table are self-explanatory, the emulation support entry warrants elaboration. The most popular laser printers are the LaserJet series, manufactured by Hewlett-Packard. This type of printer is controlled by a set of commands that form the HP Printer Command Language. Many programs were written to support the use of the HP LaserJet, so other laser printer vendors that

**Table 6.2** Laser Printer Selection Factors

| FACTOR | DETAILS |
|---|---|
| Interface | Serial, parallel, or both |
| Resolution in dots per inch | |
| Print speed in pages per minute | |
| Rated engine life in pages | |
| Pages between replacement of toner | |
| Number of built-in fonts and type | |
| Ability to accept font cartridges | |
| Standard RAM and expansion ability | |
| Number of paper trays | |
| Paper tray capacity | |
| Maximum paper size | |
| Optional accessories | |
| Emulations supported | HP LaserJet<br>Other |

offer an HP Printer Command Language (PCL) emulation capability can be used with existing programs that were developed to work with the LaserJet. Refer to the next section for information concerning the HP Printer Command Language.

# Printer Control Codes

Printer control codes are individual characters or strings of characters that are transmitted to a printer to enable or disable predefined printing features. To differentiate between data to be printed and control codes, printers either contain circuitry that examines American Standard Code for Information Interchange (ASCII) characters received, or a microprocessor and read only memory (ROM) code that performs a similar function.

Among the more common printer control codes are several ASCII characters whose decimal values are less than 32. When the ASCII character set was defined, all characters with a decimal value of 32 or less were assigned to nonprintable functions. These functions included ringing a terminal's bell (ASCII 7), performing a backspace (ASCII 8), tabbing horizontally (ASCII 9), and so on. Although the ASCII character set was defined decades prior to the manufacture of printers for use with personal computers, many of the nonprintable control codes of the character set are used by modern printers. Table 6.3 lists the nonprintable ASCII control codes and the function they perform when received by a dot matrix printer.

Several entries in Table 6.3 warrant an explanation. First, the ASCII Code column lists the mnemonics for each ASCII character. Although some are self-explanatory—such as LF for line feed—others—such as SO, SI, and DC1 through DC4—are probably not recognizable unless you are familiar with the ASCII character set. SO is the mnemonic for Shift Out, which in communications is used to select a new character set. Similarly, SI is the mnemonic for Shift In, which in communications is used to restore the original character set used. When dot matrix printers were developed, manufacturers selected SO as the control code to initiate one line of double-width printing, whereas SI was selected as the control code to select condensed printing.

The DC1 through DC4 ASCII control characters are mnemonics for Device Control 1 through Device Control 4. When the ASCII character set was originally defined, most terminals were electromechanical teleprinters that could be interfaced to paper-tape readers and punches, cassettes, and other off-line storage devices. Originally, DC1 through DC4

**Table 6.3** Nonprintable ASCII Control Codes

| ASCII CODE | DECIMAL VALUE | FUNCTION |
|---|---|---|
| NUL | 00 | Null character |
| BEL | 07 | Sound beeper |
| BS | 08 | Backspace |
| HT | 09 | Horizontal tab |
| LF | 10 | Line feed |
| VT | 11 | Vertical tab |
| FF | 12 | Form feed |
| CR | 13 | Carriage return |
| SO | 14 | Select double-width printing (one line) |
| SI | 15 | Select condensed printing |
| DC1 | 17 | Select printer |
| DC2 | 18 | Cancel condensed mode |
| DC3 | 19 | Deselect printer |
| DC4 | 20 | Cancel double-width printing (one line) |
| CAN | 24 | Cancel |
| ESC | 27 | Escape |
| SP | 32 | Space |

control codes were designed to activate such devices. With the development of more modern printers, the DC1 through DC4 control codes were reserved to perform the functions indicated in Table 6.3.

Although most of the ASCII control codes listed in Table 6.3 will work with all types of dot matrix printers, there are some exceptions. Among the major exceptions are the control codes that select and cancel double-width and condensed-mode printing. Double-width printing results in the printing of characters twice the width of a normal character, whereas condensed-mode printing causes characters to be printed at about 60 percent of their normal width. Both of these print modes are only applicable to dot matrix printers that have a printhead containing pins that are activated in correspondence to the print mode selected. If you have a letter quality printer, its print pattern is fixed. Thus, the transmission of control codes to vary the print mode is either ignored by a letter quality printer or produces unexpected results.

Because the IBM personal computers use extended ASCII, you can add 128 to each of the decimal values listed in Table 6.3 to perform the listed functions. This occurs because the eighth bit position of an 8-bit extended ASCII character is ignored by most ASCII printers that support characters whose values range from 0 through 127. Thus, ASCII 07 or ASCII 135 could, as an example, be sent to a printer to sound its beeper.

## Escape Sequences

Because most modern dot matrix printers are built to perform a large number of functions, a logical question is how those functions can be activated if ASCII 33 through 127 are printable characters that represent data. The answer is by using escape sequences that printers are constructed to interpret.

An escape sequence begins with the ASCII ESC character, whose decimal value is 27. The ESC character is then followed by one or two alphanumeric character codes that define the print function to perform. To illustrate the similarities and differences that can exist among escape codes recognized by printers, the IBM Proprinter and Epson LQ-850/1050 printers were examined. Table 6.4 lists common escape code sequences recognized by each printer. As you read the entries in Table 6.4, note that although the operations performed by each printer are similar for many escape code sequences, there are also differences. Most of these differences concern the physical construction of the printer, such as each one's tolerance for incrementing line spacing. Other differences between these two printers, as well as most dot matrix printers, concern the character sets supported. Some printers have several built-in character sets that are also known as *fonts*. Other printers are designed to accept one or more font cartridges that contain ROM, which defines how each character will be printed. When you use a printer that has two or more built-in character sets or that supports font cartridges, you must either send an appropriate code to the printer to select the desired character set or press a button on the printer's control panel.

Due to the subtle but important differences between escape code sequences printers are built to recognize, several software firms that develop printer drivers sold to word processing software developers have found a

**Table 6.4** Common Escape Code Sequences

| CODE | DECIMAL VALUES | DESCRIPTION | PRINTER |
|---|---|---|---|
| ESC 0 | 27 48 | Select 1/8-inch line spacing | Both |
| ESC 1 | 27 49 | Select 7/72-inch line spacing | IBM |
| ESC 2 | 27 50 | Start text line spacing set by ESC A | IBM |
| ESC 2 | 27 50 | Select 1/6-inch line spacing | Epson |
| ESC 3 n | 27 51 n | Graphics line spacing (n/216 inch) | IBM |
| ESC 3 n | 27 51 n | Graphics line spacing (n/180 inch) | Epson |
| ESC 4 | 27 52 | Set top of form | IBM |
| ESC 4 | 27 52 | Select italic mode | Epson |
| ESC 5 n | 27 53 n | Automatic line feed (1=on,0=off) | IBM |
| ESC 5 | 27 53 | Cancel italic mode | Epson |
| ESC 6 | 27 54 | Select character set 2 | IBM |
| ESC 6 | 27 54 | Enable printable characters | Epson |
| ESC 7 | 27 55 | Select character set 1 | IBM |
| ESC 7 | 27 55 | Enable upper control codes | Epson |
| ESC : | 27 58 | 12 CPI printing | IBM |
| ESC : | 27 58 | Copy ROM to RAM | Epson |
| ESC A n | 27 65 n | Select n/72-inch line spacing | IBM |
| ESC A n | 27 65 n | Select n/60-inch line spacing | Epson |
| ESC B n..n | 27 66 n..n | Set vertical tabs n..n | Both |
| ESC C n | 27 67 n | Set form length (n lines) | Both |
| ESC C 0 n | 27 67 0 n | Set form length (n inches) | Both |
| ESC D n..n | 27 68 n..n | Set horizontal tabs n..n | Both |
| ESC E | 27 69 | Start emphasized printing | Both |
| ESC F | 27 70 | Cancel emphasized printing | Both |
| ESC G | 27 71 | Start double-strike printing | Both |
| ESC H | 27 72 | Cancel double-strike printing | Both |

significant market for their products. Although most word processing programs support a wide range of printers, they do not support *all* printers. Thus, by knowing how to send control codes to your printer you may be able to use your printer to perform certain functions the word processor or other application program you are using does not support.

## HP Printer Command Language

The Hewlett-Packard LaserJet Printer Command Language is similar in construction to most dot matrix printer control languages. Each command begins with the ESC character (ASCII 27) followed by either one or two characters, numerical data, and a terminating letter. All letters in a command string with the exception of the terminating letter are in lowercase. The last letter in a command string must be a capital letter, which both further defines the function to be performed and serves to inform the printer that the command has ended. Refer to the *Hewlett-Packard Technical Reference Manual* for the LaserJet for specific information covering the Printer Command Language codes and the specific functions each code performs. Knowing those codes you can use the information presented in the next section to control your laser printer with a BASIC language program.

## Control via BASIC

Because BASIC is provided on each DOS diskette, it's convenient for you to examine the control of the operation of your printer using that language. Here the key to controlling printer functions is the BASIC LPRINT statement and the CHR$ function.

## LPRINT Statement

The LPRINT statement provides you with the ability to print information under program control. The format of this statement is

```
LPRINT [list of expressions]      {[;]}
                                  {[,]}
```

The expressions listed in an LPRINT statement may be numeric or string; however, string constants must be enclosed in quotation marks or they are considered to be variables.

If a semicolon (;) is used as an item separator, the value of the next item is printed directly after the previous item. If you use a comma (,) as an item separator, the value of each item is placed into predefined positions called *print zones*. IBM BASIC is similar to most BASIC implementations in that a print line is divided into six print zones. If more than six items are in the list of expressions and you are using commas as separators, the values of the seventh through twelfth items will be printed on the next line in zones 1 through 6, and so on. If you terminate an LPRINT statement without a comma or semicolon, BASIC automatically generates a carriage return and line feed. Then, the next LPRINT statement prints the next chunk of information on a new line. If you include a comma or semicolon at the end of the LPRINT statement, the carriage return and line feed are suppressed, and the next LPRINT statement prints information on the same line.

## CHR$ Function

The CHR$ function can be used in an LPRINT statement to send the ASCII character represented by the decimal value contained in the function to the printer. When you use it in an LPRINT statement, the format of the CHR$ function is

```
CHR$(expression)
```

The expression can be a decimal number or a mathematical expression that BASIC evaluates. Because IBM personal computers use an extended ASCII character set in which each character is represented by 8 bits, the expression can range in value from 0 to 255.

Now that you have reviewed printer control codes, the BASIC LPRINT statement, and the CHR$ function, try actually creating some small program segments to demonstrate how to operate some printer functions under program control. Suppose you have a dot matrix printer that is capable of NLQ printing but that cannot be placed into that printing mode by a switch or button on the control panel of the printer. If your word processor does not support the NLQ printing mode of your printer, you can still use this capability by creating a small BASIC program to set that print mode. Then you can use the program each time you power on your computer to set your printer to its NLQ print mode.

If you have an IBM Proprinter I, that printer's NLQ print mode is also called double-strike printing. Using Table 6.4, you can determine that the Proprinter requires ESC G (decimal 27 71) to switch to its NLQ print mode. You could send this code sequence to your printer by executing the following LPRINT statement, which uses line number 100 for reference because each BASIC line requires a line number.

```
100 LPRINT CHR$(27) CHR$(71)
```

To print in NLQ print mode on a regular basis, you can avoid repeatedly entering and executing the LPRINT statement by creating a small file. If you want to execute a non-BASIC application after you set the NLQ print mode of your printer, you can add a second line, so your program looks like

```
100 LPRINT CHR$(27) CHR$(71)
110 SYSTEM
```

Here the BASIC SYSTEM command causes the program to exit back to DOS. Now that you have created the two-line BASIC program, assume you saved it, using the name NLQ.BAS. By typing SYSTEM without a line number you can exit BASIC and return to DOS. Now you can create a short batch file that automatically executes the previously created NLQ.BAS program. The batch file, named NLQ.BAS here, consists of

```
COPY CON: NLQ.BAT
BASICA NLQ.BAS
^Z
```

The batch file simply executes advanced BASIC (BASICA) using the previously created NLQ.BAS program file as input. The BASIC NLQ program file then sends an ESC G printer control sequence to your printer, placing it into its NLQ printing mode of operation. Once you have created the NLQ.BAS and NLQ.BAT files, you can simply enter the command NLQ at the DOS prompt, assuming your current directory is the directory that contains the NLQ.BAT file. Thus, each time you want to use your printer's NLQ print mode, you can power on your printer and computer and enter the batch command NLQ.

## Expanded Printer Control

Upon occasion you may want the ability to control specific features of your printer. You can develop a BASIC program that provides an easy mechanism to set and reset desired printer features.

This section provides an example of the use of the BASIC language to control a printer's mode of operation. You will see how to create a small program to control double-width, condensed, emphasized, and double-strike printing on both an IBM Proprinter and an Epson LQ-850/1050 printer.

Based on the control codes listed in Tables 6.3 and 6.4, there are four 1-character control codes and four 2-character control code sequences that must be transmitted to either printer to enable and disable the four desired printer modes of operation. Table 6.5 summarizes the control codes as BASIC CHR$ functions that must be incorporated into LPRINT statements. The following listing is a short BASIC program that controls the four printing modes.

```
100 CLS
110 PRINT "*** PRINTER SETUP UTILITY ***"
120 PRINT
130 PRINT " 1-Start double width"
140 PRINT " 2-Cancel double width"
150 PRINT " 3-Start condensed"
160 PRINT " 4-Cancel condensed"
170 PRINT " 5-Start emphasized"
180 PRINT " 6-Cancel emphasized"
190 PRINT " 7-Start double strike"
200 PRINT " 8-Cancel double strike"
210 PRINT " 9-Exit to DOS"
220 PRINT
230 INPUT "Enter selection 1 to 9";X
240 ON X GOTO 310,320,330,340,350,360,370,380,390
310 LPRINT CHR$(14);
315 GOTO 100
320 LPRINT CHR$(20);
325 GOTO 100
330 LPRINT CHR$(15);
335 GOTO 100
340 LPRINT CHR$(18);
345 GOTO 100
350 LPRINT CHR$(27) CHR$(69);
355 GOTO 100
360 LPRINT CHR$(27) CHR$(70);
```

```
365 GOTO 100
370 LPRINT CHR$(27) CHR$(71);
375 GOTO 100
380 LPRINT CHR$(27) CHR$(72);
385 GOTO 100
390 SYSTEM
```

Line 100 of the program clears the display screen. Lines 110 through 220 display the selection menu and the numeric code you enter to start or cancel one of the four printing modes or to exit BASIC to DOS. The INPUT statement in line 230 displays the message Enter selection 1 to 9 and then assigns the numeric value entered to the variable X.

In line 240 the ON-GOTO conditional branching statement causes execution to branch to the appropriate line among those shown in the statement, based on the value of the X variable. That is, if X has a value of 1, a branch to line 310 occurs; if X has a value of 2, a branch to line 320 occurs; and so on. Each branch location uses an LPRINT statement with the CHR$ function to transmit the appropriate printer control code to the printer.

Although the program only controls four printing modes, you can easily add additional printing modes following the same logic. You may have other types of printers than the IBM Proprinter or the Epson LQ-850/1050 printer, and if so, you should review your printer manual to determine the control codes required to perform any printer control functions you may require. Then you can develop a program similar to the one just listed to control the printer modes of operation you require.

Table 6.5 CHR$ Functions for Selected Printer Modes

| PRINTER MODE OF OPERATION | BASIC CHR$ FUNCTION |
|---|---|
| Start double width | CHR$(14) |
| Cancel double width | CHR$(20) |
| Start condensed | CHR$(15) |
| Cancel condensed | CHR$(18) |
| Start emphasized | CHR$(27) CHR$(69) |
| Cancel emphasized | CHR$(27) CHR$(70) |
| Start double strike | CHR$(27) CHR$(71) |
| Cancel double strike | CHR$(27) CHR$(72) |

CHAPTER 7

# Modem Installation, Operation, and Selection Considerations

The purpose of this chapter is threefold. First, we will examine the process by which modems are either directly installed in the system unit of a personal computer or connected via a cable to a serial port of the computer. In examining serial ports, we will investigate the addition of hardware to obtain a serial port capability if your computer either lacks this feature or an existing serial port is being used to support a previously acquired device. Second, we will focus on the modulation process to obtain a basic understanding of the method by which modems convey information. Third, because the modulation process is only one of three technological areas that must be considered to ensure compatibility among products, we will also discuss methods by which modems detect and correct errors and compress data. In addition, because the command set of a modem is its key for supporting "intelligent" operations under the control of a computer, we will examine the Hayes Microcomputer Products modem command set in this chapter. To conclude the chapter, we will summarize the previously presented information in key selection factors to consider before you purchase a modem.

## PC Series System Unit

The system unit of each member of the IBM PC series is similar to the others in many respects. Once the cover of the system unit is removed, a series of expansion slots becomes visible in the upper left-hand portion of the unit. The functionality of one's PC, including communications support, is obtained by installing various adapter boards in these expansion slots.

The procedures required to remove the system unit covers of IBM PCs, PC XTs, and PC ATs are very similar. Regardless of the personal computer model you have, prior to disassembling any equipment you should ensure that the power switch of the system unit and any externally connected devices are off. Then, you should unplug the system unit power cable from the wall outlet and disconnect any cables from the rear of the system unit that will interfere with the removal of the cover of the unit. As an example, if an IBM monochrome display is connected to your system unit, you will have to move the display prior to removing the system unit cover. To move the monochrome display, you disconnect the display's power cable connected to the system unit, as well as the cable connector that attaches the display to the monochrome display and parallel printer adapter previously installed in your system unit.

Figure 7.1 illustrates the preliminary steps required to remove the system unit cover of an IBM PC. Note that the keyboard connector should only be removed if the keyboard is relocated more than six feet from the PC or PC XT to obtain space to remove the system unit cover. If you have a PC AT, its longer keyboard cable may permit you to easily relocate the keyboard without disconnecting the keyboard connector from the system unit.

After you have positioned the system unit to allow access to its rear panel, remove the cover mounting screws that fasten the cover to the system unit. Early versions of the IBM PC used two screws to fasten their system unit cover to the system unit. One screw was located in each of the lower left- and right-hand corners on the rear of the system unit. PCs manufactured after mid-1982, as well as all PC XTs and PC ATs, have five cover-mounting screws fastening the cover to the system unit. As illustrated in Figure 7.2, these screws can be removed using a flat-blade screwdriver, turning the screwdriver in a counterclockwise direction.

Once the screws holding the system unit cover are removed, simply lift off the cover.

If you have a PC or PC XT, first slide the system unit cover away from the rear, as illustrated in Figure 7.3. When the cover will go no further,

Modem Installation, Operation, and Selection Considerations **235**

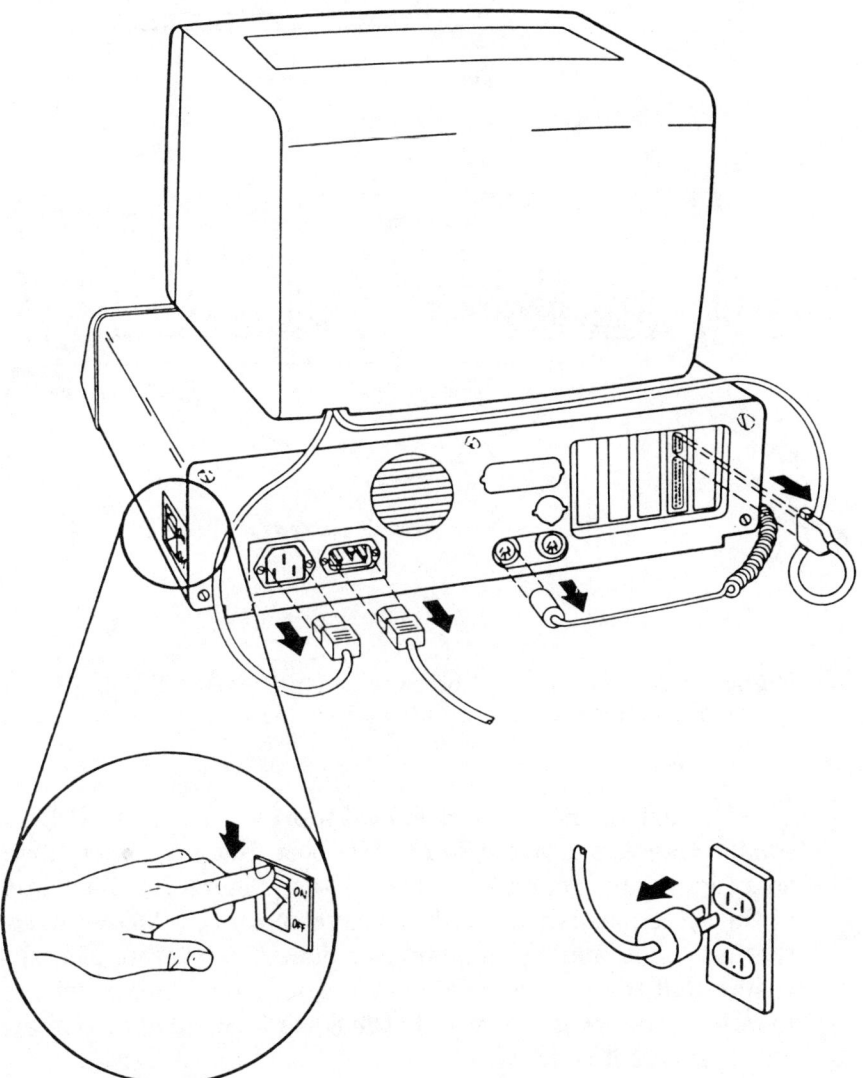

**Figure 7.1** Preparing to Remove the System Unit Cover—Before you remove the system unit cover, ensure that all power cables are disconnected and the power switch is off.

tilt it up at approximately a 15-degree angle and lift it away from the base of the system unit. If you have a PC AT, you only have to slide the cover directly away from the rear, as illustrated in Figure 7.3.

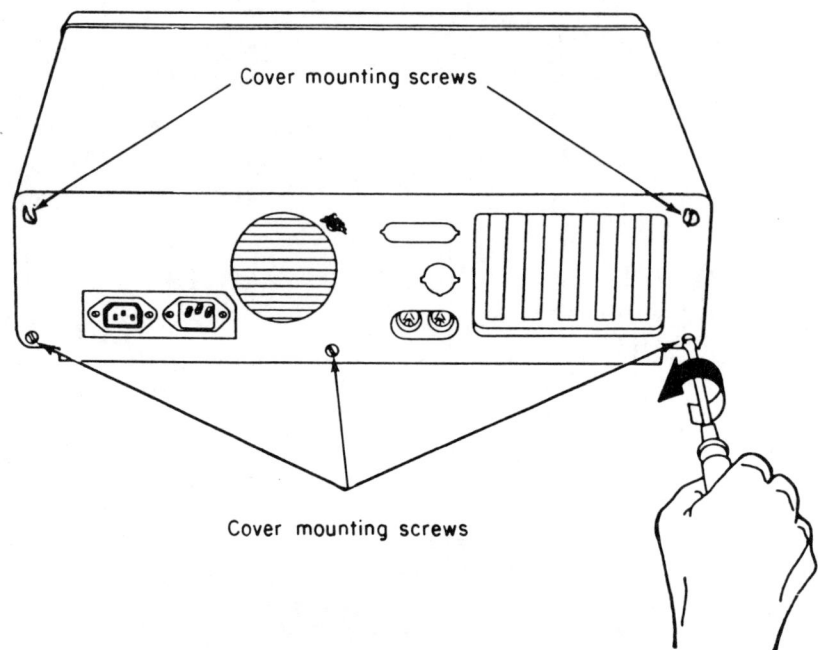

**Figure 7.2** Unfastening the System Unit Cover—Turning the cover mounting screws counterclockwise will unfasten the cover of the system unit.

Similar to the PC series, desktop models in the PS/2 family of personal computers have a system unit cover that you remove prior to installing adapters in its system expansion slots. Figure 7.4 illustrates the removal of the system expansion unit cover from a PS/2 Model 50 computer. Note that after you unplug all computer power cords from electrical outlets and ensure that the cover lock is unlocked, you must loosen the two cover screws to remove the cover. Then slide the cover forward approximately two inches and then lift it upward.

Just as with the PC series, most desktop members of the PS/2 family of personal computers have their system expansion slots located at the left rear of the system unit, with each expansion slot mounted vertically onto the system board. The primary exception to this method of expansion slot structure is the PS/2 Model 30, which has three horizontal expansion slots as previously described in Chapter 2.

One major difference between the IBM PC and the PC XT and PC AT is the number of system expansion slots. The PC has five system expansion slots; the PC XT and the PC AT each have eight. The PS/2

Modem Installation, Operation, and Selection Considerations  **237**

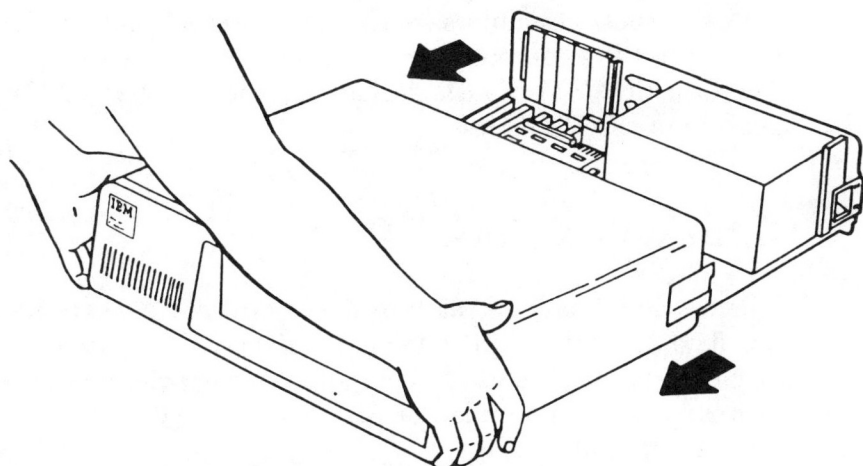

**Figure 7.3** Removing the System Unit Cover—If you have a PC or PC XT, slide the cover away from the rear until it will go no further. Then, tilt the cover up at a 15-degree angle to remove it from the base of the system unit. If you have a PC AT, you only have to slide the cover away from the rear of the system unit.

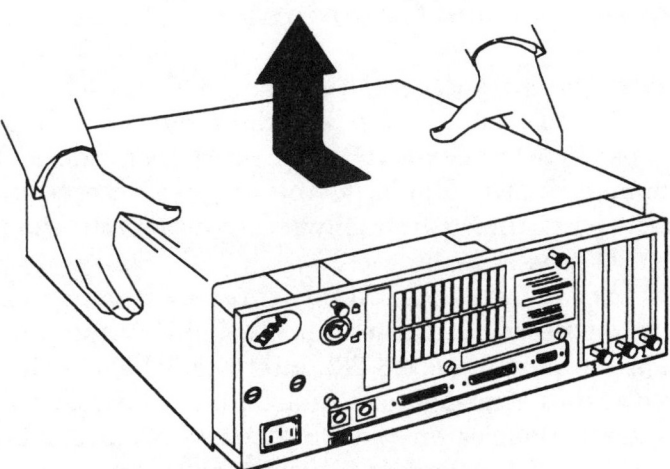

**Figure 7.4** PS/2 Desktop Computer Cover Removal.

Models 25 and 30 use an 8-bit bus, so adapters designed for most PCs can be used in those computers. Unfortunately, the Micro Channel bus used in other members of the PS/2 series precludes the use of adapters designed for PCs in those computers. Similarly, a Micro Channel adapter designed for use in a PS/2 computer that supports the use of that interface cannot be used in the PS/2 Models 25 and 30, nor in the PS/2 Model 30 286 or members of the PC series.

## Obtaining a Serial Port

Modems can be classified as external or internal. An external modem contains its own power supply and is manufactured as a stand-alone unit that is cabled to the serial port of a computer. In comparison, an internal modem is manufactured as an adapter designed for installation in an expansion slot of a personal computer.

Because an external modem requires the availability of a serial port, we will first focus on obtaining this feature for PC and PS/2 computers. Then we will examine the installation of an internal modem so we can compare and contrast each device.

### Asynchronous Communications Adapter

Figure 7.5 is a photograph of the IBM Asynchronous Communications Adapter that, among other functions, converts the parallel data flow of 8 bits per byte inside an IBM PC or PC XT into a serial data stream for communications. Similarly, the adapter accepts a received serial data stream and converts 8 serially received bits into a parallel formed byte for internal processing by the PC.

In examining the IBM asynchronous communications adapter, several components warrant attention. Although almost everyone will use this adapter to obtain an RS-232 interface, which is the standard method by which external modems are cabled to computers, positioning the lower four pluggable modules on the RS-232/20mA current loop interface selector module to the upper four positions will change the interface to a 20-mA current loop. This enables teletype type devices operating with a current loop interface to be connected to the PC or the PC to be connected to a current-loop mainframe computer port via the PC's asynchronous communications adapter.

Prior to installing the asynchronous communications adapter or any other adapter in the system unit, you must remove a system expansion

Modem Installation, Operation, and Selection Considerations  **239**

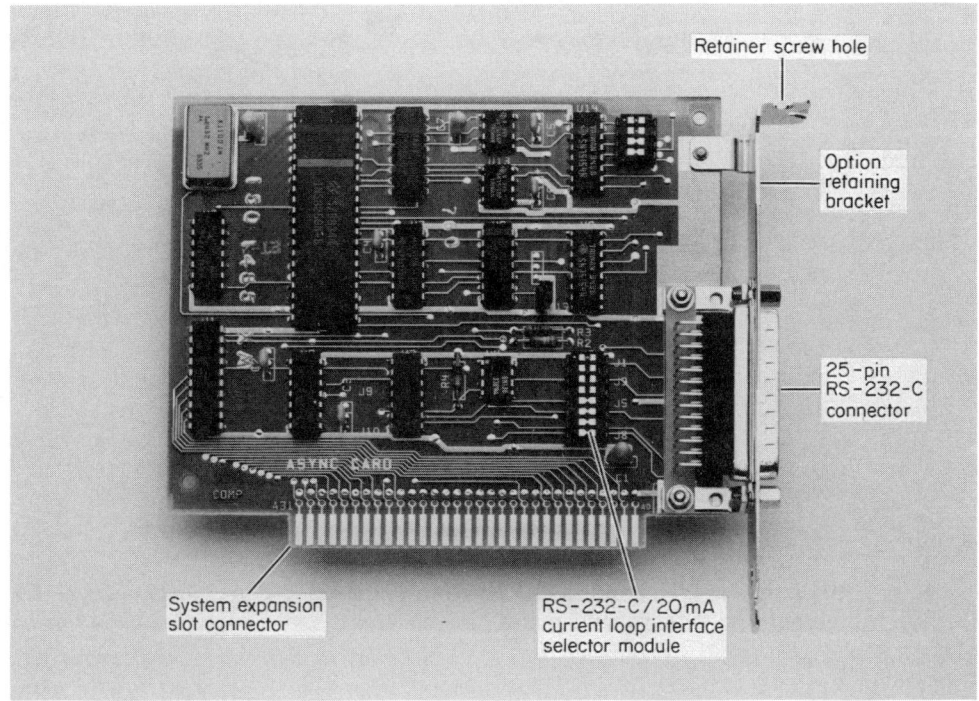

**Figure 7.5** IBM Asynchronous Communications Adapter. *Photograph courtesy of IBM Corporation.*

slot cover, as shown in Figure 7.6. Be sure to turn the screw holding the cover counterclockwise. The screw holding the expansion slot cover will be used to fasten the adapter to the system unit, so you should save this screw.

To install the asynchronous communications adapter or any other adapter after the slot cover is removed, hold the board by its top corners and press it firmly into the expansion slot. Next, align the hole in the option-retaining bracket of the adapter card with the hole in the rear panel of the system unit that contained the slot cover screw. Now insert this screw into the hole in the option-retaining bracket and turn it clockwise to fasten the adapter to the system unit. This process is illustrated in Figure 7.7. Assuming the asynchronous communications adapter was installed in system expansion slot 3 of an IBM PC, Figure 7.8 illustrates how the RS-232 connector would appear at the rear of the system unit. This connector can then be cabled to a modem or a serial printer.

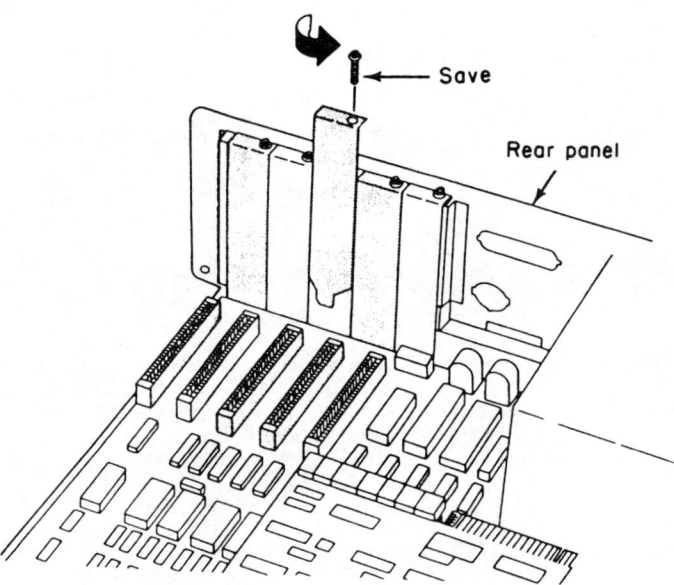

**Figure 7.6** Removing the System Expansion Slot Cover—Turn the screw that fastens the system expansion slot cover in the counterclockwise direction.

## Serial/Parallel Adapter

For the PC AT, IBM markets a serial/parallel adapter whose serial interface provides asynchronous communications support. Both the asynchronous communications adapter and the serial/parallel adapter are similar in that they regulate the data transmission rate at a predetermined fixed rate between 75, 9600, and 19200 bps and support data rates of 75, 110, 150, 300, 600, 1200, 1800, 2400, 4800, 9600, and 19200 bps, which are selected by the asynchronous communications software.

Because by definition asynchronous communications is not continuous, each character must contain its own timing information in the form of start and stop bits. Both devices add a start bit to each character being transmitted and delete this bit from each character received. To inform the other end of the link of the termination of a character requires a stop bit to be appended to each transmitted character. Under program control, each adapter adds a stop bit 1, 1.5, or 2 bit times in length to the end of each transmitted character, where it is removed by the adapter at the other end of the link. Normally, a stop bit 2 bit times in length is used at data rates of 110 bps or less; a stop bit of 1 bit times in length is used with

Modem Installation, Operation, and Selection Considerations   **241**

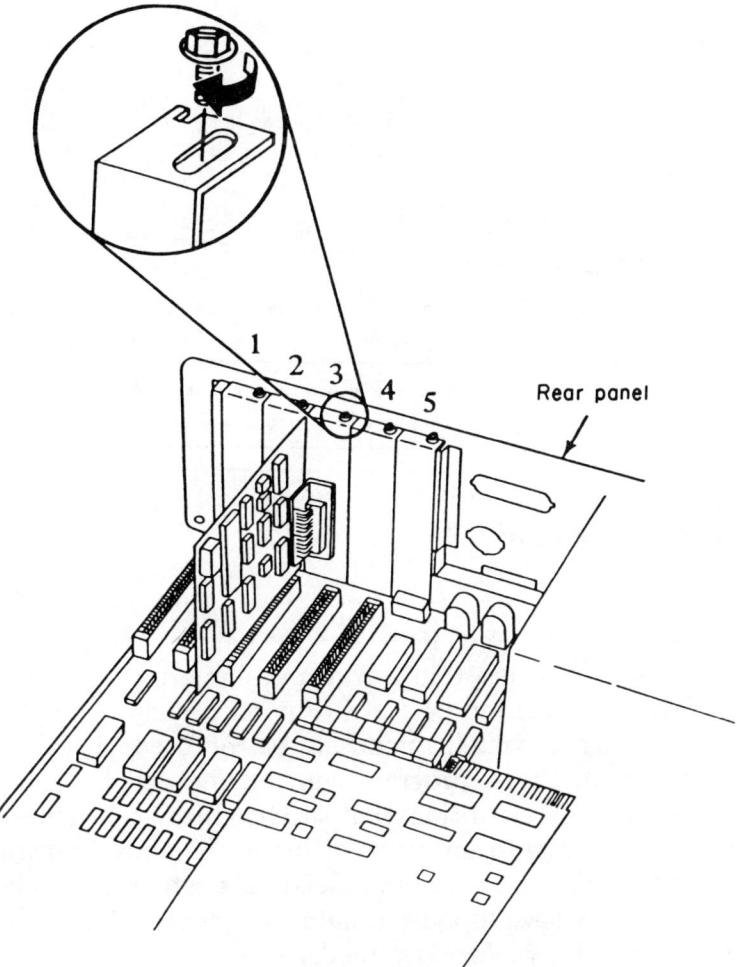

**Figure 7.7**  Fastening the Adapter to the System Unit—Use the screw from the system expansion slot cover to fasten the adapter card to the system unit.

data rates of 300 bps and above. A stop bit of 1.5 bit intervals is normally used when a PC is used to emulate older types of terminals.

In addition to the previously discussed timing information, each adapter can be controlled by software to add a parity bit to each transmitted character. Through the addition of a parity bit, the total number of bits per character can be set to an even or odd count via program control. Doing so will enable the receiving adapter to check the received character

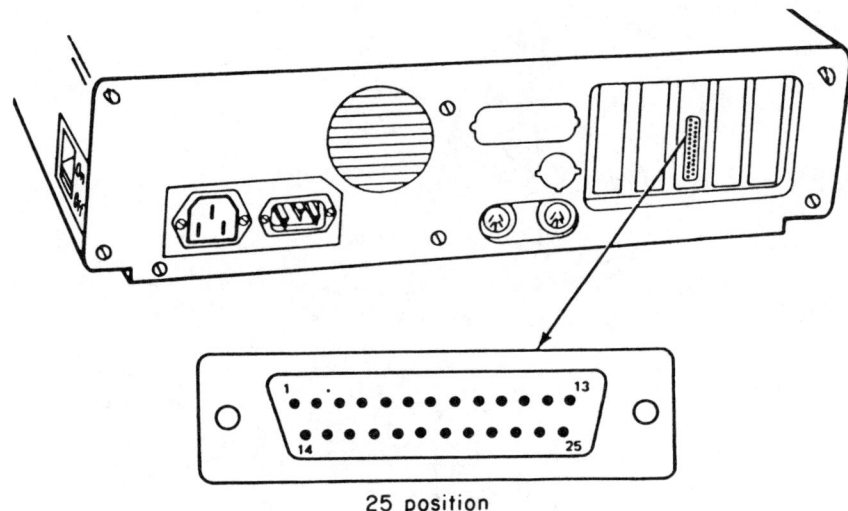

**Figure 7.8** The RS-232 Connector.

for a parity error and, if detected, to signal the user through the communications software that a transmission error has occurred.

Another function performed by each adapter card is the generation of a break signal, which should not be confused with the break key on the PC keyboard. Under program control, the adapter generates a 20-millisecond marking condition that is recognized by many mainframe computers as a signal to interrupt or break the activity being performed.

Although the maximum official data rate of each adapter is 9600 bps, both adapters have supported data rates up to 19200 bps when connected to high-speed asynchronous modems.

As the name implies, the IBM PC AT serial/parallel adapter includes a parallel port and a serial port on one adapter card. The rear of the adapter contains a 9-pin D-shell connector at the top of the card that is classified as an RS-232 port. The serial port of the PC AT serial/parallel adapter card illustrating the numbering of the 9 pins is illustrated in the upper right of Figure 7.9. Table 7.1 lists the relationship between the pins on the 9-pin D-shell connector and the RS-232 25-pin connector equivalents.

Because modems normally have an RS-232 interface, you cannot directly cable the 9-pin connector on the PC AT serial/parallel adapter card with a straight-through conductor cable to a modem. As Table 7.1 indicates, pin #2 on the adapter must be routed to pin #3 on the 25-pin connector connected to a modem, pin #3 on the 9-pin connector must be

Modem Installation, Operation, and Selection Considerations  243

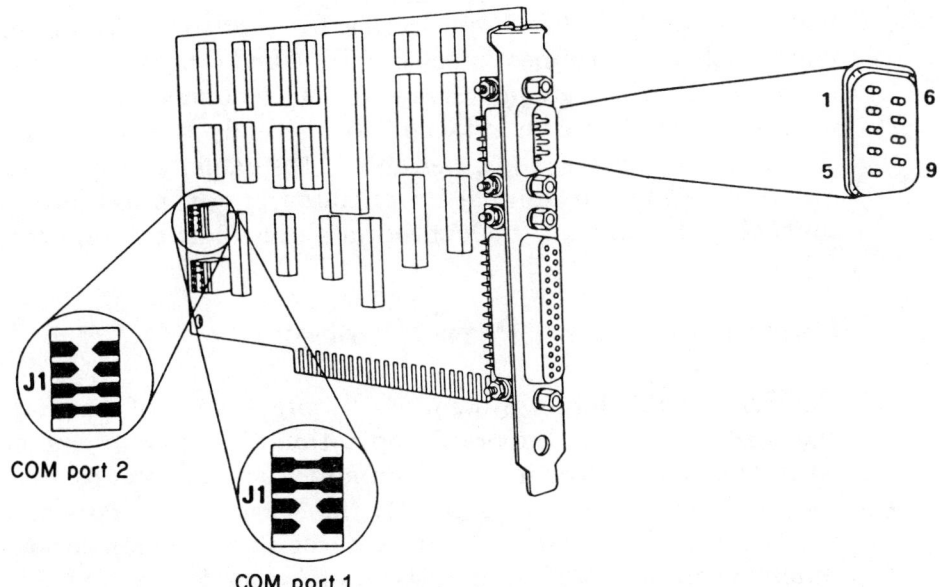

**Figure 7.9**  PC AT Serial/Parallel Adapter Card.

**Table 7.1**  PC AT Serial/Parallel Adapter Serial Port Pin Assignment

| 9-PIN CONNECTOR PIN NUMBER | RS-232 CIRCUIT | 25-PIN CONNECTOR EQUIVALENT |
|---|---|---|
| 1 | Carrier Detect | 8 |
| 2 | Receive Data | 3 |
| 3 | Transmit Data | 2 |
| 4 | Data Terminal Ready | 20 |
| 5 | Signal Ground | 7 |
| 6 | Data Set Ready | 6 |
| 7 | Request to Send | |
| 8 | Clear to Send | 5 |
| 9 | Ring Indicator | 22 |

routed to pin #3 on the 25-pin connector, and so on. To obtain compatibility with 25-pin connector devices, IBM and other vendors market what is known as a *serial adapter connector*. This connector is actually a cable with a 25-pin connector attached to one end of the cable and a 9-pin connector attached to the other end of the cable. The conductors in the cable are wired to ensure that the circuits from the pins on the 9-pin shell connector are routed to the appropriate pins on the 25-pin connector.

## Communications Port Numbers

The Basic Input-Output System (BIOS) of members of the IBM PC Series and PS/2 family can support the operation of up to four communications ports. Unlike the asynchronous communications adapter that has the fixed address of communications port 1, the serial output port of the serial/parallel adapter card can be addressed as either communications port 1 or communications port 2. The lower portion of Figure 7.9 illustrates the appropriate positioning of the J1 jumper on the serial/parallel adapter card to address the serial output port.

If you install more than one adapter card containing a serial port in the system unit of a PC, take care to prevent an addressing conflict. If an addressing conflict occurs due to two or more adapter cards or ports on adapter cards having the same address, your computer will probably "freeze" the first time you attempt to use one of the ports that share the same address. This results in the loss of any data in memory and causes you to reboot the system. Addressing conflicts can be avoided by ensuring that a different port address is assigned to each similar type port on additional adapter cards that are to be installed in your system unit.

To conserve expansion slots, many third party vendors offer multifunction boards. These boards typically contain additional memory capacity as well as one or more serial and parallel ports and a clock/calendar. The serial port on these multifunction boards is normally equivalent to a stand-alone asynchronous communications adapter or the serial interface on the serial/parallel adapter. Their use in place of an IBM adapter is normally transparent to the user.

Figure 7.10 illustrates a block diagram of the Quadram Corporation Quadboard. This adapter board enables you to expand the memory of your PC or PC XT system in increments of 64K bytes, adding up to 384K bytes of memory to your personal computer. In addition to memory, the adapter board contains a clock/calendar, parallel port, and serial port. By confi-

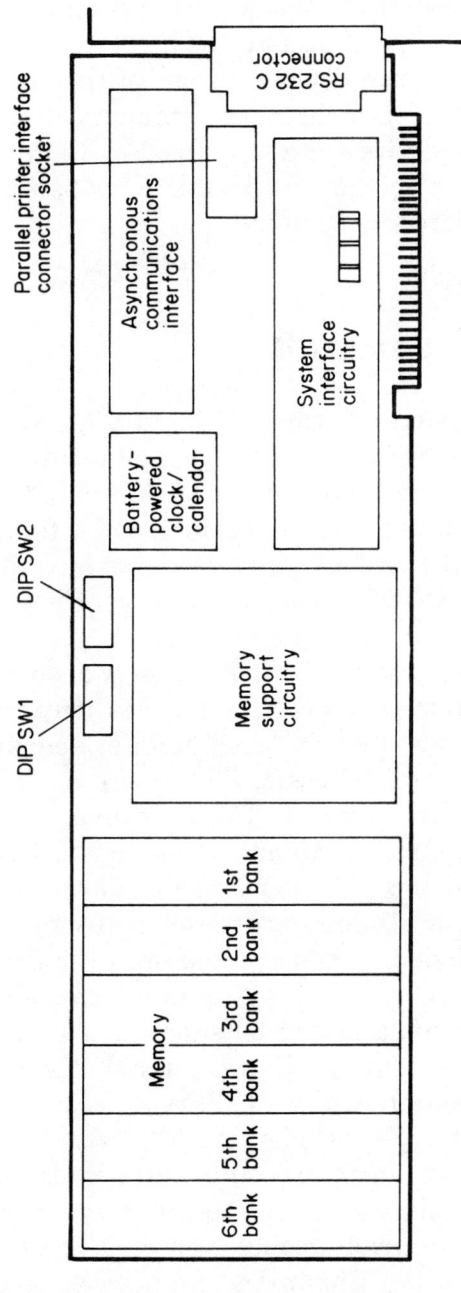

**Figure 7.10** Quadram Corporation Quadboard—The serial port on this multifunction board can be configured to be addressed as COM1 or COM2 by setting elements on DIP switch 2.

guring appropriate elements on DIP switch 2 (SW2) on the adapter, you can configure the serial port on the board to be addressed as device COM1 or COM2, or you can disable the use of the port. Thus, if you previously installed an IBM asynchronous communications adapter in your PC or PC XT whose device address is fixed as COM1, you would set the DIP switch elements on the Quadboard to configure its serial port as COM2 to avoid an addressing conflict.

## PS/2 System Unit

The major difference between PC and PS/2 system units in their use of a modem is the fact that all PS/2 computers include a built-in serial port. This means you may not have to obtain an adapter card that contains a serial port or have to use an expansion slot to install the card.

The serial port built into the system unit of a PS/2 computer is accessed via a DB-25 connector. This connector is mounted at the lower rear of the system unit.

If you are using the built-in serial port to connect a serial printer or another device to your PS/2, you must then install an adapter card that includes a serial port in your computer's system unit to support an external modem. Similar to PC users, PS/2 users can consider a variety of IBM and third party adapter cards to obtain an additional serial port capability for their computer. As noted in Chapter 5, IBM markets a dual asynchronous serial port Micro Channel adapter, whereas third party vendors market single, dual, and quad serial port cards as well as multifunction cards that include a serial port. You must use the IBM Reference Diskette to reconfigure your hardware to prevent an addressing conflict. However, unlike serial cards that can be swapped among different PCs, you must determine the specific PS/2 computer that will use the additional serial port prior to obtaining a card. This is because PS/2s support the use of three different types of adapters—PC bus, PC AT bus, and the Micro Channel bus. Fortunately, 8-bit adapter cards designed for use in the PC and PC XT can be used in the 16-bit PC AT and the PS/2 Model 30 286. Thus, you can normally reduce your serial port adapter card acquisitions to PC bus and Micro Channel adapters based on the type of PS/2 to which you wish to add a serial port.

## Internal Modem

Although called an *internal modem,* this device can actually be considered as a multifunction board, because it combines the functions of a communications adapter and modem onto one adapter card. Because the cost of an internal modem is normally less than the cost of a separate communications adapter and a stand-alone external modem, you may prefer to install this device in your computer's system unit. In addition to economic savings of one device compared to two, an internal modem eliminates the cable required to connect a port of an asynchronous communications adapter to a stand-alone modem, which can add an additional $10 to $20 to your communications cost. Another advantage of an internal modem compared to separate devices is the fact that it eliminates the footprint of a separate modem on your desk. In certain situations, this fact by itself may be a governing factor for selecting an internal modem.

Figure 7.11 contains a photograph of Digital Communications Associates' Fastlink single-board modem. Note the edge connector on the

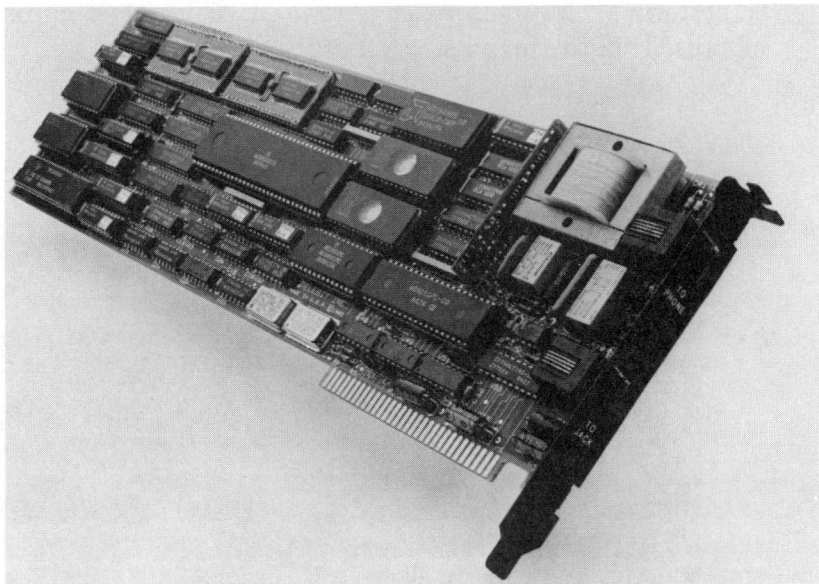

**Figure 7.11** Digital Communications Associates' Fastlink Single-Board Modem. *Photograph courtesy of Digital Communications Associates.*

right part of the photograph that is the bottom of the board. By installing the board into one of the system expansion slots in the PC or PC XT, you can obtain both an asynchronous communications adapter and internal modem occupying only one slot. This modem is really four modems in one, capable of operating at industry standard data rates of 300, 1200, and 2400 bps as well as its proprietary data rate that can range in small increments of bps up to 19200 bps. This adapter is similar to other internal modems designed for use in PC bus computers in that it does not contain a skirt. Thus, you can install this adapter in any system expansion slot of a PC AT that can accommodate a full-length adapter as well as such members of the PS/2 family, including the Model 30 and Model 30 286, that use PC bus expansion slots. If you have a Micro Channel bus PS/2, you must obtain an internal modem manufactured as a Micro Channel adapter for your computer.

Figure 7.12 contains a photograph of the Hayes Smartmodem 2400, which is one of the most popular "intelligent" modems marketed for use with personal computers. This stand-alone external modem is cabled to an asynchronous communications adapter installed in the system unit of a PC or the serial port built into a PS/2 and recognizes a set of commands to perform such functions as automatic dialing and automatic answering of calls. Due to the number of software programs written to be "Hayes

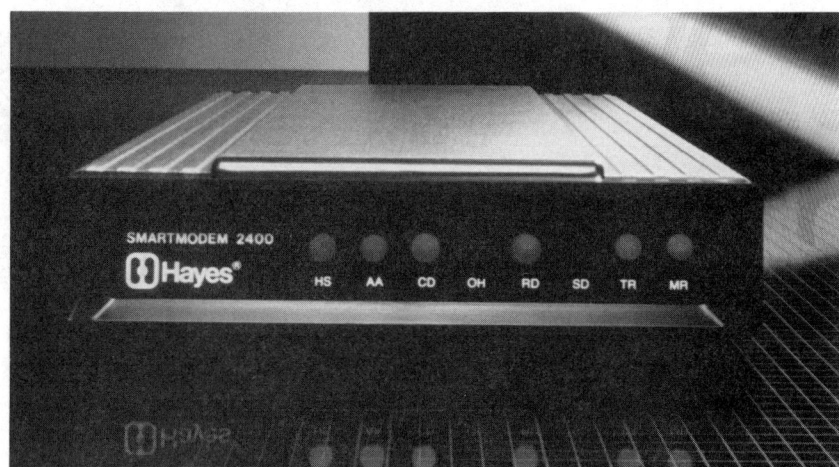

**Figure 7.12** Hayes Smartmodem 2400. *Reproduced by permission of Hayes Microcomputer Products, Inc.*

compatible," most hardware vendors offering modems have designed their devices to recognize the Hayes command set.

## Modem Modulation Methods and Operational Classification

Today, despite the introduction of a number of all-digital transmission facilities by several communications carriers, the analog telephone system remains the primary facility for data communications. Personal computers produce digital pulses, whereas telephone circuits are designed to transmit analog signals that fall within the audio spectrum used in human speech, so a device to interface the digital data pulses of personal computers with the analog tones carried on telephone circuits becomes necessary to transmit data over such circuits. Such a device is called a *modem,* which is a contraction of the two main functions of such a unit—modulation and demodulation. Although *modem* is the term most frequently used for such a device, *data set* is another common term that is synonymous.

Basically, a modem consists of a power supply, a transmitter, and a receiver. The power supply provides the voltage necessary to operate the modem's circuitry. In the transmitter a modulator; amplifier; and filtering, waveshaping, and signal control circuitry convert digital direct current pulses. These pulses, originated by a computer or terminal, are converted into an analog, wave-shaped signal that can be transmitted over a telephone line. The receiver contains a demodulator and associated circuitry that reverse the process by converting the analog telephone signal back into a series of digital pulses acceptable to the computer or terminal device. This signal conversion is illustrated in Figure 7.13.

### The Modulation Process

The modulation process alters the characteristics of a carrier signal. By itself, a carrier is a repeating signal that conveys no information. However, when the carrier is changed by the modulation process, information is impressed on the signal. For analog signals, the carrier is a sine wave, represented by

$a = A \sin(2\pi f t + \theta)$

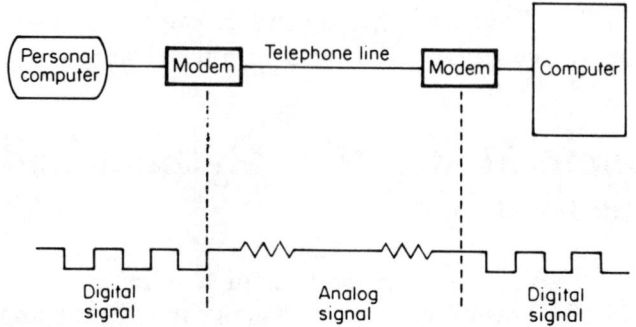

**Figure 7.13** Signal Conversion Performed by Modems—A modem converts a digital signal to an analog tone (modulation) and reconverts the analog tone (demodulation) into its original digital signal.

where:
- a = instantaneous value of voltage at time t
- A = maximum amplitude
- f = frequency
- $\theta$ = phase

Thus, the carrier's characteristics that can be altered are the carrier's amplitude for amplitude modulation (AM), the carrier's frequency for frequency modulation (FM), and the carrier's phase angle for phase modulation ($\theta$M).

## Amplitude Modulation

The simplest method of employing amplitude modulation is to vary the magnitude of the signal from a zero level to represent a binary 0 to a fixed peak-to-peak voltage to represent a binary 1. Figure 7.14 illustrates the use of amplitude modulation to encode a digital data stream into an appropriate series of analog signals. Although pure amplitude modulation is normally used for very low data rates, it is also employed in conjunction with phase modulation to obtain a method of modulating high-speed digital data sources.

## Frequency Modulation

Frequency modulation refers to how frequently a signal repeats itself at a given amplitude. One of the earliest uses of frequency modulation was in

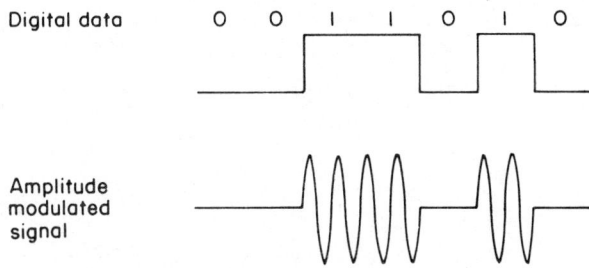

**Figure 7.14** Amplitude Modulation.

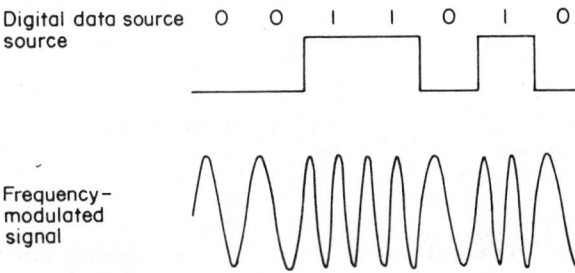

**Figure 7.15** Frequency Modulation.

the design of low-speed acoustic couplers and modems where the transmitter shifted from one frequency to another as the input digital data changed from a binary 1 to a binary 0 or from a 0 to a 1. This shifting in frequency is known as frequency-shift keying (FSK) and is primarily used by modems operating at data rates up to 300 bps in a full-duplex mode of operation and up to 1200 bps in a half-duplex mode of operation. Figure 7.15 illustrates frequency-shift (keying) frequency modulation.

## Phase Modulation

Phase modulation is the process of varying the carrier signal with respect to the origination of its cycle, as illustrated in Figure 7.16. Several forms of phase modulation are used in modems, including single- and multiple-bit phase-shift keying (PSK) and the combination of amplitude and multiple-bit, phase-shift keying.

In single-bit, phase-shift keying, the transmitter simply shifts the phase of the signal to represent each bit entering the modem. Thus, a binary 1 might be represented by a 90-degree phase change, whereas a 0

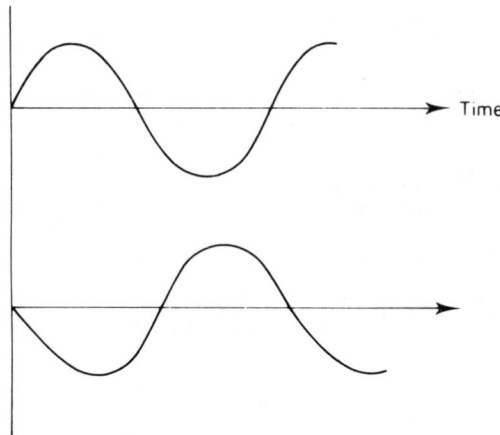

**Figure 7.16** Phase Modulation—*Phase* is the position of the wave form of a signal with respect to the origination of the carrier cycle. Here, the bottom wave is 180 degrees out of phase with a normal sine wave illustrated at the top.

bit could be represented by a 270-degree phase change. Due to the variance of phase between two phase values to represent binary 1s and 0s, this technique is also known as two-phase modulation.

Prior to discussing multiple-bit, phase-shift keying we will examine the difference between the data rate and signaling speed and the basic parameters of a voice circuit. This will enable you to understand the rationale for using multiple-bit, phase-shift keying, where two or more bits are grouped together and represented by one phase shift in a signal.

## Bits per Second Versus Baud

*Bits per second (bps)* is the number of binary digits transferred in one second and represents the data transmission rate of a device. Baud is the signaling rate of a device such as a modem. If the signal of the modem changes with respect to each bit entering the device, then one bps equals one baud. Suppose a modem is constructed such that one signal change is used to represent two bits. Then the baud rate would be one-half the bps rate.

When two bits are used to represent one baud, the encoding technique is known as *dibit encoding.* Similarly, the process of using three bits to represent one baud is known as *tribit encoding,* and the bit rate is then one-third of the baud rate. Both dibit and tribit encoding are known as *multilevel coding techniques* and are commonly implemented using phase modulation.

## Voice Circuit Parameters

*Bandwidth* is a measurement of the width of a range of frequencies. A voice-grade telephone channel has a passband, which defines its slot in the frequency spectrum, ranging from 300 to 3300 Hz. Thus, the bandwidth of a voice-grade telephone channel is 3300 − 300, or 3000 Hz.

As data enters a modem it is converted into a series of analog signals, with the signal change rate of the modem known as its baud rate. In 1928, Nyquist developed the relationship between the bandwidth and the baud rate on a circuit as

$$B = 2W$$

where:
 $B$ = baud rate
 $W$ = bandwidth in Hz

For a voice-grade circuit with a bandwidth of 3000 Hz, this relationship means that data transmission can only be supported at baud rates lower than 6000 symbols or signaling elements per second, prior to one signal interfering with another and causing intersymbol interference.

Because any oscillating modulation technique immediately halves the signaling rate, this means that most modems are limited to operating at one-half of the Nyquist limit. Thus, in a single-bit, phase-shift keying modulation technique, where each bit entering the modem results in a phase shift, the maximum data rate obtainable would be limited to approximately 3000 bps. In such a situation the bit rate would equal the baud rate because there would be one signal change for each bit.

To overcome the Nyquist limit, engineers needed to design modems that first grouped a sequence of bits together, examined the composition of the bits, and then implemented a phase shift based on the value of the grouped bits. This technique is known as *multiple-bit, phase-shift keying* or *multilevel, phase-shift keying*. Two-bit codes called *dibits* and three-bit codes known as *tribits* are formed and transmitted by a single phase shift from a group of four or eight possible phase states.

Most modems operating at 600 to 4800 bps employ multilevel, phase-shift keying modulation. Some of the more commonly used phase patterns employed by modems using dibit and tribit encoding are listed in Table 7.2.

## Combined Modulation Techniques

Because the most practical method to overcome the Nyquist limit is placing additional bits into each signal change, modem designers have combined modulation techniques to obtain very high-speed data transmission over voice-grade circuits. One common combined modulation technique involves both amplitude and phase modulation. This technique, *quadrature amplitude modulation (QAM)*, results in four bits being placed into each signal change, with the signal operating at 2400 (baud). Thus, the data rate becomes 9600 bps.

The first implementation of QAM involved a combination of phase and amplitude modulation, in which 12 values of phase and 3 values of

**Table 7.2** Common Phase-Angle Values Used in Multilevel Phase-Shift Keying

|  | BITS TRANSMITTED | POSSIBLE PHASE-ANGLE VALUES (DEGREES) | | |
|---|---|---|---|---|
| Dibit encoding | 00 | 0 | 45 | 90 |
|  | 01 | 90 | 135 | 0 |
|  | 10 | 180 | 225 | 270 |
|  | 11 | 270 | 315 | 180 |
| Tribit encoding | 000 | 0 | 22.5 | 45 |
|  | 001 | 45 | 67.5 | 0 |
|  | 010 | 90 | 112.5 | 90 |
|  | 011 | 135 | 157.5 | 135 |
|  | 100 | 180 | 202.5 | 180 |
|  | 101 | 225 | 247.5 | 225 |
|  | 110 | 270 | 292.5 | 270 |
|  | 111 | 315 | 337.5 | 315 |

amplitude were employed to produce 16 possible signal states, as illustrated in Figure 7.17. Note that the resultant 16 states are obtained by varying both the amplitude and phase value of the signal. One of the earliest modems to use QAM in the United States was the Bell System 209, which modulated a 1650-Hz carrier at a 2400 baud rate to effect data transmission at 9600 bps. Today, most 9600-bps modems manufactured adhere to the Consultative Committee for International Telephone and Telegraph (CCITT) V.29 standard. The V.29 modem uses a carrier of 1700 Hz, which is varied in both phase and amplitude, resulting in 16 combinations of 8 phase angles and 4 amplitudes. Under the V.29 standard, fallback data rates of 7200 and 4800 bps are specified.

In addition to combining two modulation techniques, QAM also differs from the previously discussed modulation methods by its use of two carrier signals. Figure 7.18 illustrates a simplified block diagram of a modem's transmitter employing QAM. The encoder operates on four bits from the serial data stream and causes both an in-phase (IP) cosine carrier and a sine wave that serves as the quadrature component (QC) of the signal to be modulated. The IP and QC signals are then summed and result in the transmitted signal being changed in both amplitude and phase, with each point placed at the X,Y coordinates representing the modulation levels of the cosine carrier and the sine carrier.

If you plot the signal points previously illustrated in Figure 7.17, which represent all of the data samples possible in that particular method of

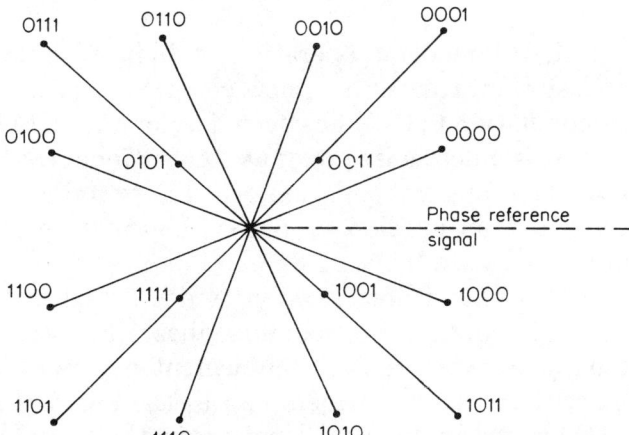

**Figure 7.17** Quadrature amplitude modulation produces 16 signal states from a combination of 12 angles and 3 amplitude levels.

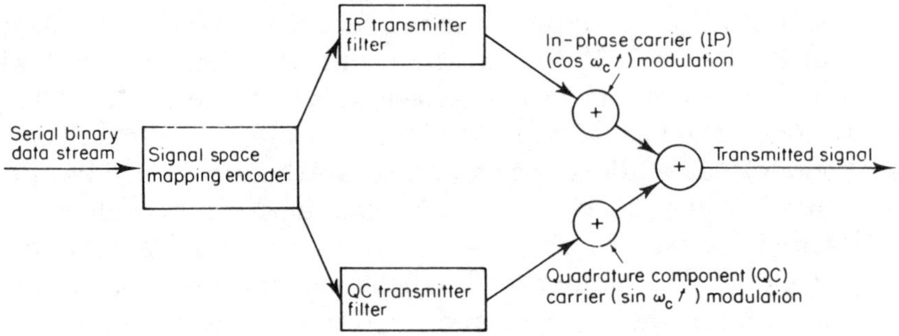

**Figure 7.18** QAM Modem Transmitter.

QAM, the series of points can be considered to be the signal structure of the modulation technique. Another popular term used to describe these points is the *constellation pattern.* By examining the constellation pattern of a modem, you can predetermine its susceptibility to certain transmission impairments. As an example, phase jitter that causes signal points to rotate about the origin can result in one signal being misinterpreted for another, which would cause four bits to be received in error. Because there are 12 angles in the QAM method illustrated in Figure 7.17, the minimum rotation angle is 30 degrees, providing a reasonable immunity to phase jitter.

## Trellis-Coded Modulation

Because QAM modems operating at high data rates are susceptible to transmission impairments, a new generation of modems based on trellis-coded modulation (TCM) has been developed. TCM modems tolerate more than twice as much noise power as conventional QAM modems, permitting 9600 to 14400 bps transmission over the switched telephone network and reliable data transmission at speeds ranging from 14400 to 19200 bps over good-quality leased lines.

To understand how TCM provides a higher tolerance to noise and other line impairments (including phase jitter and distortion), consider what happens when a line impairment occurs with conventional QAM modems. Here the impairment causes the received signal point to be displaced from its appropriate location in the signal constellation. The receiver then selects the signal point in the constellation that is closest to what it received. Obviously, when line impairments are large enough to cause the received point to be closer to a signal point that is different from the one transmitted, an error occurs. To minimize the possibility of such errors, TCM employs an encoder that adds a redundant code bit to each symbol interval.

As an example of the operation of TCM, consider a 14400 bps modem that includes this modulation capability. At 14400 bps, the transmitter converts the serial data stream into six-bit symbols and encodes two of the six bits employing a binary convolutional encoding scheme as illustrated in Figure 7.19. The encoder adds a code bit to the two input bits, forming three encoded bits in each symbol interval. As a result of this encoding operation, three encoded bits and four remaining data bits are then mapped into a signal point that is selected from a 128-point ($2^7$) signal constellation.

The redundancy introduced by the encoder results in only certain sequences of signal points being valid. Thus, if an impairment causes a signal point to shift, the receiver compares the observed point to all valid points and selects the valid signal point closest to the observed signal. As a result, a TCM modem is only half as susceptible to as much noise power as a conventional QAM modem, and its use can reduce your error rate by approximately three orders of magnitude.

Thus, a conventional QAM modem that might require one of every 10 data blocks to be retransmitted could be replaced by a TCM modem, with the result that only 1 in every 10,000 data blocks might then be received in error.

## Mode of Transmission

If the transmitter or the receiver of the modem is such that the modem can send or receive data in one direction only, the modem will function

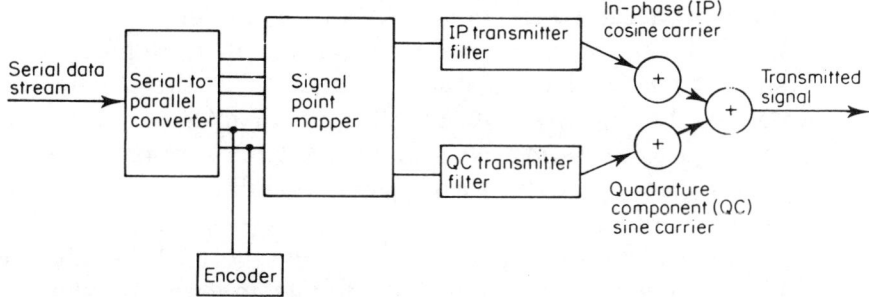

**Figure 7.19** Trellis-Coded Modulation.

as a simplex modem. If the operations of the transmitter and the receiver are combined so that the modem may transmit and receive data alternately, the modem functions as a half-duplex modem. In the half-duplex mode of operation, the transmitter must be turned off at one location, and the transmitter of the modem at the other end of the line must be turned on before each change in transmission direction. The time interval required for this operation is referred to as *turnaround time*. If the transmitter and receiver operate simultaneously, the modem functions as a full-duplex modem. This simultaneous transmission in both directions can be accomplished either by splitting the telephone line's bandwidth into two channels on a two-wire circuit or by using 2 two-wire circuits, such as are obtained on a four-wire leased line.

## Transmission Technique

Modems are designed for asynchronous or synchronous data transmission. Asynchronous transmission is also referred to as *start/stop transmission* and is usually used when the time between character transmissions occurs randomly. In asynchronous transmission, the character being transmitted is initialized by the character's start bit as a mark-to-space transition on the line and terminated by the character's stop bit, which is converted to a "space-marking" signal on the line. The digital pulses between the start and stop bits are the encoded bits that determine the type of character transmitted. Between the stop bit of one character and the start bit of the next character, the asynchronous modem places the line in the "marking" condition.

Upon receipt of the start bit of the next character the line is switched to a mark-to-space transition, and the modem at the other end of the line starts to sample the data. The marking and spacing conditions are audio tones produced by the modulator of the modem to denote the binary data levels. These tones are produced at predefined frequencies, and their transition between the two states as each bit of the character is transmitted defines the character. Asynchronous transmission was usually used at data rates up to 2400 bps. Now many modems support data rates of 9600 to 19200 bps through the use of several modulation schemes that are described later in this chapter.

Synchronous transmission permits more efficient line use because the bits of one character are immediately followed by the bits of the next character, with no start and stop bits required to delimit individual characters. In synchronous transmission, groups of characters are formed into data blocks, with the length of the block varying from a few characters to a thousand or more. Often, the block length is a function of the physical characteristics of the data to be transmitted. As an example, for the transmission of data that represents punched-card images, it may be convenient to transmit 80 characters of one card as a block, because there would be that many characters if you constructed the card image from an 80-column punched-card deck. In synchronous transmission, the individual bits of each of the characters within each block are identified based on a transmitted timing signal that is usually provided by the modem and that places each bit into a unique time period.

## Modem Operations and Modulation Compatibility

Many modem manufacturers describe their product offerings in terms of compatibility or equivalency with modems manufactured by Western Electric for the Bell System prior to its breakup into independent telephone companies or with the recommendations of the CCITT. The CCITT, which is part of the International Telecommunications Union based in Geneva, has developed a series of modem standards. These recommendations are primarily adapted by the Post, Telephone, and Telegraph (PTT) organizations that operate the telephone networks of many countries outside the United States. However, due to the popularity of certain CCITT recommendations, they have also been followed in designing certain modems for operation on communications facilities within the United States. The following examination of the operation and compatibility of the major types of Bell System and CCITT modems is based on their operating rates.

### 300 Bits per Second

Modems operating at 300 bps use a frequency-shift keying (FSK) modulation technique. In this technique, the frequency of the carrier alternates between two frequencies, one frequency representing a space or a zero bit, the other frequency representing a mark or a one bit. Table 7.3 lists the frequency assignments for Bell System 103/113 and CCITT V.21 modems that represent the two major types of modems that operate at 300 bps.

Bell System 103 and 113 series modems are designed so that one channel is assigned to the 1070-1270-Hz frequency band, whereas the second channel is assigned to the 2025-2225-Hz frequency band. Modems

**Table 7.3** Frequency Assignments (Hz) for 300-bps Modems

| MAJOR MODEM TYPES | ORIGINATE | ANSWER |
|---|---|---|
| Bell System | Mark 1270 | 2225 |
| (103/113 type) | Space 1070 | 2025 |
| CCITT V.21 | Mark 980 | 1650 |
| | Space 1180 | 1850 |

that transmit in the 1070–1270-Hz band but receive in the 2025–2225-Hz band are designated as originate modems, whereas a modem that transmits in the 2025–2225-Hz band but receives in the 1070–1270-Hz band is designated as an answer modem. When you use such modems, their correct pairing is important, because two originate modems cannot communicate with each other. As an example, Bell System 113A modems are originate-only devices that should normally be used when calls are to be placed in one direction. This type of modem is mainly used to enable teletype-compatible terminals and PCs to communicate with mainframe systems when the terminal or PC only originates calls. Bell System 113B modems are answer-only and are primarily used at computer sites where users dial in to establish communications.

Other modems in the Bell System 103 series—103A, E, F, G, and J modems—can transmit and receive in either the low or the high band. This ability to switch modes is denoted as "originate and answer," in comparison to the Bell 113A, which operates only in the originate mode, and the Bell 113B, which operates only in the answer mode.

As indicated in Table 7.3, modems operating in accordance with the CCITT V.21 recommendation employ a different set of frequencies for the transmission and reception of marks and spaces. Thus, Bell System 103/113 type modems and CCITT V.21 devices can never communicate with one another.

The two pairs of frequencies used by the modems listed in Table 7.3 permit the bandwidth of a communications channel to be split into two subchannels by frequency. This technique is illustrated in Figure 7.20 for Bell System 103/113 modems. Each subchannel can permit data to be transmitted in a direction opposite that transmitted on the other subchannel, so this technique permits full-duplex transmission to occur on the switched telephone network, which is a two-wire circuit that normally can only support half-duplex transmission.

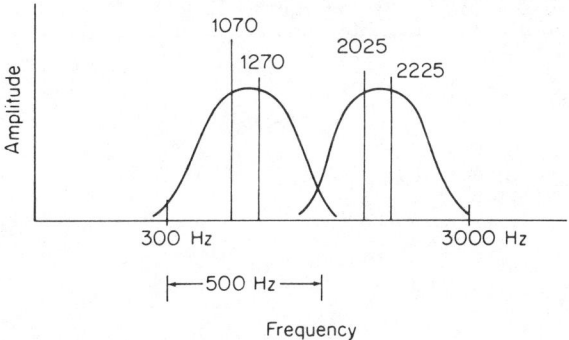

**Figure 7.20** FSK Operation for 300-bps Modems.

## 300 to 1800 Bits per Second

There are several Bell System and CCITT V series modems that operate in the range 300–1800 bps. Some of these modems, such as the Bell System 212A and CCITT V.22 devices, can operate at either of two speeds. Other modems, such as the Bell System 202 and the CCITT V.23, operate at only one data rate. We will examine these modems in pairs, enabling their similarities and differences to be compared.

## Bell System 212A and V.22 Modems

The Bell System 212A modem permits either asynchronous or synchronous transmission over the public switched telephone network. The 212A contains a 103-type modem for asynchronous transmission at speeds up to 300 bps. At this data rate, FSK modulation is employed, using the frequency assignments previously indicated in Table 7.3. At 1200 bps, dibit phase-shift keyed (DPSK) modulation is used, which permits the modem to operate either asynchronously or synchronously. The phase-bit encoding of the 212A type modem is illustrated in Table 7.4.

One advantage in the use of this modem is that it permits the reception of transmission from terminal devices at two different transmission speeds. Before the operator initiates a call, he or she selects the operating speed at the originating set. The manner in which the operating speed is selected depends on the type of 212A modem used. If the modem is what is now commonly referred to as a "dumb" modem, the operator selects the higher operating speed by pressing an "HS" (high-speed) button on the front panel of the modem. If the modem is an "intelligent" modem built

**Table 7.4** 212A Type Modem Phase Shift Encoding

| DIBIT | PHASE SHIFT (DEGREES) |
|---|---|
| 00 | 90 |
| 01 | 0 |
| 10 | 180 |
| 11 | 270 |

to respond to software commands, the operator can either use a communications program or send a series of commands through the serial port of the PC to the modem to set its operating speed. Due to the substantial use of intelligent modems with personal computers, these modems will be reviewed as a separate entity later in this chapter.

When the call is made, the answering 212A modem automatically switches to the operating speed of the originating modem. During data transmission, both modems remain in the same speed mode until the call is terminated, when the answering 212A can be set to the other speed by a new call. The dual-speed 212A permits both terminals connected to Bell System 100 series data sets operating at up to 300 bps or terminal devices connected to other 212A modems operating at 1200 bps to share the use of one modem at a computer site. Thus they can reduce central computer site equipment requirements.

The V.22 standard, which is primarily followed in Europe, is for modems that operate at 1200 bps on the Public Switched Telephone Network (PSTN) or leased circuits and has a fallback data rate of 600 bps. The modulation technique employed is four-phase PSK at 1200 bps and two-phase PSK at 600 bps, with five possible operational modes specified for the modem at 1200 bps. Table 7.5 lists the V.22 modulation phase shifts with respect to the bit patterns entering the modem's transmitter. Modes 1 and 2 are for synchronous and asynchronous data transmission at 1200 bps, respectively, whereas mode 3 is for synchronous transmission at 600 bps. Mode 4 is for asynchronous transmission at 600 bps, and mode 5 represents an alternate phase change set for 1200 bps asynchronous transmission.

In comparing V.22 modems to the Bell System 212A devices it should be apparent that they are totally incompatible at the lower data rate, because both the operating speed and modulation techniques differ. At 1200

**Table 7.5** V.22 Modulation Phase Shift vs. Bit Patterns

| DIBIT VALUES (1200 BPS) | BIT VALUES (600 BPS) | PHASE CHANGE MODES 1,2,3,4 | PHASE CHANGE MODE 5 |
|---|---|---|---|
| 00 | 0 | 90 | 270 |
| 01 | — | 0 | 180 |
| 11 | 1 | 270 | 90 |
| 10 | — | 180 | 0 |

bps the modulation techniques used by a V.22 modem in modes 1 through 4 are exactly the same as those used by a Bell System 212A device. Unfortunately, a Bell 212A modem answers a call by sending a tone of 2225 Hz on the line that the originating modem is supposed to recognize. This frequency is used due to the construction of the switched telephone network in the United States and other parts of North America. Under V.22, the answering modem first sends a tone of 2100 Hz, because this frequency is more compatible with the design of European switched telephone networks. Then, the V.22 modem sends a 2400-Hz tone that would not be any better except that the V.22 modem also sends a burst of data whose primary frequency is about 2250 Hz. This frequency is close enough to the Bell standard of 2225 Hz that many Bell 212A type modems will respond. Thus, some Bell 212A modems can communicate with CCITT V.22 modems at 1200 bps. Other 212 type modems may not be able to communicate with V.22 devices, with the ability to communicate successfully based on the tolerance of the 212 type modem to recognize the V.22 modem's data burst at 2250Hz.

## Bell System 202 Series Modems

Bell System 202 series modems are essentially obsolete devices that were designed for speeds up to 1200 or 1800 bps. The 202C modem can operate on either the switched network or on leased lines, in the half-duplex mode for switched networks and the full-duplex mode for leased lines. The 202C modem can operate half-duplex or full-duplex on leased lines. This series of modems uses FSK modulation, and the frequency assignments are such that a mark is at 1200 Hz and a space at 2200 Hz. When either modem is used for transmission over a leased four-wire circuit in the full-duplex mode, modem control is identical to the 103 series modem in that both transmitters can be strapped on continuously, which alleviates the necessity of line turnarounds.

The 202 series modems do not have separate bands, so for switched network usage half-duplex operation is required. This means that both transmitters (one in each modem) must be alternately turned on and off to provide two-way communication.

The Bell 202 series modems have a 5-bps reverse channel for switched network use, which employs amplitude modulation for the transmission of information. The channel assignments used by a Bell System 202 type modem are illustrated in Figure 7.21, where the 387-Hz signal represents the optional 5-bps AM reverse channel.

Due to the slowness of this reverse channel, its use is limited to status and control function transmission. Status information such as "ready to receive data" or "device out of paper" can be transmitted on this channel. Due to the slow transmission rate, error detection of received messages and an associated NAK and request for retransmission is normally accomplished on the primary channel. Even with the turnaround time, the request can be completed at almost the same rate obtainable with the reverse channel. Non-Bell 202-equivalent modems produced by many manufacturers provide reverse channels of 75 to 150 bps. Such channels can be used to enhance overall system performance. Reverse keyboard-entered data, as well as error detection information, can be practically transmitted over such a channel.

Although a data rate of up to 1800 bps can be obtained with the 202D modem, transmission at this speed requires that the leased line be conditioned for transmission by the telephone company. The 202S and 202T

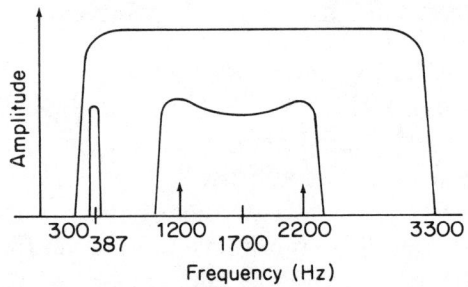

**Figure 7.21** Bell System 202 Type Modem Channel Assignments.

modems are additions to the 202 series and are designed for transmission at 1200 and 1800 bps over the switched network and leased lines, respectively. At speeds in excess of 1400 bps, the 202T requires line conditioning when interfaced to either two- or four-wire circuits, whereas for a two-wire circuit, conditioning is required at speeds in excess of 1200 bps when an optional reverse channel is used.

### V.23 Modems

The V.23 standard—like the V.22 standard—is primarily followed in Europe and is for modems that transmit at 600 or 1200 bps over the PSTN. Both asynchronous and synchronous transmissions are supported using FSK modulation. An optional 75 bps backward or reverse channel can be used for error control. Figure 7.22 illustrates the channel assignments for a V.23 modem. In comparing Figure 7.22 with Figure 7.21, it is obvious that Bell System 202 and V.23 modems are incompatible with each other.

### 2400 Bits per Second

Examples of modems that operate at 2400 bps include the Bell System 201, CCITT V.26 series, and the V.22 bis modem. Here the term *bis* is from the French and means "second." Thus, V.22 bis is a second V.22 standard. The Bell System 201 and CCITT V.26 series modems are designed for synchronous bits-serial transmission at a data rate of 2400 bps, while the V.22 bis standard governs 2400-bps asynchronous and synchronous transmission.

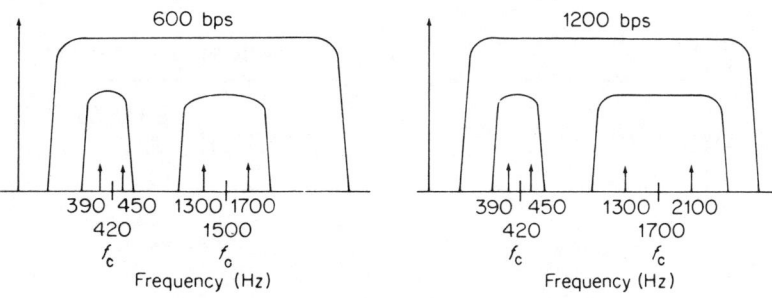

**Figure 7.22** V.23 Channel Assignments.

### Bell System 201 B/C

Members of the 201 series include the 201B and 201C models. Both of these modems use dibit phase-shift keying modulation, with the phase shifts based on the dibit values listed in Table 7.6.

The 201B modem is designed for half- or full-duplex synchronous transmission at 2400 bps over leased lines. In comparison, the 201C is designed for half-duplex, synchronous transmission over the PSTN. A more modern version of the 201C is AT&T's 2024A modem, which is compatible with the 201C.

### V.26 Modem

The V.26 standard, which is primarily followed in Europe, specifies the characteristics for a 2400-bps synchronous modem for use on a four-wire leased line. Modems operating according to the V.26 standard employ dibit phase-shift keying, using one of two recommended coding schemes. The phase change based on the dibit values for each of the V.26 coding schemes is listed in Table 7.7.

Table 7.6  Bell System 201 B/C Phase Shift vs. Bit Pattern

| DIBIT VALUES | PHASE SHIFT |
|---|---|
| 00 | 2250 |
| 10 | 3150 |
| 11 | 450 |
| 10 | 1350 |

Table 7.7  V.26 Modulation Phase Shift vs. Bit Pattern

| | PHASE CHANGE | |
|---|---|---|
| DIBIT VALUES | PATTERN A | PATTERN B |
| 00 | 0 | 45 |
| 01 | 90 | 135 |
| 11 | 180 | 225 |
| 10 | 270 | 315 |

Two similar CCITT recommendations to V.26 are V.26 bis and V.26 ter. Here *ter* is from the French and means "third." Thus, V.26 ter is a third version of the V.26 standard. The V.26 bis recommendation defines a dual-speed 2400/1200 bps modem for use on the PSTN. At 2400 bps, the modulation and coding method is the same as the V.26 recommendation for pattern B listed in Table 7.7. At the reduced data rate of 1200 bps, a two-phase shift modulation scheme is employed, with a binary 0 represented by a 90-degree phase shift while a binary 1 is represented by a 270-degree phase shift. The V.26 bis recommendation also includes an optional reverse or backward channel that can be used for data transfer up to 75 bps. When employed, frequency-shift keying is used to obtain this channel capacity, with a mark or 1 bit represented by a 390-Hz signal and a space or 0 bit represented by a 450-Hz signal.

The V.26 ter recommendation uses the same phase shift scheme as the V.26 modem but incorporates an echo-canceling technique that enables transmitted and received signals to occupy the same bandwidth. Thus, the V.26 ter modem is capable of operating in full-duplex at 2400 bps on the PSTN. Echo canceling is described later in this chapter when the V.32 modem is discussed.

## V.22 bis

The CCITT V.22 bis recommendation governs modems designed for asynchronous and synchronous data transmission at 2400 bps over the PSTN, with a fallback rate of 1200 bps.

Similar to other low-speed modems, a V.22 bis modem uses two channels separated by frequency to obtain a full-duplex transmission capability on the PSTN. At 2400 bps, one carrier frequency occurs at 1200 Hz, and a second carrier frequency at 2400 Hz is used for transmission in the opposite direction.

When operating at 2400 bps, a V.22 bis modem groups data into four consecutive bits or a quadbit. The first two bits are encoded as a phase change relative to the quadrant occupied by the preceding signal element. Table 7.8 denotes the phase quadrant change used by V.22 bis modems operating at 2400 bps based on the value of the first two bits in the quadbit.

The last two bits in the quadbit define one of four signaling elements associated with the new quadrant selected based on the value of the first two bits. Figure 7.23 illustrates the signal constellation of a V.22 bis modem, noting the four signaling elements in each quadrant that create a 16-point constellation pattern.

**Table 7.8** V.22 bis Phase Change

| VALUE OF FIRST TWO BITS IN QUADBIT | RESULTING PHASE | QUADRANT CHANGE |
|---|---|---|
| 00 | 1 → 2<br>2 → 3<br>3 → 4<br>4 → 1 | 90 degrees |
| 01 | 1 → 1<br>2 → 2<br>3 → 3<br>4 → 4 | 0 degrees |
| 11 | 1 → 4<br>2 → 1<br>3 → 2<br>4 → 3 | 270 degrees |
| 10 | 1 → 3<br>2 → 4<br>3 → 1<br>4 → 2 | 180 degrees |

The V.22 bis defines operations at 1200 bps to follow the V.22 format, so communications capability with Bell System 212A type modems at that data rate may not always be possible. This is due to an answer tone incompatibility usually encountered between modems following Bell System specifications and CCITT recommendations. In addition, V.22 bis modems manufactured in the United States are usually not compatible with such modems manufactured in Europe at fallback data rates. This is because V.22 bis modems manufactured in Europe follow the V.22 format, with fallback data rates of 1200 and 600 bps. At 1200 bps, the incompatibility among most European telephone networks (which are designed to accept only 2100-Hz answer tones) and the U.S. telephone network (which usually accepts an answer tone between 2100 and 2225 Hz) may preclude communications between a U.S.- and a European-manufactured V.22 bis modem at 1200 bps. At a lower fallback speed, the European modem will operate at 600 bps, whereas the U.S. V.22 bis modem operates at 300 bps, ensuring incompatibility.

In spite of the previously mentioned problems, V.22 bis modems can be considered a de facto standard for use with personal computers communicating over the PSTN. This is due to several factors, including the

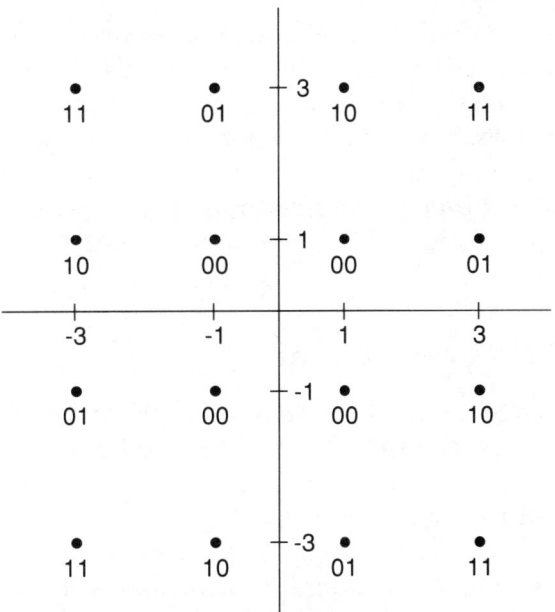

**Figure 7.23** V.22 bis Constellation Pattern.

manufacture in the United States of V.22 bis modems that are Bell System 212A compatible, permitting PC users with such modems to be able to communicate with other PCs and mainframe computers connected to either 212A or 103/113 type modems. In addition, at 2400 bps, US V.22 bis modems can communicate with European V.22 bis, in effect, providing worldwide communications capability over the PSTN.

## 4800 Bits per Second

The Bell System 208 series and CCITT V.27 modems represent the most common types of modems designed for synchronous data transmission at 4800 bps. The Bell System 208 Series modems use a quadrature amplitude-modulation technique. The 208A modem is designed for either half-duplex or full-duplex operation at 4800 bps over leased lines. The 208B modem is designed for half-duplex operation at 4800 bps on the switched network. Newer versions of the 208A are offered by AT&T as the 2048A and 2048C models, which are also designed for four-wire leased line operation.

Both Bell 208 type modems and CCITT V.27 modems pack data three bits at a time, encoding them for transmission as one of eight phase angles.

Unfortunately, since each type of modem uses different phase angles to represent a tribit value, they cannot talk to each other. Table 7.9 lists the V.27 modulation phase shifts with respect to each of the eight possible tribit values. The most common use of 208 and CCITT V.27 modems with personal computers is when the PC is functioning as a remote job entry computer. Several manufacturers offer internal and external 208A/B modems, permitting PCs to communicate at 4800 bps over the PSTN or on a leased line.

## 9600 Bits per Second

Three common modems that are representative of devices that operate at 9600 bps are the Bell System 209 and the CCITT V.29 and V.32 modems. Modems equivalent to the Bell System 209 and CCITT V.29 devices are designed to operate in a full-duplex, synchronous mode at 9600 bps over leased lines. The Bell System 209A modem operates by employing a quadrature amplitude modulation technique as previously illustrated in Figure 7.17. Included in the Bell System modem is a built-in synchronous multiplexer that combines up to four data rate combinations for transmission at 9600 bps. Other vendors market similar modems with and without the built-in multiplexer.

With the exception of Bell System 209 type modems, a large majority of 9600-bps devices manufactured throughout the world adhere to the CCITT V.29 standard. The V.29 standard governs data transmission at 9600 bps for full- or half-duplex operation on leased lines, with fallback

**Table 7.9** V.27 Modulation Phase Shift Versus Bit Pattern

| TRIBIT VALUES | PHASE CHANGE |
|---|---|
| 001 | 0 |
| 000 | 45 |
| 010 | 90 |
| 011 | 135 |
| 111 | 180 |
| 110 | 225 |
| 100 | 270 |
| 101 | 315 |

data rates of 7200 and 4800 bps allowed. At 9600 bps, the serial data stream is divided into groups of four consecutive bits. The first bit in the group is used to determine the amplitude to be transmitted. The remaining three bits are encoded as a phase change, with the phase changes identical to those of the V.27 recommendation listed in Table 7.9.

Table 7.10 lists the relative signal element amplitude of V.29 modems, based on the value of the first bit in the quadbit and the absolute phase, which is determined from bits 2 through 4. Thus, a serial data stream composed of the bits 1100 would have a phase change of 270 degrees and its signal amplitude would be 5.

The resulting signal constellation pattern of V.29 modems is illustrated in Figure 7.24.

Although the V.29 modem was originally designed for use on leased lines, its modulation scheme has been successfully adapted for use on the

**Table 7.10** V.29 Signal Amplitude Construction

| ABSOLUTE PHASE | 1ST BIT | RELATIVE SIGNAL ELEMENT AMPLITUDE |
|---|---|---|
| 0,90,180,270 | 0 | 3 |
|  | 1 | 5 |
| 45,135,225,315 | 0 | $\sqrt{2}$ |
|  | 1 | $3\sqrt{2}$ |

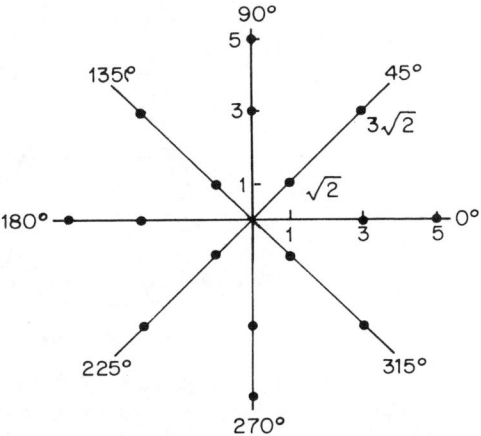

**Figure 7.24** V.29 Signal Constellation Pattern.

switched network. A variety of vendor modems that use asymmetrical transmission are based on V.29 technology. In addition, several vendors have incorporated data compression into V.29 modems, boosting their data rate over the PSTN to 19.2 Kbps when a high rate of compression is achievable. Both data compression and asymmetrical transmission are covered later in this chapter.

A relatively new CCITT recommendation that warrants attention is the V.32 standard. V.32 is based on a modified quadrature amplitude modulation technique and is designed to permit full-duplex 9600 bps transmission over the switched telephone network. A V.32 modem establishes two high-speed channels that operate in opposite directions, as illustrated in Figure 7.25. Each of these channels shares approximately the same bandwidth. An echo-canceling technique is employed by V.32 modems that permits transmitted and received signals to occupy the same bandwidth. This is made possible by designing intelligence into the modem's receiver that permits it to cancel out the effects of its own transmitted signal. This feature enables the modem to distinguish its sending signal from the signal being received.

Unfortunately, echo-canceling requires sophisticated circuitry, which causes the cost of V.32 modems to be approximately twice the cost of V.29 modems that offer the same data rate on leased lines.

A summary of the operational characteristics of Bell System and CCITT V series modems is given in Table 7.11.

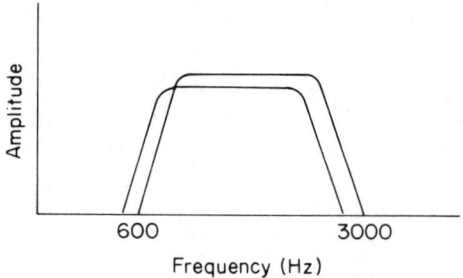

**Figure 7.25** V.32 Channel Derivation—A V.32 modem obtains high-speed full-duplex transmission by deriving two channels that share approximately the same bandwidth using an echo-canceling technique. Table 7.11 summarizes the operational characteristics of Bell System and CCITT V series type modems.

Table 7.11  Modem Operational Characteristics

| MODEM TYPE | DATA RATE | TRANSMISSION TECHNIQUE | MODULATION TECHNIQUE | TRANSMISSION MODE | LINE USE |
|---|---|---|---|---|---|
| BELL SYSTEM | | | | | |
| 103 A,E | 300 | Asynchronous | FSK | Half, Full | Switched |
| 103 F | 300 | Asynchronous | FSK | Half, Full | Leased |
| 201 B | 2400 | Synchronous | PSK | Half, Full | Leased |
| 201 C | 2400 | Synchronous | PSK | Half, Full | Switched |
| 202 C | 1200 | Asynchronous | FSK | Half | Switched |
| 202 S | 1200 | Asynchronous | FSK | Half | Switched |
| 202 D/R | 1800 | Asynchronous | FSK | Half, Full | Leased |
| 202 T | 1800 | Asynchronous | FSK | Half, Full | Leased |
| 208 A | 4800 | Synchronous | PSK | Half, Full | Leased |
| 208 B | 4800 | Synchronous | PSK | Half | Switched |
| 209 A | 9600 | Synchronous | QAM | Full | Leased |
| 212 | 0–300 | Asynchronous | FSK | Half, Full | Switched |
| | 1200 | Asynchronous/Synchronous | PSK | Half, Full | Switched |

Table 7.11 Modem Operational Characteristics (continued)

| MODEM TYPE | DATA RATE | TRANSMISSION TECHNIQUE | MODULATION TECHNIQUE | TRANSMISSION MODE | LINE USE |
|---|---|---|---|---|---|
| CCITT | | | | | |
| V.21 | 300 | Asynchronous | FSK | Half, Full | Switched |
| V.22 | 600 | Asynchronous | PSK | Half, Full | Switched/Leased |
| | 1200 | Asynchronous/Synchronous | PSK | Half, Full | Switched/Leased |
| V.22 bis | 2400 | Asynchronous | QAM | Half, Full | Switched |
| V.23 | 600 | Asynchronous/Synchronous | FSK | Half, Full | Switched |
| | 1200 | Asynchronous/Synchronous | FSK | Half, Full | Switched |
| V.26 | 2400 | Synchronous | PSK | Half, Full | Leased |
| | 1200 | Synchronous | PSK | Half | Switched |
| V.26 bis | 2400 | Synchronous | PSK | Half | Switched |
| V.26 ter | 2400 | Synchronous | PSK | Half, Full | Switched |
| V.27 | 4800 | Synchronous | PSK | | |
| V.29 | 9600 | Synchronous | QAM | Half, Full | Leased |
| V.32 | 9600 | Synchronous | QAM | Half, Full | Switched |

## Nonstandard Modems

Because today's PC users require faster transmission throughput to support file transfer and interactive full-screen display operations, several vendors have designed proprietary operating modems to achieve data rates that would have been beyond the realm of belief several years ago. Some of these modems incorporate data compression and decompression algorithms, permitting data to be compressed prior to transmission and then expanded back into its original form at the modem at the opposite end of the communications path.

Because compression decreases the amount of data requiring transmission, the modem can accept a higher data rate input than it is capable of transmitting. Thus, a V.29 operating modem incorporating data compression that has a 2-to-1 compression ratio is theoretically capable of transmitting data at 19200 bps, even though the modem operates at 9600 bps. Because the compression efficiency depends on the susceptibility of the data to the compression algorithms built into the modem, in actuality the modem operates at a variable data rate. When no compression is possible, the modem operates at 9600 bps, whereas the actual throughput of the device increases as the data input into the modem becomes more susceptible to compression.

## Packetized Ensemble Protocol

A second type of nonstandard modem reached the marketplace in 1986. More formally known as a *packetized ensemble protocol modem,* this hardware incorporates a revolutionary advance in technology. It incorporates a high-speed microprocessor and approximately 70,000 lines of instructions built into read only memory (ROM) chips on the modem board.

To better understand the operation of a packetized ensemble protocol modem, let us review the operation of a conventional modem, using the Bell System 212 device for illustrative purposes.

When a Bell 212A modem modulates data, two carrier signals are varied to impress information onto the line. One carrier signal operates at a frequency of 1200 Hz, whereas the second carrier frequency operates at 2400 Hz. This results in two paths that enable full-duplex transmission to occur on a two-wire circuit. Thus, at any instant in time data can only flow on two frequencies. Figure 7.26 illustrates the carrier use of a Bell 212A modem.

Under the packetized ensemble protocol, the originating modem simultaneously transmits 512 tones onto the line. The receiving modem evaluates the tones and the effect of noise on the entire voice bandwidth, reporting back to the originating device the frequencies that are unusable. The originating modem then selects a transmission format most suitable to the useful tones, employing 2-bit, 4-bit, or 6-bit quadrature amplitude modulation (QAM) and packetizes the data prior to its transmission.

As an example of the efficiency of this type of modem, assume that 400 tones are available for a 6-bit QAM scheme. This would result in a packet size of 400 times 6, or 2400 bits. If each of the 400 tones is varied 4 times per second, a data rate of approximately 10,000 bps is obtained. Note that the modem automatically generates a 16-bit cyclic redundancy check (CRC) for error detection, which is added to each transmitted packet. At the receiving modem, a similar CRC check is performed. If the transmitted and locally generated CRC characters do not match, the receiving modem will then request the transmitting modem to retransmit the packet, resulting in error correction by retransmission.

Some of the key advantages of a packetized ensemble protocol modem are its ability to automatically adjust to usable frequencies, which greatly increases the use of the line bandwidth, and its ability to lower its fallback rate in small increments. The latter is illustrated in Figure 7.27, which shows how this type of modem loses the ability to transmit on one or a few tones as the noise level on a circuit increases, resulting in a slight decrease in the data rate of the modem. In comparison, a conventional modem, such as a 9600 bps device, is designed to fall back to a predefined fraction of its main data rate, typically 7200 or 4800 bps.

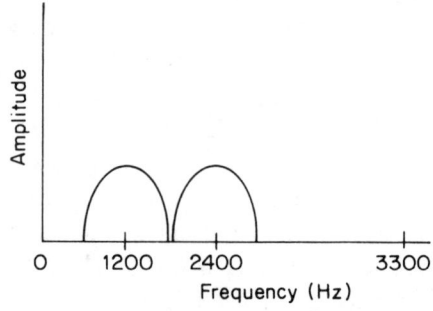

**Figure 7.26** Bell System 212A Frequency Usage.

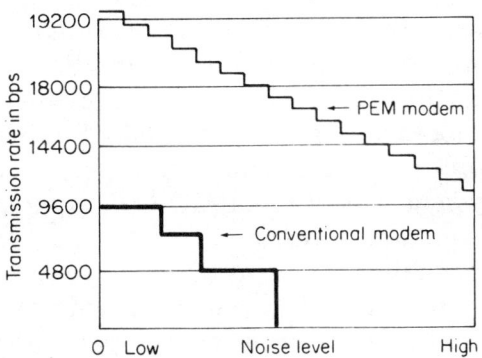

**Figure 7.27** Packetized Ensemble Modem.

**Table 7.12** Comparing Throughput Efficiencies

| ITEM TO TRANSMIT | TRANSMISSION RATE (BPS) | | | | |
|---|---|---|---|---|---|
| | 300 | 1200 | 2400 | 4800 | 10000 |
| 1 page 250 words (sec) | 40 | 10 | 5 | 2.5 | 1.2 |
| 20 pages (sec) | 800 | 200 | 100 | 50 | 24 |
| 360K byte diskette (min) | 163.84 | 40.96 | 20.48 | 10.24 | 4.92 |

To appreciate the advantages of using high-speed modems, examine the transmission of a 250-word document, 20 such documents, and the contents of a 360K-byte diskette at different data rates. A comparison of the use of 300-, 1200-, 2400-, 4800-, and 10000-bps modems is presented in Table 7.12. As indicated, a 10000-bps modem can substantially reduce the transmission time required to send long files between personal computers or a personal computer and a mainframe computer. In fact, the retail price of approximately $900 for a packetized ensemble modem can be recovered in less than one year through a reduction in communications charges. This will occur if you have a requirement to transmit via a long-distance telephone call the contents of a diskette just once every few weeks to another computer.

The original packetized ensemble modem was designed by Telebit Corporation and is marketed as the Trailblazer. Over the past few years, Telebit has entered into a variety of agreements with other vendors—Digital Communications Associates (DCA), Racal-Milgo, and VenTel. Under these agreements, vendors have marketed packetized ensemble protocol modems using the names Fastlink and Pathfinder, among others. Regardless of the name used, the key to recognizing the capability of this modem lies in its use of 512 carriers and its PEP modulation scheme. Both Telebit and the previously mentioned third party vendors market a modem card for the system unit of an IBM PC or compatible personal computer and a stand-alone unit that can be attached to any computer with a standard RS-232 communications port.

In addition to being compatible with other packetized ensemble protocol modems, these devices are compatible with V.22 bis, V.22, 212A, and 103 type modems. This compatibility enables you to use the device for high-speed file transfer operations when it is connected to another packetized ensemble protocol modem. Also, the device can access information utilities, other personal computers, and mainframes that are connected to industry standard modems. Newer versions of the Trailblazer and equivalent modems marketed by other vendors include a V.32 compatibility, so the modem can support six distinct modulation methods. Telebit markets its modem with V.32 compatibility as the Trailblazer Plus.

## Asymmetrical Modems

Borrowing an old modem design concept, several vendors have introduced asymmetrical modems for use by personal computers. These modems, in essence, contain two channels that in the early days of modem development were known as the primary and secondary channel.

Originally, modems with a secondary channel were used for remote batch transmissions, in which the primary high-speed channel was used to transmit data to a mainframe computer while a lower-speed secondary channel was used by the mainframe to acknowledge each transmitted block. The acknowledgments were much shorter than the transmitted data blocks, so it was possible to obtain efficient full-duplex transmission even though the secondary channel might have one-tenth of the bandwidth of the primary channel.

In the late 1980s, several modem vendors realized that although high-speed transmission might be required to refresh a PC's screen when the personal computer was connected to a mainframe or for a file transfer, transmission in the opposite direction is typically limited by the user's typing speed or the shortness of acknowledgments in comparison to data blocks of information. Realizing this, modem vendors developed a new category of devices that use wide and narrow channels to transmit in two directions simultaneously. The process is illustrated in Figure 7.28. The wide bandwidth channel permits a data rate of 9600 bps, whereas the narrow bandwidth channel supports a data rate of 300 bps. These asymmetrical modems differ from older modems with secondary channels in the incorporation of logic to monitor the output of attached devices and then to reverse the channels, permitting an attached PC to access the higher speed (wider bandwidth) channel when necessary. Although no standards existed for asymmetrical modems when this book was written, several manufacturers were attempting to formulate the use of common frequency assignments for channels. A 9600-bps asymmetrical modem has a retail price approximately two-thirds that of a V.32 modem, so it appears that consumer use of this type of modem will result in the development of standards.

## Intelligent Modems

The incorporation of microprocessor technology into modems has created a revolution in modem design as well as the addition of enhanced capabilities to this category of communications hardware. Through programming, the intelligence of the microprocessor was first used to develop functions a modem would initiate based on receiving predefined commands. The series of commands the modem responds to is known as its *command set* and can include automatic dialing of a telephone number, redialing the number, and terminating or disconnecting a call and similar operations.

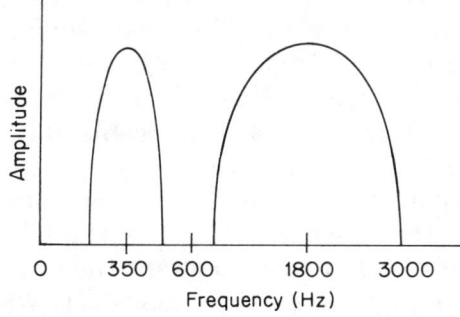

**Figure 7.28** Asymmetrical Modem Channel Assignment—An asymmetrical modem encodes data onto two carrier signals. High-speed data is encoded onto an 1800-Hz carrier; low-speed data is encoded onto a 350-Hz carrier.

In addition to functions supported by the command set, two additional operations incorporated into most intelligent modems are error detection and correction capability and data compression. This discussion first focuses on the most popular modem command set, considered to be a de facto standard—the Hayes Microcomputer Products command set. Next, due to the popularity of the Microcom MNP protocol, which incorporates both error detection and correction capability as well as data compression, we will examine each of the nine classes of that protocol. Then you can compare the MNP protocol with recent CCITT recommendations that standardize error detection and correction and data compression as well as develop an appreciation of the issues involved in ensuring compatibility between different modems.

## The Hayes Command Set

Due to the popularity of the Hayes Microcomputer Products series of Smartmodems, the command sets of those modems are the key to what the terms *intelligent modems* and *Hayes compatibility* mean. Just about all modern personal computer communications software programs are written to operate with the Hayes command set. The degree of Hayes compatibility that a non-Hayes modem provides affects the communications software that it can use. In some cases, non-Hayes modems work as well or even better than a Hayes modem if the software supports the non-Hayes features of that device. In other cases, the omission of one or more Hayes Smartmodem features may require you to reconfigure the communications software to work with a non-Hayes modem, usually eliminating a degree of functionality.

The Hayes command set actually consists of a basic set of commands and command extensions. The basic commands, such as those to place the modem off hook, dial a number, and perform similar operations, are common to all Hayes modems. The command extensions, such as using a specific operating speed, are applicable only to modems built to transmit and receive data at that speed.

The commands in the Hayes command set are initiated by transmitting an attention code to the modem, followed by the appropriate command or set of commands you want the modem to implement. The attention code is the character sequence AT, which must be specified as all uppercase or all lowercase letters. The requirement to prefix all command lines with the code AT has resulted in many modem manufacturers denoting their modems as "Hayes AT compatible."

The command buffer in a Hayes Smartmodem holds 40 characters, permitting a sequence of commands to be transmitted to the modem on one command line. This 40-character limit does not include the attention code, nor does it include spaces included in a command line to make the line more readable. Table 7.13 lists the major commands in the basic Hayes Command Set. Other modems, such as the Telebit Trailblazer, employ a command set that can be considered to be a superset of the Hayes command set. Although communications software that uses the Hayes command set can operate with this modem, such software cannot use the full potential of the modem. This is because the Hayes command set in 1990 only supported a data rate selection up to 9600 bps, and the Trailblazer modem could be set to data rates of 19200 bps by proprietary software commands.

**Table 7.13** Hayes Command Set Major Commands

| COMMAND | DESCRIPTION |
|---|---|
| A | Answer call |
| A/ | Repeat last command |
| C | Turn modem's carrier on or off |
| D | Dial a telephone number |
| E | Enable or inhibit echo of characters to the screen |
| F | Switch between half- and full-duplex modem operation |
| H | Hang up telephone (on hook) or pick up telephone (off hook) |
| I | Request identification code or request check sum |
| M | Turn speaker off or on |
| O | Place modem on-line |
| P | Pulse dial |
| Q | Request modem to send or inhibit sending of result code |
| R | Change modem mode to "originate-only" |
| S | Set modem register values |
| T | Tone dial |
| V | Send result codes as digits or words |
| X | Use basic or extended result code set |
| Z | Reset the modem |

The basic format required to transmit commands to a Hayes compatible intelligent modem is

```
AT Command[Parameter(s)]Command[Parameter(s)]...
```

Each command line includes the prefix AT, followed by the appropriate command and the command's parameters. The command parameters are usually the digits 0 or 1, which serve to define a specific command state. As an example, the command H0 tells the modem to hang up or disconnect a call, whereas H1 results in the modem going off hook—the term used to define the action that occurs when the telephone handset is lifted. A number of commands can be included in one command line as long as the number of characters does not exceed 40 (the size of the modem's command buffer). Finally, each command line must be terminated by a carriage return character.

To illustrate how to use the Hayes command set, assume you desire to automatically dial New York City information. First, you must tell the modem to go off hook, which has an effect similar to manually picking up the telephone handset. Then you must tell the modem the type of telephone system you are using, pulse or tone, and the telephone number to dial. Thus, if we have a terminal or personal computer connected to a Hayes compatible modem, we would send the following commands to the modem:

```
AT H1
AT DT1,212-555-1212
```

You can also enter ATH1 and ATDT1, because the space after AT is optional. In the first command line, the 1 parameter used with the H command places the modem off hook. In the second command, DT tells the modem to dial (D) a telephone number using tone (T) dialing. The digit 1 was included in the telephone number because it was assumed you have to dial long distance. The comma between the long-distance access number (1) and the area code (212) causes the modem to pause for two seconds before dialing the area code. This two-second pause is usually long enough to permit the long distance dial tone to be received before the modem dials the area code.

A Smartmodem automatically goes off hook when dialing a number, so the first command line is not actually required and is normally used for receiving calls. In the second command line, the type of dialing does not have to be specified if a previous call was made, because the modem will use the last type specified. Although users with only pulse dialing availability must specify P in the dialing command when using a Hayes Smartmodem, several vendors offer modems that automatically determine the type of dialing facility the modem is connected to and then use the appropriate dialing method. For other non-Hayes modems, when the method of dialing is unspecified, such modems automatically attempt to perform a tone dial and, if unsuccessful, redial using pulse dialing.

To appreciate the versatility of operations that the Hayes command set provides, assume two personal computer users are communicating with one another. If the users wish to switch from modem to voice operations without hanging up and redialing, one user can send a message via the communications program he or she is using to the other user, indicating that voice communication is desired. Then, both users simply lift their telephone handsets and type +++, press Enter, type ATH and press Enter again to switch from on-line operations to command mode (that is, to hang up). This command sequence causes the modems to hang up, turning off the modem carrier signals and permitting the users to converse.

## Result Codes

The response of the Smartmodem to commands is known as *result codes*. The Q command with a parameter of 1 is used to enable result codes to be sent from the modem in response to the execution of command lines. A parameter of 0 inhibits the modem from responding to the execution of each command line.

If the result codes are enabled, the V command can be used to determine the format of the result codes. When the V0 command is used, the result codes will be transmitted as digits. The use of a parameter of 1 causes the modem to transmit the result codes as words. Table 7.14 lists the Basic Results Codes set of the Hayes Smartmodem 1200. As an example of the use of these result codes, assume the following commands were sent to the modem:

```
AT Q0
AT V1
```

The first command causes the modem to respond to commands by transmitting result codes after each command line is executed. The second command causes the modem to transmit each result code as a word code. As Table 7.14 indicates, this causes the modem to generate the word code

**Table 7.14** Smartmodem 1200 Basic Result Codes Code Set

| DIGIT WORD | WORD CODE | MEANING |
|---|---|---|
| 0 | OK | Command line executed without error |
| 1 | CONNECT | Carrier detected |
| 2 | RING | Ring signal detected |
| 3 | NO CARRIER | Carrier signal lost or never heard |
| 4 | ERROR | Error detected in the command line |

CONNECT when a carrier signal is detected. If the command AT V0 were sent to the modem, a result code of 1 would be transmitted by the modem, because the 0 parameter causes the modem to transmit result codes as digits.

By combining an examination of the result codes issued by a Smartmodem with the generation of appropriate commands, software can be developed to perform such operations as redialing a previously dialed telephone number to resume transmission in the event a communications session is interrupted and automatically answering incoming calls when a ring signal is detected.

## Modem Registers

A third key to the degree of compatibility between non-Hayes and Hayes Smartmodems is the number, use, and programmability of registers contained in the modem. Hayes Smartmodems contain a series of programmable registers that govern the function of the modem and the operation of some of the commands in the modem's command set. Table 7.15 lists the functions of the first 12 registers built into the Hayes Smartmodem 1200, including the default value of each register and the range of settings permitted. These registers are known as S registers, because they are set with the S command in the Hayes command set. In addition, the current value of each register can be read under program control, permitting software developers to market communications programs that enable you to easily modify the default values of the modem's S registers.

To understand how useful it is to be able to read and reset the values of the modem's S registers, consider the time period a Smartmodem waits for a dial tone prior to going off hook and dialing a telephone number.

**Table 7.15**  S Register Control Parameters

| REGISTER | FUNCTION | DEFAULT VALUE | RANGE |
|---|---|---|---|
| S0 | Ring to answer on | | 0...255 |
| S1 | Counts number of rings | 0 | 0...255 |
| S2 | Escape Code Character | ASCII 43 | ASCII 0...127 |
| S3 | Carriage Return Character | ASCII 13 | ASCII 0...127 |
| S4 | Line Feed Character | ASCII 10 | ASCII 0...127 |
| S5 | Backspace Character | ASCII 8 | ASCII 0...127 |
| S6 | Dial tone wait time (seconds) | 2 | 2...255 |
| S7 | Carrier wait time (seconds) | 30 | 1...255 |
| S8 | Pause time caused by comma (seconds) | 2 | 0...255 |
| S9 | Carrier detect response time (1/10 second) | 6 | 1...255 |
| S10 | Time delay between loss of carrier and hang up (1/10 second) | 7 | 1...255 |
| S11 | Tone duration and spacing time (milliseconds) | 70 | 50...255 |

The dial tone wait time is controlled by the S6 register, so a program offering the ability to change this wait time might first read and display the setting of this register during the program's initialization. To read the S6 register, the program would generate the following command:

AT S6?

The modem's response to this command would be a value between 2 and 255, indicating the time period in seconds that the modem will wait for a dial tone. Assuming you want to change the waiting period, the communications program would then transmit the following command to the modem, where n would be a value between 2 and 255.

AT S6 = n

## Compatibility

For a non-Hayes modem to be fully compatible with a Hayes modem, command set compatibility, result codes compatibility, and modem register compatibility are required. Of the three, the modem register compatibility is usually the least important. Many users may prefer to consider only command set and response codes compatibility when acquiring intelligent modems.

The rationale for omitting register compatibility from consideration is the fact that many modem vendors manufacture compatible modems using the default values of the Hayes Smartmodem registers. This enables those manufacturers to avoid building the S registers into their modems, reducing the size, complexity, and often the price of their modems. Thus, if the default values of the S registers are sufficient and the modem under consideration is both command set and result code compatible, the issue of register compatibility can normally be eliminated as a factor.

# The MNP Protocol

The Microcom Networking Protocol (MNP) was developed by the modem manufacturer Microcom, Inc., to provide a sophisticated level of error detection and correction as well as to enhance the data transfer of modems. Microcom has licensed MNP for use by other modem vendors, resulting in a large number of manufacturers incorporating this protocol into their products. Today, the MNP error correcting protocol is considered a de facto industry standard, with over 750,000 modems including this feature at the time of this writing.

## Layered Design

The MNP protocol was designed in a layered fashion and includes link, session, and file transfer layers. The MNP link layer is responsible for establishing a connection between two devices. Included in the link layer is a set of negotiations that are conducted between devices to enable them to agree on such factors as the transmission mode (full- or half-duplex), how many data messages can be transmitted prior to requiring a confirmation, and how much data can be contained in a single message. After these values are established, the link layer initiates the data transfer process as well as performing error detection and correction through the use of a frame checking scheme that uses cyclic redundancy checking.

## Cyclic Codes

When a cyclic error-detection scheme is employed, the message block is treated as a data polynomial $D(x)$, which is divided by a predefined generating polynomial $G(x)$, resulting in a quotient polynomial $Q(x)$ and a remainder polynomial $R(x)$, such that

$$D(x)/G(x) = Q(x) + R(x)$$

The remainder of the division process is known as the cyclic redundancy check (CRC) and is normally 16 bits in length or two 8-bit bytes. The CRC checking method used in the MNP protocol results in the remainder of the division process being appended to each block of data to be transmitted. The receiving modem uses the same predefined generating polynomial to generate its own CRC based on the received message block and then compares the "internally" generated CRC with the transmitted CRC. If the two match, the receiving modem transmits a positive acknowledgment to the transmitting modem, which not only informs the distant modem that the data was received correctly but also informs the modem to send the next block of any additional blocks of data. If an error has occurred, the internally generated CRC will not match the transmitted CRC, and the receiving modem will transmit a negative acknowledgment, which informs the transmitting modem to retransmit the block previously sent.

Figure 7.29 illustrates the format of an MNP frame of information. Each frame contains three bytes that act as a "start flag." The SYN character tells the receiver that a message is about to arrive, the combination of data link escape (DLE) and start of text (STX) informs the receiver that everything following is part of the message. The first header describes the user data, such as the duplex setting and number of data messages before confirmation. The session header defines additional information about the transmitted data, which enables the automatic negotiation of the level of service that can be used between devices communicating with one another. Currently there are nine versions or classes of the MNP protocol, with each higher level adding more sophistication and efficiency. When an MNP link is established, the protocol assumes that the devices on both sides can only operate at the lowest level. Then, the devices negotiate with each other to determine the highest mutually supported class of MNP services they can support. If a non-MNP device is encountered, the MNP device reverts to a "dumb" operating mode,

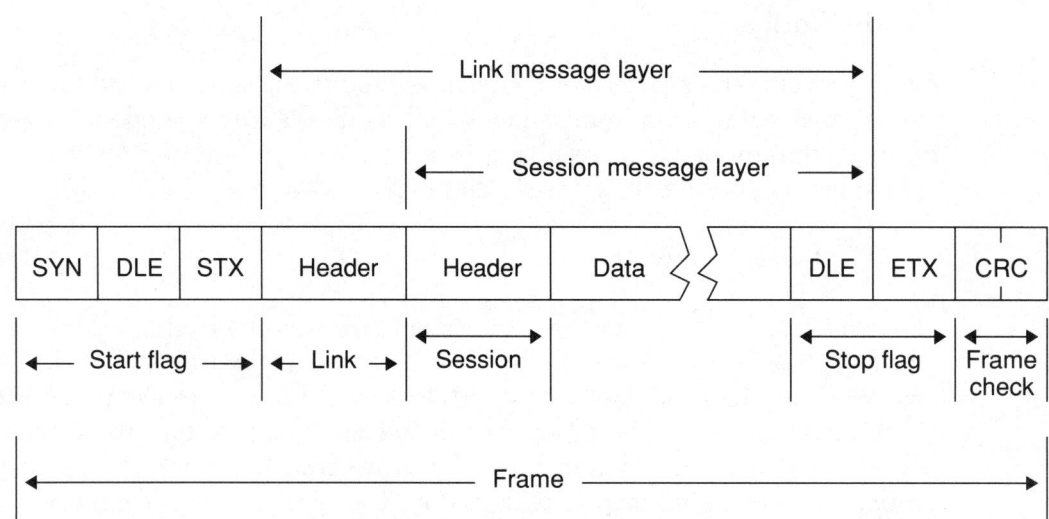

**Figure 7.29** MNP Block Format.

providing an MNP modem with the ability to be used with non-MNP devices, assuming their modulation methods are compatible. Table 7.16 describes the nine MNP protocol classes.

# Modem Selection Considerations

A large number of parameters may be considered by some PC users in the modem selection process, while other users, due to their application requirement, may be content to examine only a limited number of parameters. The following lists the major modem-selection parameters to consider as well as some of the more popular choices available for selection for many parameter categories:

Compatibility: modulation, command set, error detection and correction, and data compression method
Alternate voice/data switch
Automatic features: autodial, autoanswer, and redial
Asynchronous character bit length
Bundled software
Configuration: stand-alone or card
Data rate: 300, 1200, or 2400

**Table 7.16**  MNP Protocol Classes

| PROTOCOL CLASS | DESCRIPTION |
|---|---|
| Class 1 | Lowest performance level; uses an asynchronous byte-oriented, half-duplex data exchange. The protocol efficiency of a Class 1 implementation is about 70%. (A 2400-bps modem using MNP Class 1 will have a 1690 bps throughput.) |
| Class 2 | Uses asynchronous byte-oriented, full-duplex data exchange. The protocol efficiency of a Class 2 modem is about 84%. (A 2400-bps modem will realize 2000-bps throughput.) |
| Class 3 | Uses synchronous bit-oriented, full-duplex data exchange. This approach is more efficient than the asynchronous, byte-oriented approach, which takes 10 bits to represent 8 data bits because of the "start" and "stop" framing bits. The synchronous data format eliminates the need for start and stop bits. Users still send data asynchronously to a Class 3 modem, but the modems communicate with each other synchronously. The protocol efficiency of a Class 3 implementation is about 108%. (A 2400-bps modem will actually run at a 2600-bps throughput.) |
| Class 4 | Adds two techniques—adaptive packet assembly and data phase optimization. In the former technique, if the data channel is relatively error free, MNP assembles larger data packets to increase throughput. If the data channel is introducing many errors, then MNP assembles smaller data packets for transmission. Although smaller data packets increase protocol overhead, they concurrently decrease the throughput penalty of data retransmissions—more data is successfully transmitted on the first try. Data phase optimization is a technique for eliminating some of the administrative information in the data packets, which further reduces protocol overhead. The protocol efficiency of a Class 4 implementation is about 120%. (A 2400-bps modem will effectively yield a 2900-bps throughput.) |
| Class 5 | Adds data compression, which uses a real-time adaptive algorithm to compress data. The real-time capabilities of the algorithm allow the data compression to operate on interactive terminal data as well as file transfer data. The *adaptive algorithm* refers to its ability to continuously analyze user data and adjust the compression parameters to maximize data throughput. The effectiveness of data compression algorithms depends on the data pattern being |

**Table 7.16** MNP Protocol Classes (continued)

| PROTOCOL CLASS | DESCRIPTION |
|---|---|
| Class 5 (continued) | processed. Most data patterns benefit from data compression, with performance advantages typically ranging from 1.3 to 1.0 and 2.0 to 1.0, although some files may be compressed at an even higher ratio. Based on a 1.6-to-1 compression ratio, Microcom gives Class 5 MNP a 200% protocol efficiency, or 4800-bps throughput in a 2400-bps modem installation. |
| Class 6 | Adds 9600-bps V.29 modulation, universal link negotiation, and statistical duplexing to MNP Class 5 features. Universal link negotiation allows two unlike MNP Class 6 modems to find the highest operating speed (between 300 and 9600 bps) at which both can operate. The modems begin to talk at a common lower speed and automatically "negotiate" the use of progressively higher speeds. Statistical duplexing is a technique for simulating full-duplex service over half-duplex high-speed carriers. Once the modem link has been established using full-duplex V.22 modulation, user data streams move via the carrier's faster half-duplex mode. However, the modems monitor the data streams and allocate each modem's use of the line to best approximate a full-duplex exchange. Microcom claims that a 9600-bps V.29 modem using MNP Class 6 (and Class 5 data compression) can achieve 19.2-Kbps throughput over dial circuits. |
| Class 7 | Uses an advanced form of Huffman encoding, enhanced data compression. Enhanced data compression has all of the characteristics of Class 5 compression; in addition, it predicts the probability of repetitive characters in the data stream. Class 7 compression, on the average, reduces data by 42%. |
| Class 8 | Adds CCITT V.29 Fast-Train modem technology to Class 7 enhanced data compression, enabling half-duplex devices to emulate full-duplex transmission. |
| Class 9 | Combines CCITT V.32 modem modulation technology with Class 7 enhanced data compression, resulting in a full-duplex throughput that can exceed that obtainable with a V.32 modem by 300%. Class 9 also employs selective retransmission, in which error packets are retransmitted, as well as piggybacking, in which acknowledgment information is added to the data. |

Data format: asynchronous or synchronous
Half/full-duplex on two-wire lines
Interface to the telephone network
Originate/answer mode
Power source
Security features: dialback or password
Self-testing features and indicators
Stored log-on/telephone numbers
Telephone dialing method: pulse or rotary

In reviewing the list, note that compatibility was placed on the top of a list whose remaining entries are in alphabetical order. Although your requirements will govern the weight assigned to each parameter, compatibility is by far the most important item to consider.

## Compatibility

The complexity of features added to modems through the incorporation of microprocessor technology no longer ensures compatibility based simply on the method of data modulation. Modem users must now consider modulation as well as the command set of the modem, its method of error detection and correction, and the type—or lack—of data compression support.

Concerning modulation, while differences in high-speed transmission techniques may preclude compatibility between modems manufactured by different vendors, such modems may be able to communicate with each other at lower data rates. One example of this downward compatibility is the ability of asymmetrical and packetized ensemble protocol modems to operate as V.22 bis devices. These two modems are totally incompatible with one another in their high-speed data transfer mode. Once they are placed in their V.22 bis mode, however, they can communicate with each other as well as with other proprietary and nonproprietary modulation modems that include a V.22 bis support capability.

The error detection and correction method is a second key factor to consider in investigating modem compatibility. Although all modems with an error detection and correction feature can disable this feature, doing so simply removes error detection and correction as a compatibility issue. Users that want to ensure data integrity during transmission will probably prefer to obtain a modem that incorporates the same error detection and correction algorithm as the modem they will usually communicate with. The selection of two modems that support the MNP protocol ensures compatibility between modems, but the CCITT recently promulgated what is referred to as the V.42 standard. This standard defines the Link Access Protocol M (LAP-M) as the primary error detection and correction method, whereas MNP is considered as a secondary method. Thus, it is entirely possible that new modems may be manufactured with LAP-M error detection and correction capability, making them incompatible for error-free operation with MNP modems. Similarly, a packetized ensemble protocol modem that does not support the MNP protocol cannot communicate with an MNP modem in an error-free mode of operation.

At the time of this writing, more than 60 modem vendors incorporated data compression algorithms in their products. Most vendors either licensed MNP from Microcom or competing data compression algorithms from two other firms. Unfortunately, the three leading data compression algorithms are incompatible with one another. Because data compression is normally implemented in a modem's high-speed data transfer mode, it is quite possible, as an example, for two V.32 modems to be incompatible with one another due to differences in the compression algorithms used. To obtain compatibility, users would have to disable the data compression feature on each modem or obtain a second modem that supports both the V.32 modulation standard and the data compression algorithm used by the modem they wish to communicate with.

Although several vendors, including AT&T and IBM, have introduced proprietary command sets, the Hayes command set has, by far, the most support with respect to software programs. In spite of this, you should take care to ensure that the program you anticipate using with your modem fully supports the modem. This is because many modems that are "Hayes command set compatible" were designed with extensions to that command set to support proprietary features, such as enabling or disabling error detection and correction. Verify both the command set supported by the modem and the modem supported by your software. Now that we have examined compatibility issues, let us examine the remaining selection parameters.

## Alternate Voice/Data Switch

Alternate voice/data capability is normally accomplished by a switch on the modem or via software control. If you want to use your PC to switch between voice and data, this feature should be considered.

## Automatic Features

Automatic modem features run the gamut from automatic dialing and answering of calls to line sound monitoring and redialing of the last number dialed. Normally, the command set used to implement the features is more important than any one feature offered by a specific modem vendor. This is because asynchronous communications programs are written to operate with the Hayes command set, and if your automatic modem features do not correspond to this command set your software choices may be limited.

## Asynchronous Character Bit Length

The asynchronous character bit length actually refers to the number of data bits and stop bits an asynchronous modem supports. Typically, most modems support 7 or 8 data bits and 1 or 2 stop bits.

## Bundled Software

Concerning software bundling, many modem vendors package an asynchronous communications program with their hardware. Although such packages offer a convenient—and usually more economical—method of obtaining hardware and software, just as all modems are not equal, neither are all communications programs. Thus, you should carefully check the features of the communications software if its acquisition is of major importance.

## Configuration

As discussed earlier in this chapter, you can obtain an external (stand-alone) modem or a modem built onto a card that must be inserted into an expansion slot in the computer's system unit. There are many advantages to internal modems, including eliminating the cable requirement between the computer and modem as well as its "nonfootprint." Because 2400-bps modems consume much more power than 300- or 1200-bps modems, you should examine the power consumption of other devices installed if you own a PC. This is because a PC has a 65-watt power supply, whereas the PC XT has a 135-watt power supply and the PC AT has a 192-watt power supply.

## Data Rate

Although a 2400-bps modem can transmit and receive information twice as fast as a 1200-bps modem, a higher data rate may not always be best. Because no one can type at the rate of 300 characters per second, it makes little sense to access an information utility at 2400 bps for interactive query-response applications if the utility charges more per connect hour at the higher data rate.

On the opposite side of the spectrum, if you expect to transmit and receive a large volume of data, higher-speed modems, such as those operating at 2400 or 9600 bps, may be more appropriate. In such cases, the savings from reduced transmission durations may exceed the cost of the higher-speed modem after several months of usage.

## Data Format

To communicate synchronously, you must use a synchronous modem. Although most PCs presently communicate asynchronously, synchronous transmission normally permits a higher level of data transfer to occur and offers the ability for a personal computer to emulate a batch terminal. Some modems, such as the Bell System 212A and compatible devices, can operate either asynchronously or synchronously based on the setting of a switch in the modem or through receipt of an appropriate command. Due to advances in technology, by the end of the decade one might expect 9600-bps modem cards to cost no more than 300-bps modem cards cost today.

## Half/Full-duplex on Two-wire Lines

The switched telephone network represents a two-wire circuit, so you cannot have two transmissions in opposite directions at the same time. In comparison, a four-wire leased line consists of 2 two-wire pairs, allowing the simultaneous transmission and reception of data to occur on each two-wire pair.

Modems are able to transmit in full-duplex on a two-wire circuit by splitting the bandwidth of the circuit by frequency. Doing so results in two derived channels, each containing a segment of frequency. Thus, a modem that splits a two-wire circuit by frequency is capable of full-duplex transmission on the switched network. Because simultaneous transmission and reception allows blocks of data to be quickly acknowledged, a full-duplex modem provides a higher level of throughput than a half-duplex modem.

## Interface

Most modems currently marketed can be interfaced to the telephone network via a modular plug that is inserted into a wall-mounted jack. The most popular jacks used are RJ11, RJ12, and RJ13. Normally if you are making a single line connection, your cable from the modem will be inserted into an RJ11 wall jack. For a multiline installation, the cable is usually connected to an RJ12 or RJ13 telephone jack. The information pages in the front of your local telephone book usually contain a detailed explanation of the type of telephone jack required and the requirements for notifying the telephone company of the installation of the modem to the telephone line.

## Originate/Answer Mode

If you expect to originate and answer calls, an originate/answer mode modem is an absolute requirement. Otherwise, the frequency assignments between your modem and the distant device will be incompatible, because the distant modem would most likely be an originate mode modem. As previously explained, an originate modem cannot communicate with another originate mode modem.

## Power Source

Although most external modems obtain power from a transformer with a wall plug that directly plugs into a standard AC outlet, several manufacturers offer a series of modems that obtain power from their connection to the telephone line. This feature may not appear to be significant, but it can alleviate the necessity of long extension cords when you want to connect a modem to a telephone jack that is remotely located from a conventional power outlet. Modem boards obtain power from the system unit of the computer they are installed in. Because a 1200-bps modem usually requires four times the power of a 300-bps modem, you are cautioned to check the power requirements of all components in a fully populated PC; the sum of the power of all components in operation can conceivably exceed the maximum output of the PC's 65-watt power supply.

## Security Features

Due to the mass media exposure of various "hackers" and the popularity of movies like *War Games,* several vendors market security modems. These modems usually incorporate such features as dialback to the transmission originator to verify the location of the call's origination party or a password-checking mechanism. Such modems are normally sold for use at a mainframe computer center, but they can also be considered for use with a PC that operates as a corporate bulletin board or with a multiuser PC system that permits dial-in access. By using this type of modem, you can reduce the probability of unauthorized access.

## Self-Testing Features and Indicators

Although self-testing features are usually associated with expensive high-speed modems, many manufacturers of low-speed modems have incorporated this feature into their products. By pressing a button, issuing a command, or toggling a switch, you can place the modem in its self-test mode. If the modem performs a local test, a word generator in the modem transmits a predefined message to the transmitter that is then strapped to the receiver, bypassing the telephone line—hence the term *local test.*

    The receiver demodulates the data, which is then sent to a word comparator in the modem that checks the message content against the content it expects to receive. If the transmitted message matches the expected message, a green light is normally displayed to indicate that the modem has passed its self-test. If the message demodulated by the receiver does not match the value in the word comparator, a red light is usually displayed, indicating that the modem failed its self-test and that it requires service.

Other modems have diagnostic features built in that permit the device to be tested via the telephone from a remote diagnostic center. This permits the vendor or a company's technical control center to remotely check the operational status of the modem.

Most external modems contain a series of light-emitting diode (LED) indicators on the front panel of the device that display the status of the modem's operation. Typical indicators include a power indicator, which is illuminated when power to the modem is on; a terminal-ready indicator, which is illuminated when the attached PC or terminal is ready to send or receive data; a transmit data indicator, which illuminates when data is sent from the attached device to the modem; a receive data indicator, which illuminates when data is received from a distant computer or terminal; and a carrier detect signal, which illuminates when a carrier signal is received from a distant modem. Other indicators on some modems include an off-hook indicator, which illuminates when the modem is using the telephone line, and a high-speed indicator on dual-speed modems, which illuminates whenever the modem is operating at its high speed. Table 7.17 lists the most common modem indicator symbols, their meaning, and the resulting status of the modem when the indicator is illuminated on the front panel of the modem.

## Stored Log-on/Telephone Numbers

Although most modems obtain the telephone number to be dialed from a dialing directory in a software program, several modems can store both telephone numbers and log-on sequences required to access mainframe computers. These modems usually contain a limited amount of complimentary metal oxide semiconductor (CMOS) storage whose low power requirements are satisfied by a small battery in the modem.

## Telephone Dialing Method

A large part of the United States has tone dialing, but a few areas exist that can only accept rotary or pulse dialing. Normally, a modem that provides autoselect touch tone or pulse dialing is preferable, because it provides the PC user with the ability to access long-distance discount telephone services such as MCI or Sprint, whose access may require tone dialing. Even if you do not use a long distance service requiring tone dialing

**Table 7.17** Common Modem Indicator Symbols

| SYMBOL | MEANING | STATUS |
| --- | --- | --- |
| HS | High Speed | ON when the modem is communicating with another modem at 2400 baud. |
| AA | Auto Answer/Answer | ON when the modem is in Auto Answer mode and when on-line in Answer mode. |
| CD | Carrier Detect | ON when the modem receives a carrier signal from a remote modem. Indicates that data transmission is possible. |
| OH | Off Hook | ON when the modem takes control of the phone line to establish a data link. |
| RD | Receive Data | Flashes when a data bit is received by the modem from the phone line, or when the modem is sending result codes to the terminal device. |
| SD | Send Data | Flashes when a data bit is sent by the terminal device to the modem. |
| TR | Terminal Ready | ON when the modem receives a Data Terminal Ready signal. |
| MR | Modem Ready/Power | ON when the modem is powered on. |
| AL | Analog Loopback | ON when the modem is in Analog Loopback Self-Test mode. |

and are presently located in an area serviced by pulse dialing, the auto-select feature will provide you with the capability to take advantage of the quicker dialing capability of touch tone if it should be offered in your area without having to replace your modem.

With modem technology one of the most rapidly evolving technical fields, be aware that the parameters presented here should be used as a guide and not as an all-inclusive list to consider in selecting the most appropriate modem.

CHAPTER 8

# *Clone Construction*

The unqualified success of the IBM PC series can be judged by the large number of firms that developed compatible computers. The demand for PCs, XTs, and ATs resulted in hundreds of suppliers manufacturing components ranging in scope from system boards to power supplies that compose PC "clones." Recognizing the demand by individuals for IBM PC-compatible computers, a large number of electronic supply stores, mail order marketers, and other retailers started purchasing PC components in quantity from manufacturers and reselling them to individuals. Today, every component necessary to assemble a PC clone, including Basic Input-Output System (BIOS) modules that legally mimic the operation of IBM's BIOS, are readily available for purchase.

Unfortunately, only a few computer manufacturers had licensed IBM Micro Channel technology at the time this book was written, which inhibited the development of a secondary market in Micro Channel components. It will probably be several years or more before PS/2 components become commodity items. Until that time, clone construction will probably remain restricted to members of the PC series.

There are two basic methods of constructing a clone that provides the performance and compatibility of a member of the IBM PC series. You can purchase the individual components, such as a chassis, power supply, memory board, memory chips, adapter cards, monitor, and printer. Then you can assemble the individual components into a system in a manner similar to assembling a machine from an electronics kit. As an alternative to purchasing all components individually, you can acquire a system unit consisting of a power supply, system board, memory, and perhaps a few adapter boards bundled and sold as a minimally configured PC-compatible system. Then, you can tailor these minimum system processing requirements by adding other adapter cards, a monitor, and printer.

In this chapter we will examine both methods of clone construction. Since the second method of clone construction is actually hardware tailoring we will use that term where appropriate.

# Individual Components

The individual components of a personal computer are designed to fit together using a few screws and connectors; soldering is not normally required. The biggest problem involved in assembling individual components is to ensure that they are compatible with one another when they are purchased. Ensuring compatibility among components includes such functions as verifying that the system board can fit into, and be fastened to, the chassis and that when you fasten the power supply to the chassis, it does not interfere with the system board.

## System Board

The following lists the major features that you should consider before purchasing a system board:

Type of board
Type of microprocessor
Processor clock rate
Method of clock speed switching
Number of layers
Math coprocessor socket
Amount of memory
Memory capacity
Type of memory chips used
System BIOS used
System expansion slots

Although we are examining these features with a view to acquiring individual components, you should give them just as much attention if you are purchasing a minimally or fully configured and assembled compatible IBM PC system. We'll comment on each of these features in turn.

The *type of board* normally refers to its physical dimensions, which govern the type of chassis or case into which you insert the board. Basically, there are four common types of IBM PC series clone system boards: conventionally sized XT and AT type system boards, and space-saving XT and AT system boards that are designed to fit into a chassis approximately two-thirds the size of a conventional XT or AT system unit.

By mid-1987, most vendors had abandoned the manufacture of PC-type system boards with only five expansion slots in favor of PC XT-type system boards with eight slots. A few vendors, who market rugged-ized PC-compatibles for industrial purposes, offer an unusual system board: an adapter card that plugs into a passive PC-bus backplane that may have as many as twelve slots. These vendors use very large-scale integration (VLSI) gate arrays to compress, into two or three chips, all of the support logic that you normally find on a system board. The advantages of the system are ease of repair and ease of upgrading. If the computer malfunctions, you just replace each card in turn with a known-good card of the same type, and the computer is up and working again within a few minutes. You can upgrade from a PC XT type system to a PC AT system merely by changing the processor board.

The *type of microprocessor* included on the system board affects both the *processor clock rate* and the *method of clock speed switching*. Various versions of the Intel 8088 are used on most XT-type system boards. Although the Intel 8088 used in the IBM PC operated at 4.77 MHz, other versions of the 8088 can operate at 8 MHz and 10 MHz. Normally, system boards that incorporate other than the original 4.77 MHz 8088 microprocessor are known as turbo boards. These boards permit the operator, either through software or via the keyboard, to switch the operating rate of the microprocessor. In its standard mode of operation the Intel 8088 microprocessor operates at 4.77 MHz, permitting speed-sensitive software, which includes some games and most copy-protected programs, to function correctly. When switched into its turbo mode of operation, the 8088 will operate at either 8 MHz or 10 MHz, the turbo speed being dependent upon the type of 8088 and clocking circuitry included on the system board.

For AT type system boards, you can select a fixed-speed 80286 microprocessor operating at 6, 8, 10, or 12 MHz. Turbo AT system boards typically permit 6/8 MHz, 8/10 MHz, or 8/12 MHz operating rate selection.

Although no members of the original PC series used the Intel 80386 microprocessor, many vendors now market system boards with an 80386 or 80386SX microprocessor that can be installed in PC XT or PC AT type cases. The 80386 is a true 32-bit microprocessor that accesses memory and transfers data 32 bits at a time. The 80386SX accesses memory 32 bits at a time but performs I/O operations 16 bits at a time, permitting it to be easily adapted for use with the 16-bit bus system expansion slots used with the PC AT. The 80386SX has a lower wholesale cost than the 80386, which translates into an approximate $500 retail savings between system boards based upon the 80386 and 80386SX. No standard 32-bit expansion slot exists for PC type systems, so most 80386-based system boards are also designed to work with 16-bit expansion slots. Thus, you should probably consider purchasing an 80386SX-based system board rather than an 80386 based system board if you require the processing speed of an 80386 microprocessor.

The *number of layers* refers to the physical construction of the system board. Most boards are constructed with either two or four layers bonded together. Four-layer boards are slightly more expensive than two-layer boards; however, the additional layers provide more immunity to electrical noise that might adversely affect the operation of the personal computer.

Although every system board examined by the author contained a *math coprocessor socket*, the type of coprocessor supported varied considerably. Because the mathematical coprocessor must be compatible with the operating rate of the microprocessor, a considerable difference in the cost of the coprocessor can occur. As an example, an Intel 80287-2 designed to operate at 6 MHz costs approximately $100 less than an Intel 80287-3, which is designed to operate at 8 MHz.

The *amount of memory* included on the system board can range from 0K to 1M byte. In the case of the former, you must purchase RAM separately. In the case of the latter, if additional memory is required, you obtain it through the use of one or more adapter boards. In between the two extremes many system boards are sold with a portion of available "onboard" memory populated, requiring the purchaser to insert memory chips in all available locations of the system board prior to installing adapter cards. If additional memory can be installed on the system board, the type and speed of memory chips required to populate memory should be ascertained. Because 64K-bit chips are approximately one-third the cost of 256K-bit chips, it is slightly less expensive to populate system board RAM with 256K-bit chips than with 64K-bit chips.

The *type of BIOS* included on the system board is perhaps the ultimate factor that governs the compatibility of the resulting personal computer with a member of the IBM PC series. When the original IBM PC was introduced a few vendors simply copied its BIOS, resulting in several well-publicized copyright infringement actions initiated by IBM. Although some third party manufacturers, such as Compaq Computer Corporation, designed their own BIOS, many manufacturers selected BIOSs developed by a few companies that independently developed a legal emulation of IBM's BIOS. Among the most prominent vendors that market BIOS to system board and personal computer system manufacturers are Phoenix Technologies Ltd. and Award Software. A large portion of advertisements, both for system boards and for clone systems, include the terms "Phoenix BIOS" or "Award BIOS," indicating the source of the BIOS.

Phoenix BIOS is actually used in more personal computers than IBM and Compaq combined. Over 180 manufacturers rely on Phoenix, as their firmware enables personal computer vendors to focus upon the unique features and benefits that set their products apart from the competition while avoiding the months of in-house development that would be required to develop their own BIOS.

Phoenix PC XT compatible ROM BIOS supports the Intel 8086 and 8088 microprocessors as well as NEC V20, V30, and V40 microprocessors. Processing speeds from 4.77 through 9.54 MHz are supported as well as the optional use of the keyboard to change the speed of the clock. The company's BIOS supports internal and external 3½-inch 720K-byte diskette drives, providing storage compatibility with the IBM Convertible as well as members of the IBM PS/2 series. The company also markets an 80286 AT compatible ROM BIOS and an 80386 ROM BIOS, the latter enabling third party vendors to develop AT compatible systems that use the 80386 microprocessor.

Because different versions of ROM BIOS have been manufactured by companies specializing in this field, it is a good idea to verify which version is included on the system board under consideration. The major difference between most BIOS revisions is in the area of support for 3½-inch diskettes. Thus, purchasers who do not require this capability may be able to eliminate the BIOS version from consideration if the BIOS is produced by one of the major firmware developers.

Although the IBM XT and AT system boards both contain 8 *system expansion slots*, third party system boards can be obtained with 6, 7, 8, 10, and 12 expansion slots. When obtaining an AT type system board, you should check the number of 16-bit slots, as well as the total number of system expansion slots built into the system board.

In addition to determining the number of expansion slots and their type (8-bit or 16-bit), you should verify that they are I/O compatible with the IBM PC XT and AT buses. This compatibility will ensure that most expansion cards can be used in the resulting system unit.

## Power Supply

The following lists four of the major power supply features that you should consider for building a clone. Of the four features listed, the first two are the most important; the latter two are merely convenience features:

Wattage
Physical dimensions
Number of power connectors
Monitor power receptacle

## Cabinets

Cabinets or chassis are manufactured in a variety of shapes and sizes. Some cabinets are the exact size of the IBM PC XT and AT system units; other cabinets are reduced-size, space-saving chassis that create a smaller desktop footprint than similar IBM system units.

Both portable and desktop cabinets are readily available, with the type of chassis to be selected determined by your requirement for an easily transportable personal computer. Another important consideration in selecting an appropriate cabinet is the capacity of the device housing areas, which are usually expressed in terms of the number of half-height devices they can accept. Unfortunately, the reliance upon the device housing area capacity by itself can provide a false indication of the ultimate storage capacity of the cabinet. This false indication results from some cabinets having a built-in metal cage that can be used for the installation of one or more fixed disks, similar to the metal cage in the IBM PC AT. Thus, more appropriate measurements of the number of storage devices that can be installed within a cabinet are both the capacity of the device housing areas and the size of any metal cages included in the interior of the cabinet.

One of the most convenient features of a personal computer cabinet is often overlooked. This is the method required to open the cabinet to obtain access to the system board for the installation of adapter cards, memory, or storage devices. Members of the IBM PC series use a cover that requires either two or five screws to be unfastened from the rear of the system unit to enable the cover to be removed. Cabinet covers made by other vendors pop off or are held in place by latches, expediting the cover removal process. Note that most cases with flip-top lids are not FCC approved for Class B (home) use.

The following lists the major features that should be considered in acquiring the cabinet to house the individual components of a personal computer:

Size/footprint
Portable or desktop
Storage device capacity
Method required to open cabinet

Once the system board, power supply, and cabinet are selected, actual configuring of the system by the addition of adapter boards, internal and external devices, and peripherals is exactly the same for both methods of clone construction covered in this chapter. The next section examines the actual configuration process.

# Clone Tailoring

Until mid-1983—a few years after the introduction of the IBM PC—the purchase of a clone was viewed by many business organizations as akin to heresy. Many clones were only partially compatible with software that operated on the IBM PC and the "litmus" test of operating the Lotus 1-2-3 and Microsoft Flight Simulator programs was no guarantee that other software would operate, that the BIOS was legal, or that the vendor would not go out of business. Today, low-cost clones lure both the home buyer and corporate purchasing agent alike, in many instances providing a considerable price-performance advantage over members of the IBM PC series. IBM clones have transformed the personal computer marketplace into a multitude of shopping sources for commodity products. Over 100 companies primarily located in the United States, Japan, Korea, and Taiwan manufacture one or more personal computer clones.

The following lists the major features you should consider in selecting a clone system. Note that the first three features to be considered actually refer to those items previously discussed in describing the system board, power supply, and cabinet features in this chapter:

System board
Power supply
Cabinet/system unit housing
Keyboard type
Bundled software
Bundled hardware
Documentation
Warranty

## Keyboard

Although most clone systems include a keyboard, some vendors enable you to select from either an "AT style" keyboard or an "enhanced" keyboard, the latter containing function keys as well as light emitting diodes (LEDs) to indicate the state of the Caps Lock, Num Lock, and Scroll Lock keys.

## Bundled Software

Bundled software, or software packages included with the hardware purchase, can vary considerably between clone systems. Some vendors include a version of DOS and GW BASIC with their system; other vendors market such software as options. If DOS is offered, be sure to ascertain the version, because one or more commands in one version of DOS may not be included in another version.

Two versions of disk BASIC are included with every DOS diskette sold for use with members of the IBM PC series. Both of these BASIC interpreters require the use of internal, proprietary, read only memory on the system board of an IBM Personal Computer. This ROM code is known as Cassette BASIC. It was originally developed to limit the amount of RAM a BASIC interpreter would require because the system board of the original IBM PC contained a maximum 64K bytes of memory. The dependency on the use of ROM-based Cassette BASIC resulted in incompatibility of the BASIC interpreters on an IBM PC DOS diskette for operation on a clone. As a result of this incompatibility, Microsoft developed GW BASIC, which is a completely diskette-based version of the language that does not require the use of any code in ROM. Vendors marketing clone systems either bundle or separately sell a version of PC DOS designed for use with clones. This version of DOS is known as MS-DOS and includes GW BASIC either on the diskette or as a separate option.

A second type of software that some vendors bundle with clones is application software. Such software can range in scope from a word processor to an electronic spreadsheet or an integrated application program that may contain word processing, database, spreadsheet, and telecommunications capability.

## Bundled Hardware

The adage that "an IBM PC without adapter cards is a bargain" holds true for clone systems. By purchasing a minimally configured clone system, you obtain the flexibility to configure a system to satisfy your specific data processing requirements. Most clone systems offer a high degree of configuration flexibility, because a diskette controller and one diskette drive is usually included with the system, with an additional diskette or fixed disk storage being optional. Similarly, many clone systems do not bundle a display adapter or a monitor with the system, permitting you to select the most appropriate hardware to satisfy your display requirement.

Most adapter cards and storage devices are commodity items, so clone purchasers can easily tailor their system from hardware obtained from a variety of sources. Later, this chapter discusses the purchase of a minimally configured clone system tailored to the author's processing requirements through a variety of third party devices. Although clone tailoring provides a high degree of flexibility, on occasion it may be more appropriate to acquire a complete system. Many clone vendors advertise a system that includes 256, 512, or 640K bytes of RAM installed on the system board, a diskette drive adapter and one or two diskette drives, a graphics card, and monitor at a lower cost than you can obtain by separately purchasing the components. In such situations it is economically advantageous to purchase this type of system—if it meets all or most of your processing requirements. As an example, a system including a diskette controller, two diskette drives, and a monochrome display adapter and monochrome monitor would not satisfy your requirements if you needed 20M bytes or more of storage with a fixed disk. If the basic system satisfied all or most of your other requirements, it would be simple to obtain a fixed disk card from another vendor and install it into the clone system to satisfy your storage needs.

## Warranty

The type of warranty provided with clone systems varies considerably among vendors. Although most vendors warrant their system for a period of 1 year, some vendors offer 90-day or 15-, 18-, and 24-month warranty periods. The terms of vendor warranty can vary, so they should be carefully checked. Some vendors permit purchasers to bring their malfunctioning system to a local computer store, whereas other vendors require the system to be returned to the manufacturer. Still other warranties may provide on-site service for an initial period after purchase. In addition, some warranties cover parts and labor; other warranties only cover parts. Although the difference may appear trivial, the expenses associated with the repair of a personal computer can vary considerably. Under a worst-case scenario, the isolation and replacement of a $10 chip on the system board could involve $200 worth of labor, resulting in a parts-only warranty paying $10 for the repair, whereas a parts and labor warranty would cover the full $210 repair cost.

## Purchasing Sources

Prior to discussing the purchasing and tailoring of a clone system, the method used to consider different vendor products warrants attention. In examining different clone systems, I first conducted a literature search to determine the available features and cost of vendor products. One of the key sources of information on current product offerings was the classified advertising section of *PC Week*, which is considered "The National Newspaper of IBM Standard Microcomputing." Each week the "Hardware Mart" section of *PC Week* classifieds contains hundreds of advertisements, ranging in scope from the sale of individual components to clone systems. Another source I used was *Computer Shopper*, a monthly publication so large that it can require the better part of an afternoon to read.

The following lists the names and addresses of several publications you may wish to examine prior to purchasing either a clone system or one or more clone components.

*Computer Shopper*
407 S. Washington Avenue
Titusville, FL 32796

*InfoWorld*
1060 Marsh Road
Menlo Park, CA 94025

*Data Preference Used News*
1164 Triton Dr.
Foster City, CA 94404

*PC Week*
One Park Avenue
New York, NY 10016

*The Processor*
P.O. Box 85518
Lincoln, NE 68501

*Data Preference Used News* is a publication of Data Preference Inc., formerly Leasametric Inc., which, as the original name implied, lists used equipment. Such equipment is normally returned from the vendor's rental program, and on occasion you can find some excellent offerings of IBM, Compaq, and other personal computers as well as monitors, printers, and adapter cards. Most equipment is refurbished by Data Preference and has a 30-day warranty.

*The Processor* is another most interesting publication. Each issue lists hundreds of wholesale advertisements of dealers marketing a variety of computers ranging in scope from mainframes to micros. With patience and perseverence, you may be able to locate $1000 printers selling for $200 and PC XT systems with 20M-byte hard disks priced under $500!

Although any of the previously mentioned publications as well as numerous other trade magazines are excellent sources to determine the cost and capability of different clone products, I am old-fashioned and like to become familiar with hardware prior to purchasing it, especially if it has a considerable price tag. After all, how many persons purchase a new automobile without first taking a short test drive?

Perhaps the best source for comparison shopping where you can operate equipment as well as intelligently discuss the merits of products with vendor sales personnel is the Comdex exhibitions, sponsored by the Interface Group.

Comdex is an acronym for Computer Dealer Exhibition. Since the first Comdex exhibition approximately 12 years ago, which had an attendance of 3000 persons, this show has almost geometrically expanded to the point where over 50,000 persons attend Comdex (usually held in Atlanta) in the spring and 100,000 persons clog the exhibits in Las Vegas during the fall show.

Although many people attend Comdex for free using complimentary exhibitor passes, if you cannot obtain a pass, the $40 exhibits-only pass can actually save you several times the cost of attending the show. This is because many vendors have show specials and show promotional prices that can result in significant savings as compared to purchasing their products through retail channels.

In shopping for computer hardware at a trade show, be as cautious and inquisitive as if you were purchasing by mail. First, scrutinize vendor promotional advertisements. As an example, 640K-byte *capacity* on the motherboard does not tell what amount of memory, if any, is installed! Other common fine-print items to look for include shipping fees, Visa or Mastercard surcharge fees, and assembly and test fees. One unusual fee I encountered was for a packing carton. So "let the buyer beware" is most appropriate when you shop for a personal computer.

# Assembly Techniques to Consider

One of my requirements for purchasing a clone system was to find a vendor that sold a basic startup kit consisting of a power supply, system unit case, and an XT-turbo type system board with Phoenix BIOS. This startup kit was preferred to purchasing a complete system, because my consulting group had an ample stock of other components, including keyboards, multifunction cards, and fixed disk cards, which could be used to expand a low cost clone into a system that would exceed the processing and storage capacity of an IBM PC XT.

At the Comdex exhibition in Atlanta in early June, I examined numerous basic IBM PC XT and PC AT clone systems. After an avid comparison of systems, it was noted that at least 10 vendors were marketing clones based upon the use of a common system board made in Taiwan. Because an IBM PC XT Turbo Clone would provide the processing capability required by the author, cost became a primary consideration. Five computers examined in detail were exactly the same with the exception of the label placed on the exterior of the system unit.

## Clone System Board

Figure 8.1 illustrates the layout in schematic form of the system board used in the clone I purchased. Note that banks 0, 1, and 2 are designed to accommodate either 64K-bit or 256K-bit memory chips, and in bank 3, 64K-bit memory chips must be used. Although populating banks 0 through 2 with 256K-bit chips and bank 3 with 64K-bit chips results in 832K bytes of on-board memory, the design of the system board is such

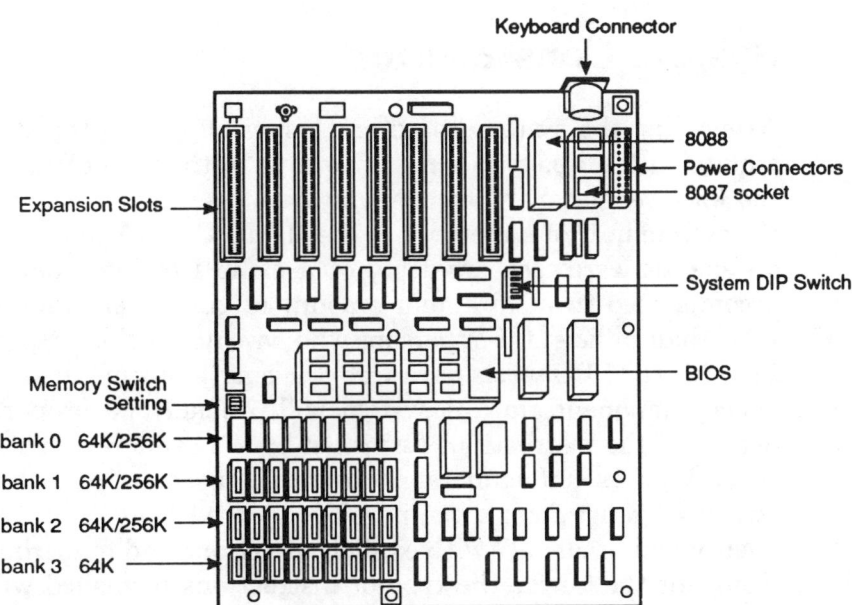

**Figure 8.1** Taiwan Manufactured Turbo System Board—The memory switch informs the system board of the type of chips used in each bank. The system DIP switch elements define whether a coprocessor is installed, the memory on the system board when 64K-bit chips are used, the default monitor, and other system features.

that only 640K bytes of RAM is recognized, regardless of the types of memory chips used to populate the sockets. I already had a 384K-byte multifunction card, so only the first memory bank (bank 0) was populated using 256K-bit chips, resulting in a total of 640K bytes of RAM on the system after the multifunction card was added.

Two important considerations in configuring the system board to operate correctly with on-board memory and the memory installed via an adapter card are the appropriate settings of DIP switches on the system board and the adapter card. If the system board permits the use of two types of RAM chips, there are usually two DIP switches on the system board that must be set. The first DIP switch controls the recognition of the type of memory chips used in each bank—64K or 256K bits—whereas the second DIP switch indicates the total amount of memory installed, whether an 8087 coprocessor is installed, the default monitor, and other common IBM PC type system functions, such as the number of disk drives and whether a self-test is to be performed upon power-on or system reset.

## System Construction

Assembling the system board and power supply to the system unit case required a Phillips type screwdriver due to the type of screws supplied by the kit's vendor. For persons who have previously removed the cover of the system unit of a member of the IBM PC series and added or replaced an adapter card, the assembly of a clone from its components can be accomplished in a minimum amount of time. Ten minutes is probably more than sufficient. For persons who have no previous experience in working with IBM PC series hardware, the length of time required to assemble clone components into a system will probably be proportionate to the quality of the instructions furnished by the vendor(s) of the components. Some vendors unfortunately provide no instructions; other vendors' instructions range from a one-page overview without illustrations to a high-quality "minimanual" with explicit directions and numerous illustrations. Thus, for the novice the type of instructions furnished with the components of a kit system should be an important consideration.

In assembling the components I purchased, two screws were required to fasten the system board to the system unit case, whereas four screws were required to fasten the 150-watt power supply to the system unit. Then two 12-pin connector power cord cables from the power supply were fastened to two 12-pin sockets located at the upper right corner of the system board.

After the system board and power supply are fastened to the system unit case, the builder installs any RAM chips in the appropriate memory banks on the system board. This memory installation normally precedes the installation of adapter cards, because the use of full-length adapter cards in system expansion slots one through five blocks access to the sockets into which the RAM chips are installed.

Once all on-board memory additions are complete, the kit builder should make a list of the adapter cards and on-line storage devices to install in the system. This information should be used to set the appropriate elements of the DIP switch(es) on the system board prior to the installation of the adapter cards, because the DIP switches can be difficult to reset once a full complement of adapter cards is installed. Prior to installing the adapter cards, the on-line storage devices should be installed in the device housing areas and connected to the appropriate cables that will be later fastened to the adapter cards. Screws in the metal cage on the left device housing area are blocked from turning with a screwdriver when full-length adapter cards are installed in the system expansion slots. The following lists the assembling sequence in constructing an IBM PC XT or compatible computer system:

1. Remove system unit cover from system unit.
2. Fasten system board to case.
3. Fasten power supply to case.
4. Install memory chips as required.
5. Partially install on-line storage devices in device housing areas.
6. Connect power connectors and adapter cables to storage devices.
7. Set system DIP switch and memory switch if necessary.
8. Secure on-line storage devices to device housing areas with screws.
9. Remove system expansion slot covers and install adapter cards.
10. Fasten system unit cover to system unit.
11. Connect keyboard to system unit.
12. Connect monitor cable to appropriate adapter card connector and monitor power cable to power source.
13. Connect system unit power cable to system unit and power source.

## The Assembly Process

Although the system units of clone PC XTs and PC ATs differ slightly, several common procedures can be followed in constructing a system. First, if you purchased individual components, the system unit cover should be unfastened and removed from the system unit. First note the type of screws used to fasten the system unit cover to the system unit—single cut or Phillips screws. Using either a flat-blade screwdriver or Phillips screwdriver, the screws should be turned in a counterclockwise direction as illustrated in Figure 8.2. Note that most system unit covers are held in place by five screws, as illustrated in Figure 8.2; however, some covers may have latches or fewer screws.

After the system unit cover mounting screws are removed, turn the unit to face you and slide the cover to the front. If the system unit is similar to an IBM PC or PC XT system unit, when it cannot slide forward any farther you should tilt it upward to remove the cover from its base. If the system unit is similar to an IBM PC AT system unit, the cover should slide fully forward, with no tilting required to remove it from its base. Once you remove the cover from its base, set the cover aside while you install the individual components in the base of the system unit.

If you purchased a system board separately, it should be inserted into the system unit. Normally, the base of most system units is manufactured with a number of plastic prongs, onto which you place the system board holes to guide the system board into a semisecure position by pressing the

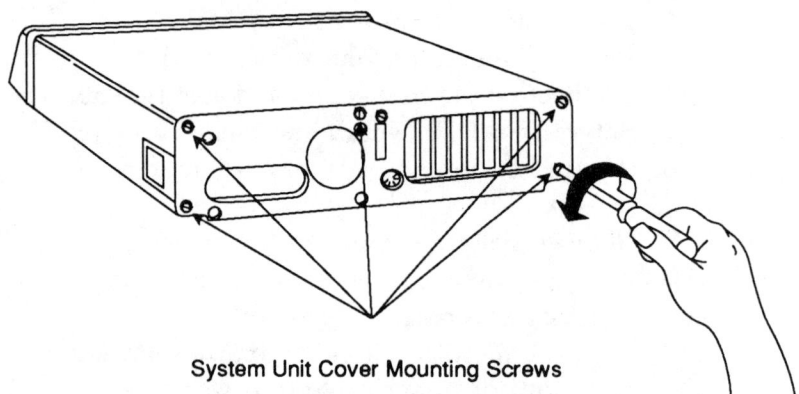

System Unit Cover Mounting Screws

**Figure 8.2** Removing the System Unit Cover Mounting Screws.

system board onto the plastic prongs. Next, fasten two or more screw holes on the system board, identified by metal squares with holes, to the system unit with screws. Figure 8.3 shows the guide holes and two screw holes on the system board I purchased.

Once the system board is connected to the system unit base, you are ready to install the power supply. Figure 8.4 illustrates the placement of the power supply into the system unit of a PC or PC XT type system unit base. In this illustration four screws are used to fasten the power supply to the rear of the system unit base. However, note that the actual number of screws can vary based upon the type of power supply and system unit.

After the system board and power supply are connected to the base of the system unit two 12-pin power supply connectors should be cabled to the power connector sockets that are normally located in the upper right corner of the system board as illustrated in Figure 8.3.

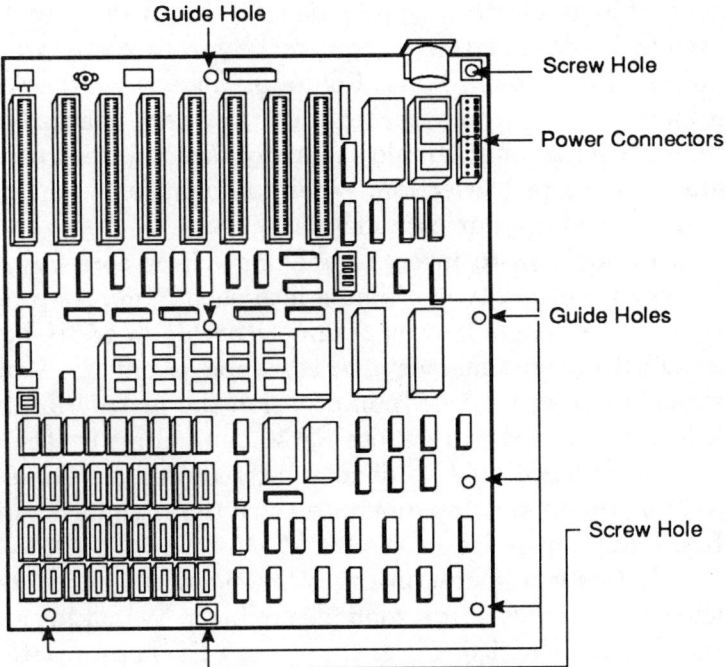

**Figure 8.3** System Board Guide Holes and Screw Holes—The system board is correctly positioned in the system unit by placing the guide holes on the board over the plastic prongs protruding from the base of the system unit.

**316** The PC Upgrader's Manual

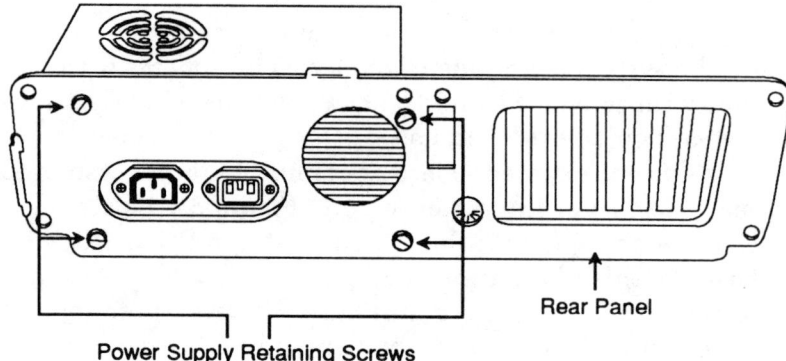

**Figure 8.4** Installing the Power Supply—Four screws fasten the power supply to the rear panel of the system unit base.

Prior to installing any required memory chips, you should ensure that each chip is correctly positioned for insertion into the sockets on the system board and that the correct type of chips are to be used in the appropriate memory bank. Figure 8.5 illustrates the correct placement of a memory chip into a socket on the system board. Note that the notch on each RAM chip should normally face the rear of the system unit to ensure its correct insertion. When in doubt follow the mask on the system door or consult your user manual.

In addition to inserting memory chips correctly, it is important to insert the correct type of chips into each bank. As previously mentioned, some clone system boards permit either 64 or 256K-bit RAM chips to be installed in some memory banks, whereas only 64K-bit chips can be installed in other banks. Upon occasion the instruction book obtained with the system board will denote RAM bank chips by the chip code, labeling a memory bank 4164 to denote the requirement to use 64K-bit chips or 41256/4164 to denote a memory bank that can have either 256 or 64K-bit RAM chips installed in the bank.

Before you install on-line storage devices in the device housing areas and adapter cards, it is a good idea to begin by making a list of the hardware that will be installed. Then you can set the appropriate DIP switch(es) on the system board, because it may be difficult to do so after other devices are installed.

Figure 8.6 illustrates the typical face plates that cover the device housing areas on most system units. By either pulling off retaining clips

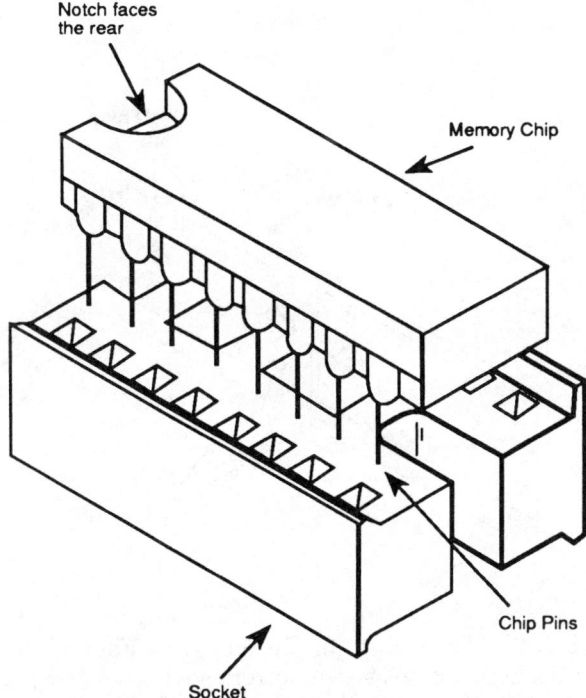

**Figure 8.5** Inserting Memory Chips—The notch of each RAM chip normally faces the rear of the system unit prior to its insertion in a memory bank socket.

or pushing a plastic retainer, the face plates can be removed, permitting the installation of full- or half-height storage devices. The storage devices can then be partially slid into the device housing areas. Later, you fasten them with two or more mounting screws to the metal cages that form each housing area. Prior to actually fastening the storage devices to the metal cage, fasten a 4-pin power connector from the power supply to each storage device. In addition, you should fasten the appropriate cables from the adapter card or cards required to operate each storage device to the storage device prior to securing the storage device to the metal cage of the device housing area. This is because there is only a small amount of room between the rear of each storage device and the power supply, which makes the cabling of the adapter cards to the storage device and the power supply connector to the power socket on the storage device almost an impossible task if the storage device is placed completely into the device housing area.

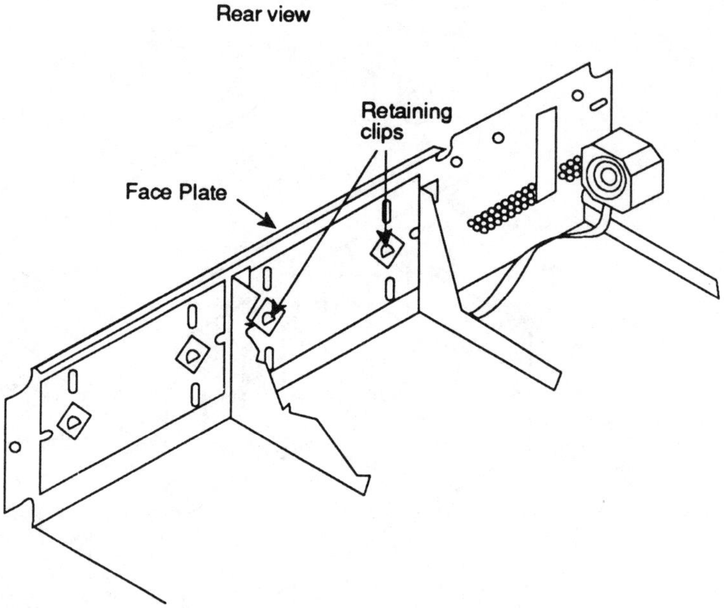

**Figure 8.6** Removing the System Unit Face Plates—The face plates covering the device housing areas can be removed by either pulling off a retaining clip or pushing a plastic clip to the side of the fastener.

Before you install adapter cards, remove the expansion slot covers, as illustrated in Figure 8.7. The removal of the expansion slot cover enables you to insert each adapter into the expansion slot by holding the card by its top and pressing it firmly so the edge connector of the card slides into the connector on the system board. Figure 8.8 illustrates the placement of an adapter card into an expansion slot after the expansion slot cover has been removed.

Once the adapter card is installed, use the screw from the expansion slot cover to fasten the adapter card to the rear panel of the system unit. Assuming that the adapter card installed in expansion slot 5 was a diskette drive controller, you should then cable the controller to the end of the cable previously connected to the diskette drive or drives. After all adapter cards are installed, refasten the system unit cover to the system unit. Then connect the keyboard and monitor to the system unit. You are now ready to power on your clone!

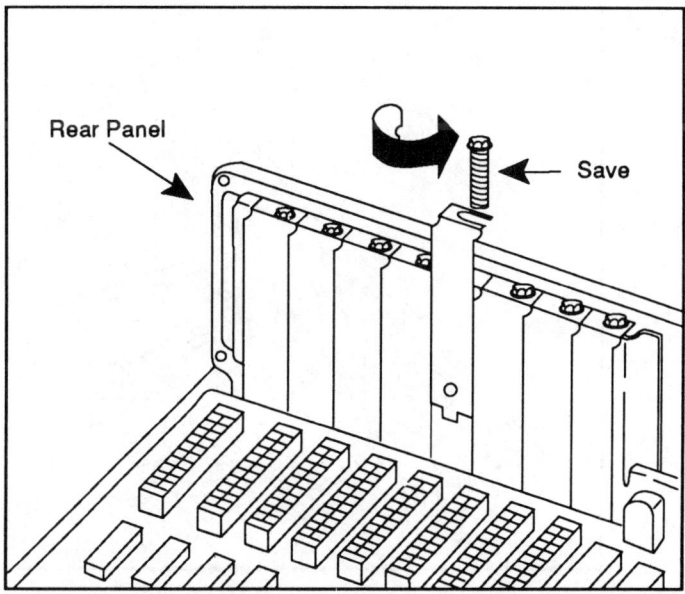

**Figure 8.7** Removing the Expansion Slot Cover—Prior to installing an adapter card in an expansion slot the expansion slot cover must be removed.

# Clone Operation

## Precautions to Consider

Note and follow the precautions in the instructions furnished with your equipment concerning power and static electricity. The power switch on the power supply attached to the system unit should be placed into the off position and the power cable should not be plugged into a wall outlet until the system unit is completely assembled and the cover is placed back onto the unit. Before you install memory chips, ground yourself by touching the metal case of the system unit or a similar object, then insert the chips into their sockets.

## Turbo Mode Operation

The "Turbo" system board I selected can be operated at either the standard 4.77 MHz rate of the IBM PC and PC XT or at a Turbo rate of 8 MHz,

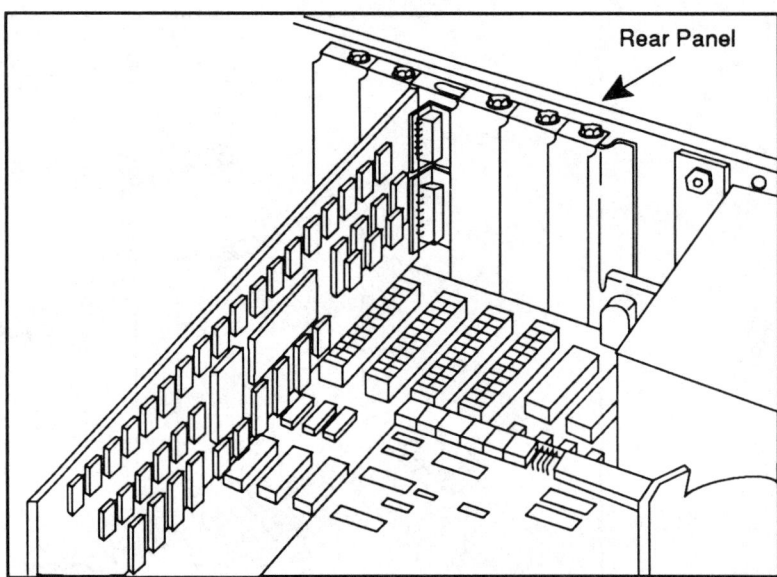

**Figure 8.8** Installing an Adapter Card—After the expansion slot cover is removed, the adapter card can be installed by pressing it firmly into the expansion slot socket.

the latter providing an increase of almost 40 percent in the speed of program execution. Some programs, such as communications and copy-protected software, are execution time sensitive, so manufacturers of most, if not all, Turbo boards provide an easy mechanism to switch between the Turbo mode and the normal mode of processing. The system board I acquired used a set of jumpers to enable the operating speed of the 8088 microprocessor to be varied either by software or hardware, with the latter permitting operating modes to be switched by pressing predefined key sequences on the keyboard.

If Phoenix BIOS is installed on the system board, pressing the Ctrl and Alt keys and the + key on the numeric keypad serves as a toggle between the Turbo and the normal 4.77 MHz operating modes. To visually inform you of the mode you are using, the appearance of the cursor on the monitor is changed from a rectangle (Turbo mode) to an underline (normal mode) or vice versa each time the Ctrl-Alt-+ key sequence occurs. If another BIOS is used on the system board, the Ctrl and Alt keys and the minus (−) key on the keyboard are used to toggle between the Turbo and normal operating modes.

**Table 8.1**   IBM PC XT Clone Cost Estimator

| | COMPONENT | NORMAL COST RANGE | ACTUAL COST QUOTED |
|---|---|---|---|
| | Keyboard | $ 40–$ 60 | _____ |
| | System Board | 80– 100 | _____ |
| | Power supply | 50– 75 | _____ |
| | Case | 30– 50 | _____ |
| | Diskette drive controller | 25– 40 | _____ |
| | Diskette drive | 65– 90 | _____ |
| | Fixed disk controller | 80– 110 | _____ |
| or { | 20M-byte fixed disk | 200– 260 | _____ |
| | Fixed disk on a card | 330– 350 | _____ |
| or | Monochrome display adapter with parallel printer port | 50– 75 | _____ |
| or | Color graphics adapter | 60– 80 | _____ |
| or | Enhanced graphics adapter | 200– 280 | _____ |
| | Video Graphics Adapter | 180– 300 | _____ |
| Select as appropriate to obtain required RAM | 64K-bit memory 9 chips | 7– 11 | _____ |
| | 256K-bit memory 9 chips | 30– 35 | _____ |
| | 384 multifunction card | 80– 110 | _____ |
| | Monochrome monitor | 60– 110 | _____ |
| | Color monitor | 200– 250 | _____ |
| Select one | Enhanced color monitor | 350– 400 | _____ |
| | VGA analog monitor | 300– 600 | _____ |
| | Multisync monitor | 500– 600 | _____ |
| | Shipping | 0– 25 | _____ |
| | Visa/Mastercard Surcharge | 0%–3% | _____ |
| | Shipping cartons | 0– 20 | _____ |

## Cost Considerations

Although my consulting group had many of the key components required to build a complete IBM PC XT compatible system, many people must purchase everything required. To assist such individuals in obtaining a "target" cost estimate of items that will be required, Table 8.1 lists those hardware and miscellaneous "extra" costs you must consider to budget correctly.

If a fixed disk is not required, a second diskette drive should be substituted for the fixed disk controller and fixed disk or a fixed disk card that includes a built-in controller. Assuming that a 640K-byte RAM turbo dual diskette system is required, a total under $500 is possible if a monochrome monitor is used. For a fixed disk system with two diskette drives, a total cost of under $650 is achievable for a monochrome system. In comparison, a dual drive IBM PS/2 Model 30 with a monochrome display has a list price in excess of $2000, and an IBM PS/2 Model 50 with a monochrome display lists for in excess of $2500 as of the time of this writing. Thus, from an economic perspective, the purchase of a clone system offers significant economic advantages over the purchase of current IBM-manufactured personal computers.

CHAPTER 9

# Problem Resolution

Included with every member of the IBM PC series and some compatible computers are two diagnostic aids that assist you to determine the cause of computer malfunctions. These two aids are the built-in power-on self-test (POST) and a diagnostic program included in the *Guide to Operations* manual provided with each IBM personal computer. Another set of diagnostics marketed by IBM is included in the vendor's *Hardware Maintenance and Service* publication for specific IBM personal computers. The diagnostic diskette included in *IBM's Hardware Reference Library* is labeled Advanced Diagnostics, to distinguish it from the conventional diagnostic diskette included with the vendor's *Guide to Operations* manual.

## POST

Every time an IBM personal computer is powered on, a sequence of diagnostic tests contained in ROM BIOS is executed; hence they are known as built-in test routines. In addition, whenever a member of the IBM PC series is reset by the Ctrl-Alt-Del key sequence, all tests with the exception of a RAM test are conducted. Because a system reset is typically used to rapidly clear a software error that previously froze the computer, and a

RAM test can take up to 45 seconds to perform (depending upon the amount of memory installed in the computer), this test is omitted during reset operations.

No matter what the source of the initiation of the built-in tests—power-on or system reset—if a test fails, the computer will issue an unusual sequence of beeps and most likely display a cryptic error code on the monitor. This is a signal that the computer has malfunctioned and a hint as to the source of the problem. To understand the signals and messages that indicate a malfunction, it is a good idea to review an activity we normally take for granted—the sequence of events and resulting activity when an IBM personal computer operates correctly.

When the POST is initiated and everything is operating correctly the cursor should begin to blink on the computer's monitor a few seconds after power is applied to the system. As POST checks the system board, memory, keyboard, and some adapter cards, the cursor should continue to blink on the computer's display. After a period of time that can range up to 45 seconds on fully populated 8088 systems the light emitting diode (LED) on drive A will come on and the speaker will emit a short beep. Next, the LED will go out for a few seconds and then turn back on, resulting in the boot record of a diskette in drive A being read. If there is no diskette in drive A and the computer has a fixed disk, BIOS will next attempt to read data from drive C, first looking for a configuration file and then looking for an AUTOEXEC.BAT file.

As previously stated, when a malfunction occurs the computer's speaker will normally respond in some manner other than one short beep as an audio signal to the operator. Table 9.1 lists the POST audio error signals you may encounter and the probable cause of the audio indicated malfunction.

Depending on the type of malfunction and the version of BIOS installed in the computer, a POST error code may also be displayed. Because

**Table 9.1** POST Audio Error Signals

| ERROR INDICATOR | MEANING |
| --- | --- |
| Nothing happened | No power to computer |
| Continuous beep or repeating short beep | Power supply |
| 1 long, 1 short beep | System board |
| 1 long, 2 short beeps | Video adapter |

IBM diagnostic programs generate the same error code number that is displayed when a POST error is detected, the diagnostic programs can be used to both verify and isolate POST errors. Table 9.2 lists the major POST/Diagnostic Program Error Codes, with the letter X used to represent any number.

## Parity Check Errors

One of the more common errors that can occur on a member of the IBM PC series is a problem during the parity check. As the computer checks its RAM, the cursor will either continue to blink (IBM PC) or display

Table 9.2 POST/Diagnostic Program Error Codes

| ERROR CODE | PROBABLE ERROR SOURCE |
| --- | --- |
| 1XX | System board |
| 2XX | RAM |
| 3XX | Keyboard |
| 4XX | Monochrome display |
| 5XX | Color display |
| 6XX | Diskette drive |
| 7XX | Math coprocessor |
| 9XX | Printer adapter |
| 11XX | Asynchronous communications |
| 12XX | Alternate asynchronous communications |
| 13XX | Game control adapter |
| 14XX | Graphics printer |
| 15XX | SDLC adapter |
| 17XX | Fixed disk |
| 18XX | Expansion unit |
| 20XX | Binary synchronous communications adapter |
| 21XX | Alternate binary synchronous communications adapter |

memory in 16K-byte increments to indicate that that segment of memory has been successfully checked (PC XT and PC AT). The display of a PARITY CHECK 1 error denotes that a RAM parity error occurred on the system board, whereas the display of a PARITY CHECK 2 denotes that a RAM parity error occurred on a memory board. When either error occurs, ROM BIOS generates the parity check message in the upper left corner of the monitor, followed by an error message that can be used to ascertain the location of the failed chip. After the parity error occurs, an interrupt is generated to halt the operation of the microprocessor, in effect freezing the computer. Although many adapter boards permit you to disable parity checking by the appropriate positioning of a DIP switch, it cannot be disabled for memory on the system board of an IBM personal computer. Thus, to be able to resume operations, you must always replace a failed chip on the system board.

## Troubleshooting Parity Errors

Some POST errors—such as a 201 error, which identifies a RAM error—can include a sufficient level of information to enable you to isolate and replace a failing chip. When a memory failure occurs, a four- or seven-character alphanumeric code followed by the digits 201 can be used to ascertain both the bank and the bit position on the bank where a chip has failed. To understand how the error codes can isolate a failing chip, let us first review how system board memory is arranged.

Figure 9.1 illustrates the arrangement of system board RAM by banks and bit chips. Here the term *bit chips* is used to denote the nine memory chips required to contain character data. Each chip is either a 16K X 1-bit, 64K X 1-bit, or 256K X 1-bit chip that can store the indicated number of bits of information. By forming a row of nine bit chips to include parity, 16K-, 64K-, or 256K-byte characters can be stored in a memory bank. Note that the first bank is referred to as bank 0, and the fourth and last bank of system RAM is referred to as bank 3. Thus, additional memory included on adapter cards would commence with bank 4. Also note that the nine bit chips in each bank are labeled P for parity and 0 through 7. Thus, by knowing the bank and bit position of a chip we then know its exact location.

When four alphanumeric characters prefix the 201 RAM error code, the format of the error display is as follows:

ABCD 201

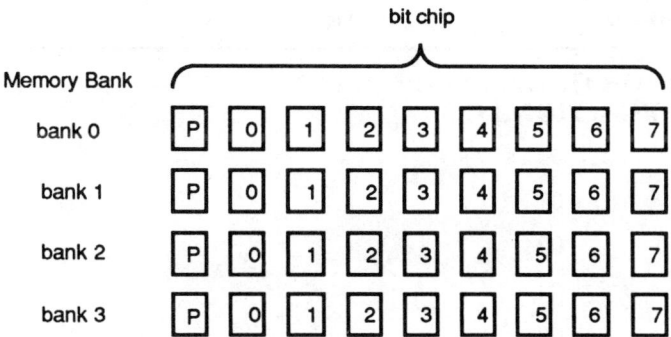

**Figure 9.1** System Board RAM Arrangement.

The A position is the bank identifier when 64K- or 256K-byte chips are used on the system board. The digits 0 to 3 correspond to the four physical banks on the system board while numbers in excess of 3 correspond to memory banks installed on adapter cards.

If an original IBM PC with 16K-byte memory chips is used, the B position becomes the bank identifier. Valid digits in the B position are 0, 4, 8, and C, which are used to denote errors occurring in memory banks 0, 1, 2, and 3 on the system board.

For both types of chips (64/256K- and 16K-byte) positions C and D identify the location of the chip in the bank that failed. Table 9.3 lists the values for positions CD in the four-digit 201 error code and the equivalent chip number the position value references.

The last two error code values in Table 9.3 actually denote an improper DIP switch setting, which indicates a bank of memory to be used that was not populated. Instead of replacing a specific chip, these error messages can be corrected by either populating an empty memory bank or by resetting the DIP switches on the system board to reflect the correct amount of memory installed.

When seven characters are included in a 201 error code, the display format appears as follows:

```
ABCDE FG 201
```

Here position A has the same values as previously described for the four-digit 201 error code. Similarly, positions F and G have the same values as positions C and D described for the four-position 201 error code.

**Table 9.3** Bank Chip Location

| ERROR CODE VALUE (POSITIONS CD) | CHIP LOCATION |
|---|---|
| 00 | Parity |
| 01 | data bit 1 |
| 02 | data bit 2 |
| 04 | data bit 3 |
| 08 | data bit 4 |
| 10 | data bit 5 |
| 20 | data bit 6 |
| 40 | data bit 7 |
| 80 | data bit 8 |
| AA | empty bank |
| FF | empty bank |

# Keyboard Malfunctions

Similar to the display for RAM errors, POST will display a code that can assist you in rectifying many problems when keyboard circuitry malfunctions. A keyboard malfunction causes POST to display the error message xx 301, where xx represents the hexadecimal value of the scan code of a malfunctioning key.

To illustrate how you can easily repair a malfunctioning keyboard, first examine the scan codes associated with the original IBM PC keyboard that are listed in Table 9.4. Note that the scan code for lowercase c is 2E. Next, perform a system reset operation if your computer is powered on or turn on power to your computer and press the letter C key down while POST is performed. This causes the error message 2E 301 to be displayed in the upper left corner of your screen and two short beeps to sound. In this example, POST is informing you that your keyboard malfunctioned as well as that the letter C is the culprit. If this error were caused by a stuck key, you would then unfasten the key. Because this error was self-inflicted, you can clear it by performing a system reset operation.

**Table 9.4** IBM PC Keyboard Scan Codes

| KEY NUMBER | KEY LABEL | SCAN CODE | KEY NUMBER | KEY LABEL | SCAN CODE |
|---|---|---|---|---|---|
| 1 | Escape | 01 | 27 | ] | 1B |
| 2 | 1 | 02 | 28 | Enter | 1C |
| 3 | 2 | 03 | 29 | Ctrl | 1D |
| 4 | 3 | 04 | 30 | a | 1E |
| 5 | 4 | 05 | 31 | s | 1F |
| 6 | 5 | 07 | 32 | d | 20 |
| 7 | 6 | 07 | 33 | f | 21 |
| 8 | 7 | 08 | 34 | g | 22 |
| 9 | 8 | 09 | 35 | h | 23 |
| 10 | 9 | 0A | 36 | j | 24 |
| 11 | 0 | 0B | 37 | k | 25 |
| 12 | - | 0C | 38 | l | 26 |
| 13 | = | 0D | 39 | ; | 27 |
| 14 | Backspace | 0E | 40 | , | 28 |
| 15 | Tab | 0F | 41 | ' | 29 |
| 16 | q | 10 | 42 | Shift | 2A |
| 17 | w | 11 | 43 | \ | 2B |
| 18 | e | 12 | 44 | z | 2C |
| 19 | r | 13 | 45 | x | 2D |
| 20 | t | 14 | 46 | c | 2E |
| 21 | y | 15 | 47 | v | 2F |
| 22 | u | 16 | 48 | b | 30 |
| 23 | i | 17 | 49 | n | 31 |
| 24 | o | 18 | 50 | m | 32 |
| 25 | p | 19 | 51 | < | 33 |
| 26 | [ | 1A | 52 | > | 34 |

Table 9.4  IBM PC Keyboard Scan Codes (continued)

| KEY NUMBER | KEY LABEL | SCAN CODE | KEY NUMBER | KEY LABEL | SCAN CODE |
|---|---|---|---|---|---|
| 53 | / | 35 | 69 | Num Lock | 45 |
| 54 | Shift | 36 | 70 | Scroll Lock | 46 |
| 55 | Prt Sc | 37 | 71 | 7 | 47 |
| 56 | Alt | 38 | 72 | 8 | 48 |
| 57 | Space | 39 | 73 | 9 | 49 |
| 58 | Caps Lock | 3A | 74 | - | 4A |
| 59 | F1 | 3B | 75 | 4 | 4B |
| 60 | F2 | 3C | 76 | 5 | 4C |
| 61 | F3 | 3D | 77 | 6 | 4D |
| 62 | F4 | 3E | 78 | + | 4E |
| 63 | F5 | 3F | 79 | 1 | 4F |
| 64 | F6 | 40 | 80 | 2 | 50 |
| 65 | F7 | 41 | 81 | 3 | 51 |
| 66 | F8 | 42 | 82 | 0 | 52 |
| 67 | F9 | 43 | 83 | Del | 53 |
| 68 | F10 | 44 | | | |

# The Diagnostic Disk

When an error code appears, one of the first things you should do is record the error number and determine its meaning. Some errors, such as a 301 keyboard error without a hexadecimal prefix, can result from the failure to properly connect the keyboard cable to the system unit. Therefore, it is a good idea to check the cables to the system unit from the keyboard and monitor either if a keyboard error occurs or if there is no display on the monitor. For isolating other errors that may not be as obvious, the diagnostic disk should be used.

The diagnostic disk included with the *Guide to Operations* manual can be used to perform a much more thorough testing of the computer than performed by POST. You can execute tests multiple times, which is necessary to detect intermittent errors.

Another area that warrants attention when you attempt to detect the cause of errors is the length of time that the computer has been powered on. Most integrated circuits that are on the verge of failure can be placed into an inoperative state after the computer has been operating a sufficient amount of time for the heat buildup in the system unit to cause a failure. Thus, if an error occurred on the computer in the morning and it was turned off until later in the day when the diagnostic disk program was executed, there is a reasonable probability that the program may not detect the error. To prevent this situation from occurring, attempt to run diagnostics after an error code is displayed or after the computer has been in a power-on state for at least 15 minutes.

You are referred to the *IBM Guide to Operations* manual for information concerning the operation and use of the diagnostic diskette, but there are certain features of the program that warrant attention here. First, the diagnostic program is executed by placing the diskette in drive A and performing a system reset or applying power to the system unit. If Cassette BASIC is displayed whenever the computer is powered on, it is most likely that either the diskette controller or drive A has malfunctioned. Under this situation, the diagnostic program cannot be executed. Assuming the diagnostic program can be executed, when the program reaches the point where it will test the diskette drives the operator should have a scratch diskette available for insertion into the drive. This scratch diskette is required because the diagnostic program writes and then reads predefined data, destroying any data previously recorded onto the diskette. Finally, it is a good idea to log errors to the printer, especially when you are executing multiple tests, because this lets you leave the computer unattended while it is performing a multiple number of tests.

## Troubleshooting Tips

Due to the use of audio tones and diagnostic error codes, determining the cause of a malfunction is not as difficult as it may appear. By first treating the personal computer in a manner similar to other electronic devices some of the most frequent causes of problems can be avoided. Specifically, two common problems are a lack of power and loose or improperly attached connectors.

If your computer or separately powered peripheral device appears to be completely inoperative, the primary cause of failure is either a power supply or the lack of power at the outlet. Prior to taking apart the system unit and expending time and money on what may be the unnecessary replacement of a power supply, the obvious should be checked—is the power plug inserted correctly into the outlet and is power available at the outlet? Upon occasion, connectors get bent from the insertion and removal of the power cord in and from different outlets. In such situations, a small vibration may be enough to cause contact to be broken between the outlet and cable, resulting in the loss of power. Simply removing the power cable and slightly bending the power tongs may be sufficient to remedy the previously mentioned situation. To determine if the outlet is working the operator can plug another device into the outlet, such as a lamp or electric clock. Then, if the other device doesn't work, the fusebox or circuit breaker box should be checked.

If the monitor, printer, expansion unit, or another type of external peripheral device appears inoperative both the power cables to the device and its cable connector to the system unit should be checked. Doing so may rapidly isolate the cause of an easily corrected problem.

# Internal Failures

When a problem occurs inside the system unit one of the first reactions of many users is to take the computer to a computer store. Although in many cases the assistance of a professional technician may be required, by spending some time the computer operator may be able to isolate the probable cause of a malfunction. Doing so may result in both a considerable cost saving and a sense of accomplishment attained by isolating and correcting the malfunction.

As an example of problem isolation let us assume that upon power-on Cassette BASIC is displayed and the LED on drive A fails to light. Although the probable cause of failure is either the diskette drive controller or the diskette drive, there is a possibility that a chip on the system board failed. Prior to calling a technician or packing the computer for delivery to the nearest computer store it may be possible to isolate the failure.

After turning the power switch of the system unit to the off position and disconnecting the power cable, an investigation and a simple recabling or "reseeding" operation may be able to isolate the cause of the malfunction. Once the cover of the system unit is removed you should check the cable connectors from the power supply to the diskette drives and the cable from the diskette drive controller to the diskette drives. The latter is usually one cable with two or more connectors that are designed to snap onto the edge connector of the diskette drive. During this check you should verify that the connectors are fastened correctly to both the diskette drive controller adapter and the diskette drives.

Another area that could be causing the previously mentioned problem is the improper "seeding" or placement of the diskette drive controller adapter in a system expansion slot. If the adapter does not appear to be straight from a vertical view, it should probably be removed and reinstalled, which to a technician is known as the process of "reseeding a board."

If the connectors and diskette controller appear to be properly installed, attempt to verify that drive A is the culprit. Without physically swapping drives A and B you could swap their cable connectors. Then, if the system boots from the drive B physical location, you would know that the malfunction is with drive A. At this point you can leave physical drive B connected as drive A and remove drive A from the system unit for appropriate repairs. Unfortunately, if swapping the connectors did not permit the other drive to operate, the problem is now isolated to either the diskette controller or the system board. At this point a friend that could lend a diskette controller adapter would be very valuable! As an alternative, it may be possible to borrow a diskette controller from a computer store, or you might consider purchasing a spare card. The rationale for purchasing a spare card is based upon the advertised price of diskette generic controllers being under $30, whereas the cost for a computer store technician to examine the system unit may be easily double or triple that amount prior to performing any required repairs. Thus, if the replacement of the diskette drive controller card alleviates the malfunction the expenditure of a minimum amount of time and approximately $30 could permit the avoidance of a much higher repair expense.

In general, the prices of many of the components that are used to construct a personal computer are so low that repairs often cost more than the purchase price of a new adapter card or diskette drive. Only for a system board or fixed disk failure is it of a definite economic advantage to repair the failed component in lieu of its replacement. Even when the fixed disk begins to generate data errors a trip to the repair shop may not be necessary. After ensuring that a current backup of the contents of the fixed disk exists, a simple reformat of the disk may be the solution to the problem. This is because the reformatting process results in the operating system denoting bad sectors, which are then eliminated from use.

## Summary

From reading this chapter and noting the long list of error codes, you might expect to encounter a number of equipment failures each year. In actuality, the opposite is true, because personal computer malfunctions are normally an exception to normal operations and in effect are quite rare. When a malfunction occurs, both POST and the IBM diagnostics diskette can be used to isolate many errors. By using the process of elimination in conjunction with available diagnostic tools the personal computer user may be able to isolate the cause of the problem and take corrective action. When all else fails, there are thousands of computer stores with trained technicians who can provide assistance.

# APPENDIX A

# PC Components to Consider

The major components for the construction or upgrade of a member of the IBM PC series or a compatible personal computer are listed in this appendix. Entries in this appendix were first grouped into such distinct equipment categories as system cases, power supplies, keyboards, and other components. Next, each category of equipment was described and a dash was positioned to the right of the description to permit you to review the entries in a checklist manner. Thus, by placing checkmarks on the appropriate entries, you can use the material presented in this appendix to develop a requirement list of components necessary to satisfy your specific goal—be that one of constructing a new computer system or upgrading an existing system.

To extend the utility of the checklist in Table A.1, two columns labeled Vendor A and Vendor B have been added. These entries enable you to perform a comparison of the price of components between two vendors once the appropriate component is deemed to be required by entering a check in the column labeled "Required" for a specific component.

As you examine the entries in this appendix you will notice that several components include a dash in the description of the item. In such cases the dash is followed by the storage indicator M for millions of bytes. Because the capacity of hard disks and tape units varies considerably it was felt that providing you with the ability to indicate storage capacity requirements for these devices would be preferable to attempting to list all possible hard disks and tape units based upon storage capacity.

Finally, note the presence of footnotes for certain categories of personal computer equipment whose explanation is designed to prevent or minimize potential ordering problems. When you order equipment, do not hesitate to ask questions concerning both the installation and compatibility of the component or components you anticipate ordering with other components you may either already have or anticipate ordering. As the old adage states, "Proper planning prevents poor performance" or to modernize the adage, "Proper planning provides personal computer expansion and operation."

| PC COMPONENT CATEGORY/COMPONENT | REQUIRED | VENDOR A | VENDOR B |
|---|---|---|---|
| **System Cases** | | | |
| XT-Style Case (Slide-Top) with 4 exposed half-height drive bays | _____ | _____ | _____ |
| XT AT-Style Case with XT footprint and height, keylock, 2 exposed and 2 hidden half-height drive bays | _____ | _____ | _____ |
| AT-Style Case with keylock, 2 exposed and 2 hidden half-height drive bays | _____ | _____ | _____ |
| AT-Style Case with keylock, 3 exposed, and 2 hidden half-height drive bays | | | |
| Baby-AT Case with XT footprint, keylock, 2 exposed and 2 hidden half-height drive bays | _____ | _____ | _____ |
| Baby-AT Case with XT footprint, keylock, 3 exposed and 2 hidden half-height drive bays | _____ | _____ | _____ |
| **Power Supplies** | | | |
| PC Power Supply (65 W) | _____ | _____ | _____ |
| XT Power Supply (150 W) | _____ | _____ | _____ |
| XT Power Supply (200 W) | _____ | _____ | _____ |

| PC COMPONENT CATEGORY/COMPONENT | REQUIRED | VENDOR A | VENDOR B |
|---|---|---|---|
| AT Power Supply (200 W) | _____ | _____ | _____ |
| Baby-AT Power Supply (180 W) | _____ | _____ | _____ |
| **Keyboards** | | | |
| AT-Style for XT only with 10 function keys in two columns on left of keyboard | _____ | _____ | _____ |
| AT-Style for XT only with 10 function keys across top of keyboard | _____ | _____ | _____ |
| AT-Style for XT only with 12 function keys across top of keyboard | _____ | _____ | _____ |
| AT-Style XT/AT Auto-switching with 10 function keys in two columns on left of keyboard | _____ | _____ | _____ |
| XT/AT Switchable 10 function keys across top of keyboard | _____ | _____ | _____ |
| XT/AT Switchable 10 function keys in two columns on left of keyboard | _____ | _____ | _____ |
| XT/AT Switchable 12 function keys across top of keyboard | _____ | _____ | _____ |
| **Motherboards** | | | |
| XT Motherboard, 4.77-MHz and 8-MHz switchable 8088 processor | _____ | _____ | _____ |
| XT Motherboard, 4.77-MHz and 10-MHz switchable 8088 processor | _____ | _____ | _____ |
| AT Motherboard, 6/8-MHz switchable 80286 processor | _____ | _____ | _____ |
| AT Motherboard, 6/10-MHz switchable 80286 processor | _____ | _____ | _____ |
| AT Motherboard, 6/12-MHz switchable 80286 processor | _____ | _____ | _____ |
| AT Motherboard, 16-MHz 80386 processor | _____ | _____ | _____ |
| AT Motherboard, 16-MHz 80386SX processor | _____ | _____ | _____ |

## PC COMPONENT CATEGORY/COMPONENT

| Component | REQUIRED | VENDOR A | VENDOR B |
|---|---|---|---|
| Baby-AT Motherboard with XT footprint 6/8-MHz switchable 80286 processor | _____ | _____ | _____ |
| Baby-AT Motherboard with XT footprint 6/10-MHz switchable 80286 processor | _____ | _____ | _____ |
| Baby-AT Motherboard with XT footprint 6/12-MHz 80286 | _____ | _____ | _____ |
| Baby-AT Motherboard with XT footprint 16-MHz 80386 | _____ | _____ | _____ |
| Baby-AT Motherboard with XT footprint 16-MHz 80386SX | _____ | _____ | _____ |

### Diskette Drives

| Component | REQUIRED | VENDOR A | VENDOR B |
|---|---|---|---|
| 360K 5¼-inch full-height | _____ | _____ | _____ |
| 360K 5¼-inch half-height | _____ | _____ | _____ |
| 1.2M 5¼-inch half-height | _____ | _____ | _____ |
| 720K 3½-inch half-height (normally requires frame kit to fit into 5¼-inch device housing area) | _____ | _____ | _____ |
| 1.44M 3½-inch half-height (normally requires frame kit to fit into 5¼-inch device housing area) | _____ | _____ | _____ |

### Internal Hard Disk Drives

| Component | REQUIRED | VENDOR A | VENDOR B |
|---|---|---|---|
| PC XT__M byte full-height | _____ | _____ | _____ |
| PC XT__M byte half-height | _____ | _____ | _____ |
| PC XT__M byte disk on card | _____ | _____ | _____ |
| PC AT__M byte half-height | _____ | _____ | _____ |
| PC AT__M byte full-height | _____ | _____ | _____ |
| PC AT__M byte on a card | _____ | _____ | _____ |

### External Hard Disk Drives

| Component | REQUIRED | VENDOR A | VENDOR B |
|---|---|---|---|
| PC XT__M byte | _____ | _____ | _____ |
| PC AT__M byte | _____ | _____ | _____ |

## PC Components to Consider

| PC COMPONENT CATEGORY/COMPONENT | REQUIRED | VENDOR A | VENDOR B |
|---|---|---|---|
| PC XT __M byte with __M byte tape backup unit | _____ | _____ | _____ |
| PC AT __M byte with __M byte tape backup unit | _____ | _____ | _____ |
| **Internal Tape Drive** | | | |
| PC XT __M byte | _____ | _____ | _____ |
| PC AT __M byte | _____ | _____ | _____ |
| **External Tape Drive** | | | |
| PC XT __M byte | _____ | _____ | _____ |
| PC AT __M byte | _____ | _____ | _____ |
| **Disk Drive Controller Cards** | | | |
| PC XT 2 internal diskette drive support | _____ | _____ | _____ |
| PC XT 2 internal/2 external floppy drive support (useful for connecting a portable tape backup unit to the rear of the PC) | _____ | _____ | _____ |
| PC XT Diskette and hard disk controller card supports up to 2 floppies and 2 hard drives | _____ | _____ | _____ |
| PC AT Diskette and hard disk controller card supports 360K and 1.2M floppies, up to 2 floppies and 2 hard drives | _____ | _____ | _____ |
| **Multifunction and I/O Cards** | | | |
| PC XT Disk I/O Card controls 2 floppy drives, includes game port, clock/calendar with battery backup, 1 serial, 2 parallel ports | _____ | _____ | _____ |
| PC AT Multidisk I/O Card controls 2 floppy drives, 1 serial port, 1 parallel port with optional second serial port and game port | _____ | _____ | _____ |

| PC COMPONENT CATEGORY/COMPONENT | REQUIRED | VENDOR A | VENDOR B |
|---|---|---|---|
| PC AT Multi-I/O Card includes serial and parallel port | _____ | _____ | _____ |
| PC XT Serial/Parallel Card includes 1 parallel port and 1 serial port | _____ | _____ | _____ |
| PC XT Memory card with one or more serial and parallel ports, clock/calendar, and game port | _____ | _____ | _____ |
| PC AT Memory card with one or more serial and parallel ports and clock/calendar | _____ | _____ | _____ |
| PC XT Parallel printer port | _____ | _____ | _____ |
| PC XT Serial port card (also called asynchronous communications adapter) | _____ | _____ | _____ |
| PC XT Serial/Parallel Port | _____ | _____ | _____ |

**Memory Cards**[1]

| | REQUIRED | VENDOR A | VENDOR B |
|---|---|---|---|
| PC XT Memory expansion to 576K/640K bytes | _____ | _____ | _____ |
| PC XT EEMS RAM card with __M bytes of expanded memory | _____ | _____ | _____ |
| PC AT 126K-byte Memory expansion to populate 640K bytes | _____ | _____ | _____ |
| PC AT EEMS RAM card with __M bytes of expanded memory | _____ | _____ | _____ |

**Memory Chips**[2]

| | REQUIRED | VENDOR A | VENDOR B |
|---|---|---|---|
| PC 16K-bit Memory Chips | _____ | _____ | _____ |
| __150 NSEC | _____ | _____ | _____ |
| __120 NSEC | _____ | _____ | _____ |
| __100 NSEC | _____ | _____ | _____ |

[1] Note: Some memory cards are sold with 0K installed, requiring the purchaser to obtain and install memory chips.
[2] Note: When used on the motherboard the speed of the memory chips should be compatible with the clock rate of the microprocessor.

| PC COMPONENT CATEGORY/COMPONENT | REQUIRED | VENDOR A | VENDOR B |
|---|---|---|---|
| PC XT 64K-bit Memory Chips | ———— | ———— | ———— |
| __150 NSEC | ———— | ———— | ———— |
| __120 NSEC | ———— | ———— | ———— |
| __100 NSEC | ———— | ———— | ———— |
| PX XT 256K-bit Memory Chips | ———— | ———— | ———— |
| __150 NSEC | ———— | ———— | ———— |
| __120 NSEC | ———— | ———— | ———— |
| __100 NSEC | ———— | ———— | ———— |
| PC AT 64K-bit Memory Chips | ———— | ———— | ———— |
| __150 NSEC | ———— | ———— | ———— |
| __120 NSEC | ———— | ———— | ———— |
| __100 NSEC | ———— | ———— | ———— |
| __80 NSEC | ———— | ———— | ———— |
| PC AT 256K-bit Memory Chips | ———— | ———— | ———— |
| __150 NSEC | ———— | ———— | ———— |
| __120 NSEC | ———— | ———— | ———— |
| __100 NSEC | ———— | ———— | ———— |
| **Coprocessor Chip**[3] | | | |
| PC/PC XT__MHz 8087 | ———— | ———— | ———— |
| PC AT__MHz 80287 | ———— | ———— | ———— |
| **Monitors**[4] | | | |
| High Resolution Monochrome Green | ———— | ———— | ———— |
| High Resolution Monochrome Amber | ———— | ———— | ———— |
| CGA RGB Color | ———— | ———— | ———— |

[3] Note: The speed of the coprocessor must match the operating rate of the motherboard selected and be compatible with the microprocessor.
[4] Note: All monitors can be purchased as a fixed base unit or with a tilt/swivel base. Some monitors have a power plug that will fit into the power receptacle in the power supply; other monitors have a power plug that must be inserted into a wall outlet or power strip.

| PC COMPONENT CATEGORY/COMPONENT | REQUIRED | VENDOR A | VENDOR B |
|---|---|---|---|
| CGA High Resolution Color | _____ | _____ | _____ |
| EGA 640 * 350 Color | _____ | _____ | _____ |
| EGA Multiscan | _____ | _____ | _____ |
| EGA Multiscan Digital or Analog input | _____ | _____ | _____ |
| VGA Monochrome White | _____ | _____ | _____ |
| VGA Color | _____ | _____ | _____ |

**Video Adapters**

| | | | |
|---|---|---|---|
| Monochrome Display | _____ | _____ | _____ |
| Monochrome Display & Parallel Printer | _____ | _____ | _____ |
| Monochrome Graphics | _____ | _____ | _____ |
| Monochrome Graphics & Parallel Printer | _____ | _____ | _____ |
| Color Graphics | _____ | _____ | _____ |
| Color Graphics & Parallel Printer | _____ | _____ | _____ |
| EGA | _____ | _____ | _____ |
| EGA & Parallel Printer | _____ | _____ | _____ |
| EGA Auto-switch | _____ | _____ | _____ |
| EGA Auto-switch & Parallel Printer | _____ | _____ | _____ |
| VGA | _____ | _____ | _____ |
| VGA + Resolution Support | _____ | _____ | _____ |

**Modems**

| | | | |
|---|---|---|---|
| __BPS Internal | _____ | _____ | _____ |
| __BPS External | _____ | _____ | _____ |

| PC COMPONENT CATEGORY/COMPONENT | REQUIRED | VENDOR A | VENDOR B |
|---|---|---|---|
| **Cables[5]** | | | |
| Parallel cable to connect parallel printer port to printer | ———— | ———— | ———— |
| Floppy/Hard Disk Controller cable to connect controller to floppy and hard disks | ———— | ———— | ———— |
| Serial cable to connect serial port to modem, plotter, or other serial device | ———— | ———— | ———— |

[5] Note: For parallel and serial cables, you should determine the type of connector required at each end of the cable (9-pin, 25-pin, or centronics) as well as the gender (F or M) and cable length. Common cable lengths are 6, 10, and 12 feet.

# APPENDIX B

# Vendors to Consider

This appendix lists the names, addresses, and telephone numbers of nine vendors of IBM compatible personal computers and components. The author of this book previously purchased one or more products from each of the vendors listed in this appendix and was impressed by their technical and sales ability. However, you are cautioned that policies can change and key technical personnel that may have been able to correctly answer purchaser questions may now be working elsewhere. Due to this, you should consider developing a series of questions to ask each vendor or answer for yourself by reviewing vendor advertisements and sales literature. These questions should be answered to ensure that you will be dealing with an organization whose policies with respect to the method of purchase, technical support, and product warranty satisfy your requirements.

To assist you, Table B.1 lists what the author of this book feels are some of the key questions to consider prior to making a purchasing decision that could involve hundreds to thousands of dollars. Similar to the method of considering the major components of a personal computer that was presented in appendix A, note that entries were positioned to enable the comparison of responses between vendors. Thus, you may wish to make a copy of this table and use it in your equipment selection process.

**Table B.1.** Vendor Purchasing Questions to Ask

|  | VENDOR A | VENDOR B |
|---|---|---|
| Do you offer a product warranty? | _____ | _____ |
| If so, what are the terms of the warranty? | _____ | _____ |
| Do you offer an extended product warranty? | _____ | _____ |
| If so, what are the terms and cost of the warranty? | _____ | _____ |
| Is the product in stock and available for immediate shipment? | _____ | _____ |
| If not, when will it be available? | _____ | _____ |
| What credit cards do you accept? | _____ | _____ |
| Do you add a surcharge to credit card purchases? | _____ | _____ |
| If so, what is the surcharge percent or fee? | _____ | _____ |
| Do you offer a satisfaction guarantee? | _____ | _____ |
| If so, what are the terms of the guarantee? | _____ | _____ |
| How do you ship orders (UPS, Postal Service, Overnight Courier)? | _____ | _____ |
| Is there a surcharge for shipping? | _____ | _____ |
| If so, what is the surcharge? | _____ | _____ |
| Is there a discount for quantity purchase of an item, orders exceeding a dollar value, or for payment by check? | _____ | _____ |
| If so, what is the discount? | _____ | _____ |
| Do you accept APO, FPO, or international orders? | _____ | _____ |
| If so, do you add a surcharge to such orders? | _____ | _____ |
| What is the surcharge? | _____ | _____ |
| Do you have a restocking fee for items returned? | _____ | _____ |
| If so, what is the fee? | | |

The following list of vendors is presented in alphabetical order with comments based upon the author's experience in dealing with each firm indicated when appropriate after the vendor's address.

**Bestek International, Inc.**
4252 Bluebonnet Drive
Stafford, TX 77477
713/240-0818

Did you ever wonder where many of the vendors that advertise IBM PC compatible computer systems and such individual components as power supplies, motherboards, and system cases obtain their products? Bestek International is probably one of their wholesale sources.

Bestek is a large importer of components from whom you can purchase the parts necessary to build your own system or you can request the company to assemble the components into a system for a nominal fee. Although the more economical purchases from this vendor are obtained when buying a large quantity of components or systems, the firm's unit price is normally a significant bargain in comparison to the discounted retail prices charged by many other firms. Unfortunately, Bestek ships COD and unlike other firms mentioned in this appendix does not accept credit cards.

**CMO**
477 East Third Street
Williamsport, PA 17701
800/233-8950
In Pennsylvania 717/327-9575

Computer Mail Order (CMO) markets an extensive line of name brand monitors, diskette drives and hard disks, tape backup units, printers, and multifunction and video adapter cards. In addition, CMO markets both IBM and IBM compatible personal computers as well as an extensive number of modems.

**Computer Expo**
11230 Wilcrest Green
Houston, TX 77042 800/622-3976
In Texas 713/784-7817

Calling itself "Texas' #1 IBM Compatible Computer Center," Computer Expo markets a series of IBM PC compatible computers under the

"EXPO" label. In addition, this vendor markets a wide range of adapter cards, diskette drives and hard disks, tape backup units, and other major PC components.

**47th Street Computer**
67 W. 47th Street
New York, NY 10003
800/221-7774
In New York 212/398-1410

Best known for its two full page personal computer advertisements in the Sunday edition of *The New York Times*, 47th Street Computer markets a series of IBM PC compatible computers and components under the MAXUM label. In addition, this subsidiary of 47th Street Photo markets a wide range of personal computers manufactured by other vendors as well as name brand PC hardware components and software.

**JDR Microdevices**
110 Knowles Drive
Los Gatos, CA 95030
800/538-5000
In California 408/866-6200

If you remember how you felt as a child holding a dime in a candy store, you will probably feel the same way when examining a JDR Microdevices advertisement. This company regularly advertises most, if not all, of the components necessary to construct a clone as well as a clone kit.

**PC Connection**
6 Mill Street
Marlow, NH 03456
800/243-8088

One of the leading mail order marketers of IBM PC hardware and software products, PC Connection is well known for its prompt and reliable service. Although their prices may not always be the lowest, their trained sales personnel are always extremely helpful. The hardware marketed by this vendor is normally restricted to name brand merchandise, to include AST Research boards, Amdek monitors, Epson printers, Hayes modems, and similar products.

**PC Source**
12303-G Technology
Austin, TX 78727
800/643-0992
In Texas 800/234-2537

Established in 1982, PC Source markets a series of IBM compatible personal computers under the "Standard" label as well as both brand name and "no-name" PC components.

Advertising on a weekly or monthly basis in leading trade journals, PC Source advertisements are noticeable by their photographs of such components as hard disks, adapter cards, monitors, and diskettes, as well as their low prices.

**Priority Electronics**
26122 Plummer Street
Chatsworth, CA 91311
800/423-5922

Known for its special advertising supplements that frequently appear in *Byte Magazine*, Priority Electronics markets a comprehensive selection of brand name personal computer components as well as IBM PC compatible computer systems. Products included in this vendor's special advertising supplements range in scope from hard disk cabinets and cables to graphics systems, power supplies, math coprocessors, keyboards, and accessories. For readers that do not read *Byte*, a call to Priority Electronics to receive a copy of their latest supplement is highly recommended.

**Telemart**
8804 N. 23rd Avenue
Phoenix, AZ 85021
800/426-6659
In Arizona 602/944-1037

This division of CW Marketing has been doing business since 1980 and regularly advertises IBM PC compatible computers, brand name printers, adapter boards, monitors, and components.

# Index

1.2M-byte diskette drive, 38-41, 47
25-pin connector, 23

## A
Above Board, 115-117
AC power protector, 98-99
accelerator card, 118-123, 168, 191
adapter cards, 2-3, 21-23, 25, 30, 42-44, 46-48, 70, 134-135
addressing conflicts, 95-97, 109, 142, 156, 165, 244
addressing memory, 26, 68, 94-97
amplitude modulation, 250-251
analog monitors, 59-60, 76-78
ASCII, 7, 15, 54, 56, 224-226, 229
AST Rampage, 180-182, 208
AST SixPak Plus, 106-108, 112, 140, 180-181
AST-3G, 152-153
asymmetrical modems, 278-279
asymmetrical transmission, 272
asynchronous communications adapter, 22-24, 31, 34, 38, 44, 95-97, 146, 238-242
asynchronous transmission, 258
attribute code, 54, 56
Award BIOS, 302

## B
bandwidth, 253
bank switching, 113
bar code input, 102-103
BASIC, 4-5, 149-150, 158, 228-232, 306-307
Basic Input/Output System (see BIOS)
battery, 44-46, 51, 109
baud, 252-253
Bell System modems
  103/113, 259-261
  201, 265
  202, 263-264
  208, 269-270
  209, 270-271
  212A, 261-263, 268, 275

Bernoulli Box, 176
BIOS, 7, 16-18, 20, 41, 69-70, 121, 164, 167-168, 186-187, 244, 302
bisynchronous communications adapter, 22, 24, 202
bits per second (BPS), 252-253
break signal, 242
Bridge-File, 194-198
bus, 21, 42, 70-72, 89-90, 203
bus arbitration, 71-72, 82
bus mouse, 146-147

## C

cable, 24-25
cache memory, 120-121
Caps Lock key, 5-7, 37, 100
card select signal, 30
carrier signal, 249
Cassette BASIC, 17, 41, 121, 306-307
cassette recorder, 29
CCITT modems
    V.21, 260-261
    V.22, 261-263, 268
    V.22 bis, 265, 267-269
    V.23, 265
    V.26, 265-267
    V.27, 269-270
    V.29, 270-272
    V.32, 272
CGA (see Color Graphics Adapter)
chip speed, 16-17
clock/calendar, 44-45, 51, 97, 107-109
clock rate, 66
clone construction, 299-322
cluster, 128-129
CMOS RAM, 44-45
Color Display, 52, 57, 77-78
Color Graphics Adapter, 21-23, 43-44, 47, 52, 55-58, 148, 150-152
communications software, 172-173
COM ports, 24, 97, 109, 141, 243-246
Complementary Metallic Oxide Semiconductor RAM (see CMOS RAM)

configuration switches (see DIP switches)
constellation pattern, 256
conventional memory, 113-115, 164
coprocessor, 10, 26-28, 31, 69, 120
crystal, 39, 42, 49, 66, 119-120, 167
CuRAM card, 208
current loop interface, 238
cyclic codes, 287-288
cylinder, 33, 127

## D

data compression, 275, 292
Data Migration Facility, 172
DB-9 connector, 39, 173, 242-243
DB-25 connector, 23-25, 39, 110, 173, 242, 246
debouncing, 6
device housing area, 2-3, 10-12, 29, 34-35, 37-38, 40-41, 82, 133
diagnostic disk, 323-325, 330-331
DIP switches, 10, 17-19, 30-32, 45, 71, 96-97, 140
direct memory access (see DMA)
disk operating system (see DOS)
diskette and fixed disk controller, 38, 47
diskette drive, 2-3, 13-15, 48-49
    3½ inch, 34-35, 47, 72-76, 169, 170-171, 200, 204
    5¼ inch, 9, 11, 13, 31, 38, 169, 170-171, 193-198
Diskette Drive Bus Adapter, 196, 199
diskette drive controller, 22-23, 44, 169-170, 194, 211-212
diskette format, 75, 92
display adapters, 52-59, 148-159, 201
display switch, 46
DMA, 140-141
DOS, 4, 12-15, 24, 26, 33-34, 42, 129-130, 190, 306
dot matrix printer, 215-221
dot pitch, 77, 162
driver card, 178
dual asynchronous adapter, 206
dual-inline package (see DIP switches)

## E

edge connectors, 43, 247-248
EGA (see Enhanced Graphics Adapter)
EIA RS-232, 24
Enhanced Color Display, 52, 55, 57-58
Enhanced Graphics Adapter, 22, 26, 44, 47, 52, 55, 57-59, 77, 158-159
Enhanced Run Length Limited Code (see ERLL)
Epson 850/1050 printers, 226-228
ERLL 131, 175
error codes, 324-328
escape key, 6, 8
expanded memory, 113-115, 117, 166, 181
expanded memory adapter, 200-201, 205-206
Expanded Quadboard, 112
expansion slot cover, 10, 110, 239-240, 318-320
expansion slots, 2, 10, 21-22, 30-31, 40, 42-44, 50-51, 70, 81-83, 152, 164, 178, 236-237, 318-320
expansion unit, 22, 178-179
extended memory, 113-115, 117, 166, 181
external modem, 238

## F

faceplate, 9
Fastlink, 247-248
file allocation table, 129-130
fixed disk, 2-3, 9, 11, 31-33, 35, 75, 123-133, 173-175, 189-190, 205
fixed disk card, 133-136, 202-203
fixed disk controller, 23, 31, 131-132, 174-175, 187, 190
flat ribbon, 110
format, 13, 75
frequency modulation, 250-251
frequency shift keying (see FSK)
FSK, 251-252, 259
function keys, 4-8

## G

Genoa Systems SuperVGA, 153-157
GMEC, 58

Graphics Memory Expansion Card (GMEC), 58
Graphics Memory Module Kit, 58

## H

Hayes command set, 280-286
Hercules Color card, 151-152
Hercules Graphics card, 148-150
Home key, 6
horizontal scan frequency, 77
HP Printer Command Language, 228

## I

IBM Enhanced keyboard, 2, 7-8, 37, 51, 62-63, 189
IBM PC, 2-3, 4-36, 55, 70, 105-113, 117, 119-120, 122, 133, 136, 140, 152, 164, 167, 174, 185-189, 234-238, 301
IBM PC AT, 2, 7, 21-22, 24, 36-49, 55, 67, 71, 117, 119-120, 137, 139-141, 152-153, 155, 164, 167, 171, 189-192, 194, 197, 203, 234-236, 240-242, 301
IBM PC Convertible, 34-35
IBM PC Network Adapter, 22
IBM PC XT, 2, 4-36, 55, 70, 105-113, 117, 119-120, 122, 133, 135-136, 139-140, 152, 164, 167, 189-192, 301
IBM PC XT 286, 2, 49-52, 55, 119-120
IBM Reference Disk, 73, 210, 246
IBM Token Ring adapter, 22, 80
impact printer, 214-215
index hole, 13, 14
index mark, 14
Intel
  8048, 6-7
  8086, 27, 65-67, 69, 80, 113, 119-120, 191
  8087, 10, 26-28, 31, 80
  8088, 10, 21, 26, 42, 65-67, 69, 94-96, 113, 167, 191, 301
  80286, 42-43, 49, 51, 65, 67-69, 71, 86, 94-96, 113, 119, 167, 191, 205, 301
  80287, 68-69, 205, 302
  80386, 65, 68-69, 71, 85-86, 88, 113, 119-120, 191

80386 SX, 85, 119-120, 302
80387, 69, 205
Intel Inboard, 122
interleave factor, 127-128
internal modem, 238, 247-249
interrupt, 140-142
I/O address space, 94-97

## K

keyboard, 2, 4-8, 37, 49, 62-63, 99-104, 189
keyboard malfunctions, 328-330
keyboard visual indicators, 7-8, 100
keylock, 37
Keytronic keyboards, 100-104

## L

landing zone, 130
LaserJet, 223-224, 228
laser printer, 222-224
liberty board, 115-116
LIM, 114
LPT ports, 24, 54, 95, 109, 148, 152

## M

MCGA (see Multicolor Graphics Array)
media transfer, 171-173
memory adapter, 22-23, 43-44, 47-48, 165, 205-206
memory banks, 105-108
MFM, 131
mice (see mouse)
Micro Channel, 71-72, 82, 84-89, 204-210, 248
Microcom Networking Protocol (MNP), 286-291
modems, 25, 179, 200, 202, 233-298
modified frequency modulation (see MFM)
modulation, 249-252
monitors, 2, 3, 52-59, 76-78, 159-162
Monochrome Display, 23, 29, 46, 52-54, 56-58, 78, 150
Monochrome Display and Parallel Printer adapter, 22-23, 39, 44, 47, 52-54, 56, 58, 95, 148-149

Mountain Computer tape backup, 137-139, 142-145
mouse, 24, 80-81, 145-148
Multicolor Graphics Array, 76, 80-81, 83, 160-161
multifunction card, 96, 104-113, 180-182, 203, 244-246
multi-protocol adapter, 206
multiscan monitor, 77, 79, 152-153, 159-160
multitasking, 68

## N

Num Lock key, 5-7, 37, 100
numeric keypad, 5-6, 8

## O

optical disk drive, 200-201, 205
optical mouse, 146

## P

packetized ensemble protocol (see PEP)
page frame, 113-115
paper parking, 221
parallel ports, 23-24, 39
parallel printer adapter, 22-24, 44, 57
parity, 15-16, 41, 69, 241-242
parity check errors, 325-328
Pause key, 101
PC (see IBM PC)
PC AT (see IBM PC AT)
PC hardware upgrade strategies, 163-192
PC XT (see IBM PC XT)
PC XT 286 (see IBM PC XT 286)
PEP, 275-278
PGA (see Professional Graphics Adapter)
phase modulation, 251-252
phase shift keying (see PSK)
Phoenix BIOS, 302, 320
ports, 94-97, 109-110, 140-141
POS, 71
POST, 16-17, 41, 69, 323-328
PostScript, 223

power cables, 11
power protector, 98-99
power supply, 10-11, 31, 39, 82, 117, 132, 136, 174, 187-189, 315-316
power switch, 8, 10
power-on self test (POST), 16-17, 41, 69, 323-328
Princeton Graphics System MAX-15, 210-211
printer, 2-3, 213-232
printer control codes, 224-232
printer interface, 214
printer spooler, 110-111
problem resolution, 323-324
processor performance, 167-168, 191
Professional Graphics Adapter, 52, 59
Programmable Option Select (see POS)
Proprinter Series, 216-218, 226-228
protected mode, 67, 68, 82, 113, 191
Prt Sc key, 8, 101
PS/2, 1, 18, 35, 59-92, 160-161, 236-237
PS/2 Hardware enhancements, 193-212
PS/2 Model 25, 59, 61-62, 65, 67-70, 76, 79-80, 162, 200-203, 237
PS/2 Model 30, 2, 59, 61-63, 65, 67, 69-70, 76, 80-83, 162, 195, 200-203, 236-237
PS/2 Model 30 286, 71, 76, 84, 203
PS/2 Model 50, 2, 61-65, 76, 83-84, 206, 236-237
PS/2 Model 50Z, 61, 85, 206
PS/2 Model 55, 61, 65, 85
PS/2 Model 60, 61-63, 65, 86, 206
PS/2 Model 70, 61, 65, 86-88
PS/2 Model P70, 61, 65, 88-90, 208
PS/2 Model 80, 61-63, 65, 89, 208
PSK, 251-252

# Q

QAM, 254-256
quad serial port adapter, 210
Quadboard, 110-111, 244-246
Quadboard PS/Q, 207
QuadEGA ProSync, 152-153
quadrature amplitude modulation (see QAM)
Quad386 XT, 122-123
Quietwriter, 217-219

# R

RAM, 10, 15-17, 32, 41, 54, 70, 105-108, 164-166
RAM disk, 111
random access memory (see RAM)
raster generator, 54
RCA connector, 55
read only memory (see ROM)
read/write head, 124-125, 127
real mode, 67-68, 113, 191-192
receiver card, 178
release code, 7
removable mass storage, 175-177
Reset key, 102
result codes, 283-284
reverse channel, 264-265, 267
RF modulator, 55
RGB interface, 55
RLL, 130-132, 175
Rodime R-Card, 133-134
ROM, 7, 17, 20-21, 41, 54
ROM BIOS, 10, 21
Run Length Limited (RLL), 130-132, 175

# S

scan code, 6-7
scan rate, 54, 56, 77, 160-161
Scroll Lock key, 5-7, 37
SDLC Communications adapter, 22, 24, 202
sectors, 13-14, 124
seek time, 127
segmented addressing, 18, 20, 26
serial adapter connector, 47, 244
serial mouse, 146
serial ports, 23-25, 38, 179, 238
serial/parallel adapter, 38, 47, 240-244
Setup program, 45-46
short cards, 30

SIMMs, 208-209
Single Inline Package (see SIP)
Single On-Line Memory Modules (see SIMMs)
SIP, 81
skirt, 22, 40, 43-44
Smartmodem 2400, 248-249, 282-285
soft-sectored disk, 14
speaker, 10
SSB Design Pure Power Plus, 98-99
start bit, 240-241, 258
status line, 6
STB Chauffeur HT display adapter, 150-151
stepper motor, 128-129
stop bit, 240-241, 258
synchronous transmission, 258-259
system board, 300-301, 314-315
system expansion slots (see expansion slots)
system memory map, 26-27, 41
system RAM, 70
system unit
    PC, 2, 6-9, 28-36, 234-238
    PC AT, 37-48, 234-236
    PC XT, 28-36, 234-238
    PS/2 63-72, 246

## T

tape backup unit, 2-3, 12, 41, 137-145, 198-199
TCM, 256-257
Tecmar MicroRAM, 208-209
third party hardware, 93-163
Toshiba Internal Disk Drive, 171-172
touch pad keyboard, 102-104
trace lines, 21, 70
tracks, 13-14, 40, 74, 125-127, 132
Trailblazer modem, 277-278
Trellis Coded Modulation (see TCM)
troubleshooting tips, 331-334
Tseng Labs UltraPAK-S, 150-151
turnaround time, 258

## V

ventilation grill, 9
vertical scan rate, 77
VGA (see Video Graphics Array)
VHS video cartridge, 177
Video Graphics Array, 52-53, 59-60, 76-77, 83, 153-157, 160-161, 203
voice coil motor, 128-129
voltage regulator, 98

## Y

Y cable, 134, 189

## W

wait states, 51, 85
warranty, 308

**25% OFF ALL PRODUCTS**
INCLUDING GRAPHIC CARDS, AND
TAPE BACK-UP SYSTEMS

**GENOA SYSTEMS CORPORATION**
73 E. TRIMBLE ROAD
SAN JOSE, CA 95131

PLEASE CALL 1-800-423-6211 FOR INFORMATION ON
HOW TO TAKE ADVANGAGE OF THIS OFFER
AND THE DEALER NEAREST YOU!

---

**FREE VGA CARD**
WITH PURCHASE OF A COMPLETE
386/25, 386/33 OR 486 SYSTEM
INCLUDING MEMORY, MONITOR, HARD &
FLOPPY DRIVES

**BESTEK INTERNATIONAL, INC.**
10400 ROCKLEY ROAD
HOUSTON, TEXAS
(713) 530-2395

HAVE YOUR FAVORITE DEALER CALL,
AND SPECIFY PROMO #GH-2

---

**15% DISCOUNT**
OFF ANY PRODUCTS - INCLUDING
COMPUTER PARTS FOR PC AT & 386, AND
MEMORY UPGRADER'S KIT

**DOLPHIN MICROCOMPUTER CORP.**
1234 SOUTH STREET
LONG BEACH, CA 90805
(213) 422-4444

PLEASE CALL OR WRITE FOR THE CURRENT PRICE LIST,
THEN SEND OR PRESENT THIS COUPON WITH YOUR
PURCHASE.